VOLUNTARY ASSOCIATIONS

VOLUNTARY ASSOCIATIONS
Socio-cultural Analyses and Theological Interpretation

James Luther Adams

Edited by
J. Ronald Engel

Exploration Press, Chicago

To George Huntston Williams
My former student, my colleague, my mentor

Copyright © 1986 by Exploration Press of the Chicago Theological Seminary

Printed in the United States of America

All rights reserved. No part of this book may be reproduced or transmitted in any form or by any means, electronic or mechanical, including photo copying, recording, or any information storage and retrieval system, without permission in writing from the publisher.

Exploration Press
Chicago Theological Seminary
5757 University Avenue
Chicago, Illinois 60637

ISBN: Cloth: 0-913552-34-8
       Paper: 0-913552-35-6

Library of Congress Catalog Card Number: 86-80304

Contents

Editor's Preface

Voluntary associations (independent associations, non-governmental organizations, not-for-profit associations, public-regarding associations) must be at or near the center of attention in a serious assessment of the democratic possibilities of contemporary public life. This is true for Anglo-American society; it is also true for other societies and for international relations. Recognition of the importance of voluntary associations for democratic social change calls for a kind of scholarship that takes seriously not only their political, sociological and institutional dimensions, but their religious, philosophical and ethical meanings as well.

There is no better guide for this task than James Luther Adams.

Adams is well-known for his rich and diverse contributions to theological scholarship, religious community, and social justice. However, the integrative focus of his labors, first at Meadville Theological School and the Federated Theological Faculty of the University of Chicago, and later at Harvard Divinity School, has been the history, theology, ethics, sociology and politics of voluntary associations. This volume brings together the major body of Adams' writings directly treating the subject of voluntary associations. It also includes the major portion of his writings in constructive theological and social ethics.

The essays cover a forty-five year time span, and are grouped chronologically within three major sections, preceded by an introduction in which Adams tells the arresting story of his personal journey of faith.

The first section introduces the theological and cultural analyses that inform his approach: the Judaeo-Christian tradition of voluntarism, a relational understanding of power, the emergence of persuasive love as a religious and political ideal in Western life, the contribution of the Protestant ethic to citizenship, the character of human institutions as the acid test for the meaning of ideas.

In the second section, Adams lifts up for scrutiny the living reality of voluntary associations as they function ambiguously in the promotion of democratic values. He examines them from several angles, as a prism of the human condition. Although there is repetition in these essays, each adds a significant element to our understanding of the structural and ethical dilemmas of modern associational existence.

In the third section, Adams shows the fruitfulness of a multi-disciplinary theology of voluntary associations for interpreting the wide range of personal, professional, political and economic issues in contemporary society, and for imaging new possibilities for human fulfillment.

Interpenetrating and undergirding each of these essays is Adams' central conviction that human beings are made for the life of free association, and that divine reality, the Holy Spirit, is manifest in all associations committed to the democratic pursuit of justice in the common life.

It is an esthetic as well as an intellectual delight to read these pages, for Adams, like other Unitarian clerics before him, is a master of the essay genre. The essays are reprinted in original, unedited form, with all footnotes intact. Had the method of publication permitted, it was Adams' wish to revise the essays to reflect new ethical sensibilities in matters of gender.

For many generations of students and colleagues, Adams has both taught and incarnated the highest values of free associational life. As one of many persons indebted to Jim Adams in more ways than are conceivable to name, I will gain no small satisfaction if the present book enables his life work to be better understood and more widely shared.

J. Ronald Engel
Meadville/Lombard

For Further Reference

BOOKS AND COLLECTED ESSAYS BY JAMES LUTHER ADAMS:

"James Luther Adams at 75." Edited by Herbert F. Vetter, Jr. *The Unitarian Universalist Christian* 32, Nos. 1-2 (1977).
On Being Human—Religiously. Edited by Max L. Stackhouse. Boston: Beacon Press, 1976.
Paul Tillich's Philosophy of Culture, Science and Religion. New York: Harper and Row, 1965.
The Prophethood of All Believers. Edited by George K. Beach. Boston: Beacon Press, 1986.
Taking Time Seriously. Edited by J. Bryan Allin. Glencoe, Illinois: The Free Press, 1957.

BIBLIOGRAPHIES OF WORKS BY JAMES LUTHER ADAMS:

Potter, Ralph B., Jr.; Potter, Jean; and Hunt, James D. "A Bibliography of the Writings of James Luther Adams." In *Voluntary Associations: A Study of Groups in Free Societies.* Edited by D. B. Robertson. Richmond: John Knox Press, 1966. (Chronological)
Wilcox, John R. "Bibliography." In John R. Wilcox, *Taking Time Seriously: James Luther Adams.* Washington, D.C.: University Press of America, 1978. (Alphabetical)

PUBLISHED WRITINGS ABOUT JAMES LUTHER ADAMS:

Deutsch, Judy. *Study Guide for James Luther Adams' On Being Human— Religiously.* Boston: Unitarian Universalist Association, 1978.
Hunt, James D. *James Luther Adams and His Demand for an Effective Religious Liberalism.* Ph.D. dissertation, Syracuse University, 1965.
————. "Voluntary Association as a Key to History." In *Voluntary Associations: A Study of Groups in Free Societies.* Edited by D. B. Robertson. Richmond: John Knox Press, 1966.
Muelder, Walter. "James Luther Adams as Theological Ethicist." *Andover Newton Quarterly* XVII (1977): 186-194.
Robertson, D. B., editor. *Voluntary Associations: A Study of Groups in Free Societies.* Essays in Honor of James Luther Adams. Richmond: John Knox Press, 1966.
Soper, David W. "James Luther Adams: A Theology of History and Hope." In David W. Soper, *Men Who Shape Belief: Major Voices in American Theology,* Vol. II. Philadelphia: Westminster Press, 1955.
Stackhouse, Max. "James Luther Adams: A Biographical and Intellectual

Sketch." In *Voluntary Associations: A Study of Groups in Free Societies.* Edited by D. B. Robertson. Richmond: John Knox Press, 1966.

———. "Editor's Introduction." In James Luther Adams, *On Being Human—Religiously.* Edited by Max Stackhouse. Boston: Beacon Press, 1976.

Wilcox, John R. *Taking Time Seriously: James Luther Adams.* Washington: University Press of America, 1978.

Williams, George H. "James Luther Adams and the Unitarian Denomination." *Andover Newton Quarterly* XVII (1977): 173-183.

Sources and Acknowledgements

I wish to express my gratitude to W. Widick Schroeder and Perry LeFevre of Chicago Theological Seminary for making this publication possible, and to thank the James Luther Adams Foundation for a grant of partial support. I am also indebted to John H. Nunemaker for permission to use the cover photograph. Many copyright holders generously gave permission to reprint individual essays. These are acknowledged in the list of sources below.

J.R.E.

1. "The Evolution of My Social Concern." *The Uniterian Universalist Christian* 32, Nos. 1-2 (1977): 12-24. Used by permission of the Unitarian Universalist Christian Fellowship, 110 Arlington Street, Boston, MA 02116.
2. "The Changing Reputation of Human Nature." *Journal of Liberal Religion* IV, Nos. 2-3 (1942-43): 59-72, 137-60.
3. "Theological Bases of Social Action." *Journal of Religious Thought* VIII, No. 1 (1950-51): 6-21. Used by permission.
4. "Arminius and the Structure of Society." From *Man's Faith and Freedom: The Theological Influence of Jacobus Arminius*. Edited by G. O. McCulloh. New York: Abingdon Press, 1962, pp. 88-112. Copyright © 1962 by Abingdon Press. Used by permission.
5. " 'The Protestant Ethic' with Fewer Tears." From *In the Name of Life—Essays in Honor of Erich Fromm*. Edited by Bernard Landis and Edward S. Tauber. New York: Holt, Rinehart and Winston, 1971, pp. 174-90. Copyright © 1971 by Bernard Landis and Edward S. Tauber. Reprinted by permission of Holt, Rinehart and Winston, Publishers.
6. "The Use of Symbols." From *On Being Human—Religiously*. Edited by Max Stackhouse. Boston: Beacon Press, 1976, pp. 88-112. Copyright © 1976 by Beacon Press. Reprinted by permission of Beacon Press. This essay is a retitled and edited version of Adams' 1969 presidential address for the Society for Christian Ethics, "The Pragmatic Theory of Meaning."
7. "The Political Responsibility of the Man of Culture." *Comprendre*, No. 16 (1956): 11-25. Used by permission.
8. "The Indispensable Discipline of Social Responsibility." *Journal of the Liberal Ministry* 6 (Spring 1966): 80-86.
9. "Voluntary Associations in Search of Identity." *Journal of Current Social Issues* 9, No. 6 (1971): 15-22. Used by permission.
10. "The Voluntary Principle in the Forming of American Religion." From *The Religion of the Republic*. Edited by Elwyn Smith. Philadelphia: Fortress Press, 1971, pp. 217-46. Copyright © 1971 by Fortress Press. Used by permission.
11. "The Geography and Organization of Social Responsibility." *Union Seminary Quarterly Review* XXIX, Nos. 3-4 (1974): 245-60. Used by permission.
12. "Mediating Structures and the Separation of Powers." From *Democracy and Mediating Structures*. Edited by Michael Novak. Washington, D.C.: American Enterprise Institute, 1980, pp. 1-33. Copyright © by American Enterprise Institute for Public Policy Research. Used by permission.
13. "Voluntary Associations." From *The Westminister Dictionary of Christian Ethics*. Edited by James F. Childress and John Macquarrie. Philadelphia: The Westminster Press, 1986. Used by permission.

14. "Notes on the Study of Gould Farm." *Cooperative Living* VII, No. 1 (1955-56): 8-10.
15. "Some Notes on the Ministry of the Clergy and the Laity." *Teamwork: Journal of the Universalist Ministers Association,* December, 1957.
16. "The Social Import of the Professions." *Bulletin of the American Association of Theological Schools,* No. 23 (June 1958): 152-68. Used by permission.
17. "The Place of Discipline in Christian Ethics." *Crane Review* IX, No. 3 (1967): 138-48.
18. "Civil Disobedience: Its Occasions and Limits." From *Political and Legal Obligations: Nomox XII.* Edited by J. Roland Pennock and John W. Chapman. New York: Atherton Press, 1970, pp. 293-331. Reprinted by Permission of the Publishers, Hebrew Publishing Company, Copyright © 1970. All rights reserved.
19. "Social Ethics and Pastoral Care". From *Pastoral Care and the Liberal Churches.* Edited by James Luther Adams and Seward Hiltner. Nashville: Abingdon Press, 1970. Copyright © by Abingdon Press. Used by permission.
20. "The Vocation of the Lawyer." *Mercer Law Review* 31 (Winter 1976): 531-44. Copyright © Mercer Law Review. Used by permission.
21. "God and Economics." From *Belief and Ethics.* Edited by W. Widick Schroeder and Gibson Winter. Chicago: Center for the Scientific Study of Religion, 1978, pp. 89-105. Used by permission.

The Evolution of my Social Concern

JAMES LUTHER ADAMS

I WAS reared in a Plymouth Brethren home where the name of
Darby was a household word and where the Scofield Reference
Bible, with its *heilsgeschichtliche* footnotes on the dispensations
was the daily food. Indeed, the food at table always followed the
spiritual repast of the Bible-reading. In accord with Scofield's footnotes, my father's constant attention was devoted to interpreting
apocalyptically the signs of the times. This whole apparatus, and
even the interest in the Bible, disappeared from my consciousness for
a time when evolutionary humanism and then classical humanisn
(under Irving Babbitt) took their place.

Considering the early training, I find it no accident that following
upon my student years at Harvard in theology my experiences in face
of Nazism assumed crucial significance. I would like to ask your
indulgence here as I relate an incident of some importance for me.
In the summer of 1927, six years after Hitler became head of the
movement and six years before the Party came into power, I visited
Nuremberg just at the time when thousands of people, young and
old, were in the city for the annual Nazi festival. On the day of the
great parade in the streets of Nuremberg, history as it was being
made at that juncture gave me personally a traumatic jolt. Standing
in the jostling crowd and watching the thousands of singing Nazis
with their innumerable brass bands as they passed along the street,
I inadvertently got into a conversation with some people who turned
out to be Nazi sympathizers. Out of curiosity as to what they would
say, I asked a bystander the meaning of the swastika that was everywhere evident. Within a few minutes I found myself in a heated
conversation with more and more people joining in, particularly
when the discussion turned to the Jewish question. As I bore down
in the argument against these defenders of Nazism, asking more and
more insistent questions, I was suddenly seized by the elbows from
behind, and pulled vehemently out of the crowd. No one made an
effort to help me. I immediately thought I was being taken into
custody. I could not see who it was who, after extricating me from
the crowd, marched me vigorously down a side street and then
turned up into an alley. On reaching the dead end of the alley,
my host, a young German workingman in his thirties, wheeled me
around and shouted at me, "Don't you know that when you watch a
parade in Germany today you either keep your mouth shut or get
your head bashed in?"

My palpitation mounted even higher at this moment, and I was all

1

the more puzzled when my captor smiled and said, "Don't be frightened. I have saved you."

"Saved me from what?"

"From being sandbagged. In about five minutes more of that argument on the curb, they would have knocked you out, flat on the pavement."

This man was an unemployed worker and an anti-Nazi. He immediately invited me to take dinner with him at his home. I accepted gladly. Then came the second shock: the walk into the slums, the trudge up four flights of a rundown tenement house, where some of the stairs were missing, and even some of the bannisters. The dinner was just as far from normal. In the few hours I spent with this man and his family I learned at first hand about the *Sitz im Leben* of the rising Nazism.

The experiences in Germany during that summer became crucial for me, but they did not assume full significance in my consciousness until in the middle Thirties I spent some months in the so-called "underground" movement of the Confessing Church in Germany. Meanwhile, I had resumed graduate studies at Harvard. These were years in which my acquired religious liberalism came under the scrutiny that we associate with that period in American Protestantism. The awareness of the thinness of its theology was in part stimulated by the Whiteheadean concern for metaphysics, by Irving Babbitt's vigorous attack upon Romantic conceptions of human nature, and by von Huegel's emphasis upon the theological, the historical, the institutional, and the devotional elements in Christianity. The depression and the early Roosevelt years, along with a markedly unideological interest in the writings of Marx, an increasing interest in the problems of unemployment and of the labor movement, participation as a minister in the activities incident to the great textile strike in Salem, Massachusetts — all these things conspired to develop a social concern, both theoretical and practical, which had previously been relatively peripheral. At the same time, the awareness of the fissiparous individualism and the unprophetic character of conventional middle-class, humanitarian religious liberalism served to increase my concern for the nature and mission of the church and especially for the *ecclesiola in ecclesia* as indispensable for the achievement of significant and costing consensus relevant to the historical situation.

Some of us Unitarian ministers initiated a study group just before I went to Germany in 1927. The group undertook a vigorous year-round discipline of reading, discussion, and the writing of papers. We collectively studied major literature of the time in the fields of theology, Bible, historical theology, social philosophy, art, liturgy, prayer, ever seeking consensus and seeking common disciplines

2

whereby we could implement consensus in the church and the community. During one entire summer, for example, we read thoroughly and discussed at length Troeltsch's *Social Teaching of the Christian Churches.* Reinhold Niebuhr and Karl Mannheim, of course, figured largely in our study. Such groups have increased through the years, and they continue in several parts of the country. I speak of this group discipline here, because in my conviction the concern for group participation and group responsibility became increasingly crucial in the quest for identity.

These multiple concerns were brought to a convergence by my second, more prolonged visit to Europe, a year of study of theology, of prayer and liturgy, of fascism and its persecution of the churches. During a period of several months at the Sorbonne, also at the Protestant theological faculty, and at the Catholic Institute, I lived in the home of a retired professor of the Sorbonne. Another paying guest in this home was a right-wing nationalist student. Many an hour we spent arguing the issues between democracy and fascism. I soon became aware of the fact that he would hesitate not a moment to shoot me down in cold blood if his wave of the future came to flood tide. I cannot enter here into detail about the experiences of those days. Listening to lectures daily at the hands of a liberal theologian, of an orthodox Calvinist, and of the principal Parisian Barthian — none of them making any analytic effort to interpret the signs of the times, signs that were the chief interest of the secularists — the Fascists and the Marxists. Meanwhile, I was also under the tutelage of an eminent Jesuit spiritual director at the Roman Catholic Seminary of Saint-Sulpice. Each week I posed my questions on prayer, and the following week he answered them. But always I felt the gap between the cultivation of mental prayer and the bludgeonings of a period of history that was swiftly moving into the storms of our time. I recall an experience not dissimilar to the one of 1927 in Nuremberg. Early one morning I went to the Pantheon to watch the formation of a United Front parade. When it began to move, I could not get out of the jam. Willy nilly I marched; no escape was possible. Every cross street was filled with crowds of people, obstructed also by a police cordon. For two hours I marched, pushed along as if I had been seized by the elbows and at every moment seeing people giving the Communist salute from the windows of the buildings. On the day when Hitler marched into the Rhineland, I was in the home of Edgar Ansel Mowrer. We stayed up all night.

It is perhaps not surprising that soon after this in Geneva I adopted the counsel of the young Visser 't Hooft. "You are to study in the German universities? I hope that is not all! I am going to give you the advice that I constantly give to churchmen going to Germany. But

3

none of them takes my advice. I say you should get into the underground of the Confessing churches and learn the meaning of the Synod of Barmen."

I took his advice, though I also attended the lectures of Bultmann and Heiler, of Jaspers and Barth and Brunner, of Heim and even of Wilhelm Hauer, the founder of the German Faith Movement. I cannot here narrate the melodramatic experiences of the underground, largely in company with or under the auspices of a former Harvard friend, Peter Brunner, who had served time in the Dachau Concentration Camp and who is now Professor of Theology at Heidelberg. For several months, during an interim, I spent two or more hours a day with the retired Rudolf Otto at Marburg, at the same time taking the lectures of Bultmann and others in the University. In view of my connections with leaders in the Confessing Church, Rudolf Otto saw to it that I should get acquainted with German Christians, Nazis among the clergy whom he deemed to be insane.

It is extremely difficult to pass over a description of the maelstrom of this whole experience in Germany, an experience that brought fearful encounter with the police and even a frightening encounter two years later with the Gestapo. The ostensible charge made by the Gestapo was that I was violating the law by walking on the street with a deposed Jewish teacher and by visiting a synagogue. The word existential came alive in those hours of bludgeoned questioning and of high palpitation. It is difficult, I say, to suppress giving an account of incidents in connection with the Nazis, the anti-Nazis, and the hidden underlings. It is even more difficult to determine how to compress into brief statement what all this did for the evolution of my "social concern."

One way to do this is in terms of the ideological battles, specifically in terms of symbols. The ideological battle, as Schelling would say, was a war of the gods, a war between myths. Here I express indebtedness to Paul Tillich, whose reputation and writing I began to encounter at this time, seeing in him a German counterpart to Reinhold Niebuhr. I wish I could pause here to speak of the lectures of Jaspers and Heidegger and Bultmann. But let me hasten on. As between Bultmann and Otto, I was the more greatly attracted to Otto. The gnostic existentialism of Bultmann, despite his heroic stand against Hitler, did not speak directly to my condition. Like others in the Confessing church, he possessed only an abstract conception of concreteness and decision with respect to *positive* action in history. Indeed, his aversion to concern for the historical Jesus and his preference for *kerygma* alone seemed to me to be part and parcel of a really inchoate non-historical outlook, despite the frequent admonition of openness to the future. His concern for anthropology

4

to the exclusion of ontology seemed to me to urge the cart without the horse. The increasing criticism of Bultmann today, even among his quondam disciples, insists on a more historical understanding of history, on the resumption of the quest for the historical Jesus, and on the centrality of ontology.

What gave focus to the whole experience in Germany was Rudolf Otto's *The Kingdom of God and the Son of Man*. The conception of the kingdom as more than judgment, as redemptive dynamics, as the seed that grows of itself in struggle against the demonic powers, the Son of Man as suffering servant, the kingdom as both present and future — all of this represented a turning point away from the consistent eschatology of Schweitzer. In the course of studying simultaneously the anti-prophetic organic symbolism of the Nazi myth, I, like everyone else, became more vividly aware than hitherto of the role of myth in religion and culture, but more specifically I became aware of the *types* of symbolism. Later on I was to recognize the ontological significance of myth, particularly at the hands of Schelling, Tillich, and Heidegger. Later on, too, I was to see the anthropological significance of symbolism — the view that language is a decisive medium for the expression of the freedom of man. But at the time I was particularly frustrated by the pietistic, individualistic symbolism of Kierkegaard and of American individualism. Heinrich Frick of Marburg (whom I saw a great deal) suggested in his *Vergleichende Religionswissenschaft* a distinction between symbols drawn from history — dynamic symbols oriented to time — and symbols drawn from nature — static symbols oriented to space. The pertinence of dynamic symbolism had earlier been impressed upon me by the study of Whitehead.

But more significant than this sort of typology was the distinction between symbols that relate the concept of the kingdom of God to the inner life or the life of the individual and that relate the concept of the Kingdom of God to institutions, that is to the church and to other institutions. Quite decisive for me was the recognition of the *political* character of Biblical symbolism. As political, this symbolism, particularly in the Old Testament, expressed the sovereignty of God over all of life, including the institutional structures. From this time on I saw, with the aid of Troeltsch, the narrowing of Christian obligation which in Lutheranism resulted from the two-kingdom theory — a bifurcation of political symbolism which makes a dichotomy between the church and culture and thus reduces the tension between them.

In conjunction with a doctrine of vocation oriented only to daily work, the two-kingdom theory released the eschatological tension and also prevented the doctrine of vocation from including dynamic political obligation. Likewise, the merely interpersonal emphasis on the priesthood of all believers crowded out dynamic functioning of a doctrine of the prophethood of all believers in face of institutions. In contrast to this institutional orientation of political symbolism, one can readily observe the merely interpersonal orientation of the doctrine of justification by faith or the doctrine of forgiveness. I still offer a prize to students in my classes if they can bring in a report that the Sunday morning Lutheran Hour on TV finds any symbol of the power or the demand of God other than the power and the demand of God to forgive. It is difficult to work out a social ethics on the basis of a doctrine of forgiveness. Toward this end, the doctrine must be related to political symbolism. One must emphasize, of course, that both the personal and the institutional belong together in soteriology and in a theological anthropology. To separate them is to violate the sovereignty of God. One sees these two corresponding forms of distortion in Kierkegaard and Marx. Both of these thinkers are unthinkable without the Bible, but in their reduction of ethics exclusively to the personal or to the institutional they are both of them unbiblical. Looking at them, one must say there is nothing so much like a swelling as a hole. Kierkegaard, despite his astute attack upon so-called Christendom, is in Christian circles a form of infidelity to the sovereignty of God over institutions, a sophisticated form of pietism, that is, a form of political and ecclesiastical irresponsibility. In industrial society, pietism tends to support by default the primacy of the economic life over the political.

These considerations underscore the fact that Christians possess almost infinite capacities of dissolving the political symbolism of covenant and kingdom. These forms of dissolution include the reduction of Christian ethics to personalism, systematic theology that has no reference to institutions, psychotherapy that possesses no sociological framework, abstract existentialism that talks about concreteness and decision but does not drive towards actualizing concreteness and decision in the social-historical situation.

Why is it so extremely easy for Christians to become pietistic, in the sense that they see little connection between Christian ethics and structural institutional analysis or between Christian ethics and responsibility for the character and influence of economic and political institutions? One reason for this is the ease with which pietism can appeal for sanction to the Gospels. The first sentence of Troeltsch's *Social Teaching of the Christian Churches* asserts that primitive Christianity was not a social movement. In one of his long essays, *The Social Philosophy of Christianity*, he argues that primitive Christianity had no social philosophy, no articulated theology of social institutions which could provide a critical and positive interpretation of ongoing economic and political institutions. Accordingly, he asserts that early Christianity turned to pagan natural-law doctrine in search of a basis for a social philosophy. I do not need to examine this issue here. I would like to say only that the angelology and the doctrine of Christ the King recently under debate among New Testament scholars offers some challenge to Troeltsch's view. A masterly essay by G. Dehn on the doctrine of the Kingship of Christ appeared in the Barth *Festschrift* of 1936; through the years I have asked my students to familiarize themselves with my translation of this essay. According to this view, the state, for example, is seen to be in a fallen condition and under the aegis of fallen angels; under Christ the King, it and other social forces are in the end to be restored to their essential nature. Thus salvation is for society as well as for the individual. In a recent essay, Amos Wilder has suggested that the doctrine of the Kingship of Christ could serve as a new Christian theological basis for Rauschenbusch's Social Gospel. I mention this here only in order to suggest that a continuing problem for Christian ethics is the place of political symbolism. The Nazi movement and the Communist movement have given new urgency to the explication of the political symbolism of the Bible and of later articulations of Christian ethics. It is striking to observe how little the Bultmann School has contributed to contemporary understanding of the political symbolism of the Bible. One must question the adequacy of the Heideggerian anthropology as a framework for demythologizing the Gospel.

I must now return to consider another aspect of the impact of Nazism upon my social concern. This consideration, if fully set forth, would entail the discussion of the sociology of religion, the philosphy of history, the relations between Christianity and democracy, as well as between Christianity and capitalism and religious socialism. But I must spare you the full rehearsal of those themes. I must be highly selective.

Let me repeal reticence so far as to say that the experience of Nazism induced a kind of conversion. I recall a conversation with Karl Jaspers at his home one day in Heidelberg in 1936. I asked him what he deemed to be the contemporary significance of liberal Christianity. He replied with unwonted vehemence, "Religious liberalism has *no* significance. It has *Zwang* — no costing commitment."

He was thinking of the liberals who had become German Christians (Nazis), the while overlooking the impotence and silence of orthodoxy and neo-orthodoxy in the burgeoning period of Nazism, overlooking also the collaboration of the Catholic Center Party and the Vatican with Fascism and Nazism — a collaboration that is now at last receiving candid discussion precisely in Catholic circles in Germany. So Jaspers now offered me some advice. "If I were a young man of liberal preferences today, I would return to the most orthodox branch of my heritage."

Immediately I asked him if he planned to do this himself. He flushed, he blushed, and replied, "I am not making a personal confession. I am giving you a sociological judgment." So spoke the pupil of Max Weber!

I did in those days recover a sense of the centrality of the Bible and of the decisive role in history of both the sacramental and the prophetic elements. I mention only in passing here the influence of Christian art, and especially of Bach, upon me. In addition, I pressed upon myself the question, "If Fascism should arise in the States, what in your past performance would constitute a pattern or framework of resistance?" I could give only a feeble answer to the question. My principal political activities had been the reading of the newspaper and voting. I had preached sermons on the depression or in defense of strikers. Occasionally, I uttered protests against censorship in Boston, but I had no adequate conception of citizen participation.

I must now turn to this theme. The German universities, supposedly independent entities, had been fairly easily Nazified. My American acquaintance, Edward Yarnall Hartshorne, later killed in Marburg when serving as American Military Government director of the universities at Hesse-Nassau, wrote a well documented account of the Nazification of the universities: *The German Universities and National Socialism* (Harvard University Press, 1937). Hitler also liquidated the trade unions. The persecuted Confessional Seminary I attended in Elberfeld occupied an abandoned Masonic building. The order was forbidden to hold meetings. Repeatedly I heard anti-Nazis say, If only 1,000 of us in the late twenties had combined in heroic resistance, we could have stopped Hitler. I noticed the stubborn resistance of the Jehovah's Witnesses. I observed also the lack of religious pluralism in a country that had no significant Nonconformist movement in the churches. Gradually I came to the conviction that a decisive institution of the viable democratic society is the voluntary association as a medium for the assumption of civic responsibility. Ernst Troeltsch's treatment of voluntarism of associations, his account of the free-church movement and of the associational creativity of the Calvinists began to flood back into memory. I read Max Weber's *Proposal for the Study of Voluntary Association* and his typology of Associations. In his "Proposal" Weber said it had been the genius of the Prussian government to drain off the national energies into Singing Academies, thus diverting attention away from public policy and from civic responsibility. More than Troeltsch, I, the former sectarian (Plymouth Brethren), began to appreciate the role of the aggressive sect in Western history and of its grandchild, the secular voluntary association concerned with public policy.

You will forgive me if I mention here quickly the important

8

ingredients of this development of social concern. I plunged into voluntary associational activity, concerning myself with race relations, civil liberties, housing problems. I joined with newly formed acquaintances in the founding of the Independent Voters of Illinois, and I began to learn at first hand about Moral Man and Immoral Society. I traveled to Washington fairly often to consult with men like Adlai Stevenson, Jonathan Daniels, and Harold Ickes regarding Chicago politics. At the same time I participated in precinct organization, becoming a doorbell ringer and also consulting with party leaders in the back rooms. There is nothing intrinsically unusual about all this. It was only unusual for the Protestant churchman or clergyman. Equally significant for me was the new motivation for sociological understanding. The social sciences acquired an existential quality; and increasingly they figured in my thinking, in my associations, and in my courses.

Moreover, this combination of impulses conditioned my historical studies. I turned to the history of the Radical Reformation, to the influence of English Independency and Quakerism on the rise of democracy. From Bourgeaud I first learned to appreciate the epic sweep of what Whitehead had called the diffusion of opportunity and what I called the dispersion of power, the capacity to participate in social decision. Here with considerable excitement I pursued the theme through modern history — the transfer of radical concern from the Independents and the Levellers to the initiation of rationally devised public agitation and to the initiation of political parties, the spread of this voluntarism into education, and under Methodist leadership the rise of the British labor movement, and so on. In a memorable address by Whitehead before the American Academy of Sciences in 1941, he spoke of the *gap* between Statesmanship and Learning, between the processes of social coordination and the activities of the vocations and professions. The voluntary association in manifold ways fills in these gaps. Indeed, voluntary association stands between the individual and the state, providing the *opportunity* for achievement and implementation of consensus. It provides, alas, other opportunities, depending on the goals, the constituency, the internal organization of the association. I can mention here the American Medical Association, the name of James Hoffa, or the Board of Trustees of a suburban church in captivity.

Max Weber adumbrated a philosophy of history in terms of his typology of authority — traditionalist, rational legal, and charismatic (relying here in part upon Sohm's *Kirchenrecht*). Troeltsch offered a typology of religious associations — church, sect, and mystical type — which became the basis of a philosophy of church history. He has also offered a typology of Christian political theory, arranged according to the degree of reliance upon individual spontaneity or upon the external shaping disciplines. In a general way, all of these philosophies of history may be traced back to Joachim of Flora's theory of the three ages of the church, but more immediately the father of this associational theory of history and its periods is Otto von Gierke. In his magnum opus *Genossenschaftsrecht*, we may recognize a special kind of anthropology. Men are associating beings. Their differences may be determined by observing the associations they form, and by observing the relations between their voluntary and their involuntary associations, the types of participation they give to these associations. Accordingly, Gierke offers a theory of the periodization of Western history from the time of Charlemagne to the eighteenth century, a theory that characterizes the periods in terms of the dominant types of association.

Now the ramifications of associational theory are of course manifold. Maitland and Jenks have traced the history of England in terms of associational theory and practice. Gierke and Fred Carney have shown the great significance of the Calvinist Althusius for Protestant theory. Troeltsch and Weber really presuppose Gierke in their works. H. Richard Niebuhr in his neo-Troeltschean work on the *Social Sources of Denominationalism* traces the development of Protestantism in terms of the structure and dynamics of associations.

I would like now at the end to list some theses and some problems. First, some theses very briefly put.

Considering the associational character of human existence, we may say that the social meaning of a theological idea is to be determined in a crucial way by the type of association it calls for in the minds of the believers. Here we have a special application of the pragmatic theory of meaning. By their groups, their associational fruits, shall ye know them. If the theological or the theological ethical commitment does not issue in associational preference or transformation, it is to this extent not yet clear or meaningful.

Let me give two illustrations. R. B. Braithwaite, the British linguistic philosopher, in his book *An Empiricist Approach to Religion* argues that we can determine the meaning of Christianity by observing its consequence for behavior. To be a Christian, he says, means that one is committed to an agapaistic way of life. This view, like Bultmann's openness to the future, is extremely abstract. A Roman Catholic, a Presbyterian, and a Quaker might provisionally agree with Braithwaite. But consider the wide breach of differences they exhibit in their doctrines of the church. We can most quickly determine the meaning of a theological outlook by examining its doctrine of the church.

A second illustration. H. Richard Niebuhr has offered a typology of the relations between Christ and Culture. Here he gives the now familiar rubrics Christ Against Culture, Christ Over Culture, Christ

Transforming Culture. The rubrics are scarcely sufficient. Within each of these classifications one can find a considerable variety of associational theories, and in several of the classifications one can find thinkers who would hold very similar associational theories. This fact shows us, on the one hand, that no timeless associational theory may be taken as definitively normative for the Christian. On the other hand, one does not know enough about a particular type of Christian ethos at a given time if one does not know the type of associational arrangements that are preferred. From this perspective the man from Mars could be misled if he accepted William Adams Brown's claim that the Protestant and the Catholic worship the same God. The man from Mars would do well to look into Sohm's *Kirchenrecht* or into K. Barth's *Christengemeinde und Bürgergemeinde.* At the same time we must say that the Christian ethos can appear in a considerable variety of types of association. To this extent and by this means the Christian ethos is differentiated. It is also differentiated by the types of non-ecclesiastical associations in which the Christian participates. Associational theory contributes to the analysis of meaning by reminding us, "By their groups shall ye know them." Here the social sciences have their contribution to make by assisting in the study of the types, the structure and dynamics, and the pathology of associations. So much for the pragmatic theory of meaning when applied to associations.

A second thesis I do not need to spell out. Christian vocation extends beyond the job to the church and the community. The means by which the church goes into the world is through the voluntary associations. That is, the responsibility of the Christian is to participate in the associations that define and re-define the actual situation, in the associations that give utterance and body to prophetic protest, and to social change or to social stability in associations that provide the occasion for the Christian and the non-Christian to enter into dialogue and even to achieve a working consensus — in short, in the associations that contribute to the shaping of history. Indeed, it is from these associations that the Christian can carry back to the church experience, significant fact, informed concern, insight demanding interpretation at the hands of the *koinonia.*

Now for some problems.

We do not have, and we probably shall not be able to get, an adequate study of the history of voluntary associational activity in the various countries, including our own. Arthur Schlesinger, Sr., following the lead of de Tocqueville, has outlined the history of American associations under the title of *A Nation of Joiners.* Great changes with respect to associations have come about in the twentieth century. Many of the changes that were implemented during the nineteenth century within the context of voluntary philanthropic activity have been taken over by the welfare state. There yet remain thousands of associations in the United States. Some of them, like labor unions and the American Medical Association, are scarcely voluntary, and their internal structures exhibit Michel's iron law of oligarchy — the tendency of political organizations to come under the control of a small group of "eager beavers." Doctors who deplore the tight bureaucratization despairingly say that in order to break the hierarchy, they would have to expend more energy than they can afford — they trained to be doctors and they want to be doctors. Some of the associations provide the opportunity to cross racial and class lines, in order to work for the general welfare. The NAACP, which has lost some of its dynamic, has done much to elevate the status of the Negro and to extend democracy. Many civic associations function to bring about minor reforms or to serve as watchdogs. On the other hand, many associations serve only special and narrow interests. Pressure groups with enormous budgets enter into collusion in state legislatures and in the national legislature, to promote or obstruct legislation. On the whole, participation in associations concerned with public policy is a middle class phenomenon, and even then in special interest groups. Philanthropic associations in large degree have this middle class constituency. Rev. Robert Cowell of Denver, in his study published in the *Harvard Business School Bulletin* shows that business and professional people, so far from breaking through class and race barriers, more deeply entrench themselves in their own perspectives by participation in philanthropic and service organizations. Like the churches, voluntary associations of this sort shape the society into isolated grooves or channels. Mirra Komarovsky, in her studies of associations in New York City, shows that the average of membership in associations apart from the church is less than one per person. Some indication of the trend in the USA is revealed by the fact that from 1892 to 1948 the percentage of eligible voters who participated in national elections declined from 87 per cent to 57 per cent — hardly credible. This fact alone reveals the character and extent of the opportunity for the operation of the political machine. Komarovsky has suggested that nonmembership and nonparticipation in associations concerned with public policy is the criterion for the appearance of the mass man. Add to these facts the structure and power of the American business corporation community, and the largely centralized control of the mass media of communications, and we see the dimensions of domination in American society; we see the measure of the impotence of the churches in face of the principalities and powers.

I share the conviction that Christian ethics must be promoted in direct confrontation with these principalities and powers. These principalities and powers have to be analyzed with the assistance of the behavioral sciences, which in turn are promoted by persons who, like us, are under the grip, even under the spell of the principalities and powers. From certain quarters we hear the term "the end of the ideologies." This term itself bespeaks an ideology. If we observe the confusion brought to a focus by the indictment of General Electric, Westinghouse and other corporation executives; if we observe the extreme difficulty one encounters in the attempt to secure basic information regarding poverty in the United States; if we ask the question as to the contribution of the United Fruit Company to the rise of Castro; if we ask the question how the mass media are to be freed from their bondage to the processes of marketing, we should be brought to an awareness of the epochal structural dimensions of our economy, and thus to an awareness of demands that the Lord of history places upon us at this time and in this place.

The Changing Reputation of Human Nature

JAMES LUTHER ADAMS

"Modern Liberalism, whether political or religious, needs nothing so much as a realistic and credible doctrine of man. We pride ourselves on the open-mindedness of our kind toward all sciences and their findings. But at this particular point most of us have a hereditary or a willful blind spot."

Few things in human history are fixed. Least of all, reputations, As Santayana remarks of Hamlet, the reputations both of the great figures of fiction and of their creators have usually had an evolution and a history. One age extols Shakespeare as abiding our every question, and another devotes itself to "improving" him. One age wishes Milton could be living at this hour; another regards him as the blight of English poesy. One "school" honors Plato as the "father of all orthodoxy;" another excommunicates him as the "source of all heresy." Hence, the admonition "Let us now praise famous men" raises again and again the questions, Which men? and How praise them?

But not only individual reputations change. The reputation of the whole species also changes. Indeed, it has been changing a good deal of late. The reasons for this are legion. One reason is, of course, that among men above the primitive level some change of outlook is always taking place. It may be slow or devious, but it is inevitable. There is a sort of dialectic in the history of ideas which over and over again manifests itself in a dissatisfaction with "established" views and in a demand for novelty. Moreover, every idea that persists in history has what Hegel calls its own "cunning." No idea can remain static, not even the conception of man. The values and insights of a given orientation or emphasis seem to

---

[1]This essay is an expansion of the Berry Street Conference Address delivered in Boston, Mass., at the annual "May Meetings" of the American Unitarian Association, May 21, 1941.

Since the delivery of this address a number of ministers have suggested that when published the paper should provide references to significant literature on the topics discussed.

The author wishes to thank Professor Gerhard E. O. Meyer and Professor Wilhelm Pauck of The University of Chicago for the criticisms and suggestions they have generously provided.

The epigraph is taken from Dean Sperry's provocative essay, "Liberalism," *Christendom*, V (1940), 185.

exhaust themselves, and the moving finger of time points in a new direction,—and sometimes in the opposite direction. Another reason for the change in the reputation of man is the fact that many of the generalizations applied to human nature in one period of world history have only a restricted validity in another period. The structure of society at a given time in large measure determines which aspects of human nature shall receive fuller expression and which shall be suppressed or called very little into play.[2]   But there are also reasons for changes in the reputation of human nature which are peculiar to our age. For one thing, both the natural and the social sciences have in the recent past brought forth new knowledge about human nature which is affecting its reputation. Equally significant as a cause for the changes taking place today in this area is the profound change in the whole historical situation. History has its "cunning" too, and this affects man's estimate of the human condition. Hence, the current revolt against the older Liberal estimate of man is partially due to the fact that the so-called Age of Liberalism has culminated in a terrifying crisis.[3]

This change in the reputation of human nature presents a serious problem for every "established" philosophy. Old and encrusted forms of thought are being subjected to radical criticism. Some of them are being broken and transformed; some are even being replaced by new forms or by revised versions of old forms of thought. In such a situation it is inevitable that the attempted changes should encounter resistance, especially where the "established" philosophy has enjoyed a wide acceptance. For there is in every "established" historical movement a resistance to movement.

This resistance to movement is not necessarily a sign of ossification. Particularly in periods of crisis, prophets always abound who take a melodramatic attitude toward history and toward their own younger selves. These melodramatic prophets urge their fellows to repudiate all the doctrines that have prevailed in the

---

[2] Cf. Karl Mannheim, *Man and Society in an Age of Reconstruction* (New York, 1940), for a brilliant exposition of this thesis.

[3] In view of the fact that the present essay is concerned with certain changes that are taking place or are imminent within religious liberalism, it seems advisable for the sake of clarity to follow the practice of referring to the eighteenth and nineteenth-century philosophy of individualism and progress as Liberalism (with a capital L) and of referring to the ongoing broader movement for the freedom of the Christian mind and conscience in a just order of society as liberalism (with a small l). Both of these types

recent past and frequently they offer salvation through a return to the good old days of the Mishpat or of primitive Christianity or of the Middle Ages. In the face of these invitations to somersault, resistance may serve a valuable purpose. It may help to give continuity and stability to the processes of history and thus aid an excited generation to resist the temptation simply to pass from one extreme to another.

Just this sort of resistance one might hope will be provided by religious liberalism in a time of stock-taking such as ours. Indeed, if religious liberalism does not fulfill this function today it will in the end be rightly adjudged as the salt that has lost its savour.

But the resistance to change that is found in every historical movement may also serve as an obstruction to the emergence or appreciation of new insights. Liberalism is not unlike other "established" philosophies in this respect. Having enjoyed success for so long, it is now prone to assume glibly that it has "arrived." Hence many liberals today, instead of recognizing the inevitability of change in the reputation of human nature, are inclined to doubt whether the changes they do not like are really significant. They prefer to think that time's wingéd chariot only carries coals to Newcastle. What Professor E. E. Aubrey has characterized as the conservative tendency of reason plays a large role here. Thus the attitude of dogged resistance to change or criticism is often symptomatic of a change that has already taken place imperceptibly and even unconsciously,—the change from a dynamic movement of growth to a static position of defense. Among liberals this sort of resistance is in some instances motivated by the notion that the best interests of liberalism will be threatened if one concedes that it is rightly subject to radical criticism. This kind of resistance appears where liberalism has become an "ideology." Its adherents

---

of liberalism, of course, have taken a secular as well as a religious form.

The confusion that obtains with regard to the use of the word "liberalism" is, of course, nothing new. For a brief study of its many meanings in the past and in current usage see Guido de Ruggiero, "Liberalism," *Encyclopedia of the Social Sciences*, Vol. 9, 435-441; see also James Truslow Adams, "Liberals," *Dictionary of American History*, Vol. III, 269-270; Willard L. Sperry, *op. cit.*, pp. 181 ff.; John Dewey, *Liberalism and Social Action* (New York, 1935); Frank H. Knight, "Ethics and Economic Reform. I. The Ethics of Liberalism," *Economica*, February, 1939; Ruth Anshen (ed.), *Freedom—Its Meaning* (New York, 1940) and Frank H. Knight's review of it in *Ethics*, LII (1941), 86-109; David E. Roberts and H. P. van Dusen (eds.), *Liberal Theology* (New York, 1942).

use, or rather abuse, it to protect some vested intellectual or material interest.

Another type of regressive resistance to movement in liberalism is the sort that arises from the identification of it with some particular doctrines that are believed to be once for all delivered and thus not subject to criticism. This sort of resistance appears where a philosophy has become orthodox, and it plays right into the hands of those critics of liberalism who identify it with some particular doctrine and then, because of the alleged inadequacy of this doctrine, urge us to have done with liberalism of every form. By means of this ruse such critics give the impression that they were right in always having opposed liberalism, and thus they the more easily persuade their adherents that the world should attempt to assuage its guilt by casting its sins upon a scapegoat "constructed" for the purpose, a scapegoat that they call "liberalism."

In the face of this sort of attack the liberals have (as we have suggested) a very significant positive role to play in maintaining resistance, especially in maintaining it against those forces that threaten to destroy the enduring values of liberalism and that lead towards fanaticism, obscurantism, and authoritarianism. Certainly, the religious liberals should protest vigorously against the claim that they must either retain the old Liberalism in its entirety or give up liberalism altogether. They should also insist that such a false statement of the alternatives bespeaks a complete misunderstanding of the nature of liberalism. The modification or abandonment of some particular doctrine of an earlier Liberalism is not tantamount to the betrayal of liberalism. Far from it. It may be actually the practice of liberalism.

This fact becomes evident if we consider a pungent criticism of modern Liberalism written by an eminent theologian of our day. Attacking the traditionally over-optimistic doctrine of man in the older Liberalism and at the same time appealing to a liberal principle as the basis for his criticism, this theologian writes:

Turning now to the criticism of Liberalism from within, to which its own creative principle gives rise, we must seriously question whether it can bear the weight of the tragedies of human existence. Does not its amiable faith in inherent goodness appear ghastly mockery when confronted by the facts of life? Believing in the immanent God, it must seriously consider what sort of God it is that nature reveals. We cannot be so enamoured of the loveliness of nature as to be blind to its terrible aspects. And what of human sin? Here more than anywhere else the weakness of Modern Liberalism shows itself. It may be conceded that traditional theology made too much of sin, but surely that was better than to make light of it. To a serious thinker, Modern Liberalism often seems too jocund for life as it actually is. . . . We would not have Modern Liberalism return to a belief in the devil—that is too easy a solution to the problem—but it must deal more justly with the crushing tragedies of life, with evil and sin, if it is to command the respect of candid and thoughtful men. The saviors of the world have always been and always will be men of sorrow and acquainted with grief."

This paragraph was not written by an adherent of any one of those groups that are, according to some accounts, today leading a retreat into the "dark backward and abysm" of Calvinism. It was written by a representative Unitarian. Nor was it written by one whose vision was distorted by "post-war pessimism." It appeared not in the year 1942, but in 1913. And its author was undoubtedly a liberal,—the late William Wallace Fenn of the Harvard Divinity School.[4]

It would be wrong to suppose that Dean Fenn's criticism stands alone in the literature of liberalism or that his criticism is illiberal in spirit or consequence. It is of the essence of liberalism to criticize itself. Moreover, among religious liberals there is and there has always been a considerable variety of opinion about human nature as well as about many other matters. In other words, although religious liberals have been at one in espousing certain liberal principles, such as freedom of inquiry and freedom of conscience, they have not all brought forth the same ideas in their exercise of these freedoms. Thus we see that the liberal method or attitude is one thing, the specific content of liberalism is another. Hence, the liberal doctrine of man may change while the non-authoritarian method of liberalism remains in fundamental respects the same.[5] Indeed, if some particular doctrine of man—or of God— held among liberals should be viewed as final in its form of expression and as exempt from criticism or change, the principle of freedom in liberalism would thereby be surrendered. Only if the

---

[4]The quotation is taken from Dean Fenn's article "Modern Liberalism," *The American Journal of Theology,* XVII (1913), 509-519. Walter Marshall Horton has characterized this article "by a great Unitarian thinker" as "the most incisive criticism of liberalism." See his *Realistic Theology* (New York, 1934), p. 33.

[5]In his book *The Religious Prospect* (London, 1940), V. A. Demant, the eminent British Anglo-Catholic theologian, has recognized and has succinctly delineated certain of the differences between the method of lib-

conception of man or God were altered to an extent requiring a fundamental revision of the liberal method, would liberalism as we cherish it be threatened. In this respect, the method and the content of liberalism are correlative and interdependent. Within these limits, then, both variety and change in the stated doctrines of religious liberalism are at once inevitable and legitimate.

Three Rival Conceptions

Two things should strike the attention of any one interested in the changing reputation of human nature. The first is that the reputation of human nature in any epoch or movement is closely associated with a general world-view, and it cannot be understood apart from this world-view. The second is the fact that in modern times the major changes in this reputation represent to a large extent variations on a few very old themes. A completely novel fundamental idea does not appear often in human thought, whether that thought be concerned with man, nature, or God. Granted that always an element of novelty is added whenever an old and basic conception is "revived" in a new intellectual and social context, it is nevertheless necessary to recognize over the centuries the fundamental continuity in the great rival metaphysical doctrines. Only a few basic conceptions have been developed, and most of these we have inherited from ancient times.

When the reputation of human nature changes, then, it is almost inevitable that either some variation of the prevalent attitude toward human nature and existence or a new version of a neglected earlier conception should emerge. This latter trend has been taking place in our day. In the very process of assimilating the new knowledge of man which has resulted from the application of modern scientific methods and which has accrued from viewing man in a changed historical situation, many people have been led to a new appreciation of certain earlier estimates of human nature and the human situation.

---

eralism and its content (or doctrines) at any particular time. It is to be regretted that some of the present-day critics of religious liberalism have not taken into account this distinction between method and content.

It should be noted here that although the religious liberal renounces authoritarianism, he adopts some positive doctrine of authority. Indeed, the conception of the nature of authority as held in earlier liberalism is ripe for re-examination in the light of certain new insights of our day concerning "the seat of authority" in a religious fellowship.

We now turn our attention to a consideration of three of these basic rival conceptions. Our purpose in presenting these rival conceptions is not merely to provide an orientation for the consideration of the current changes in the reputation of human nature, but also to indicate the relative merits of these conceptions and to draw from such a study an indication of the changes needful in the older Liberal doctrine of man.

In the ancient Greek tradition we find two of these typical estimates of human nature and the human situation. The one view is associated with the classical philosophers; it is usually called the intellectualistic or rationalistic view, the Apollonian view. According to this view, reason is the masterful principle of creation, and thus the cosmos is a moving shadow of a world of eternal ideas, essences, or forms. Correspondingly, man's primary, distinguishing faculty is his reason, and through it he can release a vitality that will enable him to achieve control of himself and of the human situation by subjecting them to clearly envisaged forms. What is to be especially noted here is the tendency of this intellectualistic view, first, to interpret existence in terms of a rational, unified, harmonious structure, and, second, to exalt the cognitive, non-affective aspects of the human psyche. The conjunction of these two elements leads to a preoccupation with the forms and structures of being and to a "theoretical attitude of distance" which aims at the development of the form and harmony of the Olympian calm. Thus the vitality of nature, man, and history is assumed, and creativity is identified with the operations of reason.

The other view of human nature in the Hellenic tradition interprets existence more in terms of vitality than of form, a vitality that is both creative and destructive, that imbues every form but that also eludes and bursts the bounds of every structure. It is associated with one of the major traditions in popular Greek religion, with certain pre-Socratic philosophers very close to this religious tradition, and in certain respects, with the great tragedians. It has sometimes been characterized as the Dionysian view. In recent decades this view and certain modern variations of it have been spoken of as "voluntarism."[6]

------

[6]The term "voluntarism" was coined by the German sociologist Ferdinand Tönnies in 1883 and was given wide currency by Friedrich Paulsen in his *Introduction to Philosophy* (1st American from 3rd German ed.; New York, 1895). In its popular and rather loose meaning it refers to any conception

In general, this view exalts the dynamic aspects of existence; therefore it conceives of man's proper goal as the fulfillment of the life-giving powers inherent in existence. But here the elements of struggle, contradiction, and tragedy rather than the element of harmony is emphasized. Thus in popular Greek thought and even among certain of the élite, a large place is assigned to Fate. Man is believed to be confronted by divine and demonic forces that either support and inspire, or thwart and pervert him in his attempt to fulfill his destiny. Although there is here a keen sense of tragedy, man does not in this view necessarily lose his dignity and worth. Quite the contrary. In the great Greek tragedies, for example, the tragic element is discovered at the very point at which human great-

---

of human nature or of the human situation which stresses the significance, the actual or potential strength, of will. In its more technical meaning it denotes any theory that asserts that will or creativity is the decisive factor in human nature and that will is the ultimate constituent of reality. Perhaps the most widely familiar statement of the position is the assertion of the primacy of the will over the intellect.

As an epistemological method voluntarism may be said to depend upon the view that the substantial character of reality cannot be understood merely by achieving clear and distinct ideas. For reality should determine the ideas and not the ideas the reality. Hence, scientific positivism as well as modern philosophical realism belongs within the tradition of voluntarism, though certain types of rationalistic positivism have veered away from it. Another way of stating this epistemological principle is to say that epistemology must have an ontological basis in the creativity that characterizes "the living universe." Hence, knowledge is an active understanding and a participation in creativity.

The use of the term "voluntarism" in psychology does not connote an acceptance of the old faculty psychology. The word "will" has to a great extent disappeared from the psychology textbooks except in the discussions of the freedom of the will. The words conation, striving, impulse, desire, and action have largely replaced it. Cf. "Will," *Dictionary of Psychology*, ed. Howard C. Warren (Boston, 1934). For an exposition of certain aspects of voluntaristic psychology since Nietzsche, see the valuable study by Dr. Erich Fromm, "Selfishness and Self-Love," *Psychiatry*, II (November, 1939), 507-523.

In recent decades the term voluntarism has sometimes been employed by sociologists to denote an emphasis upon the decisive significance of "the social will" in the development of society. For a survey of modern European and American voluntaristic sociology see Paul Barth, *Die Philosophie der Geschichte als Soziologie* (Leipzig, 1915), pp. 437-505; also, Ernst Troeltsch, *Historismus und seine Probleme* (Tübingen, 1922); Edward H. Redman, "A Study of Ernst Troeltsch's Theory of Historicism" (Unpublished B.D. dissertation, The Meadville Theological School, 1941).

The term "voluntarism" also denotes any theory that stresses the role of the will or of decision in religious knowledge, in faith, and in religious experience. The Pauline and Augustinian doctrines of grace may be taken as illustrations of a voluntaristic theology and psychology. In the Augustinian tradition, especially in the Middle Ages, the voluntaristic attitude toward religious experience is expressed in the view that blessedness is ness and the divine sphere come into conflict. It is precisely human greatness that makes possible tragic guilt and self-destruction. Indeed, according to this view, not only man is plagued by a Fate that drives him to tragic grandeur and self-destruction, but even the gods are subject to it, since no one of them can be identified with the highest principle. Fate is considered to be sovereign over both man and the gods just because it is viewed as a causal manifestation of a primordial creative principle. The point to be stressed, however, is that man is here understood in terms of the dignity and fate of a human agent confronted by a will or power that cannot be brought under control by any human technique.[7] The tragic process is master of all forms, causing them to undergo change and transformation and even destruction.

This tragic view of the human condition, as it was held among the Greeks, was largely ignored in eighteenth and nineteenth-century "Hellenism," as was also the fact of its affinity with ancient Hebrew conceptions. The Hellenism that has been influential since the Renaissance has taken its nourishment chiefly from the intellectualistic tendency in Greek life and thought.[8] Nietzsche

---

a state of activity. For a recent discussion of the points at issue between certain types of intellectualism and voluntarism in current theological controversy over the Augustianian theology, see Harris Harbison's article, "Will versus Reason," in *The Journal of Bible and Religion,* IX (November, 1941), 203-216. Cf. also on this whole problem, Paul Tillich, *The Interpretation of History* (New York, 1936) ; H. Richard Niebuhr, *The Meaning of Revelation* (New York, 1941).

For a history of voluntarism in Germany since the Renaissance, see the valuable work by the distinguished religious liberal, Kurt Leese, *Die Krisis und Wende des christlichen Geistes* (Berlin, 1932). On Leese's philosophy, see James L. Adams, "Kurt Leese and German Liberalism," *The Christian Register,* 116 (August 5, 1937), 463-465.

For a brief history of the various types of voluntarism and of the struggle between intellectualism and voluntarism in European philosophy and theology, see Heinz Heimsoeth, *Die sechs grossen Themen der abendländischen Metaphysik* (Berlin-Steglitz, 1934), chapter VI. Cf. also "Voluntarism," *Dictionary of Philosophy,* ed. Dagobert D. Runes (New York, 1942), and articles on "Voluntarismus" in *Religion in Geschichte und Gegenwart* (2nd ed., Tübingen, 1927-1931), Vol. V, and in R. Eisler, *Wörterbuch der philosophischen Begriffe* (Berlin, 1927-1930), Vol. III.

[7]On the Greek views of tragedy see Gilbert Norwood, *Greek Tragedy* (Boston, 1920) ; Prosser Hall Frye, *Romance and Tragedy* (Boston, 1922) ; article, "Moira," Pauly-Wissowa, *Real-Encyclopädie der classischen Altertumswissenschaft,* Vol. XV (1932), 2449-2472.

[8]It must be noted, however, that during both the Renaissance and the Romantic period there was considerable conflict among the Hellenizers, that is, between the rationalists and those who held the tragic view. But despite the revival of certain elements of the Greek tragic view in Roman-

and Burckhardt were among the first influential modern historians to become aware of the great significance of the tragic, Dionysian tendency in Greek thought.[9] The work of later scholars like Butcher and Diels has contributed much to the achievement of a new appreciation of what Butcher has characterized as "the melancholy of the Greeks." Nevertheless, the "Apollonian" interpretation of Hellenism as set forth by Matthew Arnold has continued to exercise a wide influence, and it has veiled from the eyes of many the predominantly tragic attitude of the Greeks, an attitude much more similar to that of the Hebrews than Arnold recognized. The Hellenism described by Arnold deserves the praise he bestows upon it. But we should bear in mind that it was shared by only a small élite in ancient Greece and also that it was only for a short time able to maintain the optimistic attitude that we associate with the glory that was Greece.

In the light of what has been said, it should be clear that we cannot properly understand the third influential attitude toward man and existence—the Judeo-Christian view—if we interpret it as constituting a complete contrast with "the Greek view of life." It is true that there is little in common between the Jewish-and-early-Christian view and the Apollonian attitude. In so far as Matthew Arnold confines attention to these two points of view he is a reliable guide when he emphasizes the contrasts between Hellenism and Hebraism. Also, in addition to the differences that Arnold describes, we should note that another contrast between the Judeo-Christian and the sophisticated Greek outlook is to be discerned in their contrasting views of time and history, the one looking upon history as "forward-moving" toward an End (*eschaton*) and the other viewing it as "cyclic."

On the other hand, the Greek Dionysian view and the Judeo-Christian attitude bear a resemblance to each other in their

ticism, the intellectualistic view of Hellenism was the more influential in the nineteenth century, as, for example, in Hegel and Matthew Arnold. Both these writers, despite fundamental divergencies, conceive of Hellenism as an aesthetic, harmonious outlook rather than as a "tragic" one.

[9] See Nietzsche's essays *The Birth of Tragedy* (1870-1) and *Philosophy during the Tragic Age of the Greeks* (1873); also Jakob Burckhardt, *Griechische Kulturgeschichte* (Leipzig, 1929). For a brilliant characterization of the Apollonian and the Dionysian tendencies in ancient Greek culture, see also Charles W. Morris, *Paths of Life* (Harper, 1942). For a psychological typology based on these two tendencies, see C. G. Jung, *Psychological Types* (New York, 1923), chapter III.

possession of a "tragic sense of life" as well as in their emphasis upon the dynamic elements in the world and in human life. According to the Judeo-Christian view, God is a righteous will fulfilling his purpose in history; man and nature are fallen; man's natural will is at variance with the divine will, and man's sin and guilt and his conflict with the principalities and powers of this world are an inextricable part of human experience. Thus in both the Greek tragic view and the Jewish prophetic and primitive Christian outlook there is an awareness of an ontologically as well as psychologically grounded tendency in man to rebellion, perversion, and self-destruction, and thus there is an assertion of the universal guilt of man. Moreover, in both views the attention is centered upon the dynamic, creative-destructive aspects of existence and upon the affective aspects of the human psyche.

Yet, there are also certain fundamental differences to be observed between the Judeo-Christian and the Greek "tragic" view. Two of these differences may be noted here. The first has to do with the ultimate valuation they place on existence.

The Judeo-Christian doctrine of creation involves the idea that in substance the world is good, for it is God's creation. Nothing in existence is absolutely anti-divine. In order for anything to exist it must have something of the divine in it. *Esse est bonum qua esse*. The Christian confession: "I believe in God the Father Almighty, the Creator of heaven and earth," has this idea as its real import. Even suffering may be a means of grace. Indeed, the Cross is the highest revelation of the character of God, for through it divine providence overcomes sin and death. Likewise, the Pauline belief in original sin is outweighed by the emphasis on providence and the hope of redemption. Thus faith points beyond tragedy; ultimately, existence and history are not tragic.[10] On the other hand, the Greek popular view from pre-Homeric times was unable to find a principle of transcendence beyond the

---

[10]One is reminded here of Father Tyrrell's statement that Christianity is an ultimate optimism based upon a provisional pessimism. Cf. also Reinhold Niebuhr, *Beyond Tragedy* (New York, 1937).

As J. B. Bury has pointed out, the modern belief in progress represents a rationalized adaptation of the Christian doctrine of providence. H. Richard Niebuhr has suggested that the idea of progress was also implicit in the neo-Calvinist doctrine of providence which became influential after the Great Awakening. Cf. *The Kingdom of God in America*, (Chicago, 1937), p. 192.

tragedy of existence. This view finds philosophical expression in the famous fragment of Anaximander: "Things perish into those things from which they have their birth, as it is ordained; for they pay to one another the penalty of their injustice according to the order of time." For Anaximander, "the separate existence of things is, so to speak, a wrong, a transgression which they must expiate by their destruction."[11] The contrast between Judeo-Christian optimism and the "melancholy" of the Greeks cannot be discussed in further detail here.[12]

The other major difference between the Judeo-Christian and the Dionysian view concerns their contrasting attitudes toward reason and morality. The Dionysian view was strongly characterized by "enthusiastic" irrationalism and amoralism, defects made familiar to most of us through the diatribes of Euripides against Dionysianism. The Judeo-Christian mentality in its formative period made no virtue of irrationalism and it strongly opposed amoralism. Whether we think of the Old Testament prophets, of the writers of the Wisdom literature, or of the great rabbis of normative Judaism, whether we think of Jesus, of Paul, of the author of the Fourth Gospel, or of the Greek fathers or Augustine—the main line of the Christian tradition—we find no exaltation of irrationalism and we find a great emphasis placed on conformity to the righteous will of God. With respect to the attitude toward reason, it is no accident that the Christian outlook could be merged with Greek theology. It is largely because of this coming together of Judeo-Christian voluntarism and Greek intellectualism that Christianity became the transmitter of much of the best in both the ancient Semitic and the ancient Greek tradition.

Apart from the fact that the *pagan* tragic view was effectually overcome in the Middle Ages,[13] the views that prevailed in the

[11] Cf. Eduard Zeller, *A History of Greek Philosophy,* trans. S. F. Alleyne (London, 1881), I, 256.

[12] It must suffice to direct the reader's attention to one of the best treatments of these contrasts in S. H. Butcher's two volumes, *Some Aspects of the Greek Genius* (New York, 1893) and *Harvard Lectures on Greek Subjects* (New York, 1904). See also Paul Tillich, "The Meaning of Our Present Historical Existence," *The Hazen Conferences on Student Guidance and Counselling,* 1938, pp. 19-29, and Reinhold Niebuhr, *The Nature and Destiny of Man:* I. *Human Nature* (New York, 1941), chap. 1.

[13] A fascinating account of this struggle between the pagan idea of Fate and the Christian idea of Providence is to be found in H. R. Patch, *The Tradition of Boethius; A Study of His Importance in Medieval Culture*

Middle Ages, in the Renaissance and the Reformation, and even in the periods of the Enlightenment and of Romanticism are to be interpreted as modern developments, combinations, or perversions of motifs already present in these ancient Greek and Hebrew traditions. The increasingly dominant force in modern Western culture, however, has been in the rationalistic tradition. Although intellectualism reached its high points in Thomism, in the Cartesian tradition, and in early eighteenth-century rationalism, and although it met with strong opposition in Romanticism—a form of Dionysianism which was later in vitalism "to go on all fours," it has in many quarters continued to hold its own. To be sure, it has in this process undergone certain transformations. Indeed, its "success" is perhaps due to this very fact. Thus the earlier static rationalism was in the eighteenth century replaced by a dynamic, progressive rationalism that has exercised a considerable variety of influence. This dynamic rationalism is to be seen, for example, in the revolutionary rationalism of the late eighteenth century; it has served as the core of modern bourgeois democracy; and, alongside the influence of empiricism, it has also decisively affected eighteenth and nineteenth-century science and technology. This change to a dynamic rationalism took place at the time when the bourgeois man was freeing himself from the feudal system and bringing about in its place the modern industrialist society. This fact has no small bearing on the character that modern rationalism has assumed in its various stages.

Meanwhile, the voluntaristic view has also undergone many changes. Its peregrinations may be roughly identified with the pilgrimage of the Augustinian point of view through its many variations, as in Bonaventura, Duns Scotus, and Luther, and through essential changes, as in Schelling and Nietzsche. A list of the significant figures who in the modern period have in one way or another stressed the role of creative will and conflict rather than of unitary reason and harmony would be long and imposing. Yet it would for the most part include philosophical outlooks that have been subdominant in modern thought until recent decades. Some of these thinkers have set forth a basically irrational philosophy, others have stressed the role of the non-rational or the

(New York, 1935). See also E. K. Chambers, *The Mediaeval Stage* (2 vols., Oxford, 1903).

a-logical, and still others have attempted to combine rational analysis with a "metalogical" recognition of the decisive role of the will.[14]

In general, however, we may say that whereas intellectualism as a consequence of its having centered attention on the cognitive aspects of human nature has emphasized rational poise, harmony, and "a theoretical attitude of distance," voluntarism, although for the most part insisting upon the basic significance of the intellectual disciplines, has tended to stress the dynamic and contradictory elements in existence and the affective aspects of human nature. Consequently, voluntarism has sensed more keenly the "embarrassments" of existence, and thus it has favored what is today called the existential attitude, that is, "an ultimate concern about the meaning of being for us, demanding an attitude of decision."[15] In the light of these contrasts in typology we must interpret the age-old conflict between those who assert the primacy of the intellect and those who assert the primacy of the will.[15a] And

---

[14]The wide range of interpretation possible here can be suggested if we note that in the list of voluntarists the following thinkers have been included (in addition to those already named in the text) : Calvin, Boehme, Pascal, Jonathan Edwards, Hume, Kant, Kierkegaard, Schopenhauer, Marx, James, Babbitt, Dewey, Bergson, Freud, Troeltsch, Otto, Berdyaev, Tillich, Leese, Tennant, Klages, van Holk, and Mannheim.

The distinguished Orientalist Deussen in *Die Philosophie der Bibel* (Leipzig, 1913), pointed out the affinities between this type of thought and that of the Bible. The American Orientalist, Duncan B. MacDonald, has dealt with the same themes in his *The Hebrew Philosophical Genius* (Princeton, 1936), showing the voluntarist elements in the Old Testament.

Modern psychologists have recognized the significance and originality of Augustine for the theory of the primacy of the will in psychology. Even in that Thomist stronghold, the Latin Church, voluntarist influences have been evident not only among the Scotists but also among those deeply influenced by the Bible and modern realism and pragmatism. Especially significant in this respect are the writings of P. Laberthonnière and Maurice Blondel.

[15]Cf. Paul Tillich's review of Reinhold Niebuhr's *The Nature and Destiny of Man*, in *Christianity and Society*, VI (Spring, 1941), 34.

[15a]The author regrets that only after the present essay was completed did he see the essay on "Power and World Organization" by Dr. Carl Mayer, Professor of Sociology at the New School for Social Research, published in *Christianity and Society*, VII (Winter 1942), 11-18. This article gives an exceptionally fine statement of certain of the contrasts between what have been called here the intellectualist and voluntarist positions, and the author would have liked to adopt certain of Professor Mayer's formulations. With most of his theoretical analysis the present author is in entire agreement. The principal objection to be raised concerns the questionable views set forth concerning the nature and role of power. As Reinhold Niebuhr has pointed out, Dr. Mayer's contention that "power is of itself evil" is untenable "unless life itself be regarded as evil. For life is power." The point at issue here is dealt with briefly in the present essay, *infra*, pp. 26, 35-36.

it must be noted again that the voluntaristic tradition, especially in Christian theology, has stressed the fateful, tragic aspects of human existence. Indeed, in its most extreme forms voluntarism has asserted the arbitrary sovereignty of God and the helpless corruption of human nature, and in secular thought it has asserted the arbitrary sovereignty of some particularist loyalty to tradition, blood, class, or nation.

The Rise of Liberalism

The modern development of intellectualism must be understood as a reaction against these extreme forms of voluntarism. In large degree the Renaissance was a revolt against obscurantist and authoritarian elements in medieval culture and against certain earlier forms of voluntarism, though it must be added that the Renaissance also gave birth to a variety of conflicts between different types of intellectualism and of voluntarism. Finally, the intellectualism of later centuries served as a means of revolt against the extreme forms of voluntarism found in orthodox Calvinism and Lutheranism.

Indeed, religious liberalism itself can be understood in its proper perspective only when interpreted as an aspect of this opposition. In religious liberalism the rationalistic view of human nature and of the human situation appeared as a revolt against the older forms of authoritarianism, a revolt in the name of the principles of freedom of mind and freedom of conscience. But concomitantly the liberal movement represented also a revolt against the Protestant dogma of the total depravity of human nature, that is, against a depraved, lopsided, rationalized form of the Christian doctrine of original sin. In short, it was a revolt against a voluntarism that had gone to seed.

The Unitarians and their predecessors were among those who were in the vanguard of this revolt against the pessimistic Reformation conception. In opposition to the Calvinist view, and in no small measure utilizing the dialectical powers inherited from Calvinism, the Unitarians asserted that man's possession of the faculty of reason gives him the dignity of a child of God; and they held that by means of this faculty man could eliminate the superstitions and unworthy accretions of the Christian tradition, and bring about both a fulfillment of the human spirit and a return to "pure Christianity."

The fruits of this struggle and of the great humanitarian impulse of the nineteenth century represent no mean cultural accomplishment. This fact can scarcely be over-emphasized. Moreover, contemporary Protestantism owes primarily to religious liberalism the social emphasis that in the past century has been reintroduced into Protestant thought and action.

But, unfortunately, not all the fruits issuing from the new movement were actually intended or expected by its proponents. Nor was the movement able to maintain in the main body of its adherents the prophetic power of its early days. The new intellectualism, which in its early stages was powerfully dynamic, more and more moved in the direction of emphasizing again the merely, that is the static, cognitive aspects of human nature, "the theoretical attitude of distance," and of neglecting the affective side of human nature and "the attitude of decision."[16] The influence of the scientific method, despite its value in other respects, played no small role in accelerating this tendency.

Perhaps this trend in religious liberalism can best be brought into relief by an illustration drawn from an early phase of its development. At the time of the Great Awakening in the middle of the eighteenth century, there was a sharp division of opinion concerning the value and validity of the "visible upsets of grace" that attended the revivalist movement, a movement that had arisen partially as an attempt to stem the tide of the Enlightenment. Certainly, little can be said in defense of the methods of the revivalist preachers of the time. The significant thing to be noticed,

[16]Other aspects of this revolt and of certain consequences that have not been "favorable to piety" were discussed by Professor Perry Miller in his address on "Individualism and the New England Tradition" at the annual meeting of the Unitarian Ministerial Union at King's Chapel, Boston, Mass., May 18, 1942. This address was published in the Summer 1942 issue of this JOURNAL.

Professor Miller in his essay on "The Marrow of Puritan Divinity," *Publications of the Colonial Society of Massachusetts*, XXXII (1935), 247-300, has shown that the rationalistic revolt against the Calvinist emphasis on the inscrutability of the divine decrees emanating from the will of God, began among the Puritans in early seventeenth-century England and was widely prevalent among the first Puritan divines of New England. Indeed, Jonathan Edwards was the first strictly Calvinist theologian in New England; he looked upon the earlier divines as heretics.

however, is the particular form that the opposition to the new movement took. This opposition to the New Lights was led by Charles Chauncy of the First Church in Boston.[17] Chauncy was justly impatient with the irrational extravagances of the movement. He charged that it was "a plain stubborn Fact, that the Passions have generally in these times, been apply'd to, as though the main Thing in Religion was to throw them into Disturbance." "The plain truth," he insisted, is that "an enlightened Mind, and not raised Affections, ought always to be the Guide of those who call themselves men; and this, in the affairs of religion, as well as other things." "Reasonable beings," he declared, "are not to be guided by passion or affection, even though the Object of it should be God and the things of another world." Chauncy's preference for the restraints of reason as against "raised affections" indicates the trend of his thought. He did still believe that some fundamental change of heart and will—a conversion—is necessary for one who would become a Christian, but his own preoccupation and the increasing preference of his age were with more intellectual matters. As time went on man's reason and not the quality of his will was more and more widely assumed to be of primary importance. As one historian has phrased it, regeneration was now felt to be far too big a word to describe the difference that religion should make.[18] No doubt one reason for this change of attitude was the improved social status and the increased security of the people concerned. "Conversion" was more and more relegated to the underprivileged classes, and middle-class Liberalism became increasingly a form of accommodation to the ways of the world. The elapse of a century and a half of capitalism with its concomitant marriage of convenience with "religion" and the rise of new religious and secular forms of protest were required to make these facts plain. But in the long run the increase in the power of the middle class served to replace the idea of the

---

[17]See his *Seasonable Thoughts on the State of Religion in New England* (Boston, 1743). The controversy is well described in the Introduction to C. H. Faust and Thomas H. Johnson, *Jonathan Edwards, Representative Selections* (New York, 1935). For a spirited discussion of this period of the rise of American religious liberalism, see Joseph Haroutunian, *Piety versus Moralism—The Passing of the New England Theology* (New York, 1932).

[18]W. P. Paterson, *Conversion* (New York, 1940), p. 123.

necessity of conversion with another ideal: the formation of a "respectable" type of "religious" and moral character through "reasonable" and increasingly secularistic (and "safe") education.

What was happening here may be taken as characteristic of one important element in the modern movement of rationalism since Descartes. The emphasis on the quality of the will, on the disposition of the *entire* personality, was being replaced by a one-sided emphasis on "reason." The attitude of Greek rationalism as mediated through Stoicism and scholasticism and transformed by modern rationalism, was taking the place of the older Augustinian emphasis on the will and the affections. Here we find, then, the element that has given to Unitarianism its reputation for being intellectual. The appeal to affective experience, the belief in the necessity for conversion, and the use of the emotive symbols of the religious tradition were more and more deprecated.[19] Thus religious Liberalism, in the name of *intellectual* integrity, tended to neglect the deeper levels both of the human consciousness and of reality itself. As a consequence, it gradually became associated with an ascetic attitude toward the imagination as well as toward enthusiasm and gripping loyalties. Instead of confronting men with the demand of inner commitment to the tenets of prophetic religion, it more and more provided a cosmic or religious sanction for the interests of a particular group. In the end "the attitude of distance" won the day, and Liberalism achieved poise by living at the low temperature of "detached, middle-class common sense."[20]

These tendencies were not the consequence of a loss of faith. They were merely the negative aspects of a new faith. Nor was this a faith merely in human reason or in man alone. It was a faith that found its support in a new idea of the character of the universe and of man as a part of that universe.

---

[19]Cf. Gerald Birney Smith, "Liberal Theology," *A Dictionary of Religion and Ethics,* ed. S. Mathews and G. B. Smith (New York, 1921).

[20]The "attitude of distance" is, of course, indispensable for both science and religion. But it is scarcely sufficient for religion. In this connection see G. E. O. Meyer's discussion of the I-Thou relationship, "The Religious Socialist in the World Crisis," THE JOURNAL OF LIBERAL RELIGION, III (Spring, 1942), 196. Cf. also the Jewish mystic, Martin Buber, *I and Thou* (Edinburgh, 1937); Philip Wheelwright, "Religion and Social Grammar," *Kenyon Review,* IV (Spring, 1942), 202-216; H. Richard Niebuhr, *op. cit.,* chap. 2.
On the religion of the low temperature, and of "detached, middle-class common sense," see A. N. Whitehead, *Religion in the Making* (New York, 1926), pp. 52 ff.

This faith and its supporting conception of the universe is what is generally referred to when the modern historian of culture speaks of Liberalism (with a capital L). It is against this type of Liberalism and its contemporary residues that much of the current criticism of religious liberalism is directed. In so far as it is valid this criticism does not involve a repudiation of the liberal ideal of liberating the human spirit from the bondage of economic, social and ecclesiastical tyrannies. It is directed against the view of human nature and of the nature of reality which is explicit in eighteenth and nineteenth-century Liberalism and which is still implicit in much liberal thought of today. Hence, it is directed also against the tendency of this type of Liberalism to become associated too closely with the interests of one class in society. Let us now examine these conceptions.

The Philosophy of Liberalism

Dean Fenn has pointed out that the "favorite concept" of modern rationalistic Liberalism is its belief in the unified structure of the world.[21] This belief is the modern counterpart of the Greek rationalistic view of ultimate reality as a unified pattern behind phenomena, a pattern with which the rational soul feels itself akin. It has found a great variety of expression, as in Descartes' faith in the existence of a divine power that harmonizes mind and nature, or in Spinoza's view that thought and extension are different attributes of the same substance and that God is that substance, or in Leibniz's theory of a pre-established harmony that preserves unity despite apparent diversity, or in his view that the individual is a unified whole within the macrocosm.

We are all familiar with the result of this whole tendency. Because of the pre-established harmony, separative individualism was given a divine sanction, and the modern Liberal's over-optimism concerning human nature and its progressive and ultimate perfectibility was born. Mandeville does, to be sure, recognize the contrast between the selfish desire of the bourgeois man and his desire for order and education. But he resolves the conflict by appealing to the pre-established harmony: hence, he says private vices are public virtues. Shaftesbury and Hutcheson discover a moral sense in everybody. This moral sense, they say, is an

---

[21]*Op. cit.*, pp. 517 ff.

32

invariant norm, the violation of which would alone introduce discord. Helvetius even goes so far as to assert that self-love leads ultimately to the love of others. Condillac says that the brain is a *tabula rasa,* but the laws of matter operative in brain vibrations will bring forth truth. How? Through the pre-established harmony. And many of the scientists of the eighteenth and nineteenth centuries, following the lead of Francis Bacon, believed that if only the scientists would individually specialize and then pool their findings the kingdom of man would be ushered in. Finally, Liberal economics proclaimed the faith that if markets were made free and state interference were reduced to a minimum, the rationality of economic forces would do the rest and harmonious well-being for everybody would ensue.[22] This view was supported by the doctrine of the harmony of interests, according to which the individual could be relied on to promote the interests of the community for the reason that those interests were identical with his own. The harmony was believed to be none the less real if those concerned were unconscious of it. The pre-established harmony would operate willy-nilly. According to an often quoted passage in Adam Smith's *Wealth of Nations,* the individual "neither intends to promote the public interest, nor knows how much he is promoting it. . . . He intends only his own gain, and he is in this, as in many other cases, led by an invisible hand to promote an end which was no part of his intention."[22a]

Out of roots such as these grew the ideas of progress and perfectibility characteristic of the secular as well as of the religious Liberalism of the eighteenth and nineteenth centuries. In some

[22]For a discussion of the theory of pre-established harmony and of related ideas, see E. H. Carr, *The Twenty Years' Crisis, 1919-1939* (London, 1941), chap. 4. See also J. H. Randall, Jr., *The Making of the Modern Mind* (rev. ed.; New York, 1940), Bk. III; Wilhelm Pauck, "What Is Wrong with Liberalism?" *The Journal of Religion,* XV (1935), 146-160; Carl Becker, *The Heavenly City of the Eighteenth Century Philosophers* (New Haven, 1932); Ernst Troeltsch, *Protestantism and Progress,* trans. W. Montgomery (New York, 1912); Paul Tillich, *Sozialistische Entscheidung* (Potsdam, 1933), pp. 68 ff.
Professor Carr (*op. cit.*) shows the disastrous effect of the theory of "the harmony of interests" on international politics during the past two decades.

[22a]This and a few similar passages in Adam Smith's writings are important both as a symptom of a strain of harmonistic philosophy and as a frequently used weapon in later laisser-faire ideology. However, it is only fair to observe that frequently Adam Smith notes possible and probable discrepancies between private and public interests. Still, Smith argued that on the whole (with certain exceptions granted) laisser-faire would tend to

quarters these ideas were related to a new faith in man; in other quarters they were related to a thoroughly worked-out philosophy of history; and in still others they were rooted in a belief in "cosmic progress." Within these variations there were still others. Some liberals, for example, emphasized the natural power of Reason, while others, under the influence of Romanticism, emphasized the natural power of Sympathy. In 1885 belief in "the progress of mankind onward and upward forever" became one of the main articles of the Unitarian faith. And, as an eminent Unitarian historian says, Dr. James Freeman Clarke "leaves us in no doubt concerning the importance" he ascribed to the famous Point Five: "He did not intend 'the Progress of Mankind' to be an *omnium gatherum,* or an anti-climax; on the contrary, he regarded the belief in human progress as an essential and a summary of a true Liberal's religion." Dr. Clarke's sermon in which the "Five Points of the New Theology" were first set forth concludes with this affirmation: "The one fact which is written on nature and human life, which accords with all we see and know, is the fact of progress; and this must be accepted as the purpose of the creation." The historian already quoted comments as follows on Dr. Clarke's general position: "There is ground for believing, indeed, that Dr. Clarke was influenced by the doctrines of Herbert Spencer and August Comte regarding the inevitability of progress—a process and a consummation implicit in the course of evolution and assured by the trend of natural forces."[23]

Since the turn of the century some religious liberals have greatly altered their attitude toward the older ideas of progress and perfectibility. Indeed, some of them no longer even mention the ideas, except when singing hymns written a generation or so ago. Moreover, liberalism has taken on new forms as a consequence of the influence of scientific positivism, of ethical relativism, and even of Marxian dialectical materialism,—not to speak of the influence of Marxian Utopianism. Nevertheless, it would be

---

minimize actual discrepancies and thus produce the ultimately best harmonization of interests.

[23]Charles H. Lyttle, "The Faith of Progress," *The Meadville Theological School Quarterly Bulletin,* XIX (January, 1925), 4. For a recent discussion of the idea of progress as held among religious liberals and Unitarians between 1880 and 1895, see Daniel Day Williams, *The Andover Liberals* (New York, 1941). For a psychoanalytical interpretation of the extreme optimism of nineteenth-century religious Liberalism, see the New

wrong to suppose that the outlook on the world entertained by the majority of religious liberals has undergone radical modification in respect to belief in the unified structure of the world or in the continuous progress of the race. As operative presupposition if not as explicit doctrine the old beliefs in harmony and perfectibility still serve as a groundwork for "faith." This is especially true among the laity of all the denominations in the left wing of Protestantism, not to mention millions of people outside the churches. In short, the general outlook on life of many people continues to have its roots in the rationalistic "non-tragic" tradition, especially as it took form in the eighteenth century. It is therefore necessary for us to examine critically the basic presuppositions of this tradition in order to understand the present "changing reputation of human nature."

The Criticism of Liberalism

The major criticisms of Liberalism can be subsumed under the general objection suggested by Dean Fenn in the article referred to, that the world, man, and God are envisaged by "Modern Liberalism" as too neatly harmonized in a purely logical concept of unity.[24] In order to understand this criticism as it affects the Liberal doctrine of man, it will be instructive first to observe the application of it to the theory of nature characteristic of the old "harmonistic" rationalism and then to proceed to an application of it to the reputation of human nature.

From the point of view of the modern voluntarist, the seventeenth and eighteenth-century view of nature as a beautifully working mechanism or as a manifestation of reason was subjective,— it did not sufficiently take into account the stubborn external reality. The voluntarist, agreeing with the empiricist, holds that although nature lends itself to rational methods of inquiry, existence as *fact* comes first and man's rational interpretation only later. The conditions under which existence is maintained or modified are "given." The world might have been any one of an

---

Testament scholar Robert P. Casey's article, "Oedipus Motivation in Religious Thought and Fantasy," *Psychiatry*, V (May, 1942), 219-228.

[24]*Op. cit.*, p. 517. "Modern Liberalism will have to revise its favorite concept of unity. At present, monistic idealism is very much under the weather philosophically, and a theological system akin to it must suffer correspondingly."

infinite number of possible worlds, but actually it is the kind of world it is. This actual existence is a primary datum. Or, as the British empiricist F. R. Tennant says, it is an alogical datum. It is not legislated by reason or by necessary being.[25] Indeed, man's reason itself has roots in a being and in a history that might have been different. Nor is the alogical datum of existence identical with an idea that is "clear and distinct." Actuality is richer than thought. There is always a tension between *logos* and being. Hence, "natural laws" must be viewed as only tentative generalizations formulated on the basis of certain observed data.[26]

But the older Liberalism was not only subjective in its view of nature. It also interpreted nature in terms of form rather than of vitality, in terms of reason rather than of "the divine fecundity of nature." Moreover, structural centripetal forces rather than individual centrifugal tensions were stressed. In so far as a man bases his religious convictions upon this "rational" conception of nature he tends to develop an over-harmonious view of it, and thus also to develop a "simple" belief in the immanence of God. For this reason, I take it, Dean Fenn recommends to those who adopt a monistic view that they "seriously consider what sort of God it is that nature reveals." As he says, "we cannot be so enamoured of the loveliness of nature as to be blind to its terrible aspects." The heavens may declare the glory of God, and nature may exhibit the operation of a principle of mutual aid, yet the struggle for

---

[25]A recent writer on Whitehead expresses this idea as follows: "When we say, 'This is a bit of concrete reality,' what do we mean? We mean more than a mere assertion that 'this exists now.' According to Whitehead, we mean that 'this' is just what it is *in contrast to* what it might possibly have been. That is what 'becoming real' means—just *this* has happened, just this that *might* have been something else. At this point it might be objected that the occurrence of any event is determined by causal laws, and that therefore whatever happens could not in fact have been anything else. But this, if granted, merely pushes the inquiry a step farther back. We may explain the occurrence of event X by a causal law perhaps, but is not the causal law itself real? For the real particularity of the causal law itself exists only in contrast to what it might have been but which in fact it is not." Stephen Lee Ely, *The Religious Availability of Whitehead's God* (Madison, 1942), p. 9.

Especially valuable is the treatment of the relation between fact and idea to be found in F. E. England, *The Validity of Religious Experience* (London, 1937). Dr. England relies heavily upon Whitehead. See also F. R. Tennant, *Philosophy of the Sciences* (Cambridge, 1932), Lecture III.

[26]Sir William Bragg has said that the modern physicist must use one set of conceptions on Mondays, Wednesdays, and Fridays, and a different set on Tuesdays, Thursdays, and Saturdays.

existence in nature amply justifies Tennyson's description of it as "red in tooth and claw." No doubt it was because of this internecine struggle in nature that St. Paul as well as the ancient Hebrews looked upon even the world of nature as a fallen world, a world to be restored to love by the New Age or by the atonement of Christ. At all events, nature exhibits both creative and destructive tendencies, both a "will to harmony" and a "will to power." Neither of these tendencies appears without the other. Moreover, the power to exist and the power of love (or mutuality) do not possess perfect correlation; disharmony as well as harmony, devolution as well as evolution are to be found in nature.

* * *

Analogous objections may be directed against the older Liberalism's view of the human level of existence,—history. Here again the rationalistic conception is criticized because it is subjective and also because it overlooks the element of vitality (with its *both* creative and destructive tendencies) as it appears on the level of human freedom. That is, it ignores the alogical character of history and it rationalistically formalizes history by interpreting it as a progressive movement towards harmony. Thus it fails to take fully into account the elements of conflict and perversion; it fails to recognize that vitality in history does not issue from logic (which is a regulative and not a constitutive principle); and it fails to recognize that this vitality brings forth both harmony and disharmony, both creation and destruction.

The great liberal Ernst Troeltsch, who anticipated much of contemporary voluntarism, has decisively set forth these criticisms in his famous work, *Historismus und seine Probleme*. History, Troeltsch says, is something "given," and the forces that operate there share the alogical character inherent in existence itself. This alogical character of history is manifest both in necessity and in freedom. Neither the necessity nor the freedom can be understood merely in terms of reason with its self-evident premises. In the first place, knowledge of the character of that necessity can be acquired only by observing it inductively and not by deduction from *a priori* principles. In the second place, the very fact of human freedom gives to history a singularity peculiar to all human creations. "In history," as Troeltsch says, "a qualitative unity and originality is assumed to be originally given . . . which may be

called fate, destiny, creation, or something else." He speaks of
this aspect of history as metalogical and not logical. For whereas
organic nature is practically enclosed within the biological circle
of birth, growth, procreation, and death, history does not repeat
itself,—it generates novelty. And because of this also, it cannot
be interpreted in strictly rationalistic terms. As Bergson and
Whitehead (as well as Troeltsch) have pointed out, strict rationalism precludes the possibility of novelty.[27]

Now, there are certain implications for the nature of man which
must be seen to follow from the fact that history is the realm of
both necessity and freedom. Man is fated as well as free. As Wilhelm von Humboldt puts it, "man always ties on with what lies
at hand" (*Der Mensch knüpft immer an Vorhandenes an*). Certain
fateful conditioning factors always operate in the individual as well
as in society. Man must act in terms of the historical process and
of his psycho-physical organism. His actions must be of a certain
kind in order to be relevant and also in order that he may
avoid destruction. He cannot act merely in accordance with logical canons of an *a priori* order. Even his ethical ideals emerge
through his experience of being and of history. In this sense, it
may be said that "being is older than value." Yet, despite these
conditioning factors, man is fated also to be free; he is compelled
to make decisions. For he can transcend his situation and in
some measure he can freely change it; he can even change himself.
As a creative entity he can act to preserve or increase, destroy or
pervert, mutuality,—though it must be remembered also that conditions over which he has little control may affect the results of
his action. Thus man lives both in and above history. He is fate-
fully caught in history, both as an individual and as a member
of a group,[28] and he is also able to be creative in history.

Through the use of this creative freedom man expresses the
highest form of vitality that existence permits. Indeed, since this
creativity is a manifestation of a divinely given and a divinely
renewing power, we say that man is created in the image of God,

---

[27]On this whole problem, see Troeltsch's brief but profound article,
"Contingency," *Encyclopedia of Religion and Ethics,* ed. James Hastings,
Vol. 4, (1921), 87-89.

[28]It should be said in passing that Professor Frank H. Knight has
pointed out that economic Liberalism erred "in taking the individual's actual
endowment with means [personal capacities as well as material means] as a

that is, he participates in the divine creativity.[28a] This and not reason alone is the basis for the liberal's faith in man, and no change in the reputation of human nature could involve a denial of this fact without also repudiating the very essence of the liberal doctrine of man.

Because of this freedom, human history not only exhibits a singularity that transcends all *a priori* conceptions of the intellect; it also provides a more complex and spiritual form of conflict than that to be found on the level of nature. For history is a theatre of conflicts in which the tensions between the will to mutuality and the will to power appear in their most subtle and perverse forms.[29] In short, history is tragic. Let it be said immediately that this does not mean merely that men violate the moral code or disobey the law. That they do these things is obvious and universally recognized. The changing reputation of human nature does not depend upon any such "discovery."

It is at this point that we come to the consideration of the major deficiencies in the older Liberal doctrines of man and progress. These deficiencies can be brought into bold relief by showing concretely what is meant by the assertion that history is tragic. We shall use the Liberal epoch as an illustration of this view of history, not because that epoch is different from other epochs as a revelation of the nature of history, but rather because the tragic outcome of Liberalism in the present crisis presents the major problem confronting contemporary society and

datum," that is, "in taking the individual too much for granted" as such. Cf. his article "Religion and Ethics in Modern Civilization," THE JOURNAL OF LIBERAL RELIGION, III (Summer, 1941), 16.

[28a]Reinhold Niebuhr, in his *Nature and Destiny of Man,* fails to stress this idea in his discussion of the *Imago dei* doctrine. Cf. the author's criticism on this point in his article in *Christendom,* VI (1941), 576-580.

[29]On these two qualities of will, see the writings of Jacob Boehme, or see H. Brinton, *The Mystic Will* (New York, 1930), a study of Boehme's philosophy. Cf. also Irving Babbitt's distinction between *élan vital* and *frein vital, Democracy and Leadership* (Boston, 1924), pp. 17 ff., and Appendix B, "Theories of the Will."

A third type of will is also to be seen occasionally, namely the sort that tries to *escape* conflict by devotion to love without power. It was against this sort of weak will to love that Nietzsche inveighed in his criticism of Christianity. Cf. G. B. Foster, *Friedrich Nietzsche,* ed. Curt.s W. Reese (New York, 1931), chap. 12. See also Erich Fromm, *op. cit.,* and G. A. Morgan, *What Nietzsche Means* (Cambridge, 1941).

One may describe the extreme positions here by saying that the absolute pacifist seemingly believes in love without power; Hitler believes in power without love. See the author's article, "Man in the Light of War," *Christian Century,* LX (Mar. 3, 1943), 257-259.

also because Liberalism provides certain of the principles that are of decisive positive significance for the continued development of a democratic society and of liberal religion. In dealing with these problems we shall have to go over some very familiar ground. But it would seem worthwhile to do this, not only in order to show how the monistic, Liberal doctrines of man and progress actually contributed to the tragic outcome of the Liberal epoch but also in order later to indicate how a voluntaristic interpretation of man and history purports to correct the deficiencies of the "harmonistic" conception.

When we say that history is tragic, we mean that the perversions and failures in history are associated precisely with the highest creative powers of man and thus with his greatest achievements. One might call this the Oedipus motif in the sphere of history: nemesis is very often encountered almost simultaneously with the seemingly highest achievement. The very means and evidences of progress turn out again and again to be also the instruments of perversion or destruction. The national culture, for example, is the soil from which issue cherished treasures of a people, their language, their poetry, their music, their common social heritage. Yet nationalism is also one of the most destructive forces in the whole of human history. Progress in transportation has assisted tremendously in the raising of the standard of living: yet it has produced also a mobility in our cultural life which has brought in its train a new rootlessness and instability. Improved means of printing have made the treasures of the printed page available even to those who run as they read. But it has also made possible the appearance of the irresponsible manipulators of the idea industries, with the consequence that literacy is now also a powerful instrument for demagogy and the corruption of taste. The growth of a machine civilization has made available to the peasant objects that kings used to pine for; yet the machine doth man unking, and it has necessitated so rapid an urbanization of the population that a sense of community has been destroyed for millions of people, and intimate, colorful family life has become largely a rural phenomenon.

Or, consider another aspect of progress. There is no such thing as a unilinear development in the area of *moral* achievement. We see this in the fact that each generation has to acquire wisdom over again, and within this process "the war of the generations" arises. The son of the Philistine becomes a Bohemian, and his son becomes a communist. The mystical Body of Christ becomes an autocratic ecclesiastical hierarchy, and this in turn gives place to a spiritual anarchy or a militant secularism. There is progress here, regress and a new attempt or perversion there; one year a Revolution for the rights of man, but four years later a Reign of Terror and then a Napoleonic era; an American Revolution then, Daughters of the American Revolution now; emancipation of the slaves then, poll-tax Senators now; the extension of suffrage then, the Kelly-Nash machine now. Certainly, if there is progress, it is no simple configuration of "upward trends." At times, it looks more like a thing of shreds and patches.

The general tendency of Liberalism has been to neglect this tragic factor of history. It is true that most of the theorists of Liberalism were definitely pessimistic concerning man's worthiness of being entrusted with concentrated political power, but the general and prevailing trend of their thinking was nevertheless lopsidedly optimistic.

It is true also that in the hey-day of the idea of progress a few men expressed skepticism concerning the progress "assured by the trend of natural forces,"[29a] but they were given little heed. A poet here and there, an orthodox Calvinist or a cranky social prophet spoke out, but the idea that some men when released from bondage to superstition or to political and ecclesiastical authority, might use their newly acquired freedom and reason to build a new Bastille does not seem to have occurred to many. In America, Theodore Parker saw the handwriting on the wall. But his skepticism concerning the goodness of the new men of power has not had a perceptibly large influence among us. For as the

---

[29a]For example, Huxley, a scientist and not a "harmonizer," said in 1892: "The doctrines of predestination, of original sin, of the innate depravity of man and the evil fate of the greater part of the race, of the primacy of Satan in this world, of the essential vileness of matter, of a malevolent Demiurgus subordinate to a benevolent Almighty, who has only lately revealed himself, faulty as they are, appear to me to be vastly nearer the truth than the 'liberal' popular illusions that babies are all born good, and that the example of a corrupt society is responsible for their failure to remain so; that it is given to everybody to reach the ethical ideal if he will only try . . . that everything will come right (according to our notions) at last." (Quoted by Dean Sperry, op. cit., p. 184.)

nineteenth century "progressed," the wonders of science, the spread of education, the extension of suffrage, the success of certain types of reform legislation, the sense of emancipation from traditional restraints and ideas, the expansion of markets, the increase of production, population, and prosperity—all of these things conspired to make men think too well of themselves. Even Marxism, despite its attack upon the evils of bourgeois society, its great stress upon the class struggle and its criticism of the theory of unilinear progress, kept the faith in perfectibility by proclaiming a belief in dialectical progress towards a Utopian classless society.[30] One might suppose that the Civil War would have disturbed the American's complacency, but instead of being interpreted as an illustration of man's unwillingness to relinquish power for the sake of the pre-established harmony, it was taken mainly as evidence of the increasing emancipation of the race from bondage. And most of the colored folk, not to speak of millions of others, still remain slaves. After the publication of Darwin's *Origin of Species* the old optimism continued to prevail. What Carlyle contemptuously called "Darwin's Gorilla damnification of humanity" was exorcised by the grace of the older idea of progress. Thus the idea of evolution rather than the idea of struggle became the dominant if not the only "note" of the popular anthropology. In other words, the tragic note was softened and "harmonized."[30a]

And meanwhile, what had been happening? The rising bourgeois class, with which Unitarianism had been largely associated along with other branches of Protestantism, was gaining control of nature and commerce. A new will to power, comparable in irre-

---

[30]In "orthodox" Marxism "reliance upon 'processes at work in the order of things' became translated into the mythical language of the 'inevitability' of the development of capitalism into socialism." Sidney Hook, *Towards the Understanding of Karl Marx* (New York, 1933), p. 26.

[30a]Carr (*op. cit.*, pp. 58 ff.) points out that "the survival of the belief in a harmony of interests was rendered possible by the unparalleled expansion of production, population and prosperity, which marked the hundred years following the publication of *The Wealth of Nations* and the invention of the steam engine. Expanding prosperity contributed to the popularity of the doctrine in three different ways. It attenuated competition for markets among producers, since fresh markets were constantly becoming available; it postponed the class issue, with its insistence on the primary importance of equitable distribution, by extending to members of the less prosperous classes some share in the general prosperity; and by creating a sense of confidence in present and future well-being, it encouraged men to believe that the world was ordered on so rational a plan as the natural harmony of interests. 'It was the continual widening of the field of demand which, for

sistibility to ancient feudalism, became the main line of "progress." The principles of freedom and liberation were more and more domesticated into the service of Big Business and manifest destiny. As Professor Hocking puts it, the *feeling* for democracy that characterized the early days of Liberalism was lost. A solicitude for the dogma of "rugged individualism" has served only thinly to conceal the rigid desire to preserve economic gains. The dominant group has come to identify the interest of the community with its own interest, and any assailant of this group is told that he is working at cross purposes with his own interest as well as with the good of the community. As E. H. Carr points out in *The Twenty Years' Crisis* (p. 102) "the doctrine of the harmony of interests thus serves as an ngenious moral device invoked, in perfect sincerity, by privileged groups in order to justify and maintain their dominant position." In this way middle-class morality has become merely the product and the tool of power. The beginning of this shift in the temper of Liberalism can be traced back at least a hundred and fifty years in American history. Certainly, the old feeling for democracy had already very much subsided among the federalist Unitarians in the early days of the Republic. The commercial life of the nation was in time more and more looked upon as the supreme manifestation of its activity. In the words of Harold Laski:

The central theme of political policy thus became the supply of what commercial life required for its full expansion; and to this all effort in the community was increasingly subordinate. The religious discipline to which

---

half a century, made capitalism operate as if it were a liberal utopia.' "

Thus we see that the extremely optimistic and non-tragic attitude as well as the moralism of the Anglo-Saxon mentality have been largely a product of historical conditions, that is, a concomitant of the "success" of the British and American empires. Perhaps it was this "success" that also inspired the "prophets" of the age to believe that "mankind had discovered that secret of perpetual motion called progress." Here also we see the reason one finds so little discussion of tragedy in the literature of religious liberalism or in that of England and America of the nineteenth century. R. H. Gabriel speaks of Melville as an exception in this respect. Cf. *The Course of American Democratic Thought* (New York, 1940), chap. 6.

Professor F. O. Matthiessen of Harvard in his *American Renaissance* (Oxford, 1941), a penetrating study of art and expression in the age of Emerson and Whitman, devotes much attention to the contrasting attitudes toward tragedy, in this period. He draws one line reaching from Emerson's "rejection of tragedy" to the young Whitman's "superficial innocence of evil," and another line leading from Hawthorne's "conception of good and evil, which drove him to take the tragic view of life" on through Melville's "reaffirmation of tragedy" to the elder Whitman.

the individual had been formerly subject could then be replaced by an ethic derived predominantly from economic circumstance. [And it should be added, humanitarian movements made no essential change in this ethos.] Laisser-faire as a program was the logical counterpart in social philosophy of Protestantism in the religious, of free inquiry in the intellectual, sphere. Each came as a herald of freedom to an age hampered by obsolete principle. Each definitely enlarged by its victory the area in which the human spirit was free to voyage in self-discovery. But each in its adventure was to find that the abolition of unnecessary social restraint was not identical with the creation of necessary social control."[31]

In other words, the latest phase of the bourgeois epoch simply presents in a new form the problem that the earlier dynamic Liberalism set out to solve. The difference is that whereas formerly the demand for the free play of economic forces was made in the name of liberation from older social and political obstructions, today the same demand is made against those who would liberate men from the new bondage created by capitalism. (And it must be added that in the face of this perversion of liberty some contemporary pseudo-liberals point the way out of the new bondage by offering a Utopian society that would destroy every vestige of liberalism and bring a still greater bondage.)

Thus while many of the "emancipated" have been paying lip-service to the ideals of an autonomous society, the actual social process has been moving in the direction of a new heteronomous society, dominated on the one side by heavily concentrated wealth (which is protected by the unblushing selfishness of bourgeois ideals and practices) and threatened on the other side by the irrationalism of the masses who have been shut out of democratic participation by the moralism and "rationalism" of the "elect."

---

[31]"The Rise of Liberalism," *Encyclopedia of the Social Sciences* (New York, 1930), Vol. I, 124. Mr. Laski gives the impression in this essay that economic Liberalism has no merits except as an ethic of aggrandizement. On the enduring values implicit in the philosophy of Liberalism, see Frank H. Knight, *The Ethics of Competition* (New York, 1936), and also his article, "The Meaning of Democracy: Its Politico-Economic Structure and Ideals," *Journal of Negro Education*, X (1941), 318-332. If we do not recognize the genuine accomplishments and the enduring principles of Liberalism, we not only fail to appreciate its tragedy, we also prepare the way for still greater destruction. Quincy Wright has criticized E. H. Carr on these grounds. He asserts that Carr underestimates the accomplishments of nineteenth-century Liberalism and also that in his statement of the economic principles which should govern post-war reorganization he "weights his argument in favor of totalitarian economics." See Wright's discussion of Carr's *Conditions of Peace*, "The War and the Peace," *Ethics*, LIII (1942), 64-68.

The average middle-class citizen and his wife (and his priest) now slumber in almost immovable complacency, and many who have been awakened by harbingers of doom have thrown in their lot with those who accept the gospel according to the National Association of Manufacturers. Hence, so far from providing a machinery whereby autonomous man through the exercise of his freedom and reason might enter into the shared life, Liberal society (partly, to be sure, by its failure to cope with new and old forms of illiberalism) has given rise to a congeries of power groups that have been so deeply caught in a conflict of interests and "freedoms"[31a] that the whole fine flourish has at last shown its teeth by ushering in two World Wars. Society is thus divided against itself, and it is caught in a titanic struggle of wills which is now operating on a planetary scale. Fate—certainly a fate that we can find meaningful—has caught up with us; and in doing so it has also caught up with Liberalism, with modern "civilization," and even with our "religion."[31b] History has bequeathed us not a pre-established harmony or a natural trend towards progress but rather a fateful conflict from which none can escape,— and no one knows to what ruinous lengths the conflict will go before the savage violence can be stopped. Hence there is full justification for Troeltsch's statement that the older Liberalism was "all too credulous of harmony and all too egocentric."[32]

And there we have the tragedy of modern history. "The freedoms of the past . . . have somehow brought forth the slaveries of the present,"[33] and with them a widespread cynicism and even a doubt concerning the value of life itself.

Is it any wonder that the reputation of human nature has been changing? Is it any wonder that the old world-view of Liberalism

[31a]The false freedoms that have been defended or developed in the name of laisser-faire are well described by A. V. Dicey, *Lectures on the Relation between Law and Public Opinion in England during the Nineteenth Century* (London, 1930), Lectures VI-IX.
[31b]For a brilliant study of the role of fate in the history of philosophy and religion, see Paul Tillich's inaugural lecture at the University of Frankfurt, published in *Kantstudien*, XXXIV (1929), 300-311. This essay is especially interesting as a study of certain types of modern voluntarism.
[32]Ernst Troeltsch, *Christian Thought: Its History and Application* (London, 1923), p. 203.
For very recent indictments of Liberal culture, see E. H. Carr, *op. cit.*, and Max Horkheimer, "The End of Reason," *Studies in Philosophy and Social Science*, IX (1942), 366-388.
[33]Harris Harbison, *op. cit.*, p. 203.

is today under attack on all sides? Dean Fenn's observation that Modern Liberalism is "too jocund for life as it actually is" now reads like sardonic understatement. Thus more and more liberals are coming to agree with his statement that "Modern Liberalism . . . must deal more justly with the crushing tragedies of life, with evil and sin, if it is to command the respect of candid and thoughtful men." Undoubtedly it is for this reason that the subdominant motifs of the past two centuries as well as the motifs of the Bible and of Greek "tragic" philosophy have in recent decades gained in power and pertinence.[34] The "tragic sense of life" has been reawakened with a start. It may be too much to expect the modern secularized liberal to recognize the possible relevance of the biblical world-view "in our day and age." Yet, perhaps those who harbor a "cultured" antipathy or a "philosophical" *hauteur* toward the Bible will before long be willing to heed the admonition, "Leave your Bible closed then, and open your Sophocles."

* * *

The same sort of analysis, and with similar results, must be applied to the individual psyche. The modern psychologist, like the sociologist, has gradually moved away from the presuppositions of the older Liberalism. Reason is now seen to be conditioned by history, its conclusions depending upon the premises that the reasoner starts with and thus largely upon the individual's

---

[34]Here it must be noted that the influential trends in this direction have for a long time been coming from the anthropologists, the sociologists and the psychologists as well as from the theologians. Certainly, the religious liberal should be cautioned against accepting the oft-repeated assertion that the attack on Liberalism is the outgrowth of post-war pessimism (Dean Fenn's criticism, remember, was written in 1913) and first emerged with the dialectical theologians, Barth and Brunner. In so far as these two thinkers have had an influence on the changing reputation of human nature, it has been a belated influence. They are themselves continuators of an earlier revolt against the tenets of the old Liberalism, a revolt that appeared first in the areas of secular philosophy, psychology, and economic theory. The uniqueness of Barth's protest resides more in its extremism than in its novelty. Cf. Paul Tillich, "What Is Wrong with the 'Dialectic' Theology?" *The Journal of Religion,* XV (1935), 127-145; also, his long and critical review of Brunner's *The Mediator,* in *The Christian Century,* LI (Dec. 5, 1934), 1554-1556. It must be noted, however, that in the field of theology, Kierkegaard in his attack on Hegel one hundred years ago sowed some of the seeds that are now bearing fruit in theological gardens. But Kierkegaard was accorded little attention until after Marx and Nietzsche had planted and watered their quite different but scarcely less valuable seeds.

primary interest, (or upon the interest of the group to which he belongs), whether that be social or anti-social. Hence, the conflict between love and power exists not only in the world at large. The "war within the cave" is found in the heart of Everyman, for the inner and the outer struggles mirror each other in what Malcolm Cowley has called a psycho-social parallelism. The picture of man as a purely logical machine, who first thinks of some desirable end and then calculates the means by which that end can be attained, has given way to the infinitely more complex social concept of man as a creature of impulse and passion and emotional preference, who only through a strenuous social discipline can transcend his incompatible desires and direct them toward some intelligent end. Indeed, reason is now seen to occupy the ambiguous position of being at the same time the umpire among unruly, conflicting impulses and the producer of ideologies, that is, the rationalizing instrument whereby selfish interest is given a plausible but false justification. Basic predispositions, deep-seated conflicts between men and groups, and the tensions of the historical situation again and again draw the reason down from its unsteady pedestal. Consequently, many of our "ideas are weapons" and are conceived in the sin of mere self-interest, with an accompanying perversion of mind and abuse of liberty. This destruction of the older belief in the immaculate conception of ideas is for the liberal a far more significant turn than the destruction of belief in the immaculate conception of Jesus. We need not go all the way with cynics like Thurman Arnold and contend that the older Liberal conception of Man Thinking is a myth, or with Karl Marx and say unequivocally that existence determines consciousness rather than consciousness existence, (though we should at least recognize the great contribution that Marx has made especially in his conception of ideology, a conception that is, by the way, found also in Martin Luther's writings). Nor need we go all the way with the Freudian interpretation of the origin and function of human reason. But we must recognize that the new social psychology has uncovered sources of vitality as well as a deep, dark area of conflict and even a fatefulness in the life of the psyche which the earlier rationalistic psychology perforce neglected.[35]

---

[35]It is well to note in passing that in order to describe the conflicts of

Again we see that, although man possesses a divinely-given dignity in his freedom and creativity, he is also a creature of contradictions. He shares in the autonomy of the underlying creative will. But this means that he possesses a certain independence of God and his fellows; he can assert his own ego in a way that violates the divinely given conditions of meaningful existence. Through the abuse of freedom he becomes bound to tendencies in history which narrow the range of his freedom and which also pervert its operation so that he gives his energy and devotion more to power than to love. Thus the "gift" and ideal of freedom, "freedom with," degenerates into "freedom from." In this way man reasoning but unreasonable, inflates his freedom into the self-enclosed egoism of undisturbed security.[36]

Now, what should be noticed here is that this contradiction in human nature derives from the fact that man's will is a decisive element in his structure. And it is a will that is ambiguous in character. Power as such is necessary for existence; indeed, it is necessary also for the achievement of mutuality. The margin of man's freedom is to be found in the alternative possibilities open to him for the use of power in its various forms and degrees. He can use his freedom by expressing a will to mutuality, but he can also abuse it by exercising a will to power. Freedom is therefore both the basis of meaning and the occasion for the destruction of meaning. Here we see again the tragic nature of the human condition. The tragedy does not derive merely from the fact that man carries within him an inheritance from the jungle. It derives also (and primarily) from the fact that he has a freedom that he did not have in the jungle,[37] a freedom to exer-

---

the human psyche, Freud has drawn upon the conceptions of "tragic" Greek mythology. Hence we might add to the previous admonition this one: "When you have finished your Sophocles, turn to your Jung and your Freud."

[36]See on this topic the brilliant combination of theological commentary and literary criticism in Nicholas Berdyaev's *Dostoievsky* (New York, 1934).

[37]In this connection it is interesting to note the contrast between the popular conception of sin as rooted in the body, and Luther's more profound conception of it as rooted "not in 'the inferior and grosser affections,' but in the most exalted and noble powers of man . . . that is, in the reason and in the will." As with St. Paul, it is not the body that struggles against the spirit but rather "the flesh," a term that signifies the pride of the spirit as well as the lusts of the body." It should be added, however, that Luther, like St. Paul, did not maintain consistency with regard to this interpretation of the nature of sin and the role of "the flesh."

cise the infinitely higher powers of human nature in terms of creative love, and a freedom to waste them in mere lassitude and triviality, or to pervert them for the sake of a will to power.

It is this co-existence in man of the possibility of using his freedom *ad majorem gloriam dei* and the possibility of perverting it to
his own destructive ends which constitutes the deepest contradiction
of his nature. And this contradiction is no merely human, subjective
phenomenon. As Martin Luther suggests, man is the *Schauplatz*
of opposing cosmic forces, the forces of love and of power. Since
power is a necessary ingredient of even love or mutuality, this opposition in no way implies a Manichean dualism. The point to be
stressed is that the contradiction penetrates man's inmost spiritual
life. It goes to the very center of his being; and it reaches out
through the individual and permeates all his social relations. It is
not, as the Marxists contend, merely a precipitate of the structure of
society.

* * *

It was in connection with the sort of interpretation here set
forth that the historic Judeo-Christian doctrine of sin was developed. The "orthodox" theory of "original sin," because of its association with the notion of Adam's Fall "in whom we sinnéd all"
as well as with an ascetic conception of sex, has been rightly
abandoned by religious liberals. It is doubtful, however, if there
is any word available that has more profound metaphysical
implications than the word "sin," for the word has the theonomous
reference necessary for any truly theological category.[38] But,

---

[38]The use of the word "sin," of course, provides no *guarantee* of religious
depth or of philosophical adequacy. Many liberals who use the word have
secularized or moralized it. (And, correspondingly, many conservatives have
de-moralized it.) As Gerald Birney Smith pointed out some years ago, the
sociologizing and psychologizing of the conception of sin by modern liberalism has had the consequence of depriving the conception of its "metaphysical
content." "Sin" as a theological category is no merely ethical or sociological or psychological concept. Like the doctrine of the divinity of man, the
doctrine of sin—properly understood—attempts to give metaphysical depth
to an aspect of human nature. The two doctrines taken together epitomize
the paradoxical character of the human condition, the paradoxical relationship of man to the creativity that he both shares and perverts. Indeed, one
may say that an understanding of the metaphysical implications of the derived dignity of human nature (the doctrine of *Imago dei*) requires a correspondingly metaphysical interpretation of the universal perversion or
frustration of man's essential dignity (the doctrine of sin). H. Shelton Smith
(*Faith and Nurture* [New York, 1941], pp. 93-99) has succinctly described
the metaphysical shallowness of the conception of sin dominant in religious
liberalism in the past century.

whether the liberal uses the word "sin" or not, he cannot correct his "too jocund" view of life until he recognizes that there is in human nature a deep-seated and universal tendency for both individuals and groups to ignore the demands of mutuality and thus to waste freedom or abuse it by devotion to the idols of the tribe, the theatre, the cave, and the market place.[38a] The old triumvirate of tyrants in the human soul, the *libido sciendi,* the *libido sentiendi,* and the *libido dominandi,* is just as powerful today as it ever was, and no man can ignore its tyranny with impunity. It cannot be denied that religious liberalism has neglected these aspects of human nature in its zeal to proclaim the spark of divinity in man. We may call these tendencies by any name we wish, but we do not escape their destructive influence by a conspiracy of silence concerning them. Certainly, the practice of shunning the word "sin" because "it makes one feel gloomy and pious," has little more justification than the use of the ostrich method in other areas of life.[39]

Obviously, a correction here does not involve any lending of support to the old view of the total depravity of man, at least not among liberals. Indeed, the expression of fear in this respect would be comparable to the propagandist device of calling a New Dealer a communist. We ought to have enough faith in man and God to believe that even a "realistic and credible doctrine of man"

[38a]Here, as with the doctrine of man, it must be noted that mutuality can be properly understood only in the context of theonomy. Mutuality is three-dimensional in that it involves a relationship between man and man, between man and God, and between men and God. Hence, when it is viewed in proper perspective mutuality is not merely an ethical category. There is no true love of man for man without love for God and no love of God without love for man. Accordingly, the ignoring of the demand of mutuality involves not merely an ethical deviation; it is also a form of religious pride. Moreover, apart from this theonomous reference, the fulfillment of mutuality will itself become a perversion, a pride and a deception; that is, it will be distorted into either a moralistic straightjacket or a tribal ideology.

[39]A friend of mine who is a theologian tells of a conversation he had some time ago, after he had given an address at one of our conferences in the East. He had been stressing the centrality of the ideas of sin and repentance in the Christian religion. Following the address, a minister approached him and, after thanking him for the address, said that he was sorry to hear a discourse that was so gloomy. He said Jesus was a man whom people liked to have around and his gospel is one of joy. Whereupon my friend replied: "That is true. But I thought the ideas of sin and repentance were very much stressed by Jesus. Did he not say: 'The kingdom of heaven is at hand. Repent ye'?" The minister, not to be worsted, replied, "Oh, yes, that does stand on the record. But that was one of Jesus' weaker moments."

will not separate us from the love of God. Certainly, we ought to be willing to take the risk that we would incur by giving more serious consideration than we have in recent years to the sinful nature of man, and even to the biblical myth of the Fall as a description of the contradictions in human nature.[40]

If the earlier intellectualism exalted man into an archangel, the new voluntarism is right in viewing him, in the words of Charles Lamb about Coleridge, as an archangel slightly damaged. This change of attitude has long been evident among the poets. Malcolm Cowley in an article on "What Poets are Saying"[41] points out that

[40]Nor would we have to begin by studying the so-called "orthodox" and "neo-Calvinist" theologians. Dean Sperry some years ago set forth a sociological reinterpretation of the doctrine of original sin especially stressing the fact that every man shares the guilt for the injustices and inequalities of society. Cf. *The Disciplines of Liberty* (New Haven, 1921), chap. 4, "A Modern Doctrine of Original Sin."

On the metaphysical level, one of the most profound studies of the human condition in terms of the myth of the Fall is to be found in the essay of the German philosopher Schelling, entitled *Of Human Freedom* (1809). In this connection, Rowland Gray-Smith has performed a valuable service by the publication of his doctoral dissertation on *God in the Philosophy of Schelling* (Philadelphia, 1933). For a more popular and "literary," though metaphysical, interpretation of the Christian doctrine of original sin, see Thomas Mann's discussion in the symposium, *I Believe*, ed. Clifton Fadiman (New York, 1939), pp. 189-194. On the ethical level, one of the significant defenses of the tragic view of life and one that emphasizes (perhaps over-emphasizes) "the radically evil will of man" is to be found in Immanuel Kant's *Religion within the Limits of Mere Reason* (1793).

For the psychological level, Sigmund Freud, *Civilization and Its Dis-contents* (New York, 1930),—especially his discussion of the so-called "destruction instinct"—should not be neglected. The writings of Fromm, Horney, and Lasswell are also pertinent here. Cf. also Anton T. Boisen, "The Problem of Sin and Salvation in the Light of Psychopathology," *The Journal of Religion*, XXII (1942), 288-301. The contrast between the psychoanalytic theory of cleavages and the old Liberal doctrine of harmony of interests may be taken as typical of the great change in the reputation of human nature. Cf. on this point Lionel Trilling's review of Karen Horney's *Self Analysis* (1942) in which he criticizes her retention of the Liberal theory of "the progressive psyche," *The Nation*, Sept. 12, 1942, pp. 215-217.

For Unitarian expositions of the conception of sin, see H. W. Bellows *Restatement of Christian Doctrine* (New York, 1860), chap. 3; J. E. Carpenter and P. H. Wicksteed, *Studies in Theology* (London, 1903), chap. 5; J. W. Chadwick, *Old and New Unitarian Beliefs* (Boston, 1894), chap. 2; James Drummond, *Studies in Christian Doctrine* (London, 1908), pp. 203-239; E. Emerton, *Unitarian Thought* (New York, 1911), chap. 3; C. C. Everett, *Theism and the Christian Faith* (New York, 1909), chaps. 21-24; L. A. Garrard, *Duty and the Will of God* (Oxford, 1938); James Martineau, *The Seat of Authority in Religion* (New York, 1890), Book IV, chap. 3; S. H. Mellone, *God and the World* (London, 1919), chap. 8; T. G. Soares, *Three Typical Beliefs* (Chicago, 1937), pp. 83-90; Oliver Martin, "Sin and Sinners," THE JOURNAL OF LIBERAL RELIGION, III (1941), 3-10; Alexander Winston, "The Metaphysical Status of Evil," *ibid.*, III (1941), 100-106.

[41]*Saturday Review of Literature*, May 3, 1941.

the principal themes of contemporary verse are (1) the psycho-social parallelism to which reference has been made, (2) the sense of doom, (3) the sense of personal guilt, and (4) a sense of comradeship in the attempt to confront our common fate.

This change may seem to represent a swing toward a one-sided pessimism. If so, it may be explained as an illustration of the old adage that extremes breed extremes. Or, as Thomas Hardy once put it, when prurience thrusts the human shape beneath the stream, the first part of the anatomy that will reappear when the pressure is released will be the posterior.

But the change need not involve a shift from optimism to pessimism. The poets to whom Malcolm Cowley refers counter-balance the sense of doom with a sense of comradeship. "We must love one another or die," says W. H. Auden, a poet who has been drawn by the present cultural crisis into a new appreciation of Christian doctrine. But, unfortunately, not all the poets and not all the "Christian" theologians have achieved this balance between optimism and pessimism, a balance implicit in the Christian doctrines of sin and redemption. This lack of balance in our day takes the form of a sadistic and undiscriminating attack on all ideas of progress, and in some instances it takes also the form of a seemingly complete renunciation of even the valid principles of freedom which come to us from the older Liberalism.

The Transformation of Liberalism

In the face of these renunciations, contemporary liberalism has, as we have said, a positive, creative task to perform. To be sure, the failures and the perversions of Liberalism must be recognized before there can be a reasonable hope of moving in the direction of a truly liberal society. But humanity will only be brought to greater suffering under greater tyrannies if the liberal principles of freedom are abandoned. These principles must be given new forms that are revelant to the requirements of the modern Great Society and that will prepare the way for a transformed liberalism and a transformed liberal society.[41a]

[41a]Cf. the author's article, "Freud, Mannheim, and the Liberal Doctrine of Man," THE JOURNAL OF LIBERAL RELIGION, II (Winter, 1941), 107-11; also, Edward A. Shils, "Irrationality and Planning," *ibid.*, II (Winter, 1941), 148-153; Mannheim, *op. cit.*; Meyer, *op. cit.*; Paul Tillich, "War Aims," reprinted from *The Protestant*, 1941.

must be ever mindful of the fact that the power of God, the immanent and prevenient power of creativity, groweth not old. Such histrionic hyperboles as those just cited from the despairing preacher must be interpreted as an implicit denial of man's potentiality as a child of God, and of the ever-present possibilities of repentance and regeneration. These possibilities are always present despite perversions, tensions and tragedies. Indeed, this is one thing that is meant when it is said that faith points beyond tragedy, though, of course, "beyond tragedy" is not the same as "without tragedy." Faith does point beyond tragedy, but it also implies an acknowledgement of certain persistent tragic elements in life. This, we take it, is what Father Tyrrell had in mind when he spoke of the Christian view of the world as an ultimate optimism resting on a provisional pessimism.[41d]

* * *

But extreme pessimism is not the only danger of the tragic view of life that is now emerging. Just as rationalism had its characteristic besetting sin, namely, "feeling terribly at ease in Zion" and "cuddling up to the Almighty," so voluntarism has its own peculiar danger. Certain types of voluntarism, it must be remembered, have often been infected with irrationalism. Indeed, they

---

[41d]Writing of Hawthorne and of the demands incumbent upon the author who would present the tragedy of life, F. O. Matthiessen finely says: "Unless the author also has a profound comprehension of the mixed nature of life, of the fact that even the most perfect man cannot be wholly good, any conflicts that he creates will not give the illusion of human reality. Tragedy does not pose the situation of a faultless individual (or class) overwhelmed by an evil world, for it is built on the experienced realization that man is radically imperfect. Confronting this fact, tragedy must likewise contain a recognition that man, pitiful as he may be in his finite weakness, is still capable of apprehending perfection, and of becoming transfigured by that vision. But not only must the author of tragedy have accepted the inevitable co-existence of good and evil in man's nature, he must also possess the power to envisage some reconciliation between such opposites, and the control to hold an inexorable balance. He must be as far from the chaos of despair as he is from ill-founded optimism." (*American Renaissance,* pp. 179-180).

Prof. Matthiessen is here dealing with the *writer's* problem of *presenting* tragedy. In life itself, however, the possibilities of transfiguration and reconciliation do not depend merely upon "an inexorable balance." These possibilities, like the "inexorable balance" itself, depend upon the power 'that groweth not old,' the sustaining and alluring Alpha and Omega. Thus the ground of hope for man's fulfillment, the ground of Tyrrell's "ultimate optimism," is not merely "the mean" between despair and over-optimism. It is, in the words of our Unitarian poet Oliver Wendell Holmes, the "Lord of all being throned afar. . . . Yet to each loving heart how near!"

have even exalted irrationalism into a virtue. Duns Scotus illustrates this tendency when he urges acceptance of the Catholic faith without question and without reference to reason. National socialism takes the same attitude of authoritarian subjection to blood and soil. Observers from the Orient have long noted this tendency to irrationalism in the Christian Occident. Charles Chauncy valiantly opposed it in the New Lights, and many oppose it today as it appears in Nazism and Barthianism. But such irrationalism is not the only alternative to rationalism. We find keen rational analysis in great historic exemplars of voluntarism, for example, most of all in the Buddha, and to a marked degree in St. Paul and St. Augustine; or to cite three modern examples, in Jonathan Edwards, Ernst Troeltsch, and Rudolph Otto. What is needed, of course, is that combination of *logos* and *dynamis* which can effect a vitalizing tension between the attitude of distance and the attitude of decision. One of the best characterizations of this sort of relation between the reason and the will is suggested in the metaphor repeated by most of the voluntarists of the Middle Ages and especially by the anti-Thomists; they compared reason to a torch lighting the paths ahead, and the will (under God's grace), the whole self, they said, both guides the reason and chooses the path to be taken. We see, then, that a recognition of the large role of the will, a recognition of the fundamental significance of the basic orientation and predisposition of a man, does not necessarily involve a deprecation of reason.[42] Indeed, the voluntaristic theory of the nature of man is itself the result of an intellectual and rational analysis of the human condition.

* * *

The older Liberalism underestimated the destructive possibilities of the contradictions in human nature and was thus unrealistic. It offered salvation through the "restraints of reason." But the "restraints of reason" are inadequate for entering the "war within the cave." Merely intellectual education is not enough. The world

---

[42]Jacques Barzun wisely rejects W. T. Stace's idea (set forth in *The Destiny of Western Man* [New York, 1942]) that "Western man's destiny is to put reason and sympathy above will," that Greece represents the fountain of Reason, Palestine the fount of Sympathy, and Germany the tradition of Will. See Dr. Barzun's review in *The Saturday Review of Literature,* Mar. 21, 1942. The present writer trusts that the discussion above has shown the superficiality of generalizations of this sort.

has many educated people who know how to reason, and they reason very well; but, curiously enough, many of them fail to examine the pre-established premises from which they reason, premises that turn out on examination to be anti-social, protective camouflages of power. Where a man's treasure is, there will his heart be also. And where his heart is, there will be his reason and his premises. The "theoretical attitude of distance" needs for its completion the existential "attitude of decision." St. Paul underlines this fact when he speaks of the foolishness of the wise.[43] Their foolishness is not in their "wisdom" alone; it is also in their perversity and their impotence of will. The element of conflict inherent in man and in man's relations with his fellows can, as St. Paul knew, be dealt with only by a regenerated will, a will committed, under God, to the principles of liberty and justice and love, a will prepared by a faith, a decision, a commitment sufficient to cope with the principalities and powers of the world.[44]

Kant, who in this respect stands in the Pauline tradition, suggests that the *root* of evil must be touched. What is needed, he says, is not piecemeal reformation with minor adjustments of character and conduct, but an alteration of the basis of character and of the habitual way in which the mind works. Nor is this reformation a "conversion" of the evangelistic order, a conversion

[43]Professor Robert L. Calhoun of Yale emphasizes this point when he writes: "Schopenhauer's devastating analysis of the futility of education and all cultural refinement as a safeguard against inner frustration is in principle as true now as when he wrote it. Current history is driving home his theory with the hammer blows of fact. Current psychology is helping us to see why intellectual and moral education does not get to the root of the trouble, and how profoundly man needs to be made over. But all these insights are new variations on a very old theme, which St. Paul set out clearly in the seventh chapter of his letter to the Romans, and which has been central in Christianity ever since." *What Is Man?* ("Hazen Books on Religion," New York, 1939), p. 69.

[44]Dean Sperry says, concerning the Christian word for love: "The term *agape*—which is Paul's word—is not a word which concerns the senses or emotions. A classical scholar who has meditated much on an exact translation says that whatever else the word *agape* may mean, it means in the first instance 'a steady set of the will.'" Willard L. Sperry, *What We Mean by Religion* (New York, 1940), p. 121.

See in this connection Erich Fromm's brilliant observations on love from the point of view of a voluntaristic psychology, *op. cit.*, pp. 510 ff.

The reader should bear in mind here that the *agape* of early Christianity was viewed as a gift of grace, an aspect of the inbreaking kingdom. Cf. Rudolph Otto, *The Kingdom of God and the Son of Man* (London, 1938), and Anders Nygren, *Agape and Eros* (New York, 1932), Vol. I; also, Meyer, *op. cit.*, III (Winter, 1942), 139 ff.

that takes place at one moment and is then complete: Martin Luther came much nearer to describing it when he said that our whole life should be a repentance (*metánoia*) that brings forth fruits meet for repentance. Nor is this "conversion" merely what a man does with his solitariness. It is a conversion that affects his social relations and brings about some conversion in society.

These principles can be stated in non-theological terms also. The way in which the reason operates depends upon the aims and interests around which the personality is organized. Morality has as its basis an underived commitment to certain guiding principles and purposes. Thus the basis of choice is not irrational in the sense of being contrary to reason, but it is non-rational in that the direction taken by choice is determined by the evidence or principles that can be applied.[45] Accordingly, the decisive quality of a personality is its commitment, for the basic commitment determines the self and its interests, instead of being determined by them.[46]

The way in which a personality will interpret its freedom and use its reason depends, then, upon the character of the self and upon its relation to and attitude toward the rest of reality. A readiness even to enter into discussion for the sake of reaching agreement (or of reaching at least a common understanding) depends upon a man's total character and not upon his intellectual capacities alone. It depends, in short, upon a proper relation to the creative ground of meaning and existence. Moreover, science as well as religion, politics as well as art, properly flourish only when the primary quality of human character, integrity, is the foundation and when that integrity has a positive and critical relation to larger integrities, social and metaphysical.

We have now seen the ways in which the rationalistic tradition has optimistically taken for granted the idea of unity in the world, in society, and in the structure of the individual psyche; we have also seen how it stresses the role of reason in such a way as to offer a truncated view of the functions operative in both society

---

[45]Cf. Charner M. Perry, "The Arbitrary as Basis for Rational Morality," *Ethics,* XLIII (1939), 127.

[46]For the role of commitment in politics, see Karl Mannheim, *Ideology and Utopia* (New York, 1936); for its role in science, see J. D. Bernal, *The Social Function of Science* (London, 1939) and Robert S. Lynd, *Knowledge for What?* (Princeton, 1939).

and the individual and also in such a way as to encourage both separative individualism and "the attitude of distance." The voluntaristic outlook, we have seen, aims to correct and supplement this view by stressing the significance of the alogical factors in existence, in human nature and history, by emphasizing also "the tragic sense of life" arising from man's entanglement within its deep-going conflicts, and by stressing the significance of the creative depths of the entire personality (and of the group to which it belongs) for the dynamic achievement of relevant and vigorous action.

* * *

Theology is, in the language of Bonaventura, "an affective science," the science of the love of God, and the function of the church is to bring men into communion with a group wherein the divine power of transformation and the ethical standards rooted in it are operative. When we say operative, we mean that this power is capable of changing men, of eliciting commitment to a way of life that makes a difference in their attitude toward themselves, their fellow-men, and God; in short, it aids them in the achieving of voluntary community.[47] Only by some such commitment can we, in Channing's words, be always young for liberty. And without such a commitment, we become content with "philosophic" objectivity and "distance" that insulate us from the source of true vitality, from openness to the power of the Spirit. We become attached to the forms that have given us our cherished securities; or, as Augustine puts it, we give our devotion to creatures rather than to the creative power from which issue all forms and all true vitality. We substitute our aspirations and "virtues," our reason and our moralism, for God's power and goodness. Thus our rationalism and our moralism "miss and distort reality and the real possibilities for improvement of the human situation."[48] They give us a "poise" that freezes the knees and keeps us erect and "harmonious" in face of the divine demand for repentance, for change of heart and mind. The early Christians and the Protestant Reformers saw that the creative and redemptive power is not subject to domestication by means of these techniques. It breaks

[47]On this whole problem of the relation between decision and transformation, see E. E. Aubrey, *Man's Search for Himself* (Nashville, 1940).
[48]Meyer, *op. cit.,* p. 196.

into a human situation destroying, transforming old forms and creating new ones, manifesting the expulsive and creative power of a new affection,—the *Amor dei*.

Thus we are driven back to a view somewhat similar to the one that Chauncy opposed in 1743. It is not the "enlightened Mind" alone that is necessary for salvation, but rather the "raised Affections" inspiring, transforming and controlling both reason and vitality.[49] Nor is it that the reason needs merely the added push of vitality, but rather that both reason and vitality must be kept from perversion and from exceeding bounds. Not that information and hard thinking and technique are dispensable. Far from it. Even a St. Francis with commitment to the highest would be impotent when confronted with a case of appendicitis if he did not recognize the malady and did not know what to do. One sector of the problems of society and of solitude *is* the intellectual problems. Here no amount of good will alone can suffice. But something of the spirit of St. Francis is indispensable if the benefits of science and of society are to be in widest commonalty spread, and, for that matter, if even the intellectual problems are to be dealt with adequately. The desire to diagnose injustice as an intellectual problem as well as the power of action to achieve a new form of justice requires "raised affections," a vitality that can break through old forms of behavior and create new patterns of community. "Man becomes what he loves." But the raising of the affections is a much harder thing to accomplish than even the education of the mind; it is especially difficult among those who think they have found security. Spiritually significant change takes place only when a man discovers that he must make a decision for a way of life that distinguishes him and his whole orientation from the man who has not made such a decision. As Kant puts it, "the feelings must be raised to the pitch of enthusiasm where we are disposed to make the greatest sacrifices for the sake of principle." If religious liberals could learn that no significant change can be initiated before men become *committed* to liberal principles, a new strategy would not be far behind.

This element of commitment, of change of heart, of decision,

---

[49] As should be clear from the context of the discussion, we are, of course, using the phrase "raised Affections" in a different sense from that which it had in Chauncy's day, that is, we associate the phrase here with *Amor dei.*

so much emphasized in the Gospels, has been neglected by religious liberalism, and that is the prime source of its enfeeblement. We liberals are largely an uncommitted and therefore a self-frustrating people. Our first task, then, is to restore to liberalism its own dynamic and its own prophetic genius. We need conversion within ourselves. Only by some such revolution can we be seized by a prophetic power that will enable us to proclaim both the judgment and the love of God. Only by some such conversion can we be possessed by a love that will not let us go. And when that has taken place, we shall know that it is not our wills alone that have acted; we shall know that the ever-living Creator and Re-creator has again been brooding over the face of the deep and out of the depths bringing forth new life.

Theological Bases of Social Action

By James Luther Adams

THE decisive element in social action is the exercise of power, and the character of social action is determined by the character of the power expressed. Power has always a double character: first, as the expression of God's law and love; second, as the exercise of man's freedom. To understand power as God's law and love is to understand it as Being; to understand it as man's freedom is to understand it as his response to the possibilities of being, a response which is both individual and institutional. All response is therefore social action in the broad sense. Here we shall be concerned with social action in this broad sense and also in the narrower sense of group action for the achievement of consensus with respect to the shaping of social policy. Both of these types of social action are expressions of necessity as well as of freedom. The expression of power in the dimensions of both freedom and necessity must be understood by the Christian in terms of its theological bases. The definition of the theological bases of social action must be achieved in terms of the ultimate purposes and resources of human life; it must be achieved equally in terms of the threats to the fulfillment of these purposes. Taken together, God's law and man's freedom operate for the creation of community or, through God's wrath, for its destruction. According to the Judeo-Christian view of God's law and love, it is the destiny of men to love and to be loved; there is an interdependence of spiritual destinies; this is the "plan of salvation." All response on the part of men to God's law and love is social action in the broad sense, whether the response furthers community or perverts and destroys it.

Much social thought has misunderstood or ignored the dual character of power as God's law and man's response. The misunderstanding has come out of exclusive preoccupation with the dimension of man's freedom and the ignoring of the dimension of God's law. It is not enough to say with Henry Adams that "power is poison," or with Jacob Burckhardt that "power is by its nature evil, whoever wields it." The power that is law understood as God's is not in itself evil; it is the ground for the possibility of man's exercise of power for good or evil. Acton's assertion that "power tends to corrupt, and absolute power corrupts absolutely" is true as he understood it, namely, as applying only to man's freedom, the social-political dimension. Power can be understood to corrupt absolutely only when the social-political power is sundered from its theological ground, God's law and love. This was Acton's understanding of the meaning of his famous aphorism. Contemporary social thought has tended to lift the dictum out of its total context. When accepted so superficially, such dicta give plausibility to Candide's admonition that in a world of corruption we should simply cultivate our own garden. This interpretation has given both religious and irreligious people a spurious rationalization for a retreat from social action. Accordingly, the American temper has often been deeply anti-political, dismissing politics as necessarily corrupt. It is as the American temper has lost its theological basis and has thus failed to understand power as limitation as well as freedom that it has retreated from political action. But the retreat does not give men freedom from power. Candide could not even cultivate his garden without exercising freedom, man's power. The power to reject or disregard power is itself an expression of power as man's freedom and necessity.

The idea of power is in no way alien to religion. Religion cannot be adequately described without one's employing the conception of power; likewise, power cannot be properly described without one's employing religious concepts. Power is both the basic category of being and the basic category of social action. The crucial question for both religion and social action is the question concerning the nature and interrelation of divine power and human powers. All social action is therefore explicitly or implicitly grounded in a theology, and all theology implies a fundamental conception of social action. Politics, therefore, must consider the theology of power as much as theology must consider the politics of power. When power is not considered in its proper theological character but only in its political, it becomes demonic or empty, separated from its end. Here power in the end achieves little but its own creation and destruction, and thus virtually denies itself as creative. In the human "order" this is what the Bible calls hardness of heart. The creative element of power is divine. The destructive element of power appears wherever power is divorced from an understanding of its source in the divine.

Definitions of Power. Having conceived of power as man's freedom under God's law and love, we must now consider the varieties of man's experience of power. We must turn to an examination of the relations between the two ultimate poles of power.

"All power is of one kind," says Emerson, "a sharing in the nature of the world." We may take this to mean that all power is of one kind in the sense that all power is capacity or ability possessed or exercised within the context of existence as it is "given." One is reminded here of Plato's laconic remark, "And I hold that the definition of Being is simply power." Plato understands power as creative, as the condition and limit of man's social existence. For Plato this definition considers power as primarily law; it is transmuted in the Stoic and the Christian tradition as God's law, *Logos*. Here power is not understood differently from what is stressed in the typical modern generic definition, wherein it is simply the capacity to exercise influence. The modern definition is true so far as it goes. But it is true only with respect to the power of freedom, the power to influence others, the power to control one's own behavior (freedom). Plato observes in the *Sophist* that power is present equally in the capacity *to be influenced*. Power exhibits duality, but it is one in this duality: There is no adequate conception of power as freedom except as it is simultaneously conceived of as law and except as it is viewed in a context of interaction ultimately grounded in the divine power of being (with its possibilities in terms of free and also ambiguous response).

God is not to be understood merely as a rigid lawgiver, nor man merely in terms of freedom. As there is a dialectic between the two primary terms of power—man's freedom and God's law—there is also a dialectic within each term. Plato suggests that power is twofold: it is both active and passive. In the Christian view the active and passive powers, in both God and man, are dialectically related. God is creative, redemptive power, active power. But God takes satisfaction in man's free obedience; in this respect he is influenced by man's behavior. Man possesses creative freedom to influence himself and others; this is active power. But he is also influenced by participating in God's power, that is, by being affected by God's law and love and by other people's behavior. This is passive power. Where mutuality of influence appears, both active and passive power operate; and, ideally, coercive power is employed primarily for the maintenance of mutuality.

This dialectic of power is sometimes overlooked by the definitions employed by the sociologists. The typical sociological definition of power as the capacity to influence the behavior of others in accord with one's own intentions, is a truncated definition. It refers only to active power. Max Weber's definition, for example, makes explicit reference only to this active type of power. "Power," he says, "is the probability that one actor within a social relationship will be in a position to carry out his own will despite resistance, regardless of the basis on which this probability rests." This definition makes room for force (influence by physical manipulation or threat), for domination (influence by making explicit what is commanded or requested), and for manipulation (influence that is effected without making explicit what is wanted, as for example certain types of propaganda). But Weber's definition does not explicitly include "passive powers," the capacities possessed by those who yield to one or another kind of active influence. Chester I. Barnard's discussion of communication in his *The Functions of the Executive* is at least more comprehensive in this respect, for he interprets executive power as requiring two-way communication, that is, as requiring the yielding to influence as well as the exercise of influence.

A distinction that cuts across the distinction between active and passive powers should be noted here. We may speak of "power of" as ability (for example, the ability to learn or the ability to express oneself) and of "power over" as the capacity to dominate. In the social arena, when "power over" increases in a group of people, "power of" diminishes among those who are dominated. When "power of" is possessed by the members of a group engaged in social action, they have power in the sense that they participate in the making of a group decision, though of course the decision itself may lead to the attempt to exercise "power over" another group.

In all of these definitions, it is emphasized, then, that power does not exist *in vacuo;* it exists in some relation in nature and in man, and between men or groups of men, or between man and God, the limiting, creative, and redemptive power. As Locke observes, following Plato, "Power is twofold; as able to make, or able to receive, any change; the one may be called 'active,' and the other 'passive,' power. Thus power includes in it some kind of relation—a relation to action or change." Power is a relation and it must therefore always be stated in two terms: law and freedom. In the realm of individual psychology the two-term relation of power is readily evident. Perceiving, knowing, imagining, willing, and feeling, are expressions of freedom, the power to choose. But perception implies its object; otherwise, perception is itself the creator of its object. The object is thus the condition of perception, and necessary to it. Perception as an expression of freedom is united with the object as an expression of necessity or law. This interrelated, active and passive character of power must be taken into account in any discussion of human behavior. We turn now to a brief review of the development of the concept of power in the history of religion.

Divine Power in Primitive Religion. Explicit religion involves the belief that there are divine powers with which man must enter into relations for the maintenance or fulfillment of meaningful existence. (We must omit here the discussion of the question whether the divine power may properly be conceived to be *a* being alongside other beings.) There is no notion of God, even among primitive peoples, in which deity is not power, or does not have power.

One of the most widespread primitive conceptions of power (which may or may not be associated with deity) is the idea of Mana, a mysterious impersonal force which can be in anything and which makes that thing strikingly effective. Archbishop Söderblom has suggested that in its nature and working Mana may be compared to electricity; it is impersonal, it can flow from one thing to another, and it can do a variety of things. It is a holy power in things, animals, persons, magical incantations, and events. As Söderblom says, "Numerous phenomena which we understand to be essentially different are explained by primitive man to be the operation of Mana: poison, the power of healing, the power of nourishment in plants, the killing effect of weapons, the growth of plants, success, luck, unusual events, mysterious impressions, the effect of a word, the course of heavenly bodies, everything depends on Mana or rather is Mana" (*Das Werden des Gottesglaubens*, p. 88). Since Mana is sacred and is therefore considered to be dangerous, various taboos are established for protection against it.

Among men this power may be inherited or acquired. In either case, the possession of this "electricity"—a primitive understanding of law—can become the basis of authority and deference. In this fashion it can determine certain of the principal social patterns and even the hierarchical social structure. In addition to being an active power (in the sense we have defined) Mana sometimes is conceived to be also passive. Among the Polynesians, for example, ritual is performed partially for the purpose of regenerating or increasing the power of the gods themselves, so that while the people depend upon the gods, they are also able to strengthen the gods by their own exertions. The gods will run down if the tribe does not recharge them. Here both gods and men have the power "to do," and they may also be undone by the other. Both the gods and the men may dominate the other or be dominated by the other. In any event, the power of Mana "as electricity" is neither law nor ethics as we understand those concepts. Mana can be captured by an individual, thus raising freedom above law.

The modern, civilized man would consider quite fantastic any proposal that the conception of Mana should serve as a basis for social action. Yet millions of modern men have quite seriously accepted as a basis for social action an idea that is not entirely removed in character from Mana, namely, the idea of "blood and soil." This idea serves as the basis for a "religion" that in effect considers biological and tribal-territorial powers to be divine and therefore decisive for social action. Aggressive nationalism and "lily-white" Americanism live on these powers. Arnold Toynbee has argued that Anglo-Saxon Protestantism assimilated this kind of religion to that of the chosen people, establishing a new Canaan in the Western hemisphere. Like the religion of Mana, this modern tribalism is not in a universal sense ethical; it is pseudo-ethical because it is a law unto itself, thus contradicting the meaning of law.

Prophetic Conceptions of Divine Power. For a Christian theology of social action the definitive conception of divine power is set forth in the New Testament—the conception of power (*dynamis*) as forgiving, healing love working toward the fulfillment of the divine purpose of history. The law of grace is sovereign. This conception is a far cry from the primitive idea of Mana and from the powers on which primitive or "civilized" tribalism lives. Between the primitive conceptions and the New Testament conception there stands more than a millennium of religious experience. This period of history is very familiar territory to the reader precisely because its ideas have been decisive for Judeo-Christian theologies of social action. Despite its familiarity, however, we may, perhaps with some warrant, view it in the light of our concern with a theology of power as the basis for a theology of social action.

Conceptions of divine power very similar to the idea of Mana as well as tribalist conceptions of divine power are to be found in early Hebraic thought. But the power in which the ethical prophets placed their trust was of a different sort. Although this power was evident for them in miraculous event and in ecstatic (though not orgiastic) experience, it was a power that became peculiarly manifest in the corporate life of the People of God, a view of the divine which had its roots in an earlier deliverance from bondage and whose goal was a universal, ethical purpose. Here power is conceived of as the freedom of the Jews under the Law; they were chosen and they responded by choosing. All events are therefore both power as the freedom of man and power as the law and love of God.

This prophetic conception was not the result of merely abstract reflection. It appeared on the occasion of a power struggle, the struggle for domination undertaken by the military empires surrounding Israel. It was developed as a reaction to the military weakness of Israel in face of the overwhelming strength of the great powers. As Max Weber points out, "Except for the world politics of the great powers which threatened the Israelite homeland . . . the prophets could not have emerged" (*Gesammelte Aufsätze zur Religionssoziologie*, III, 282). In a previous interim of peace, the Palestinian "states" had appeared, and with them a sense of superiority in the Hebrews, a sense of pride in past achievement (freedom) under divine guidance (law), and a faith in a glorious future for the nation (freedom under God's law). The revival of oppression at the hands of the Mesopotamian and Egyptian empires raised the old mantic vision of the power of an ethical, national deity to the level of the international as well as the ethical. The prophets were "political theologians" concerned with the destiny and the ethical significance of the state; they viewed the power of God—law—as operating through social and political institutions and in international relations, the expression of man's freedom. This is a conception of divine power which in its magnitude staggers the imagination; indeed, it is the conception which the pietist, with his preoccupation with the immediate relations between the individual soul and God, always has greatest difficulty in comprehending or in taking seriously. Yet the pietist, like anyone else, participates in the institutionalization of powers which his society defines and redefines.

It is worthwhile to observe here, in passing, that the activity of the prophets was itself possible only because of a peculiar aspect of the social organization of the society in which they found themselves. The prophets could not have emerged had they not been able to appeal directly to the people. In this fact we may see implicit a principle of freedom which is indispensable for any Judeo-Christian theology of social action. The lines of political communication and activity were not held in monopoly by the monarchy. Unlike the "prophets" of surrounding countries, the Hebrew prophets were not an adjunct of the monarchy. Weber, in a slightly pejorative sense, calls them "demagogues." Within the social stratification of their society, they were able to be the spokesmen to and for the poor and the oppressed. In their tradition there was a separation between charismatic and traditional authority which left the way open for prophetic criticism. In other words, the freedom of the prophet presupposed a separation of powers which in a narrow way bears comparison to the modern ideal of freedom of the press. This separation of powers which permitted the liberty of prophecy was related to the fact that the covenant between God and the People was not through the monarch; the covenants between God and the People and between God and the royal house were parallel covenants, and both were subject to prophetic criticism. The divine kingship was limited by this separation of powers. The will of God could be discussed by the prophets without license from the government; it could even be expressed through the mouth of the prophet against the monarchy.

Viewing the overwhelming power of the great empires and exercising the liberty of prophesying, the prophets elevated Jahwe to the Lord of history. In the course of time they claimed that God uses the great powers (for example, "My servant Nebuchadnezzar"—political power) as instruments for the punishment, the purification, and the education of his chosen people; he was raised above the gods of the world powers; and, finally, he was said to be the one and only God.

The prophetic conception of the divine power was shaped, then, in the stress of power politics; conversely, the conception of power politics was shaped under the stress of a new vision of the divine power. To the degree that the conception of divine power changed its character, Israel reacted differently to subjugation, indeed transcended it, and found a new meaning in it. The divine power was not only ethicized. It was also interiorized; it was interpreted as operating in the most intimate aspects of psychic experience and of divine-human fellowship. Both God and men were now seen to be bound together not only in the realm of politics but also in the inner life. This remarkable interiorization of piety represents the translation of the conception of divine power into a new dimension: it represents also a deeper conception of the conjugation of the active and passive powers. These two aspects of the divine and the human powers, the ethical and the interior, are so important for a Christian theology of social action that they deserve a closer scrutiny.

Since the present brief essay aims primarily to be a constructive statement rather than a historical one, we shall not try to express the Hebrew prophetic outlook exclusively in its own vocabulary. Rather, we shall try to present it in a way that readily lends itself to an appreciation of its perennial relevance for a theology of power.

(1) The power that is worthy of confidence is the Creator of the world and man. This is a mythological formulation; in essence it means that existence is grounded in divine power—the power of being, in law—and is therefore a divinely given realm of meaning. Christian theology has succinctly expressed this basic presupposition of the doctrine of creation: *Esse est bonum qua esse.* Being as such is good; it is of God. Good is possible only within being. God offers the possibility of good. The doctrine of *Imago dei* is an application of this view to the doctrine of man. Man in freedom participates in this divine law and creativity. Recasting this affirmation in terms of a theology of power, we may say that to exist is to possess, or to participate in, the divine power of being; it is to be the beneficiary of the divine power which is the ground of order and meaning.

This means that the prophetic view renounces any radical asceticism in face of the material order. It rejects the cynic's notion that all power is evil, a notion that represents an extrapolation from the view that political power is evil. For the prophetic view, this false notion would imply that the perfect God should be perfectly impotent. On the other hand, prophetism rejects not only the fallacy that being is evil; it rejects also the fallacy that existence is simply good. There is a possibility of good or evil in existence. Both possibilities can express themselves in man's action. Prophetism therefore laid a burden of responsibility upon man. Escape from action to contemplation was rejected as a mode of irresponsibility. Escape from the material for the sake of the spiritual, the renunciation of the finite for the sake of the infinite, constituted irresponsibility in face of the divine possibility and command. There is no freedom *from* the world that is not freedom *for* the world. Matter is not a demonic power; it is not the enemy of meaning. Sin does not derive from the fact that man participates in a material world but rather from his disobedience to the divine demand for love and justice. The fulfillment of meaning is inextricably related to things earthy, to soul *and* body, for both soul and body are God's creatures. It does not appear in spite of or in protest against the earthy. The order of nature, in man as well as beyond, demands man's care and love just as it receives God's.

Yet, the Judeo-Christian doctrine of creation asserts also that the divine power is not to be identified with the world or with any part of it. It is never capsuled anywhere in the world, not in a "superior" race or nation, not in a religious tradition, not in religious ceremony, not even in the prophet's word. The attempt to capsule the divine power is the attempt to control and manipulate it, to become sovereign over it; the attempt is blasphemous. "Thou shalt have no other gods before me." Everything finite stands under the divine judgment. "Religion" itself stands under this judgment. The basic threat to "faith-ful" freedom is the threat of idolatry—giving to the creature that which belongs alone to the Creator. This view is the basis of prophetic criticism. Prophetic religion speaks out of a religious vision; it is not first and foremost a movement for social reform. But the vision issues not only in prophecy against idolatry; it lures toward positive obedience to and fulfillment of the divine law.

(2) The power that is worthy of confidence, the power that alone is reliable, has a world-historical purpose, the achievement of righteousness and fellowship through the loving obedience of its creatures. As an ethical, historical religion prophetism is not mystical in so far as mysticism is interpreted as a flight above the temporal world into timeless communion with eternity. For it, time is not the enemy, as it is in much of Hellenism; time is not the order of deterioration. It is the arena of fulfillment through law and freedom, though it is also the arena of God's judgment. The divine purpose is manifest not in abstract, timeless entities but rather in historical events and patterns of events, in events and even in periods in the life of the people. Past events become necessity in the form of judgment where once they were only elements in the arena of freedom. On the other hand, they are interpreted as evidence of the faithfulness of God. In the past God had chosen Israel and made a covenant in order to carry out his purpose in a special way. He had delivered Israel from bondage and slavery. Freedom from bondage is the working of a divine power, freedom from domination. But it brings with it the demand for a new commitment. The divine power, the reliable power in history, forms men into universal, righteous world-community. Where true community is being formed, there the divine power is working. Indeed, this is a way in

which we may identify the divine power. Prophetic religion is a historical religion not only in the sense that it is concerned with the struggle between good and evil in history but also in the sense that it looks toward the creation of a historical community of memory and hope with respect to God's working in history. Toward this end, man may be unfaithful, but God will be faithful.

(3) The power that is reliable in history places an obligation to righteousness upon the whole community of the faithful as a community, though to be sure the fulfillment is in God's own time. The response to the divine power is responsibility. The covenant of God is with the community and the individual members of it; it imposes responsibility upon community and individual for the character of the community and especially for concern with the needy and the oppressed. Religious institutions, cultus, political and economic institutions must serve God's righteous purpose. There is no enclave that is exempt from his sovereignty.

(4) The power that is reliable and sovereign in history offers itself as the basis of a fellowship of *persons*. Before working on the visible, outer side of history it generates the inner side of history and community; it manifests itself in the responsive, creative, healing powers of justice and love, of tenderness, forgiveness, and mercy. These qualities are not merely human devices. They are the capacities and feelings that express the fullness of the divine power. The interrelatedness of persons is seen to involve these interior qualities. When man does not exhibit tenderness, forgiveness, and mercy, he is in his freedom frustrating or perverting the divine power. Prophetism is not only a religion concerned with the divine power as it manifests itself in the outer events of history; it is also an interiorized religion of fellowship between God and men and between men under God. This feature of prophetism is conspicuous not only in the writings attributed to the prophets. Its literary precipitate appears also in the *Psalms,* the most intimate devotional literature of the race. Thus the power of God is strikingly personal in contrast to the merely impersonal, "electric" power of Mana. It is a passive as well as an active power; and it looks toward the expression of "power of" and "power with" rather than of "power over" (domination). The significance of this emphasis can be appreciated if we consider another aspect of the problem of the theology of social action.

The theological bases of social action cannot properly offer a blueprint for social action. The attempt to make a blueprint and to give it a divine sanction always runs the danger of issuing in idolatrous legalism. Yet the relevance of any theology of social action can become clear only when one discerns the demands that it makes upon social action and organization. Right attitudes are never sufficient alone. They must find embodiment in social institutions. Indeed, one must say that one does not even understand the meaning of "right attitudes" or even of a theology until one recognizes their implications for social organization. If no particular demands ensue with respect to social organization, "right attitudes" can be a snare and a deception, a form of organized irrelevance.

Now, when we search in the prophetic writings for an explicit statement of the principles of justice and love on the basis of which one might devise a theory of social organization, we get a rather "dusty answer." As Ernst Troeltsch says, the prophets did not work out these principles. But this does not mean that they were vague and inexplicit in their specific demands. Taken altogether their specific demands for social change are extensive; the prophets cannot be accused of being other-worldly.

Just at this point Troeltsch makes a radical criticism of the prophets as social reformers, as promoters of social action. In effect, he argues that when they became specific they tended to become also irrelevant, for they were not very willing to grapple with the actualities of the new economic and political situation in which Israel found herself; they indulged a nostalgia for an irrecoverable past. Their demands were not practical for their times and, he argues, they are not practicable for any other society in so far as that society is urban or is becoming urban. Several, if not all, of the prophets idealized an old, simple, half-nomadic, agricultural, small businessman ethic; they opposed the bigness as well as the luxury of cities; they deplored the violent force of the wars of empires, the precarious entangling alliances with foreign powers, the pomp and intrigue of the court, the loss of the simple, friendly justice administered by the elders, the impersonalism as well as the bribery of the courts of the princes, the officiousness of state functionaries, the oppression of officialdom, the law and usages and abuses that are characteristic of any urban economy. So far from being progressive radicals the prophets were reactionaries in the sense that they wanted to return to the good old days. To a large degree their "social program" was atavistic. As Troeltsch puts it, "The prophets are representatives of that Israelite mentality in which the old customs of the fathers stand in closest connection with the Jahwe cultus" ("Der Glaube und Ethos der hebraischen Propheten").

Troeltsch appears to suggest that the anti-urbanism of the prophets renders their conceptions of social justice anachronistic already in their own time. But there is a sense in which precisely this aspect of prophetism is perennially relevant, especially in an urban economy. Stated in sociological language, the yearning of the prophets for the rural ways of the idealized past was a yearning for a society in which primary, affectional relations are dominant. In the urban economy where division of labor is elaborate and social mobility is required, the total personality is not brought into play in most social relations. Secondary relations, segmented impersonal relations, tend to predominate. A certain alienation reflected in the individual's feeling of isolation, homelessness, restlessness, and anxiety is the consequence. The sense of alienation is created by the lack of intimacy, the impersonalism, the multiplicity of norms, the atomizing of obligations, the loss of communal solidarity. All of these consequences follow from the loss of primary ties. Luxury alongside neglected abject poverty, concentration of economic power, exploitation, callousness, intrigue, produce alienation of man from man, of man from the covenanted community, of man from God; they pervert man and society; in short, they alienate man from the community-forming power of God. Alienation can appear of course where primary ties are strong (divorce is not unknown); but in recommending the return to the past the prophets were trying to cope with a fundamental and characteristic problem of urban life. They were trying to correct the evils of mass society by the restoration of primary relations wherein fellowship, friendliness, intimacy, common responsibility could again prevail. They wanted the return of the power of mutuality as over against the power of domination. They saw that the power of God unto salvation can work only when men are not treated as things. They would have understood the Marxist protest against the *Verdinglichung* ("thingification") of man. This term is perhaps as good a symbol as any that could be used to characterize the major consequence of the frustration of the power of God as understood by the prophets. At any rate, no word could better indicate the pressing relevance of the prophetic ethic for the dehumanized anonymity of contemporary mass man. The prophetic ethic may be atavistic in its details. In its essence, however, it is an ethic that is especially pertinent in face of what John Stuart Mill called "the prices we pay for the benefits of civilization," the drying up of the sources of great virtues, "the decay of individual energy, the weakening of the influence of superior minds over the multitude, the growth of charlatanerie, and the diminished efficacy of public opinion as a restraining power" (Essay on "Civilization").

As against Troeltsch, we must say that the instinct of the prophets was sound. Taken together with the other aspects of their theology of social action which we have already noticed, their demand for the values, the powers that attach to intimacy of fellowship, is a perennially relevant demand to be made by every Christian theology of social action. Love and justice can prevail only where they are supported by the fellowship, the friendliness, the concern of each for all and of all for each, the sense of brotherly responsibility, found in the community of primary relations. These qualities of psychic relatedness are at the same time the working of the grace of God and the medium through which the divine power grows into history like a seed that grows "of itself," for through them the active and the passive powers of sensitivity operate in mutuality.

Conceptions of the Divine Power in the New Testament. The reference to Jesus' figure about the seed (employed by Jesus in parables that have metaphysical as well as moral depth) assists us to observe the way in which he continued, extended, and deepened the prophetic conceptions of the community-forming power of God. In his conceptions of Love and Law he emphasized, as did the prophets, the divine yearning and initiative for intimacy of fellowship between God and man and between men. But, going beyond their eschatological hopes (which we have had to leave out of our explicit discussion), he stressed the idea that the Kingdom of God has already "broken in." Moreover, Jesus transformed the Old Covenant into a New Testament, implying a new basis and a new world mission. He envisaged a more intimate relation between himself (the spearhead and earnest of the Kingdom now breaking in) and his community than that between Moses and the prophets to the People of God. The God of Jesus also seeks out after the lost and the neglected. Besides, he presents himself as a new, tangible manifestation and medium of divine power. "Moses received and gave Torah; Jesus *was* Torah, together with the power to fulfill Torah" (W. M. Horton, "The Christian Community: Its Lord and Its Fellowship, *Interpretation*, IV [October 1950], 391).

We should notice here another important difference. In his conception of the Kingdom of God, Jesus shared with the prophets, as we have indicated, the desire for intimacy of fellowship. In many respects his mentality and that of his immediate disciples was similar to that of the prophets in the sense that it was conditioned by agrarian protest against urbanization. "The gospel," says F. C. Grant "is, in fact, the greatest agrarian protest in all history." But the prophets do not appear to have formed continuing intimate groups in which their theology of power, their theology of fellowship, could find application. The Christians *did* form a social organization in which the power of the spirit, the power of love, could find organizational embodiment. Moreover, in the conception of the Body of Christ they found a new ontological basis for the working of the divine power that was in Jesus, namely, the *koinonia,* a group living a common life with Jesus Christ as its head and informing power. Participation in a believing fellowship became the soil for the working of the divine power. Again, we observe that the divine and human powers were interpreted as both active and passive; moreover, the noncoercive aspects of power were greatly stressed. The New Testament ethic is an ethic of abundance.

As touching the question of the theological bases of social action, however, we must observe that Jesus gave his direct attention to person-to-person relations. He was not a political theologian. He and the primitive church showed little direct concern for economic and political problems and institutions as such, the problems having to do with impersonal relations. This attitude is to be explained mainly by his sense of urgency with respect to the imminent coming of the Kingdom in fulness and power. St. Paul, however, gave impetus to a conservative evaluation of political and other institutions. "The powers that be are ordained of God." "I have learned in whatsoever state I am, therewith to be content." Despite these attitudes, the early church exercised an increasingly transformative power in institutions, partially as a consequence of the fact that the church itself provided an opportunity to people who had previously been excluded from exercising significant social-political power to assume responsibility in the exercise of power, that is, in participating in the divine creative-redemptive power and thus making social decisions. But beyond this, it surely must be recognized that the canon of Christian social action does not close with the New Testament.

Power and Social Action in the Democratic Society. The attitude of responsibility appropriate for achieving consensus toward the end of shaping social policy in modern democratic society is better represented by the nineteenth-century British theologian, William Whewell: "Every citizen who thus possesses by law a share of political power, *is* one of the powers that be. Every Christian in such a situation may and ought to exert his constitutional rights, so far as they extend, both to preserve the State and the Law from all needless and hasty innovation, and to effect such improvements in both as time and circumstance require; using the light of Religion as well as of morality and polity, to determine what really is improvement" (*The Elements of Morality Including Polity,* New York, 1845, Sec. 651). Although the fellowship of the *koinonia* is perhaps possible only in the church itself, the vocation it places upon the Christian in the world must presuppose the ongoing attempt to make its conception of the divine power applicable outside the *koinonia* as well as within it, in the latent as well as in the manifest church. The theological and ethical principles of Christian social action which are appropriate for the church are ultimately the criteria for judging and transforming society. The Christian looks for a society in which all men may be treated as persons potentially responsive to God's redemptive purpose for history. And in working for it, he must perforce use that kind of fellowship today called the voluntary association, where within the church and outside it consensus is formed and social action is undertaken.

But between St. Paul and William Whewell there stands a long period of development (including the Left Wing of the Reformation as a decisive period) almost comparable in significance to that which separates the period of belief in Mana from the prophetic period of the discovery of the Lord of history. Yet, the general framework of ideas provided by Jewish and Christian prophetism, together with its demand for responsible, communal fellowship, represents the orientation for the theological bases of social action which is imperative for any Christian who undertakes to fulfill the divinely given responsibility to participate in social action toward the end of offering loving obedience to the divine power, the Lord of history and of the soul of man. Christian obedience looks toward the kind of social action and the kind of society that can provide the soil out of which the creative, judging, healing power of God may like a seed grow of itself.

Arminius and the Structure of Society

James Luther Adams

Not as a total stranger does the citizen of Massachusetts visit Amsterdam, a seat of the old Dutch Republic. Not as a stranger does a member of Harvard University join in this celebration of the four-hundredth anniversary of Jacobus Arminius. Many are the spiritual children of the Dutch Republic and also of Arminius who have contributed to the heritage of Massachusetts and of America in both politics and religion. Permit me as a representative of American Unitarianism to express my hearty appreciation for the privilege of participating in this anniversary celebration and for the warm and generous hospitality I and my colleagues have enjoyed here at the hands of the Remonstrant Brotherhood.

It is now just over a century since the Boston scholar John Lothrop Motley first published *The Rise of the Dutch Republic* (1856). A few years later he published *The History of the United Netherlands,* and then about a decade later came his *Life and Death of John of Barneveld.* In honor of Motley, the Queen of the Netherlands set a house apart for his use at The Hague, where he had long labored in the archives. Motley told a Dutch scholar that in preparing these volumes he was struck with the analogies between the emergence of the United Provinces and of the United States and between William of Orange and George Washington. "If ten people in the world," he said, "hate despotism a little more and love civil and religious liberty a little better in consequence of what I have written, I shall be satisfied." By reason of the warm reception accorded his books, Motley was entitled to feel well satisfied, even though Calvinists (like Prinsterer in the Netherlands) severely criticized him for his sympathy with the Arminian cause.

Long before this time, however, the epic of the Dutch Republic and of the conflicts between the Remonstrants and the Contra-Remonstrants was a familiar story in America. Indeed, these things were well known in the American colonies from the beginning, for many of the first colonists migrated to New England only after a sojourn in Holland. Two members of the first Harvard Board of Overseers had been pastors of English churches in the Low Countries; and the first head of Harvard College, Nathaniel Eaton, was an alumnus of the University of Franeker. From Harvard's beginning in 1636 the Dutch universities and scholars were highly esteemed.

The attitude toward Arminianism which prevailed in New England in the seventeenth century, and even later, was expressed in a prayer on behalf of Harvard College which pleaded that the college might be "so tenacious of the truth that it shall be easier to find a wolf in England or a snake in Ireland than a Socinian or Arminian in Cambridge." So far as Cambridge and Harvard were concerned, however, the petition was denied in the end. In the year 1805 the Unitarian Henry Ware was appointed Hollis Professor of Divinity at Harvard, one event, among others, that signalized the successful penetration into the American colonies of ideas that were labeled Arminian. The Harvard Divinity

School as a special division of the university was established in 1816, and from the beginning the *Ars Critica* of the Arminian Jean Le Clerc was staple reading.[1] Already more than half a century before this, Charles Chauncy, the minister of the First Church in Boston and the great-grandson and namesake of the second president of Harvard College, had been a major opponent of the Calvinist Jonathan Edwards and was thus a key figure in the advancement of Arminianism.

By this time, however, the term *Arminian* had become a loose label, a *Kampfbegriff,* not always having a strict connection with the Trinitarian theology of Arminius himself and sometimes implying a Pelagianism that Arminius would have repudiated. Aside from these considerations, we should observe that Arminianism was a composite movement, composite in its historical antecedents and many faceted in its thrust in each of the countries in which it played a role. Indeed, the very openness of discussion which was initially promoted by Arminius and which has characterized the later developments gave to Arminianism its creative and dynamic tensions. Accordingly, the term "Arminian," even when carefully defined, has assumed many shades of meaning.

Consider the variety of ingredients to be found in the antecedents of Arminianism and in the early development. From the outset Arminianism transcended the boundaries of Calvinism as delineated in Geneva. Not only the Dutch Lutherans (and Melanchthon also) were a part of the formative background; Arminianism also presupposed the experience of the sectarians,

[1] Le Clerc, born in Geneva, was a teacher at the Seminary in Amsterdam. He was a friend of John Locke and of other leading Whigs in England and was also very sympathetic to the developing interest in the natural sciences. His *Ars Critica* is a study of the new historical criticism of ancient texts. Cf. Colie, *op. cit.*

the practical discipleship, and the struggle for toleration among the Anabaptists and the Mennonites. It presupposed also the spirit of Erasmus, "the philosophy of Christ," an ethical teaching that claimed to be available to reasonable men everywhere, a teaching to be appropriated through free inquiry and through the cultivation of the mind. In the famous school of the *Devotio Moderna* in Utrecht Arminius acquired his classical learning, and from it he gained also his conception of a divinely derived "good conscience" and Christian liberty. Erasmus previously had also attended this school of the Brethren of the Common Life. Moreover, already within its first generation, Arminianism became the name of a High-Church, anti-Puritan movement in the Church of England. At the same time it figured in the development of the left-wing movements of seventeenth-century England.

Subsequently, Arminianism in the various countries was to promote ideas we associate with the Enlightenment; and, later, it was to be adopted with one accent or another by Methodists, and still later by Congregationalists and Unitarians. From its outset, then, Arminianism had roots in the Renaissance and in the left wing as well as in the right wing of the Reformation.

It has been the genius of Arminianism to maintain the discussion between these perspectives and those of the Enlightenment and of the Evangelical Awakening and eventually between these perspectives and those of modern higher criticism and of the modern scientific outlook. Accordingly, the essence of Arminianism is not easy to define, for it has entered into a variety of alliances. In general, it has promoted "a free and catholic spirit" that has cherished practical morality as a sign of the Christian way. This spirit is not to be grasped merely by listing doctrines that are the opposite of those set forth in the Articles of the Synod of

Dort. We can say that it was initially informed by some such gestalt of ideas as the following: the Christian must place his confidence in the sovereignty and the mercy of God; all that is worthy in human life depends upon his grace; salvation through Christ is available to all men; faith precedes election; yet the regenerate man derives from Christ the grace to respond to the offer of salvation; and from Christ he derives also Christian liberty. These doctrines, to be sure, come short of indicating adequately the complex of ideas and practices which has appeared under the rubric of Arminianism.

Previous lectures in the symposium have delineated certain of the basic theological and ethical ideas of Arminianism. We are now to consider broadly some of the social issues that have been the rallying points of the movement. Ideally, one should attempt systematically to relate the theological doctrines to these social issues. Because of limitations of time we must in the main confine attention here to conceptions and practices that bear especially upon the internal organization of the church and also that reveal characteristic tendencies with respect to social organization in general. In the course of the narrative we shall see ample cause for the view of Motley that the whole epic bespeaks a persistent hatred of despotism and a love for civil and religious liberty. More specifically, we shall see that Arminianism has been a major force in the development of those principles of individuation (or differentiation) which belong to modern culture and a major force also in the development of that characteristic preference of a radically Protestant ethos—the preference for what is called freedom of association. Indeed, we shall see that in the history of Arminianism individual freedom and freedom of association are inseparable in principle, for they are mutually interdependent.

In the remarkable Arminius Exhibition arranged at Oudewater, Holland, for the celebration of the present anniversary, one encounters a striking cartoon of the Synod of Dort at which the Remonstrants were condemned. In this cartoon one sees Calvin's *Institutes* and the role of the Advocate John of Barneveld in the scales at the synod as if they were being weighed against each other. The *Institutes* outweighs the robe, the momentary symbol of the Remonstrants, but alongside the *Institutes* in the scale is the sword of Prince Maurice of Orange who took the side of the Contra-Remonstrants. The *sword* tips the balance. The symbols or these scales, the robe and the sword, bespeak the mixture of politics and religion in the whole controversy.

In Holland the sword of brute force had already figured largely in theological controversy for several generations preceding the Synod of Dort. Anyone who has read the Remonstrant Gerard Brandt's seventeenth-century *History of the Reformation in the Low-Countries* (1677) will have an indelible image of the torture to which the Anabaptists, the Calvinists, and other precursors of the Arminians were subjected in the preceding century. Here one encounters a striking illustration of the "natural history" of the Reformation period. So much was coercion in the ascendant that in most countries it determined the immediate victory. The Swiss historian Jakob Burckhardt has reminded us that the religious confession that prevailed in each territory of Europe was the one that commanded the strongest battalions. So also, following the Synod of Dort, the Calvinists harried the Remonstrants out of the land. Although these Calvinists had themselves previously pleaded for religious liberty in face of Roman Catholic Spanish tyranny, and although they themselves had suffered persecution, they retained the policies of the church fanatical when their turn came to control the power. In face of this heritage of coercion, Arminius and his associates a generation before the meeting of the Synod of Dort had tried, as was said of Erasmus, "to reform the Reformers and the Reformation itself." [2] They started a third Reformation.

We should not forget, however, that in attempting this reformation Arminius remained in certain fundamental respects a Calvinist. He retained the conviction of the sovereignty of God, the sense of man's ultimate dependence upon God in Christ, the protest against the idolatry that gives to the creature the devotion that belongs to God alone, the strong moral passion, and the demand for social order.

At the same time he was vividly sensitive to the power of God which manifests itself in compassion and tenderness, to the power that gives a new liberty in the gospel. Arminius took seriously the promise, "And I, if I be lifted up from the earth, will draw all men unto me." We may say that affection, attraction, or love, rather than will was the fundamental *pathos* of his life-view. Through God's providence and love man has freedom to accept or reject the power unto salvation in Jesus Christ. Sören Kierkegaard would very much have liked this element of the freedom of love in the thought and life of Arminius. Kierkegaard asserts that the omnipotence of God is to be seen not in his absolute control of creation but rather in his power to bring into being a

[2] Gerard Brandt, *The History of the Reformation and Other Ecclesiastical Transactions in and About the Low-Countries.* Trans. from the Low-Dutch (London: T. Wood, 1720), I, 73. Brandt in this work reflects the Dutch Arminianism of the latter part of the seventeenth century. Constantly appealing to Erasmus, he favors tolerance in place of coercion, mutual forbearance notwithstanding "diversity in points not fundamental," and simplicity of doctrine, sanctioned (he believes) by the practice of the early church, "the primitive model."

creature that can turn against him and that can voluntarily turn towards him.

Arminius, appealing to Lactantius, held that: "To recommend faith to others, we must make it the subject of persuasion, and not of compulsion." He insisted that the true religion from Christ does not deteriorate into dissension. In the exercise of Christian liberty there will be sincere and honest differences. These differences cannot and should not be stamped out by means of coercion. In confronting the Scripture, Christians should be able to agree on what is necessary for salvation. But when mutual consent and agreement cannot be obtained on some articles, "then the right hand of fellowship should be extended by both parties." Each party should "acknowledge the other for partakers of the same faith and fellow-heirs of the same salvation, although they may hold different sentiments concerning the nature of faith and the manner of salvation." [3] It is the obligation of the magistrates to maintain the conditions for this sort of discussion in synod. Arminius favored not only freedom of discussion and sweet reasonableness on the basis of the broad fundamentals of Christian faith; he wished also that the synod would eschew idolatry in its attitude toward itself and its decisions. He held that even if the synod were to achieve unanimous decision, it should not impose it upon others by force, for it is possible that even with unanimous decision the synod might have "committed an error in judgment." Such an error can appear in the realm of discipline as well as of doctrine. Accordingly, a synod, he believed, should leave open the way for revision of its findings. How characteristic it is for Arminius to conclude his ecclesiological *Disputation LVI* (Corollary) with this question:

[3] *Writings*, I, 188, 189.

Is it not useful, for the purpose of bearing testimony to the power and the liberty of the church, occasionally to make some change in the laws ecclesiastical, lest the observance of them becoming perpetual, and without any change, should produce an opinion of the (absolute) necessity of their being observed? [4]

Arminius wanted a church free from bondage to itself.

For Arminius the love of truth should under God liberate men from this bondage. As against those who would make the Dutch Confession mandatory, the Arminians appealed to Scripture as the broader, sounder norm of faith. As members of the Reformed movement, they were set against the idolatry of both the Roman Catholics and the high Calvinists who permitted their teachers and their confessions to separate them from direct examination of Scripture. In this they could appeal for sanction to Calvin himself. Without freedom of faith, Arminius asserts, the Reformation itself could not have come into being, and without it the Reformation could become inured to error. Therefore, he held that the presidency of the free assembly should be the Holy Spirit, "for he has promised to be present where even two or three are gathered in His name." This is "the true, free assembly most appropriate for the investigation of truth and the establishment of concord." Over the porch of the assembly, he says, this sentence, after the manner of Plato, should be inscribed in letters of gold: "Let no one enter this hallowed dome without a desire for the truth and for peace." Otherwise, he says, religion will experience "almost the same fate as the young lady mentioned by Plutarch,

[4] *Ibid.*, II, 140. I am indebted to Carl Bangs of the Olivet Nazarene College, Kankakee, Illinois, for calling this Disputation to my attention and for other instruction regarding the outlook of Arminius. His dissertation on Arminius, prepared at the University of Chicago, is to be published presently. Dr. Bangs attended the symposium and participated in the panel discussions.

who was addressed by a number of suitors; and when each of them found that she could not become entirely his own, they divided her body into parts, and thus not one of them obtained possession of her whole person." [5] Here we detect the spirit of Erasmus who strove for the Christian and human virtues of tolerance and peace and love of neighbor.

Arminius was resolved to resist the contentious spirit common in the theological debates of his time. "Invective, mutual anathematizing and execration," he felt, would not "excite the minds of people to the love and study of truth, to charity, mercy, long-suffering and concord." He took a dim view of the method of disputation which was then prevalent in the universities. He wished that the discussion of matters of faith could be conducted in such a fashion that the observer might exclaim, "See how these Christians love one another." A favorite word of Arminius was "moderation."

In demanding that toleration be protected by the magistrates Arminius was scarcely advocating a novelty, even among the Calvinists. Charles Perrot, a liberal theologian in Geneva, had advised Uitenbogaert, a friend of Arminius: "Never assist in condemning any for not agreeing in every point of religion with the established church, so long as they adhere to the fundamentals of Christianity, and are disposed to maintain the peace." To be sure, the issue that is difficult to determine is the question as to what the fundamentals are.

Among the Dutch "Churches under the Cross" the writings of Erasmus with their plea for toleration had been popular for two generations. These churches had included the magistrates and laymen in the direction of church affairs. Jasper Coolhaes,

[5] *Ibid.,* pp. 161-62 .

formerly a member of the faculty at Leiden, had been protected by the magistrates when he advocated tolerance for Lutherans and Anabaptists and even for disciples of Bèze. Arminius himself probably would not have received his appointment to the Leiden faculty if the magistrates had not been in control. Men of this tradition relied upon the magistrates, the laity, to protect diversity, for they feared the rigid conformity that would ensue if a clerically controlled consistory of the Bèze preference were in power.

Now, if we are to understand the social issues at stake here, we must view these developments within their broad historical context and implication. What we have been reviewing is part of the process of differentiation or individuation which in varying ways was emerging all over Europe, a process decisively initiated by the Renaissance and by the Reformation in its various branches. This process of differentiation distinguishes an open society from a merely traditionalist society; it is indispensable for the appearance of a free society. At the time of Arminius, however, it was a relatively new movement. Indeed, it represented a revolutionary change. The kind of toleration defended by Arminius and his forebears was moving away from the traditional conception of the Christian commonwealth, the conception of *corpus Christianum.*

According to this traditional conception (introduced by the Emperor Theodosius about the year 378), the stability of society requires uniformity of religious belief. In the Middle Ages the pope and the emperor had been theoretically partners in the task of maintaining society and church in unity. To this end the emperor had been expected to wield the sword against heretics and schismatics. Here the political and the ecclesiastical forces were in alliance, giving rise to a territorial religion. Indeed, Augustine would have called it a civic religion. This conception of territorial religion was not abandoned by the major branches of the Reformation. It was transferred as it were from the whole of Christendom to the parts. Accordingly, Dissenters were banished or persecuted. This territorialism involved state establishment, or recognition of an officially sanctioned group.

The situation was essentially the same in the American colonies, except in Rhode Island and Pennsylvania. Each colony officially recognized only one confession: in Massachusetts and Connecticut the Congregationalists, in New York and New Jersey the Presbyterians, in Maryland the Roman Catholics. The Constitution of the United States which was instituted in 1787 did not change the pattern of establishment in the states, although no religion was to be established in the nation as a whole.

The system of territorialism was mitigated by a marked degree of freedom and variety during the rise of the Dutch Republic. But territorialism was brought back with a vengeance immediately after the Synod of Dort. In this period dissenters, including the Arminians, were subjected to persecution or to legal penalties. The location in Amsterdam of the first Remontrant edifice of 1630 behind the houses of the Keizersgracht illustrates one of these penalties (familiar also in England in the succeeding period).

Arminius died over twenty years before the construction of this edifice in Amsterdam. Indeed, he died almost a decade before the Synod of Dort. In his view of the church he had not broken completely with the tradition of territorialism. He favored what is now called comprehension. This pattern permits a degree of latitude within the recognized confession; in addition, it permits some leeway to nonconforming groups, though it imposes one penalty or another upon them. The degree of freedom made possible by comprehension is well illustrated in the adoption of Arminian ideas in the Church of England during the early part of the seventeenth century, during the time of the Cambridge Platonists later in this century, and during the period of the Latitudinarians in the eighteenth century.[6]

Although this system of comprehension does not constitute complete religious liberty for all, it does represent an advance in freedom within the internal structure of the established church. The system as it operated in Holland in the seventeenth century was very complex, and we cannot deal with it in detail here. We should note, however, that by reason of the role of the magistrates, political authority was given a place that to us is questionable. We cannot accept this Erastian position. On the other hand, Arminius and his associates could find in their magistrates and their laity a spirit of tolerance rejected by the high Calvinists. Similarly, the development of the principle of comprehension in England was accompanied by giving the laity a significant role in the church, even apart from the magistracy. Moreover, the system in itself was intended as a means of providing for greater freedom within the church as a social organization and as a household of faith. It provided an opportunity for differentiation within the established church.

But freedom of association, the freedom to form new and unhampered religious organization was not yet available—the freedom to organize independent differentiation. Before the appearance of Arminianism this freedom had been demanded in

[6] Cf. the section entitled "The Laymen and the Moderates," in W. K. Jordan, *The Development of Religious Toleration in England* (Cambridge: Harvard University Press, 1941), II, 315-491. This section provides also an account of the Arminian leaders, Arminius, Uitenbogaert, Grotius, and Episcopius.

various branches of the left wing of the Reformation. After the Synod of Dort the next phase of development in Arminianism was the struggle to secure this sort of freedom of association, the struggle of a minority excluded from the territorial church.

What is involved here is much more than the demand for freedom of faith for the individual. The demand is for the freedom of the individual to associate with others in the promotion of forms of consensus which are not shared by the total community or by the territorial church. The demand is for group freedom, for the freedom of an institution. More than that, it is the demand for the freedom of a minority group. This sort of freedom of association is a watershed between the left and the right wing of the Reformation, between territorialism and voluntarism. It is the harbinger of the modern conception of the multi-group society.

We should now trace briefly the transition to the new conception of society. Following the Synod of Dort the Arminian clergy were banished from the United Provinces. Soon thereafter Uitenbogaert, formerly court preacher at The Hague, formed this scattered group of leaders into an association or society. These men from their places of exile secretly re-entered the country. Rallying the laity, they organized the Remonstrant-Reformed congregations. Uitenbogaert retained the idea of Arminius that the group should admit differences among themselves in matters not fundamental. Thus the Remonstrants distinguished themselves from the typical sectarian group. They became a nonconforming association that permitted a degree of noncomformity within itself. That is, it made room for innovation, self-criticism, differentiation within the group. But Uitenbogaert did not wish complete independence from the state. On scriptural grounds he held that the Christian magistrate should recognize and maintain "only one religion, and no other publicly." The magistrates, however, should not be intolerant advocates of an exclusive religion. They should "permit and tolerate in their dominions, other kinds of religion, by way of connivance; looking upon them, as it were, through the fingers."

It was Episcopius who markedly advanced the Remonstrant theory of associations. Although he held that the ruler is rightly responsible for all public functions in both church and state, he insisted that everyone should be free to express his own opinion on religious matters. He denied that the acceptance of a creed should be a test of loyalty. Freedom of inquiry should be encouraged. As against the Calvinists who would permit heretics only to hold private opinions, he insisted that they be allowed freedom of association and public worship so long as they did not challenge the essential authority of the ruler and of the recognized faith. Religion should be a matter of persuasion and choice, not of coercion. No one should arrogate to himself the right to determine what are heresies. Here Episcopius anticipates the Arminian John Milton in the view that truth should be pursued in open and free encounter. To the Calvinists Episcopius suggested that they should not worry about the risks involved here. In their view the reprobates are already damned, and the elect cannot be corrupted. Curiously enough, the Calvinist Roger Williams of Rhode Island would presently also use precisely this argument to defend complete religious liberty. In the view of Episcopius intolerance exacts a great and insufferable tax. It stifles conscience, it prevents reform, it promotes hypocrisy, it even gives occasion for sedition. What an eloquent defender of these principles is Episcopius. He says:

Be unwilling, O princes, that yours should be the right from God to bespatter your crown with the blood of the erring. Let it suffice that they approve your sceptre by faith, service and other fitting duties. Religion must be defended not by slaying but by admonishing, not by ferocity but by patience, not by crime but by faith.

And then comes a sharp thrust at the Calvinists who are indulging theocratic yearnings: "We hold the power of the magistrate to be great without equal; but the orthodox cherish it as the fulcrum of theirs." And of the Calvinists who in the name of the Word of God would suppress liberty of conscience he asks, "If they stood before a king who believed differently, although upon Scriptural grounds, would not their individual conscience prove their ultimate defence?"[7] But none of these views belies the conviction of Episcopius in favor of comprehension. He favors it both before and after the Synod of Dort. Like his colleagues, he wishes the Remonstrant Brotherhood to be a part of a latitudinarian national church and not to occupy the status of a minority. Episcopius does not conceive of the Brotherhood as a free church in a free state. He remained Erastian. The idea of the free church at this period stems more from the Baptists and the Congregationalists.

Nevertheless, viewed in the context of the Calvinism of his time and place, the outlook of Episcopius is impressive. He exposed clerical pretension, and he rejected coercion in religion. He emphasized the voluntary character of religion, liberty of conscience, and freedom of inquiry. He defended the rights of freedom of association even for heretics; indeed, he adumbrated the

[7] *Vedelius Rhapsodus*, chap. ix. Quoted by Nobbs, *op. cit.*, p. 103.

civil right of such freedom of association. These are views that much of the rest of Christendom have come to accept.

It is not difficult to believe that Episcopius exercised considerable influence upon the English Independents, for his works were read in England throughout the century. The specific role, however, of Arminianism in the development of democratic thought in the New Model Army and among the Levellers is far from clear. A variety of influences seems to have played a role, and Arminianism was among these influences. In a general way and without offering documentation the British scholar A. S. P. Woodhouse affirms that it weakened the theological basis of Puritan inequalitarianism, of the conception of an aristocracy of the elect, and thus undermined "the most formidable barriers separating Puritanism from democracy."[8] We have previously noted its influence in the Church of England of the time.

For my final illustration of the effect of Arminianism upon the theory and practice of religious association I shall turn to the Methodism of two centuries later. Here, too, other influences besides those coming from Arminianism (as understood by the Methodists) belong in the picture. But there is little doubt that John Wesley's Arminian belief that God has given every man the ability to respond to the gospel and his doctrines of assurance and perfection served as the principal nerve of the development of a new ethos in British and American society. This outcome, to be sure, does not become strikingly evident until the middle

---

[8] *Puritanism and Liberty* (Chicago: University of Chicago Press, 1951), p. 54. Leo Solt raises a question as to whether the influence of Arminianism among the Independents was always clearly in this direction. See his *Saints in Arms* (Stanford, Calif.: Stanford University Press, 1959), p. 67.

of the nineteenth century, about three-quarters of a century after the beginning. But when these developments do come, they affect group formations at three levels, namely, within the structure of the organization of Methodism, in the relation between Methodism and the state, and in the relations between Methodism and other associations in the community.

Alfred North Whitehead has rightly affirmed that Wesley turned the energies of Britain and America in new directions, but this did not take place without dust and heat within Methodism itself. Wesley was a Tory. He required his preachers to take a loyalty oath to the crown and he frowned upon any disposition among his followers to express political interests in the name of Methodism. Nothing could seem to be less promising for dynamic, democratic politics than Wesley's outlook. Wesley, the father of Methodism, was the autocrat of Methodism. The structure of social authority within early Methodism could not have been less democratic.

Yet Wesley, with his genius for organization, devised a social invention that was to subvert his own political standpattism and his own preference for ecclesiastical hierarchy. Within each society Wesley asked that class meetings be formed. Each class meeting was composed of a dozen members who met regularly for interpersonal discipline, for self-examination, prayer, and guidance in the daily problems of the Christian life. Women as well as men played a role here, also in positions of leadership. The class meeting was not dissimilar to the *eccesiola in ecclesia* which appeared in the left wing of the Reformation and in Pietism. It provided a face-to-face dynamic fellowship, indeed a number of such fellowships, in each congregation or town. In some places there were as many as three hundred class meetings. Moreover, each of these class meetings required assignment of organizational function. Now, if we remember also that the growth of Methodism was simultaneous with the advance of the industrial revolution, that the bulk of Methodist membership came from the lower and middle classes, many of them being humble workers, it becomes readily evident why the class meeting became a great leveler, particularly as the class constituency broadened. By necessity the class meeting, and for that matter the entire structure of Methodism, required people who would assume responsibility not only as individuals in their immediate personal relationships but also as participants in the organizational structure. These developments, to be sure, gave rise to heated dispute. Nevertheless, within one or two generations these people gained a vigorous capacity to assert their freedom, indeed to exercise power in the sense of participating in social decisions. They trained themselves in the art of self-government. We cannot here detail the ways in which they change the structure of authority within the denomination, and in which they broadened the areas for individual and group participation. The whole process is another illustration of the activation of the laity and of lay preachers.[9]

Especially striking is the fact that they began to try to change the world outside the church. Under a variety of influences emanating partly from nonconformity they did four things that illustrate the role of freedom of association as a voluntary moral discipline: they became critical of the state and separated their church from the state; they became politically active in promot-

---

[9] Elie Halévy, *A History of the English People in the Nineteenth Century,* Vol. III: *The Triumph of Reform, 1830-41,* trans. by E. T. Watkin (2d. ed.; Gloucester, Mass.: P. Smith, 1950).

ing legislation or in impeding it; they gave leadership to the labor movement in its struggle for freedom of association and for the improvement of the human condition; and they threw their energies into other nonecclesiastical associations concerned with philanthropy and social reform—prison reform, factory legislation, and the like. Not least significant in these efforts was the Sunday school, the missionary movement, and a little earlier the antislavery movement. Besides all this the Methodist movement promoted industry, thrift, and private investment. In these ways Methodism provided a powerful religious sanction to those qualities most conducive to the building of an enterprise economy. Some scholars have suggested, accordingly, that Max Weber in his search for the psychological sources of the spirit of capitalism, should have given more attention that he did to the Methodists and to the Arminians generally. Many of these same developments appeared among the Remonstrants who pioneered in social and philanthropic causes. In the United States similar transformations took place. One can see these tendencies in American Congregationalism and Unitarianism. The Social Gospel, appearing in the late nineteenth century, reflects similar motifs which cannot be clearly distinguished from the basic thrust of theological Arminianism. Towards the middle of the nineteenth century the Unitarian William Ellery Channing, shortly after setting forth his partly Arminian objections to the five points of Calvinism, wrote on "the elevation of the laboring classes" and even on the theory of voluntary associations. In Channing's study in Boston a remarkably large number of associations for the improvement of the community were formed. Under his inspiration also the first settlement house in America was formed. These are among the most important forces that in the various countries represented at the symposium helped to create the modern democratic society insofar as it is democratic.

We have covered a wide sweep of history in this brief survey of certain of the social issues of Arminianism. This survey suggests the question: Does Arminianism give rise to a special type of Protestant, to what has been called "the Arminian man"? It is not an exaggeration to say that strict Calvinism has tended to engender fanaticism, and if not fanaticism then at least arbitrary conceptions of grace and the will of God. This quality of strict Calvinism is epitomized in a slogan that became current at the end of the Cromwellian Protectorate: "Nothing is so dangerous as a Presbyterian just off his knees." This quality is no longer characteristic in Presbyterian circles. We need not attribute the change to the moderating influence of Arminianism alone. But we can say that in the seventeenth century one sees in Holland and England the development (under the aegis of Arminianism) of a conception of God which stresses the rational, benevolent attributes and of a conception of man which mitigates the doctrine of total depravity in the direction of emphasizing the capacities for response and for disciplined responsibility in man. Here was an effort to enlarge the powers of man and to reduce the element of the arbitrary in grace. By the time these ideas were expanded during the period of the Enlightenment, "Arminianism" had revealed its characteristic danger—the interpretation of God's grace as the warranty and fulfillment of the capacities of man, with less emphasis upon the view of the Reformation and of Arminius that God's grace is required precisely in the face of human limitations and sin. In strict Calvinism the sense of the glory of God is so overpowering that it issues in heteronomy. In Enlightenment "Arminianism" the sense of human capacity is so much stressed as to approach a self-sufficient autonomy. Ernst Troeltsch's term "autotheonomy" aptly indicates the essential quality of Arminian piety—an ultimate dependency upon divine grace which does not abrogate but rather grounds, limits, and fulfills autonomy.

The shift in mentality from high Calvinism to Neo-Calvinist Arminianism, we have seen, gives rise to a different conception of associations. Whereas previously the Calvinist favored a rigidly unitary and authoritarian church, the Arminians moved in the direction of seeking greater freedom within the established church ("comprehension") and of providing room within the community for greater freedom to associate even for the promotion of heresy. The Arminian thrust in history has been in the direction of pluralism, on the presupposition that flexibility and openness make way for the appropriate reception of divine grace and for the fuller response to the gospel. Freedom within associations and freedom of associations thus became the social-organizational consequence. Troeltsch has succinctly epitomized this essential element in the Arminian striving for the "holy community." He says:

Neo-Calvinism extends the principle of the formation of all fellowship by means of association to every relationship in life, and everywhere it manifests a tendency to form societies for ecclesiastical and religious ends, as well as for civic and cultural purposes. . . . Neo-Calvinism lays stress upon the co-operation of Christianity and Humanity in a sense quite foreign to the older Calvinism. From that standpoint it then proceeds to develop a pacifist international spirit and pacifist propaganda, champions the rights of humanity, encourages the anti-slavery movement, and allies itself with philanthropic and humanitarian movements. . . . The earnest Christian sections of American and English Protestantism—which, in England, under the influence of the Evangelicals, includes also a large part of the State Church—represent the humane, freedom-loving, and cosmopolitan ethic of Liberalism.[10]

In both Europe and America this associational thrust gradually freed itself from the constricting bonds of Erastianism. The Erastianism was a residue of the old territorialism which held within it a quite different associational "genius" from that which was already implicit in and was already struggling for expression in Arminius and his predecessors and followers.

Taking these features into account, we may say that the Calvinist man was "an instrumental activist." He viewed himself as an instrument in the hands of the Almighty, carrying out his will in the work of the Kingdom. This Calvinist man became almost an irresistible force in the name of God. The Arminian man was aware of freedom of choice under God, and yet he was under the command to work for the holy community. Just as God had given him freedom to choose, so he felt he should give others freedom also—freedom not only to choose but freedom also to associate. It was out of this ethos that the social issues we have adumbrated came to the fore.

I have ventured to define and illustrate the social issues of Arminianism under two sociological rubrics, the principle of individuation and the principle of freedom of and in association, presupposing throughout that the theological insights of Ar-

---

[10] Ernst Troeltsch, *The Social Teaching of the Christian Churches,* trans. Olive Wyon (New York: The Macmillan Co., 1960), p. 675. Used by permission of The Macmillan Co. and George Allen & Unwin Ltd. For a severely critical estimate of "Arminianism" see Martin E. Marty, *The New Shape of American Religion* (New York: Harper & Brothers, 1959).

minianism delineated in the previous papers in this symposium
in varying ways inform these principles. Much that has been said
here is summed up in a sentence of appreciation which comes
from the pen of a contemporary Roman Catholic scholar,
Friedrich Heer, who says in *The Third Force,* a recent book on
European spiritual history:

Everything that has accrued on Calvinist soil, from the seventeenth
to the twentieth century of the Western world, in elements of freedom, of culture of the spirit, of peace, of tolerance, of political enlightenment, and that is much, very much, is unthinkable without
the movement for freedom that set in with Arminius and his spiritual
affinities.[11]

It would be an egregious error, however, to suppose that the
situation in which we find ourselves today is very much more
favorable to Arminianism in these respects than the situation out
of which it initially emerged. We today confront new forms of
territorial religion and of psychic violence. What else is the religion of nationalism? Edward Shillito years ago called this the
modern man's other religion. We today live in a conspicuously
conformist society. What else is the world of the organization
man? What else is the society dominated by the mass media of
communications, media that are under the control of anonymous
and powerful authorities from the Hollywood to the Madison
Avenue of each country. Our churches exist within this context.
Indeed, in many ways they reflect the popular piety hidden within
these bulwarks of territory and class—and, we might add, of race.
   In face of this situation we recall the word of Schleiermacher

---

[11] Friedrich Heer, *Die Dritte Kraft* (Frankfurt au Main: Fischer, 1959), p. 577.

that the Reformation must continue. The Arminians continued the Reformation into a third reform. In the spirit of this third Reformation we of this assembly celebrate the four-hundredth anniversary of a man who taught of the mercy as well as the judgment of God and who taught that this God who groweth not old bringeth forth treasures both new and old for those who respond to him in the responsibility that belongs to Christian liberty.

"The Protestant Ethic" with Fewer Tears

James Luther Adams

In much of current usage "the Protestant Ethic" is associated with the widely influential book of Max Weber (1864–1920), first published in Germany in 1904–1905.[1] No book of its kind has elicited such a wide range of scholarly discussion, much of it a vast misrepresentation.

One of the cruder oversimplifications is offered by William H. Whyte who, in a discussion of Weber, asserts that thrift and the survival of the fittest represent "the Protestant ethic in its purest form."[2] Another misconception epitomizes Weber's thesis by the formula, "Protestantism—or Calvinism—produced capitalism."[3] By others, the slogan "Capitalism produced Calvinism" is recited as an incantation, as if to imply that Weber was a Marxist. As summaries of Weber's thesis these formulas are, at the most, quarter-truths. They overlook the fact that Weber vigorously rejected

[1] Max Weber, *The Protestant Ethic and the Spirit of Capitalism*, tr. Talcott Parsons, Foreword by R. H. Tawney (New York: Charles Scribner's Sons, 1930). Weber's views on the Protestant ethic are also set forth in a later, companion piece, "The Protestant Sects and the Spirit of Capitalism," in H. Gerth and C. W. Mills (trans. and eds.), *From Max Weber: Essays in Sociology* (New York: Oxford University Press, 1946). The former will be referred to hereinafter as *PE*.

[2] William H. Whyte, *The Organization Man* (New York: Simon and Schuster, 1956), p. 14.

[3] An exaggerated version of this stereotype appeared in a conversation I had years ago in Paris with the Russian philosopher Nicolas Berdyaev, who wrote extensively on religion and capitalism. Speaking of the Protestant ethic, he said, "One could have predicted that American civilization would one day collapse, for it is grounded in Calvinism. We see this collapse not only in your greedy businessmen but also in your gangsters. Legs Diamond is a spiritual descendant of John Calvin." Following upon a few minutes' discussion, Berdyaev said in astonishment, "What a surprise to me. Why has no one ever told me that those gangsters are not Presbyterians?"

any monocausal theory of history, whether idealistic or realistic (Marxist).

I have chosen to present this essay in honor of Erich Fromm, partly because he has had a long-standing and systematic interest in the role of Christianity, and especially of Protestantism, in Western culture. It is, of course, not my purpose to recapitulate and assess Weber's entire intention and accomplishment in his studies of "the Protestant ethic" (I shall place this term in quotation marks when referring to his conception). That task has already been undertaken by a host of scholars.

My principal concern here is twofold: 1) to remind the reader that since Weber's study was concerned with "ascetic Protestantism" in its relation to economic behavior, he by no means intended a complete account of the Protestant ethic, and 2) to show that in Weber's presentation, even within this limit, he fails to take into account important aspects of "ascetic Protestantism," and that correspondingly he does not give attention to a significant influence of the Protestant ethic, particularly with respect to an indispensable feature of Anglo-American democracy, the voluntary association. In view of the fact that Weber with tears laments the end-result (as he sees it) of "the Protestant ethic," the import of this essay is to qualify his conception of that ethic and its influence, and therefore to view it with fewer tears.[4] This evaluation must take into account Weber's philosophical presuppositions and especially certain value judgments.

Weber is not a sociologist if by that term one refers to the specialist who examines human groups only by means of surveys and statistics. Weber must be classed with such seminal figures as Marx and Nietzsche, Adam Smith and Hegel. In a letter of his earlier years he wrote: "One can measure the honesty of a contemporary scholar, and above all, of a contemporary philosopher, in his posture toward Nietzsche and Marx. Whoever does not admit that he could not perform the most important parts of his work without the work that these two have done swindles himself and others."[5]

Weber, trained initially in law and economics, was a man of strong moral convictions. He was fundamentally concerned with the values of civilization and the ways these values have been formulated and implemented or perverted. As a social scientist, however, he distinguished fact state-

[4] The present essay is a considerably altered version of a lecture delivered at the University of Mainz, published in the *Zeitschrift für Evangelische Ethik*, XII, Heft 4/5 (1968), 247–267.
[5] Eduard Baumgarten, *Max Weber, Werk und Person* (Tübingen, 1964), p. 554. Cited by Arthur Mitzman, see Note 7 below.

ments from value judgments, asserting that the social scientist must confine himself to the former. Nevertheless, he not infrequently interrupts his exposition to render a value judgment, and then to apologize before returning to the matter in hand. Here we see an acute inner tension between commitment to scientific objectivity and the values of moral integrity and individual responsibility. A similar tension obtains between his concern for individual freedom and responsibility and his concern for a strong German state.

In examining civilizational values Weber presupposed a conception of man as a historical, social being. Indeed, in the end he developed a philosophy of history. Of crucial significance is his view that the sociologist, like anyone else who aims to understand human behavior, must be concerned with the *meaning* of that behavior. The sociologist, he says, examines behavior "when and insofar as the acting individual attaches a subjective meaning to it." [6] For Weber, as for Wilhelm Dilthey before him, the concept of meaning—a sense of the relation between the parts and the whole —enabled him to probe beneath the symbolism of religious and cultural myths, in search of "a meaningful 'cosmos,'" that is, in search of fundamental social and psychological sanctions and ultimate loyalties. These ultimate loyalties he held to be "religiously conditioned" insofar as they inform "a whole way of life." Precisely because of his concern with meaning (and meaninglessness), Weber as an "objective" social scientist dealt with the most "subjective" aspects of the human venture. In a special sense, then, he was a theological sociologist, though he spoke of himself as religiously "unmusical."

In explication of a doctrine of man, Weber held that ideas are not merely epiphenomena of social conditions and struggles, but decisively affect human behavior and history. At the same time, of course, he recognized that a reciprocal relation obtains between ideas and conditioning factors. His total work is, therefore, full of tensions, and it is a paradox that, despite his rejection of determinism and because of his recognition of conditioning factors (such as the unintended consequences of ideas), he was in contrast to Marx pessimistic in his assessment of present and future possibilities.

In examining "the Protestant ethic" Weber was mindful of his previous studies of the despotism of the Roman slave plantations, of the monopolistic practices of medieval trade associations, of the narrow self-interest and

[6] Max Weber, *Theory of Economic and Social Organization*, Talcott Parsons (ed. and tr.) (New York: Oxford University Press, 1947), p. 88.

political insensitivity of the Junkers, and also of Bismarckian authoritarianism. Indeed, in his view his own father was a well-kept lackey of Bismarckian authoritarianism as well as being an insensitive, domineering husband.[7]

All of these features figured in Weber's decision to study "the Protestant ethic," but as the book title indicates, his exclusive focus was to examine the relation between that ethic and "the spirit of capitalism." In his view, both this ethic and this spirit represent unique features in the history of religions and in the history of capitalisms; moreover, these historical entities enter into reciprocal relations. Without the ethic of ascetic Protestantism the spirit of modern capitalism could not have become so readily widespread. On the other hand, "the spirit of capitalism," in turn, affected the development, indeed the transformation, of "the Protestant ethic."

The unique features of the modern situation, as Weber views them, can be seen by examining his conception of "rational capitalism" and of "the Protestant ethic." These features of modern culture were but two aspects of an all-pervasive Western rationalism, manifest also in the arts, the sciences, and the forms of social organization. Rational capitalism came into being by cutting the moorings from the political capitalism and patrimonial order of the previous period. Rational capitalism not only promotes the free organization of labor and the idea of the intrinsic merit of work, but rejects the notion that acquiring money is a necessary evil. Instead, it views the earning of money as an ethical obligation; rejecting the notion that limits should be placed upon living standards, it promotes innovation by emphasizing impersonal considerations in accomplishing economic tasks efficiently. In these respects it is critical of the inherited tradition. In short, rational capitalism requires a functioning bureaucracy involving impersonal devotion to the task, specialized division of labor and a rationalized discipline. These ingredients call for, indeed they engender, a particular kind of mentality, which Weber identifies as "the spirit of capitalism."[8]

The uniqueness of this spirit Weber sees epitomized "in almost classical purity" in Benjamin Franklin's esteem for thrift and hard work, incumbent

[7] Arthur Mitzman in *The Iron Cage: An Historical Interpretation of Max Weber* (New York: Alfred A. Knopf, 1970) gives a detailed depth-psychological account of the political and family struggles with which Weber was concerned in the period immediately preceding his work on "the Protestant ethic."
[8] Weber's use of the term "spirit" (*Geist*) bespeaks not only his concern for meaning but also his awareness of a German semantic tradition in both religion and philosophy; we think especially of Hegel.

upon men as a profound duty—and in his case "free from all direct relationship to religion." [9] This sense of duty finds expression in virtue and
proficiency in a calling. The calling demands rationality in the sense of
relating means to ends, achieving a systematic, methodical performance,
and subordinating personal to impersonal considerations. Rationality and
calculation, then, become matters of duty. Moreover, ostentatious enjoyment of rewards of success must be eschewed; it can serve only to damage
one's credit and one's standing. Similar characteristics are presented in
Weber's essay "The Protestant Sects and the Spirit of Capitalism," in describing Americans he encountered in the United States who "used" the
church as an accrediting agency in the business community and as a place
to "make contacts."

Alongside the already developing spirit of capitalism a new conception
of meaning, "the Protestant ethic," comes onto the scene. Weber musters
evidence to show that Calvinist theology and Anglo-American Puritanism
were conducive to rationalized, individualistic activity (particularly in the
economic sphere), activity undertaken not for the sake of gain but as a religious duty—to glorify God *in this world*. This vision of human existence
—this "ascetic Protestantism"—was supported by an ethic of vocation or
calling which issued in vigorous methodical activity, thus releasing a tremendous energy. This ethic was motivated by a doctrine of salvation pre-
destined through grace, a doctrine that gave rise to an anxiety that led to
a redoubling of effort. At least initially, the dominant motive was "interest" in the salvation of the individual rather than the acquisition of wealth. [10]

In Weber's view, the central motifs of this vision of life had an independent origin in an interpretation of the Bible and of the disciplines of
the Christian life. Through the spread of these ideas in England when "the
spirit of capitalism" was already developing, they present a new attitude
toward worldly activity which, in essential features, is "congruent" with
that spirit. Accordingly, the ideas of the Puritans provide a milieu that is
both receptive to the spirit of rational capitalism and able to qualify that
spirit in terms of the "interest" of the Puritan in individual salvation,
wherein a sign of grace is righteous, industrious, methodical activity in the
world—labor in a calling. In time, however, ascetic Protestantism lost its

[9] *PE*, p. 48.
[10] Space does not permit our attempting even to summarize Weber's account of the
theological foundations of the Calvinist system, the absolutely transcendent, supramundane God, salvation by grace, the theory of predestination, the consequent
"inner isolation" of the individual before God and man.

powerful religious orientation and sanctioned a simple doctrine of work in the pursuit of wealth; indeed it even sanctioned the doctrine that wealth is a sign of grace, and finally that "piety is the surest road to wealth." These changes might be called Weber's account of the devil's toboggan slide of ascetic Protestantism.[11] To be sure, these developments are traced in detail and with considerable subtlety, but much of the evidence offered has been challenged by other scholars.[12]

Three other aspects of Weber's intention remain to be stressed. First, Weber says that he is "interested . . . in the influence of those psychological sanctions which, originating in religious belief and the practice of religion, gave a direction to practical conduct and held the individual to it." [13] In the main, therefore, he was interested not so much in sociological, structural features of the societal changes taking place as in the psychological sanctions for the legitimacy of a new pattern of the individual's conduct, that is, for the legitimacy of rational economic activity considered as a duty. To be sure, social-structural changes occurred, as in the emerging independence of economic and other activities from political control, a precondition of a pluralistic society. Weber focuses attention on the personality types attracted to the new patterns and their motivations. He also

---

[11] Having outlined the Weberian conception of the rise and decline of "the Protestant ethic," we should now observe that Erich Fromm's view of the advent and the consequences of Protestantism is quite different. For him Protestantism in the Reformation was not primarily a set of ideas initiating a new movement in history. Rather, the breakdown of the feudal medieval system which gave life a meaning through nourishing "a sense of security and belonging," left the individual, especially in the middle classes, isolated and free, and hence economically insecure and anxious. Luther and Calvin rationalized, intensified, and systematized this attitude, teaching men to accept their impotence and submit. One of the components of this Protestant ethos was the individual's compulsion to work, and this became one of the productive forces in capitalistic society (Erich Fromm, *Escape from Freedom* [New York: Rinehart and Co., 1941], Chap. III). Modern man, having been freed from the bondage of medieval economic and political ties, finds himself impotent and lonely in the midst of the supra-personal forces of capital and the market; he seeks escape from loneliness in the spurious and debilitating sense of belonging offered by Nazism or by the deceptions of "democratic" capitalism which make him into a compulsive, conforming automaton while seducing him into believing he is a free, self-determining individual. Although Fromm's view and that of Weber converge or overlap at certain points, their respective conceptions of the Protestant ethic and its role in the development of modern capitalist society differ quite markedly.

[12] See, for one example, Winthrop Hudson's documented critique of Weber's presentation (and distortion) of the ideas of Richard Baxter who serves as Exhibit A in Weber's "case": "Puritanism and the Spirit of Capitalism," *Church History*, 18:1 (March, 1949), 3–17.

[13] *PE*, p. 97.

indicates ways in which individual conduct is constricted by social forces it has released.

Second, Weber attempted, as part of his method, to construct "ideal types." This method, he insisted, had long been used (indeed is inevitable in analyzing human behavior); but he felt that it required clarification. Here again the concept of meaning is of crucial significance. The ideal type is an intellectual tool, a unified analytical construct, devised by the historian or sociologist in order to characterize unique, meaning-oriented phenomena of human action, and in such a way as to give them a quality of generality whereby comparison and contrast with other meaning-oriented phenomena become possible. The concept of meaning is involved here in dual fashion. Being a construct, the ideal type in the first place reflects the value-orientation of the one who devises or uses it as a tool. In the second place, it selects and accentuates concrete, individual phenomena in a onesided way so as to achieve precision, a precision that combines generality with individuality in a context of meaning. Weber thus combines insights regarding generality and particularity which may be traced respectively to the Enlightenment and to Romanticism. Since ideal types are made up of highly abstract patterns, he speaks of their being "utopian" (not to be found anywhere in concrete detail) and also of their "artificial simplicity." They serve as "conceptual points of reference" for "experiments" in comparative cultural analysis. Major illustrations of these ideal types are such concepts as otherworldly and this-worldly asceticism; a patrimonial traditionalist social order and a rational, innovating capitalist order; and, of course, the Protestant ethic and the spirit of rational capitalism.[14] In later writings Weber developed a whole series of ideal types, such as types of authority or domination (traditional, legal-rational, and charismatic) and types of prophetism (ethical and exemplary). It has been suggested that Weber's ideal types may be compared to Hegel's logically related concepts. Weber, to be sure, rejects any "emanationist" or dialectical theory of the sort espoused by Hegelian idealism. He was not only religiously but also metaphysically "unmusical."

Obviously, the particular form of an ideal type depends entirely upon the features chosen for accentuation. Hence, an ideal type is like a wax nose to be shaped in a variety of ways. Think of the protracted debate of the past generation regarding the question, What was the Renaissance? Similarly, Weber's ideal type of "the Protestant ethic," as we shall see, is not only made of wax; it is also a bone of contention.

14 For references to ideal types in *PE*, see pp. 71, 98, 200.

Third, we must stress what we have already hinted at, namely that in Weber's view a crucial feature of Western culture is the element of rationality. He sees an anticipation of it in the universal ethical prophetism stemming from the Old Testament which in both Judaism and Christianity has served in principle to combat magic. Of course, he finds it in Greek science and logic. He also points out that, along with an ethos of work, it appears conspicuously in medieval monasticism in its methodical features.

Rationality "covers a whole world of different things." Moreover, for Weber it possesses a markedly ambiguous value: it is capable of obstructing as well as of promoting human freedom and fulfillment. If we spell out here its positive and negative aspects, we shall the more readily grasp the character of Weber's doctrine of man and his philosophy of civilization.

In its more positive aspects rationality appears in: the deliberate weighing of a methodical course of action; the process of intellectualization for the sake of clarity; self-control that overcomes instinct and "everything impulsive and irrational"; the rationalization of mystical contemplation; the shaping of means to ends; the method of scientific investigation (including the mathematization of knowledge); machine production, technology, and the mastery of the world; the division and coordination of activities for the purpose of achieving efficiency and productivity (which requires, for example, rational bookkeeping); the stability and predictability of bureaucracy; the organization of free labor to create or appeal to a market; the rational-legal acquisition of wealth by virtue of one's ability and initiative; the limitation of occupational effort to specialized work; military training; the system of counterpoint in music; the establishment of rational-legal authority; the logical ordering and rearrangement of the contents of the law; the conceiving of different types of order in society; the carrying through of radical social change; and, of course, the construction of ideal types. In all of these forms of rationality we see the combining of order and meaning. Many of these expressions of rationality have appeared in modern "rational capitalism" in its conflict with traditionalism, while many of them antedate the modern period. But rationality appears in unique fashion in "rational capitalism" and in this-worldly "ascetic Protestantism"—in its methodical and ethical conduct of life motivated by a coherent system of doctrine and commitment which is able to overcome an inherited traditionalist system.

On its negative side, rationality can be severely restrictive. It can appear in the conservative philosophy calculated to resist social change; it can claim to understand everything under a single perspective; it can reduce almost everything to specialization and to the rigidity of bureaucratic system, thus stifling individual decision and initiative; and it contributes to the "disenchantment" of the world and to the elimination of any vital sense of meaning and depth in existence. In these ways it becomes a threat to, indeed the destruction of, belief in the supra-empirical validity of an ethic rooted either in a humane sense of values or in a religious conception of the ultimate structure of things. Thus it can be the enemy of authentic personality and of commitment to "the daemon who holds the thread of its life." In these and in other ways rationality can lead to dehumanizing, compulsive behavior, to irrationality, and meaninglessness.

The positive aspects of rationality (along with individual freedom and responsibility) delineated by Weber are indispensable elements in civilization, and of course are cherished by him. The negative aspects, on the other hand, illustrate the axiom: the corruption of the best is the worst. It is no accident that the account given of the corruption of freedom and reason by Weber, a scholar learned in theological lore, should remind one of the Christian theologian's account of the corruption of the *imago dei*. In this respect one must say that Weber reveals a tragic view of history—in the Hebraic sense. Human freedom and reason are a heavy burden (as well as a gift) requiring constant vigilance; they are the pivot at once of meaning and of the possibility of the fall into unfreedom, irrationality, and meaninglessness. So fundamental for Weber is the negative dimension of rationality that it can be said to correspond to the concept of alienation in the thought of Karl Marx and Erich Fromm. Erich Fromm holds with Weber, however, that insofar as Marxism promotes monolithic bureaucracy it simply guarantees the continuation or creation of alienation. The dictatorship of the proletariat turns out to be the dictatorship of the bureaucrats.

Weber's most negative judgment on technical rationality and on the secularized, corrupted "Protestant ethic" appears in the famous passage near the end of his book:

The Puritan wanted to work in a calling; we are forced to do so. For when asceticism was carried out of monastic cells into everyday life, and began to dominate worldly morality, it did its part in building the tremendous cosmos of the modern economic order. This order is now bound to the technical and economic conditions of machine production which today determine the lives of all the individuals who are born into this mechanism, not only those directly concerned with economic acquisition, with irresistible force. Perhaps it will so determine them until the last ton of coal is burnt. In Baxter's view the care for external goods should only lie on the shoulders of "the saint like a light cloak, which can be thrown aside at any moment." But fate decreed that the cloak should become an iron cage . . . No one knows who will live in this cage in the future, or whether at the end of this tremendous development entirely new prophets will arise, or there will be a great rebirth of old ideas and ideals, or, if neither, mechanized petrification, embellished with a sort of convulsive self-importance. For of the last stage of this cultural development, it might well be truly said: "Specialists without spirit, sensualists without heart; and this nullity imagines that it has attained a level of civilization never before achieved." [15]

Then Weber goes on to make his usual apology for violating the principle that the social scientist should not inject value judgments into his presentation. "But this brings us," he says, "to the world of judgments of value and of faith, with which this purely historical discussion need not be burdened."

Despite the positive values of rationality, then, and despite the initial capacity of Puritanism to bring a new sense of meaning into life and to initiate a revolutionary process that displaced a restrictive social order, the outcome is an iron cage, a soul-less compulsive social system of specialization and bureaucratism without spirit and without heart—a nullity. This specialization and bureaucratism are closely linked with the joyless and impersonal character of work and with "its joyless lack of meaning." Moreover, capitalism, being today "in the saddle, . . . is able to force people to labour without transcendental sanctions." [16] The negative aspects of rationality have overwhelmed the positive.

In reading the long passage just quoted one is reminded of Nietzsche's prediction of the advent of "the last man," who will be a completely rationalized cog in a machine without creative vitality. This outcome, in Weber's view, is the working of the unintended consequences of initially noble impulses, and his comparative studies in the sociology of religion were intended to confirm this insight and to serve as a warning. In this connection one may think of Hegel's theory of "the cunning of reason." But whereas Hegel refers to the hidden instrument of the World Spirit unfolding and realizing a divine purpose, Weber's view is pessimistic—pessimistic also in contrast to the ultimate optimism of Marx. Weber leaves modern man

[15] *PE*, pp. 181–182.
[16] *PE*, p. 282.

in the iron cage; he questions whether there is a way out, hinting only at a variety of foggy possibilities.[17] Weber never loses his fear of perverted reason. It is strange, however, that despite his basic interest in economic forces, he says nothing here about poverty and the maldistribution of wealth. Nor does he explore the possible correction of bureaucratism. Yet, however dusty the answers he gives to the larger social issues raised, we must say with Benjamin Nelson that a major thrust of this whole study of "the Protestant ethic" is to be seen in his concluding protest against "conscienceless reason." [18]

While appreciating the immensity of Weber's accomplishment and the stimulus he has given to the study of the relations between religion and society, I want to offer three critical comments on his presentation of "the Protestant ethic."

First, let it be noted again that Weber's ideal type of "the Protestant ethic" is by intention a restricted one, in that by means of it he aims only to set forth the essential features of the relation between that ethic and economic behavior. On the last pages of the book he emphasizes this point and specifies the large areas of investigation which remain to be undertaken.[19] The ideal type constructed by Weber, then, is not an ideal type of the Protestant ethic as a whole. It excludes from consideration those types of Protestantism which do not belong under the rubric of ascetic Protestantism. Nor is it an ideal type of ascetic Protestantism as a whole.

Second, Weber stresses the point that the meaning of life in Calvinism and Puritanism was rooted in a belief in "a supramundane God" who is

[17] In his later writings Weber works out one of these possibilities in his conception of a nonrational, charismatic authority (initially a theological concept) in contrast to rational-legal and to traditionalist authority. *Charisma*, he says, rests in part "upon the belief in magical powers, revelations and hero worship," but it is destined to be routinized in the direction of bureaucracy. For a discussion of Weber's probable dependence on the church historian Rudolf Sohm for this view see the present writer's essay on "Rudolf Sohm's Theology of Law and Spirit," in Walter Leibrecht (ed.), *Religion and Culture: Essays in Honor of Paul Tillich* (Harper & Bros., 1959). The term *charisma* appears only once in *PE*.

[18] From a paper read at the 1964 Weber Centenary Conference held in Heidelberg, Germany, published in *Max Weber und die Soziologie Heute*. Otto Stammer (ed.), Tübingen, 1965.

[19] Noneconomic areas excluded from Weber's study have been investigated by Robert K. Merton (in the sphere of science), Michael Walzer (in politics), David Little (in law), and Ernst Troeltsch. Indeed, Weber himself said later on that because of Troeltsch's subsequent, massive accomplishment he did not retain his initial intention to explore other areas of social life in relation to "the Protestant ethic." *PE*, p. 284.

sovereign over the whole of life. Yet, due to his concentration on the "interests" and the conduct of the individual, Weber almost entirely ignores the Puritan concern for the social order as a whole. This deficiency in Weber's study is today receiving increasing attention. David Little, for example, has recast the Weberian thesis by directing attention to the Calvinist and Puritan demand for a new order of society.[20] In this connection we should add that Weber gives little attention to the internal life of the churches and the "pathos for order" rooted in the church fellowship.[21] Thus he fails to take into account the Calvinist view that the church and its members have the obligation to work for the establishment of a society of justice and mercy. For Calvin and for many of the Calvinists of the period, the Christian bears a *general* vocation in the world as well as having a specific calling in his daily work. This outlook is today referred to as "the totalistic impulse" of the Calvinists, and a recognition of it has given rise to a new phase of the controversy over Weber's thesis.[22] As a consequence of his not taking this "impulse" sufficiently into account, and of his centering attention on predestination and on the anxiety of the individual regarding his own salvation, Weber's finding with respect to "psychological sanctions" turns out to be inadequate.

The totalistic impulse of Calvinism is to be seen especially in the effort of the Puritans in England to take over the Establishment. When this effort failed, many of them became vigorous Dissenters, forming a variety of movements bent on reform. The totalistic impulse did not die. It was in wider commonalty spread (to adapt a phrase from John Milton). In this new situation sectarian doctrines of the church came to the fore, some of which developed into a proto-democratic doctrine of the free or voluntary church, but the demands for a new social order were not relinquished even

[20] David Little, *Religion, Order, and Law: A Study in Pre-Revolutionary England* (New York: Harper & Row, 1969).
[21] Because of this gap in Weber's investigation of Puritanism, Roger Mehl in his work on *The Sociology of Protestantism*, James H. Farley, trans. (Philadelphia: Westminster Press, 1970), questions whether Weber's study of "the Protestant ethic" can be "qualified as sociology of religion," for it fails to interpret religion as an "emanation of the social group" (p. 18).
[22] Cf. S. N. Eisenstadt, "The Protestant Ethic Thesis in an Analytical and Comparative Framework," in S. N. Eisenstadt, ed., *The Protestant Ethic and Modernization* (New York: Basic Books, 1968). In his essay Eisenstadt traces the stages of the controversy, the first stage being concerned with the question of the direct causal relation between Calvinist ethic and the development of capitalism, the second with the discussion of Protestantism's influence after it had "failed to carry out its first totalistic impulses."

though they were fragmented. In the middle of the century John Lilburne and the Levellers, for example, formed associations for political agitation, using rational techniques to appeal to public opinion. (Perhaps one can say that at that time "public opinion" as a factor in political life was born.) In some circles the idea of a democratic structure in the church was by analogy transformed into a demand for a democratic political order. Many of these efforts exhibit the continued working of the "totalistic impulses."

Of equal importance in this connection was another aspect of this development. The idea of the free or voluntary church, in order to vindicate itself in the face of the Establishment, called for a struggle for the freedom of religious association. In time this struggle was extended to a struggle for the freedom to form other voluntary associations. So noisy were some of these associations that Thomas Hobbes asserted that all such associations are subversive and dangerous—"worms in the entrails of the natural man" (Leviathan). Even the Anglicans began to form religious societies for the reformation of morals. These societies flourished for fifty years after the Restoration, and were able even to elicit cooperation from the Dissenters.[23] The Friends early in the eighteenth century refined the techniques of agitation toward the end of effecting legislation extending their religious and political freedom.[24]

Here we encounter, then, one of the most significant features of the Protestant ethic which Weber ignored by reason of the limits of his study. Ernst Troeltsch has asserted that the Calvinists were given "to an organized and aggressive effort to form associations, to a systematic endeavor to mold the life of society as a whole, to a kind of 'Christian Socialism.' "[25] Protestants in England and America in the eighteenth and nineteenth centuries formed associations to promote philanthropy, educa-

[23] Dudley Bahlman, *The Moral Revolution of 1688* (New Haven: Yale University Press, 1957).

[24] Norman Hunt, *Two Early Political Associations* (Oxford University Press, 1961). The author shows that the Friends at this time invented the essential techniques we associate today with "pressure groups." Shades of rationality!

[25] Ernst Troeltsch, *The Social Teaching of the Christian Churches*, tr. Olive Wyon (New York: Harper & Row, 1960), II, 602. We should note here that the earliest modern theorists of associations were Calvinists. Chief among them was Althusius. See Frederick S. Carney, "Associational Thought in Early Calvinism," in D. B. Robertson (ed.), *Voluntary Associations* (Richmond, Va.: John Knox Press, 1966). D. B. Robertson in his chapter on "Hobbes's Theory of Associations" characterizes Hobbes as "the greatest and most formidable enemy [of voluntary associations] in modern times."

tional reform, penal reform, factory reform, free trade, international peace, the extension of the suffrage, women's rights, the abolition of slavery and child labor, better working and living conditions, trade unions, cooperatives, the prohibition of alcoholic beverages, "municipal socialism," civil rights and liberties, lobbies, communitarian movements, know-nothing campaigns, and a multitude of other causes (including of course "antisocial causes" and "special interests").[26] Clearly, many of these associations have changed economic behavior.

In New England one can see the beginnings of these associations in the activities of the Friends in the seventeenth century, and later in the admonitions of Cotton Mather (*Bonifacius*, 1710) to form associations for philanthropic and moral purposes. Mather reports that he belonged to twenty such associations.[27] Benjamin Franklin makes it clear that in forming voluntary organizations he was initially inspired by Cotton Mather's book. Early in the nineteenth century when the United States was rapidly becoming a "nation of joiners" fairly elaborate theories of association came from the pens of leading clergymen.[28]

These associational movements for social change, anticipated in principle in seventeenth-century Puritanism, may be viewed as activities that in varying ways expressed a sense of vocation broader than that which Weber presents with respect to the vocation of daily work. They provide the citizen with the opportunity to emerge from the "iron cage" of specialization and to join fellow citizens in bringing under criticism economic as well as political and other institutions. They have served in both church and society as a principal means to promote criticism and innovation, individual and group participation and responsibility, and thus the dispersion of power. Although subject to manipulation and to rigid, soul-less bureaucratization, they have been a source of vital tension within the Protestant ethic. In the positive Weberian sense they represent a major form of ra-

---

[26] Denominational histories abound with examples of these associations. I give only one example which stresses the activities of Protestant Dissenters: Raymond V. Holt, *The Unitarian Contribution to Social Progress in England* (London: Allen & Unwin, 1938).

[27] Richard E. French, *Cotton Mather and the Development of American Values* (Harvard University Th.D. Dissertation, 1970), p. 163.

[28] For an account of three major American Protestant theorists of voluntary association, in the early nineteenth century, see the present writer's chapter on "The Voluntary Principle in the Forming of American Religion," in Elwyn A. Smith (ed.), *The Religion of the Republic* (Philadelphia: Fortress Press, 1971).

tionality in Anglo-American life, toward the end of "turning the flank of recalcitrant institutions." [29] Moreover, for more than three centuries these associations have provided a continuing critique of what Weber calls "the Protestant ethic." They represent the institutional gradualization of revolution.

Why does Weber leave this whole dimension out of his delineation of "the Protestant ethic"? The answer is that in tracing the development of individualism he left out of account the residues of the "totalistic impulses" of original Puritanism. But there is an additional reason.

In a lecture of 1911 entitled "A Proposal for the Study of Voluntary Associations," delivered in Frankfurt, Germany, at an International Sociological Congress, Weber said:

> The man of today is without doubt an association man in an awful and never dreamed of degree. Germany stands in this matter at a very high point . . . America is the association-land par excellence. In America membership in some middle-class association belongs directly to one's legitimation as a gentleman. The prototype of these associations is the sect, a union of specifically qualified people. Today the association furnishes the ethical qualification test for the businessman, certifying that he is worthy of credit. American democracy is no sand heap, but a maze of exclusive sects, societies and clubs. These support the selection of those adapted to American life; they support it in that they help such people to business, political and every kind of success in social life. In these associations the American learns to put himself over. [30]

No one can deny that this kind of association has existed in wild variety. But the association concerned with the public weal or with public policy, so far from legitimating the qualifications of those who worship at the altar of the bitch goddess Success, often elicits obloquy rather than enviable status for its members.

We have already observed that Weber views Benjamin Franklin as a manifestation of the spirit of capitalism "in almost classical purity," devoted as he was to frugality and industry for the sake of personal success. But Franklin was also the association-man par excellence. He probably

---

[29] A. D. Lindsay, *The Two Moralities* (London: Eyre & Spotiswoode, 1940), p. 85. Lord Lindsay, Master of Balliol College, Oxford, has been one of the major scholars concerned to trace voluntary associational efforts back to the Puritans.
[30] Manuscript translation by Everett C. Hughes.

formed more associations for the public good than any other American of his time: an academy for the education of youth in Pennsylvania, a voluntary fire department, the Pennsylvania Hospital, a society for the abolition of slavery, and the American Philosophical Society (which is still flourishing), and so on. If Franklin's secularized frugality and devotion to a methodical discipline of life and work were due to the influence of "the Protestant ethic," may we not say that his concern for the methodical discipline of associations calculated to promote the public good was also influenced by the Protestant ethic of "totalistic impulse"?

One might raise the question as to why Weber took such a narrow view of the voluntary association as we have just observed. The reason is perhaps that in Germany he could see few associations of the type concerned with public policy. In the lecture just cited he scores the singing academies for draining off the national energy into "warbling," thus distracting attention from public policies (a distraction which, he says, was much to the liking of the politicians in Berlin). Another reason is that in considering the sect as an agency certifying the qualifications of piety he selected characteristics belonging more exclusively to the *withdrawing sect* rather than to the Puritan *aggressive sect* bent on bringing in a new social order (the distinction is Troeltsch's).

We see, then, that "ascetic Protestantism" from the beginning possessed a more composite character than that which Weber attributes to it. No doubt it was because of the broad scope of the totalistic dynamic that Troeltsch spoke of Calvinism as the second social philosophy in the history of Christianity (the first being Thomism and medieval Catholicism). With similar perception Lord Acton was wont to say that the nerve of democracy as we know it was engendered in the small Puritan conventicles of the seventeenth century.

Weber has seen a different side of ascetic Protestantism. But by neglecting the features we have adumbrated here he has given us a lopsided conception of the Protestant ethic. With him we may properly lament the appearance of the degenerated, rationalized, "encaged" Protestantism he presents. But considering the vitalities he has failed to see, may we not be allowed to lament with fewer tears?

But that question is not the proper way to end this essay. Sixty-five years have passed since Max Weber published his study of the Protestant ethic and the spirit of capitalism. The nullity of which he spoke is more

118

readily evident today than when he pointed to it. What Weber the prophet offers us is the shock of recognition—to enable us to see the cage of the so-called affluent society. Erich Fromm with more hope has for years effectively communicated the same shock, and has tried to find ways out of the cage for the authentic man whom Nietzsche calls the self-surpassing creature, the bridge to the future.

THE USE OF SYMBOLS

I̲T WAS in the earliest seventies," Charles Sanders Peirce tells us, "that a knot of us young men in Old Cambridge, calling ourselves, half-ironically, half-defiantly, 'The Metaphysical Club'—for agnosticism was then riding its high horse, and was frowning superbly upon all metaphysics—used to meet, sometimes in my study, sometimes in that of William James. It may be that some of our old-time confederates would today not care to have such wild-oats-sowings made public, though there was nothing but boiled oats, milk, and sugar in the mess."

One of the residues of these wild-oats-sowings is what is called the pragmatic theory of meaning. We learn from Peirce that the theory was initially stimulated by the British psychologist Alexander Bain's definition of belief, as "that upon which a man is prepared to act." Peirce goes on to say that "from this definition, pragmatism is scarce more than a corollary." He gave his own formulation to this theory of meaning in two articles for the *Popular Science Monthly* entitled "The Fixation of Belief" and "How to Make Our Ideas Clear." Here he sets forth the view that the essence of a belief is a habit or disposition to act, that different beliefs are distinguished by the different habits of action they involve, and that the rule for clarifying the conceptual elements in beliefs is to refer them to "the habits of action." In extension of these ideas he says, "Thus, we come down to what is tangible and practical, as the root of every real distinction of thought, no matter how subtle it may be; and there is no distinction of meaning so fine as to consist in anything but a possible difference of practice." He wants to leave no uncertainty about this. He continues, "Our idea of anything is our idea of its sensible effects; and if we fancy that we have any other, we deceive ourselves." The rule for attaining clarity of apprehension of meaning is this: "Consider what effects, which might conceivably have practical bearings, we conceive the object of our conception to have. Then, our conception of these effects is the whole of our conception of the object."

Obviously, such a definition of the meaning of belief is a definition of only one kind of meaning. Peirce was fully aware of this limitation of the pragmatic theory of meaning. He made many attempts to express the pragmatic principle in a form that really satisfied him, in a form that would exclude nonsense without at the same time being a "barrier to inquiry." We need not here rehearse what Peirce considered the nonsense that should be excluded. We recall, however, that A. O. Lovejoy in his essay on "The Thirteen Pragmatisms" (1908) demonstrated that the pragmatists failed "to attach some single and stable meaning to the term 'pragmatism'." In face of this assertion James was actually enthusiastic. This was fine, he thought, for it proved how "open" pragmatism is—an attitude very different from Peirce's scrupulosities and soul-searchings. It must be emphasized that Peirce's pragmatic theory is not a theory of truth but a theory of meaning, one possible theory of meaning. William James carried the theory beyond this view when he asserted that it would enable us to come into better working touch with reality, and that the true idea is the idea it is best for us to have, best in the long run. Here truth becomes a subspecies of goodness. James at one time even made beauty a subspecies of goodness, for he wrote that an evening at a symphony concert has been wasted on a young man if on returning home he is not kinder to his grandmother.

More strictly within the province of the pragmatist theory of meaning is the question emphasized by the pragmatists. They asked regarding our beliefs, what difference to our practice and to our expectations it will make to believe this rather than that. William James was initially interested in the pragmatic theory of meaning as "a method of settling metaphysical disputes which might otherwise be endless"; and he held that if we examine many metaphysical hypotheses as we should examine scientific hypotheses—by considering what difference it would make to particular occurrences if the hypothesis were true—we find absolutely no difference among them. The basic intention of the pragmatic theory of meaning is to observe the relations between thought and action, or, speaking more precisely with Peirce, the relations between symbols and action. The life of man is viewed as essentially a life of action, action in the formation of symbols and action in bringing about practical consequences in terms of the symbols.

An extension of the pragmatic theory of meaning has been devised by the Oxford linguistic philosophers, under the influence of Wittgenstein. The Oxford philosophers define meaning in terms of linguistic use. The definition of meaning is put forward as a practical methodological rule. Thus, to ask how X is used, or in what context X is used significantly, is a device or "idiom," as Ryle calls it, to remind us first of the fact that words *mean* in different ways, and that the meaning of any word is always relative to the context in which it is used.

Now, it is not to my purpose, nor is it within my competence, to review even briefly the stages by which the Oxford philosophers have discriminated different meanings of meaning, descriptive and otherwise. Nor do we need to consider the utilitarianism that infects the thought of some of these linguistic philosophers. The important thing to note is that considerable emphasis has been placed on the idea that the meaning of a term is to be observed in the use or uses to which it is put, and also that expressions have meaning only in context. Thus, Nowell-Smith says that, instead of the question, "What does the word 'X' mean?" we should always ask the two questions, "For what job is the word 'X' used?" and "Under what conditions is it proper to use the word for that job?" Here, too, meaning is understood partly in terms of context. We shall return presently to this sort of question.

At this juncture I would like to refer to R. B. Braithwaite, who has formulated the pragmatic theory of meaning in a special way.

As a positivist empiricist he rejects theological statements at their face value, for example, theological statements in the Apostles' Creed; but he does not deny that they have pragmatic meaning. This meaning is to be observed in their implications for ethical behavior. Christianity, he concludes, aims to promote "an agapeistic way of life." Consequently, Braithwaite not long ago joined the Church of England, in the high-church branch. It is said that he sent out engraved invitations to his friends in Cambridge when his child was to be christened, and that following the service one of his agnostic colleagues asked him in puzzlement, "You say that you do not believe the Apostles' Creed as a theological affirmation. How, then, can you repeat it in church?" To which Braithwaite gave the ready answer, "That is simple enough. All I have to do is to omit the first two words." This response reminds one of the limitations Peirce placed upon the pragmatic theory.

Now, the central idea contained in the pragmatic theory, namely, that the meaning of a symbol is to be observed in its effect on action, on habits, is the principal, or at least the initial, text of my discussion of one approach to method in the study of Christian ethics. But I want to extend the application of the theory. We may say that the pragmatic theory of meaning is already implied in the New Testament saying, "By their fruits shall you know them." Ordinarily, however, this New Testament axiom is interpreted in terms of personal or interpersonal behavior and not in terms of institutional behavior. Probably this interpretation is wrong, for the admonition in the New Testament runs, "Thou shalt love the Lord thy God with *all* thy heart and mind and soul." In any event, the early pragmatists appear to have restricted the application of the theory. They did not use it in such a way as to include an examination of the institutional consequences of belief. William James in *The Varieties of Religious Experience*, for example, shows extremely little interest in the institutional consequences of religious experience and belief. He confines attention to consequences for individual behavior. This is true also of Braithwaite's interpretation of what he calls "the agapeistic ways of life." It is true also of many a systematic theology. Sometimes the only place where one is shown the social-organizational consequences of religious symbols may be in the section on the doctrine of the church. Otherwise, one is not shown what difference the belief or the theology makes for institutional behavior.

Here a distinction made by Ernst Troeltsch becomes pertinent. In his critique of Kohler's work on *Ideas and Persons* in Christian history he says that Kohler entertains the illusion that one can understand the history of the faith without studying the role of institutions. In his *Problems der Ethik* Troeltsch explicates what he calls the distinction between subjective and objective virtues. Subjective virtues appear in the immediate relations between the individual and God, the individual and the neighbor, and the individual and the self (in interior dialogue). Objective virtues, on the other hand, appear in those relationships that require institutional incarnation, though of course objective virtues presuppose subjective ones. From this perspective a person is not only good as such, but that person is also a good parent, a good administrator, a good citizen.

Roger Mehl of Strasbourg in his essay for the Geneva conference on Christian Ethics in a Changing World, comments tellingly on this differentiation:

> For a long time it was thought that social life was no more than the sum of relationships between individuals and that in consequence, social ethics was no different from personal ethics. . . . It is undoubtedly to the credit of the different socialist movements and ideologies that they have brought out (even at the price of indifference to the individual ethic and the virtues of the private citizen) the original character of social ethics. . . . Socialism discovered that the chief problems of social ethics are problems of structures. These are objective realities, which evolve in accordance with their own laws. (John C. Bennett, ed., *Christian Social Ethics in a Changing World*. New York: Association Press, 1966, pp. 44–45).

This statement, which points to the concern of Social Ethics with social structures, gives me occasion to present some basic presuppositions that must be borne in mind if one is to employ the pragmatic approach to the study of religious ethics. These are broad-gauged presuppositions that require more extensive consideration than is possible here. Yet, they must be mentioned at least briefly.

I. The perspectives of religious ethics depend upon theological perspectives, and these theological perspectives are *sui generis*.

124

They possess their own intrinsic character, and when best understood they exhibit an inner coherence and consistency. To be sure, considerable variety obtains with respect to the formulation of the basic perspectives, a wide spectrum that includes different types of piety. A main task of theology and of theological ethics is to achieve clarity and consistency regarding the perspective and the formulation chosen, a clarity that reflects awareness of alternative possibilities. We have already indicated that the intrinsic quality of these perspectives is not the concern of the pragmatic theory of meaning.

Now, if theological perspectives are recognized as *sui generis*, then two false conceptions must be rejected. First, the view that the controlling perspectives may be explained as merely the consequences of psychological or social conditioning. And, second, the view that theology may be collapsed into ethical demands. This reduction is illustrated by Braithwaite's conception of the meaning of Christianity as an agapeistic way of life. An analogous reduction is to be observed in the Marxist attempt to transform metaphysics into social criticism. In this view, metaphysics is only a hidden social theory; more precisely stated, it is only ideology. Even though these views must be rejected insofar as they claim to be adequate, we should add, however, that the theology that does not examine the social consequences of belief is in this respect meaningless from the point of view of the sociological pragmatic theory of meaning.

II. In the study of religious ethics a major purpose is to discern the "ordering" or the type of ordering that reflects the impact of its characteristic symbolism. This symbolism may exercise a positive influence upon the general cultural ethos, upon the structure of personality, and upon the institutional sphere. Or it may reveal the influence of these factors. Actually, the social-ethical as well as the personal-ethical content of the religious symbolism may in large measure be taken over from the immediate social milieu. In the institutional sphere, for example, both of these processes can be discerned. The symbols in the long run may exercise a clearly positive influence, even to the extent of changing the power structure; on the other hand, the power structures within which the symbols function may determine or deflect the interpretation of the symbols. The use made of a symbol may vary according to the social status or frustration or demands of particular social groups: the use made of a symbol by a ruling group will be different from the use made by a deprived group. In this whole area of analysis both substructure and superstructure must be taken into account. Both can affect the perception of the situation.

These differentiations also appear in the study of the history of Christian ethics, so much so that the history must again and again be reconceived in order to take into account new perceptions. Consider, for example, the marked changes that have taken place in the past century with respect to the definition of the Renaissance. Once the Renaissance was defined in the contours proposed by Jacob Burckhardt, the study of the symbolism and its influence was markedly affected. But when Konrad Burdach redefined the Renaissance in terms of renewal movements of the Middle Ages, the study of the symbolism and its influences changed considerably. During the past generation or two analogous differentiations have appeared with respect to the definition and influence of the Protestant ethic. Max Weber constructed his conception of it in a special way. By concentrating attention on the economic sphere and by excluding the political sphere from attention he arrived at an ideal type of Protestant ethic quite different from the type that emerges if one takes seriously into account the theocratic, political motifs in Calvinism and Puritanism. Indeed, his construction is extremely lopsided. He ignores precisely those elements in Puritanism that presented a much broader conception of vocation than the Puritanism he constructs. This broader conception of vocation, which included a political, reformist activism, not only supplemented but also brought under radical criticism the narrower conception that Weber stresses.

These problems of analysis are perennial, and thus the study of influences is bound to be tentative and even ambiguous in outcome. Nevertheless, one can say that symbolism when effective provides some sort of ordering of experience and its sanctions. Indeed, if one is to find out the meaning of religious symbolism in past or present, the pragmatic theory suggests that one must ask the believer what he in the name of the symbolism wishes changed or not changed; and one should ask also what aspects of existence are a matter of indifference. If the religious symbol does not call for change or interpretation of social structures, then to this extent it is meaningless (from the pragmatic perspective).

III.   As the Oxford linguists remind us, a variety of meanings may be attached to or be latent in a particular word or symbol or in a particular complex of symbols. This variety of meaning becomes evident when one examines the contexts within which the symbol appears. The pragmatic meaning of a belief may be interpreted in differing ways in different times and places, partly because of the great diversity of nonreligious as well as of religious conditions (or contexts) at various stages of the social process. Besides this consideration one must take into account what Schelling called "the infinity of the idea," the fact that any fundamental symbol is pregnant with, latent with, a variety of implications or connotations. This variety almost inevitably appears in time, for symbols belong to history, that is to the temporal sphere. This aspect of symbols is a mystery. Why, for example, should one have to wait until the twelfth century for a Joachim di Fiore to use the doctrine of the Trinity to devise a periodization of history according to which society was moving out of the current period, the period of the Son, to a third period, the period of the Spirit, a period of new freedom in which there would be a transfer of power from the secular to the religious clergy? That question is simply unanswerable. Nevertheless, one can say that the Joachites and their descendants exemplify the changing meaning of symbols as understood in relation to context. Presently we shall consider some other examples of change of pragmatic meaning in terms of change of context or in terms of change in purpose.

IV.   This consideration leads to a fourth observation. Certain symbols lend themselves more readily to application in the area of subjective virtues, others to application in the area of objective virtues. *Metanoia*, for example, has generally been symbolically powerful in the realm of subjective virtues, although in primitive Christianity this change of heart-mind-soul resulted in membership in a new community and thus brought about some change in the realm of objective virtues. It is worth noting here that the conservative Lutheran jurist Friedrich Julius Stahl in the nineteenth century held that the concept of conversion (as well as of redemption) must apply to society and social institutions as well as to persons. A similar duality appears in the concept of the demonic. In the New Testament the concept refers not only to a psychic phenomenon of possession but also to a social-cultural force in the world, that is, to the corruption of the culture and its institutions which is to be overcome by the Kingship of Christ. It can no longer be said that Augustine was the first to relate the concept of the demonic to both the psychological realm and the sphere of culture and institutions. This scope of reference appeared earlier in the New Testament.

The symbol, the kingdom of God, is likewise the type of symbol that readily lends itself to pragmatic meaningfulness in both the psychological and the institutional sphere. It is a metaphor drawn from the area of politics, and just as it is drawn from this area so it repeatedly finds application in the social-institutional sphere. In this respect it is like the concept of the covenant, a major integrating conception in the Bible and one of the most powerful in the Reformed tradition for the shaping of both ecclesiological and political theory. In the Old Testament the political symbols king and covenant point to the societal demands of Jahwe. Men are responsible for the total character of the society. "God hath a controversy with *his people.*" On the other hand, an interpretation popular in the past century held that "the kingdom of heaven is within you." This is a false translation and a lamentable reduction. Joel Cadbury has suggested that the saying should be translated, "the kingdom of heaven is available to you (among you)." This translation at least can avoid the reductionist interpretation that stresses only the interiorization of the kingdom which itself, to be sure, is an integral aspect of the symbol.

The broader scope and application of the concept of the kingdom is strikingly formulated by Talcott Parsons in his recent extensive article on "Christianity," in the new *International Encyclopedia of the Social Sciences:*

> the Christian movement crystallized a new pattern of values not only for the salvation of human souls but also for the nature of the societies in which men should live on earth. This pattern, the conception of a "kingdom" or, in Augustine's term, a "city" of men living according to the divine mandate on earth, became increasingly institutionalized through a long series of stages, which this article will attempt to sketch. Later it became the appropriate framework of societal values for the modern type of society.

The symbolic powerfulness and societal relevance of these political symbols have been made markedly evident in Paul Lehmann's *Ethics in a Christian Context* and in Martin Buber's *The Kingship of God.* Another political symbol should be mentioned here in passing, the concept of the warrior, which figures largely in certain sections of the Old Testament and which came to the fore again in the Middle Ages and in the Renaissance and in some measure also in Puritanism.

There is another symbol that possesses as great a variety of connotation as any of the symbols already mentioned. This is the domestic type of symbol which of course lends itself to elaborate conjugation, the concept of the family, of God and his children, of bride and groom, of brothers and sisters. The domestic symbol can point to more intimate interpersonal cathexis than the political symbol (as, for example, in Hosea's use). At the same time it can replace or serve as a surrogate for the political metaphor, to be observed especially in patriarchal theories of societal order. It is fascinating to observe the use of domestic symbolism by Friedrich Julius Stahl, a principal shaper of the Throne-and-Altar tradition in Germany in the nineteenth century. Stahl connects the patriarchal symbol with the doctrine of justification by faith: God's relation to man is personal, it is that of the father. Then by analogy he infers that the Christian state is an authoritarian one in which the emperor as father directly concerns himself quite personally for the sake of his people. The basic principle then becomes "authority, not majority." This combination of ideas he calls "the Protestant principle."

The Roman Catholic political theorist Carl Schmitt in his work a generation ago on *Politische Theologie* attempted to show the ways in which domestic symbols of a patriarchal character have figured in religious interpretations of the political order. Here he contrasts patriarchal authority that is majestically above the law and the trivial democratic leveling that issues from the rule of law. Perhaps it was the influence of his own application of the pragmatic theory of meaning that led him to support Nazism. In any event, for him the crucial struggle in the modern period is the struggle between the conception of *law* and the conception of the transcendent *person* of God and of the ruler. Here he approaches the position of Stahl with his "Protestant principle." He overlooks, however, the ways in which individualistic philanthropic liberalism has used domestic symbolism—the Fatherhood of God and the brotherhood of man—to articulate a religious conception of democracy. It is a striking thing that when the promoters of the Social Gospel wished to give a broader scope to religious and social responsibility under a sovereign God they placed a new interpretation upon a political (rather than a domestic) symbol, the Kingdom of God. This symbol was no longer to be interpreted as pointing only to the kingdom that is within (cf. Rauschenbusch's corollary, the Kingdom of God and the kingdom of evil—a societal, institutional conception).

At this point we should observe in passing that the biological or organic symbol, the body, must rank as one of the most powerful and persistent metaphors in history. It appears recurrently in both the Orient and the Occident. It figures as a psycho-political symbol, for example, in Plato, determining a hierarchical form of social organization. In this way it functions as one of the major symbols of conservatism in the history of political theory (comparable in this respect to the conception of "the chain of being"). The jurisdiction of the organic metaphor reaches from Plato and St. Paul through the Reformation and Romanticism to Vatican Council II, a span that suggests the wide range of possibilities. A similar variety of interpretation obtains with respect to the symbol of the covenant.

This variety of interpretation, obviously, is a major characteristic of the basic symbols, political, domestic, and organic, that have been used to indicate the societal consequences of respective interpretations of the divine mandate for man not only in secular society but also in ecclesiastical polity. Accordingly, one can find most of the spectrum of social theories under the rubric of each of these types of symbol, the spectrum from spiritual anarchism to monolithic authoritarianism.

The symbol that has exhibited a greater consistency of interpretation is the psychological symbol, the Holy Spirit. We have already referred to Joachim di Fiore's conception of the Third Era, the period of the new freedom under the aegis of the Holy Spirit. In general, the sanction of the Holy Spirit has been appealed to in order to break through rigid bureaucracy and to promote individual freedom. We think here of the outpourings of the Spirit in the sixteenth- and seventeenth-century Radical Reformation, in eighteenth- and nineteenth-century revivalism, and in contemporary

130

charismatic leadership and in glossalalia. Radicalizing Rudolf Sohm's conception of charisma in opposition to law, Max Weber constructed his typology of authority, making charismatic authority the innovating power that repeatedly in history breaks through traditional and legal structures. The societal impact of conceptions of the Spirit is thus shown to be a fundamental and recurrent factor in the history of social organization.

The crucial roles that societal images play gives us reason to assert that in employing the method suggested by the pragmatic theory of meaning our typologies of religious perspectives are quite inadequate if we do not take into account the implications of these various perspectives for the spheres of both the subjective and the objective virtues. It is unfortunate that such a fruitful typology as that of H. Richard Niebuhr in *Christ and Culture*, with its articulation of the different types of piety—Christ above Culture, Christ in Culture, Christ Transforming Culture, etc.—does not examine the different kinds of social organization promoted by these different types of piety. Similar types of social theory appear under the different rubrics of Niebuhr's general typology. Insofar as this is true, we may suspect that a full application of the pragmatic theory of meaning cannot be effected in terms of the types as Niebuhr defines them. But no one knew this better than Niebuhr himself. Indeed, if one wishes to find an exemplification of the pragmatic theory of meaning in the sociological sphere, one finds it ready to hand in his volume, *The Kingdom of God in America*, where he gives explicit attention to what he calls "institutionalizing the kingdom." But the point I am stressing is that typologies should include the spectrum of social-organizational, that is, of institutional consequences of the various types of piety as they find expression in integrating images. In large degree these consequences, as we have seen, are related to metaphorical images.

Whitehead, in speaking of metaphors, asserts that the fundamental choice for the metaphysician is the selection of a ruling metaphor to express his conception of reality, and he makes a strong case for the claim. He calls this procedure the method of imaginative rationality, the devising of hypotheses whereby pervasive elements and structures may be discerned. He shows, for example, how metaphors drawn from mathematics have dominated in one period and from biology in another. His own metaphysics is based upon metaphors drawn from the spheres of psychology and biology, metaphors that he explicates in his panpsychic organicism. Insofar as these central symbols play a role in his ethics, the pragmatic theory of meaning raises the question as to the psychological and sociological consequences of the use of these metaphors.

The reference to Whitehead's method reminds us that the great integrating metaphors of Christian ethics that have influenced human behavior may not properly be studied or understood by means of a narrow conceptual analysis. They by no means have alone influenced behavior. Two things we have already hinted at must be mentioned here again. First, the metaphor has to be understood in the context of convictions about the nature of man and God, the nature of history, the nature and content of faith. Indeed, the entire Gestalt of Christian theology and piety must be taken into account if the inner meaning of a particular metaphor is to be properly understood. This consideration makes the application of the pragmatic theory of meaning much less simple than the formulation of the theory at first suggests.

The second consideration is, as we have already indicated, that in order to be effective an integrating idea or metaphor possessing social-ethical implications must be given articulation in a particular historical situation. It cannot be adequately explicated in a social vacuum. Let us take an example from Ernst Troeltsch, namely, the historical situation in which a reigning conservatism is faced with protesting movements. Troeltsch's characterization of conservatism is a masterly one. Conservatism, generally employing an organic metaphor, emphasizes above all, he says, the "natural inequalities" of men. Ethical values are derived from the *acceptance* of these inequalities. For these values conservatism claims the support of a realism that is not blinded by optimistic enthusiasm. The power structure, the separation of the classes, the need for strong leadership, the fundamental skepticism regarding the wisdom of the populace, are taken to be the dispositions that God has given to men; only in the context of this hierarchical structure does the conservative expect to achieve the good life. The powers that have historically evolved are to be regarded as God's ordinances to which one must submit as to a divine institution. They exist by the grace of God and demand submission. The recognition of sin should engender humility, readiness to be obedient and to be faithful to assigned tasks. A struggle for power on the part of the lower classes in order to change the system is the consequence of sin. Those in control of power maintain it by force in the service of God and the community. Through their service the natural process is to be purified and ennobled. Freedom for the average Christian is inner freedom. It can never become the principle of a political structure. The maintenance of the system is itself taken to be the will of God.

Now, in the face of this philosophy of conservatism a protesting movement must select symbolically powerful concepts if success is to be expected. The countersymbols selected will be calculated to undermine the religious sanctions claimed by the conservatives and to provide sanctions for fundamental social change. This means that the countersymbols must serve a dual purpose: first they must reconceptualize the conservatism and thus show its injustice; and second, they must point in new directions. In both of these processes a pragmatic theory of meaning will attempt to function; first to show the inadequacy of the previous symbolism (largely by reason of its institutional consequences), and second to provide symbols that point in the direction of new institutional forms. A characteristic bifurcation can appear in this process. It may be that the countersymbols employed will serve primarily as radical criticism of the old régime and will be somewhat irrelevant or ineffective for purposes of positive construction. Moreover, a new constructive symbolization may in turn lend itself to opposite or at least to divergent interpretations. Here again bifurcation appears. Both of these types of bifurcation can be illustrated by the familiar example of the Declaration of Independence in relation to the constitutional convention that followed the Revolution. The symbols of the Declaration for the most part were effective in making attack upon the old régime. But additional symbols were required "in order to form a more perfect union." And then division appeared again. Indeed, the same symbols were appealed to in order to define the more perfect union in varying ways. In these processes differing applications of the pragmatic theory of meaning came to the fore. In all of this we see a general feature of social change; namely, that new symbols and their pragmatic meaning always take their shape in face of a particular historical situation and in face of a previously regnant symbolism. History is made by latching onto what already has happened and onto what is occurring. Accordingly, the study of the pragmatic meaning of symbols cannot be adequately undertaken merely through the analysis of concepts, as though history proceeded from book to book or from theorem to theorem. It requires analysis of concepts in their contingent social situation and in terms of the social functions of the symbols, old and new.

There is no evidence that Peirce or James or Wittgenstein or Braithwaite has been concerned about this kind of analysis, particularly as it relates to the institutional consequences of belief or of symbols. Here we may observe that in general two kinds of answers have been offered by others, and not only by Christians. Each of those answers gives a special twist to the notion that the consequences of religious belief should appear in the realm of institutions. The first answer is that the demand for institutionalization requires the slow transformation of institutions. This is the answer of gradualism, of piece-by-piece transformation. One may call this the meroscopic answer, the attack upon crucial parts or segments of the problem. The second answer is that the entire system must be transformed. This second is the revolutionary or systemic or holoscopic answer.

It must be recognized, however, that institutionalization has an ambiguous character. It may give order to social existence, but it may also impose intolerable fetters. A certain type of religious belief may in a given situation only serve to increase rigidity, to sanction petrification. Religious belief of this sort may simply redouble the intensity of adherence to the Establishment, where improved means serve unimproved ends. Here nothing fails like success. The outcome may exemplify Howard Becker's definition of primitive religion: that set of motor habits that induces automatic resistance to change. This kind of religion finds illustration in the use that, alas, has been made of every one of the symbols we have discussed. Often the outcome represents an ethos quite contrary to that which prevailed at the beginning of a movement. Max Weber had in mind this kind of exploitation of symbols when he said that the Protestant Ethic began with a doctrine of freedom in the demand for freedom of vocation and has ended by imprisoning us in the iron cage of "specialists without spirit."

Despite the ambiguities of institutionalization, we must be wary of the claim that social change simply requires a change of attitude. Attitudes do not necessarily find expression in institutional criticism and change. At least they do not do so soon enough. Something of this sort must be said about the currently burgeoning theology of hope. A theology of hope that does not indicate the specific institutional changes that are required is not yet a theology that follows through to the consequences of religious belief. It can leave us in the mood of Augustine when he prayed, "O God, make me chaste, but not yet." White suburbia today is bursting with new attitudes and with new hope but not with importunate demand for social change.

Troeltsch's description of the theology of conservatism may seem at first blush to be of something far away and long ago. But it is a transcription not only of the eighteenth-century *ancien régime*. It is a transcription also of the system of apartheid in South Africa. And for certain contingents of the Black Power movement in the United States it is a description not only of the racist system of discrimination but also of the system that keeps almost a quarter of the nation in poverty and dependency. Further, contemporary feminists can easily recognize the contours of this theology in everyday patterns of male-female relations.

If we ask the question how we are to get out of the cages in which we live, cages that are gilded with racism and sexism, we all recognize that a crucial question is that of the redistribution of power. The means to overcome our "unconquered past" of racism and sexism brings us to two fundamental aspects of our problem of the consequences of religious belief.

I. The consequences of religious belief will depend largely upon the distribution of power and whether or not the consequences are intended. If the social system is monolithic, the prevailing religious belief will have monolithic consequences. A different sort of consequence can issue only from a separation of powers that opens the space for new religious belief and for new consequences. It is a striking fact that already in the Bible one can discover this sort of shift again and again taking place. The late Henri Frankfurt discerned this separation of powers in the advent of the idea of a double covenant. The prophets, he pointed out, stood on the covenant of Jahwe with the people, and they attacked the monarchy for its betrayal of its own covenant with Jahwe. Max Weber has suggested that the Hebrew prophets, by not being attached to the court, represent an anticipation of the modern free press.

Likewise, the early Christian community broke with the Establishment, and as much with the Roman as with the Jewish Establishment. They insisted that religious organization must be independent of the civic power. These early Christians also made membership in the community transcend class, ethnic, and familial status. In short, the Christians formed a new kind of association as the proclaimer of a new freedom in Christ and an exhibition of the institutional consequence of their belief in this freedom. Thus the association could be at the same time the bearer and the institutional exemplification of its own message. An analogous outcome is to be seen in the institutional consequences of Athanasian orthodoxy at Nicaea. The Athanasians rejected the idea that the emperor, along with Christ, was a mediator: they forbade the emperor to sit in the chancel, restricting him to the nave; the arrangements were institutional consequences of religious belief. We can trace this pattern down the centuries as it recurrently challenges a monolithic Establishment—in the conciliar movement, in the abolition of the monolithic idea of "Christendom" (the dependence of civil rights upon religious confession), in the struggle for "comprehension" and for Nonconformity and Independency, in the *ecclesiola in ecclesia*, in the idea and institutional implementation of the priesthood of all believers, in the autonomy of pietistic groups, in the encouragement of freedom of inquiry, in the development of dissenting academies, in the encouragement and defense of trades unions, and in the current civil rights and womens' movements. Analogous tendencies have appeared in Roman Catholicism—initially in the emergence of religious orders, later in the principle of subsidiarity, in the responsibilities assigned to collegial configurations, and in the lay apostolate. All of these institutional consequences of religious belief have served to disperse power and responsibility. The divisions of power were at the same time consequences and causes, consequences of religious conviction and conditions for the emergence of new convictions in new situations, in short, for the emergence of mutual criticism. In the main they presuppose that no one configuration of authority and power can be trusted.

II.   What we have said of the significance of the division of power for the sake of the freedom of religious belief to find new institutional incarnation, may also be said regarding the importance of this division for the sake of the criticism of ethical ideals. If no single configuration of power may be trusted, so also no single ethical idea or virtue may be adopted as final or trustworthy. William Hazlitt once said that the trouble with the man with one idea is not that he has an idea—that is rare enough. The trouble is that he has no other. That way lies demonry. "In my father's house are many mansions." Accordingly, the consequence of religious belief under a sovereign God must always be a rejection of idolatry before any *one* ethical idea and a promotion of "free trade" and tension among ideals. Following Pascal, we might call this the ethos of opposite virtues. According to him, the Christian has the obligation to exhibit opposite virtues and to occupy the distance between them. That is, we confront the obligation to pursue simultaneously the opposite virtues of freedom and order, freedom and equality, participation and privacy, and justice and mercy. Because of the tension among the demands in the open situation, it should be clear that either in the sphere of subjective virtues or in that of objective, institutional virtues any attempt to deduce precise pragmatic judgments from a given creedal position is likely to be overzealous in intention and to reveal ideological taint—the desire to protect special privilege. Nonetheless, it is generally possible to advocate various social-ethical emphases or pragmatic meanings that derive from differing creedal positions. But the divisions and tensions of which we have spoken remain.

These divisions and tensions have never been more nobly or more powerfully depicted than by Giotto in the murals of the Arena Chapel at Padua. This chapel is a brick box, barrel-vaulted within. Over the chancel Giotto painted the Eternal, surrounded by swaying angels, and listening to the counterpleas of Justice and Mercy concerning doomed mankind; the Archangel Gabriel is serenely awaiting the message that should bring Christ to Mary's womb and salvation to earth. This is the Prologue. Opposite on the entrance wall is the Epilogue—a last judgment, with Christ enthroned as Supreme Judge and Redeemer amid the Apostles. These tensions within the divine economy bespeak the tensions and contrarieties that belong to the human condition as well. Without them, religious belief and the consequences of religious belief are doomed to degenerate into deformity, disillusion, and destruction, and to call forth from the Stygian depths both hybris and nemesis. For, ultimately, the consequences of religious belief are not in our hands.

THE POLITICAL RESPONSIBILITY
OF THE MAN OF CULTURE

BY JAMES LUTHER ADAMS

The Fourth Assembly of La Société Européenne de Culture, held in Venice October 3-6, 1954, declared that it is « plus nécessaire que jamais pour les hommes de culture d'assumer leurs responsabilités propres dans le domaine politique ». Many are the reasons that could be given to support this view. The recurrence of world wars in the twentieth century and the threat of the supreme destructiveness of atomic combat, have become possible partly because of the work of the intellectuals. Toward the end of playing a counter-role many intellectuals have recognized that their responsibility requires an equal effectiveness with respect to the achievement of peace.

This sense of responsibility has been enhanced among intellectuals as they have witnessed the horrible spectacle of the totalitarianisms of our time and their destruction of freedom and culture. In these totalitarian movements many men of culture, we must confess it, were collaborators—thus exhibiting « la trahison des clercs ». At the same time, other men (and women) of culture offered heroic resistance to totalitarianism. To these and to the many like them we owe a great debt, and we shall long give them homage. In face of their sacrifice and also of the legion of betrayals in our time, some men of culture have understandably engendered a sense of guilt because of their previous failure or their feebleness of effort with respect to « l'engagement politique ».

Where avowed totalitarianism has not prevailed and is not an imminent danger, the ravages of a mass society upon culture, the vulgarization of ideas and ideals at the hands of the new technology of communications, the forms of depersonalization incident to an industrialized society, have elicited among men of culture a deepened sense of the devaluation of man and an awareness of their own impotence not only as bearers of culture but also as members of the body politic.

In addition to these profound changes, we have witnessed in the twentieth century the crescence of the modern militarized state into a Leviathan that more and more takes under its jurisdiction policy decisions previously reserved for non-political instrumentalities. Indeed, economic as well as political instrumentalities today exhibit great centralized power, and in varying ways they manipulate the mass media of communication—the press, the cinema, and television. Thus « the engineering of consent » at the hands of power élites has become a characteristic technique of our time, in both the totalitarian and the ostensibly democratic societies. Indeed, in some sociological circles the intellectual has been defined as the manipulator of symbols and ideologies. It is not surprising that men of culture who wish not only to retain historic cultural values but also to engage in what M. Campagnolo has called the creation of new values, experience an acute sense of impotence.

The desire to overcome this impotence is not necessarily motivated by « ressentiment » on the part of men of culture, as if they wished simply to share the influence of the power élites. One must grant of course that « ressentiment » and « slave morality » can be ingredients of the desire. But let us hope that some observers may indulge « a willing suspension of disbelief » and assume that in La Société Européenne de Culture, the expressed desire to overcome the impotence issues from an awareness of the threat to human values, to the intellectual, moral and religious depth and breadth that belong to culture in its true form and substance.

The sense of impotence is particularly acute in face of political institutions, for they are again and again the tools of great economic power blocs. Accordingly, it has stimulated a disciplined and continuing consideration of « la tâche politique dont la responsabilité incombe de façon spécifique à l'homme de culture ».

At this point it will be useful to recall a distinction that has been delineated by M. Campagnolo (« Rapport du Secrétaire général, » Comprendre, 13-14, June 1955), the distinction between the cultural and the political task of the man of culture. The cultural task, he says, is to maintain « l'autonomie de l'activité créatrice ». This task is undertaken in the name of « le principe du respect des divergences d'opinion » and by means of a dialogue « qui entraîne la conscience morale et politique des interlocuteurs, les obligeant, s'il le faut, à changer leurs convictions et leurs attitudes ». This cultural task, as M. Campagnolo has said, must be supplemented by « la politique de culture ». « La politique de la culture », he continues, « vise à ce dialogue-là, qui peut maîtriser l'histoire et la rendre plus humaine. Il implique que les hommes de culture soient politiquement engagés ... C'est par l'engagement politique que la culture plonge ses racines dans la réalité sociale d'où elle tirera la force de créer des valeurs à la fois universelles et concrètes ». By means of « l'engagement politique » the cultural task finds practical fulfilment, it becomes, « une force capable d'agir sur la structure de la société ».

« L'autonomie de l'activité créatrice ». As employed by M. Campagnolo, this phrase intends to assert that in a non-authoritarian society the cultural creativity of the man of culture is not merely a function of social, political or economic forces, that it possesses a certain independence of these forces. This intent of the phrase will meet the approval of all readers except those who cannot legitimately claim that their ideas are more than a psychological or sociological secretion. But, for the theologian, the phrase itself can raise a question that takes one into a wider frame of reference than that intended at the moment by M. Campagnolo. This question is of considerable import if we are to be aware of the bond that links together men of culture in their fulfilment of their cultural and their political tasks.

From a religious point of view, may the creative activity of men of culture be considered, strictly speaking, as only autonomous? This activity is, to be sure, an expression of human freedom. But the religious consciousness will go further and assert that human freedom and creative activity are ultimately gifts of grace. Hence, to the religious man, the phrase « l'autonomie de l'activité créatrice », however pertinent it may be for indicating the *sui generis* character of the creative impulse, has the taste of the provincial, that is, of the anthropocentric.

Alfred North Whitehead viewed the Bible as an antidote to this kind of provincialism. « The Bible » he said « excels in its suggestion of infinitude. Here we are with our finite beings and physical senses in the presence of a universe whose possibilities are infinite, and even though we may not apprehend them, those infinite possibilities are actualities ». Accordingly, we may say that creative activity is open on the one side to the infinite. Just as politics may not properly be viewed as autonomous, being itself a moment of cultural activity, so culture in turn may not be viewed as merely autonomous, for it is a moment of religious activity. This means that although cultural creativity is autonomous in the sense of being in some measure an expression of human freedom, it depends upon more than human resources, and it serves higher ends than those of culture as such. It means, therefore, that man, and thus also the man of culture, is really responsible to God (and to the neighbor as child of God) for the ways in which he uses or abuses his freedom. He lives « under the Great Taskmaster's eye ». We must distinguish between merely autonomous culture and a culture that is at once autonomous and theonomous. The latter view of the relation between culture and religion is well expressed in Ernst Troeltsch's term, « auto-theonomy », and in Paul Tillich's view that « religion is the substance of culture, and culture the form of religion ».

This conception of the relation between the finite and the infinite is a normative philosophical definition of religion, that is, it is not yet a theological conception that grasps the norm of any particular, unique historical religion.

In adopting this conception, one precludes certain interpretations of the character of true religion as well as of culture. One precludes, for example, both the « religion » that is merely autonomous and the « religion » that is authoritarian or heteronomous. In merely autonomous « religion » (humanism) the free human self, the free society, or a segment of the self or of society is viewed as independent and self-sufficient. It should be added, however, that autonomous « religion » does not make absolute claims for itself; it accepts the principle of respect for divergences of opinion. In this regard, autonomous « religion » may be at least covertly open on the one side to the infinite; it may be covertly auto-theonomous. One can frequently sense this immanent-transcendent quality in works of art, also in works of abstract art. (The quality may be present even if the artist is not disposed or able to recognize it or to give it verbal articulation). On the other hand, authoritarian « religion », though it ostensibly rejects the claim to be self-sufficient, really tries to domesticate the infinite. It makes absolute claims for itself (that is, for its apprehension of the infinite); and its ideal tends to be ecclesiastical and cultural monopoly. Thus it loses the « suggestion of infinitude »; it becomes one cultural object alongside other cultural objects. Similarly to « la trahison des clercs », authoritarian « religion » can provide merely a fanatical or a more subtly covert sanction for ethnocentrism, even though it claims to be universal. This ethnocentrism is sometimes to be found in autonomous as well as in heteronomous « religion ». In this respect, both autonomous and heteronomous religion may be spoken of as forms of culture-religion.

In contrast to culture-religion, theonomous religion stresses the prophetic « suggestion of infinitude ». It holds that culture as such, including cultural expressions issuing from explicitly religious commitment, stands under the judgment of the eternal. Indeed, the ultimate orientation of prophetic religion reveals elements of vanity and idolatry in every cultural activity and also in every cultural expression of religion. Prophetic religion rejects the absolute claims of any particular religion or culture for itself as well as insisting that culture and the man of culture are deluded when they deem themselves self-sufficient. At the same time, prophetic religion provides impetus and sanction for audacious self-criticism and innovation within a culture or a religion. Accordingly, H. Richard Niebuhr speaks of « the permanent revolution of Christian faith ».

Both the rejections and the affirmations pronounced by prophetic religion issue from the view that its faith is not a faith in culture or religion, that its faith is in the Lord of history who establisheth the world upon the floods. From the point of view of prophetic religion, the man of culture has a responsibility that transcends culture as such and that transcends also any culture-religion. For this reason, prophetic religion is not content to use the term « l'homme de culture » without indicating his limitations or without demanding a larger frame of reference than « culture » or « creative activity » for interpreting his character, his orientation, and his responsibilities.

The « bond » that *idealiter* links together men of culture is more than autonomously cultural; it is also more than moral and more than religious (as popularly understood). It is trans-cultural, trans-moral, and trans-religious. It is critical of culture, morals, and religion. At the same time, the bond possesses formative power. In Schiller's words, it is « the spirit that molds » the body of culture. The achievement of sensitivity and self-consciousness with respect to this bond is an essential aspect of the vocation of men of culture, for without sensitivity and self-consciousness the whole cultural enterprise loses its élan, it loses the *unum necessarium* of human existence, it loses touch with what Gerard Manly Hopkins, in his elliptical mode of expression, has called « the dearest freshness deep down things ». Without the awareness of this latent freshness the man of culture is likely not only to fail in his cultural task. He will even be prone to neglect his political task. For without it he can be insensitive to the misery of man which longs for a community of freedom and beauty, of justice and love.

We turn now to consider the social forms by means of which the man of culture, as well as other citizens, translates the consciousness of political responsibility into objective reality. In dealing with this matter, however, we are not concerned only with the question of means. M. Campagnolo, in his « rapport », has rightly pointed out that the cultural act is « à la fois sujet et objet, moyen et fin: l'homme cultive l'homme ». The political task is not simply a means for the completion of the cultural task. It is itself a moment of creative activity, and as such it is both means and end. In the execution of the political task we not only adopt means for the implementation of goals; as citizens confronting new situations and needs we must also continually engage in a dialogue regarding these goals and their reconception. Thus the dialogue concerning the cultural task, as variously envisaged by the S.E.C., must move beyond itself to the dialogue concerning the political task, a task that is directed toward the achievement of wider human community. Out of these dialogues emerge tentative consensus and the implementation of consensus in social action.

These dialogues aim not at a complete integration (this is, after all, possible only through coercion). They aim at continuing action and discussion, at maintaining fruitful tensions that take into their purview various needs and perspectives, needs and perspectives that are economic and political, material and spiritual. Certain unities and continuities are to be sure required for viable social existence, but they are open to revision.

Among the flexible continuities peculiarly relevant for the present discussion are the various statuses and roles of the man of culture. As a citizen the man of culture, at least theoretically, does not assume the political task with special privileges; he assumes the role of citizen alongside his fellow-citizens. He may of course possess expert experience and judgment that can enhance his status as citizen in particular situations and that can make him eligible for special assignments. But as a man of culture he by definition possesses certain privileges and responsibilities. This fact has been already indicated in our reference to the « bond » that links together men of culture. Here we have in mind the peculiar privileges and responsibilities of men of culture with respect to the transmission, criticism, and transformation of the ethos that gives self-consciousness and spiritual integrity to the common life.

In the social mobility of contemporary society the men of culture possess quite different types of training and experience, and thus it is difficult to contrive a simple definition of their status. Yet, we venture the generalization that the status of the man of culture in an important respect is very similar to that of the professional man as traditionally defined. The first mark of the professional man is that he is authorized to wear the academic gown, that is, he is recognized to have been trained in the humanistic disciplines that enable him to bear self-consciously the ethos-memory of the culture, to subject memory to revaluation, and to give new meaning, direction, and articulation to the ethos.

This part of the definition of the professional man has been subjected to some change during the past century, particularly as a consequence of the increase of the natural and social-scientific disciplines in higher education, at the expense of the humanistic disciplines. For this and for other reasons, many professional men, in their training and their practice, have in some measure relinquished or redefined the ethos-bearing role of the professional man as traditionally understood. Apart from the possession of a theoretical apparatus for the understanding of specific vocational functions (the second mark of the professional man), some so-called professional men today possess a feeble awareness of general problems of culture and ethos, and they assume little responsibility with respect to the transmission, criticism, and transformation of ethos. These so-called professional men are authorized to wear the academic gown, and they want to enjoy the status that has belonged to the professional man; but they do not play the role that belongs to the status. In terms of their general cultural functions in the community they are hardly distinguishable from « vocational men ». They are not in any substantial sense « men of culture ». In part, these developments are the consequence of degeneration in institutions of « higher learning » and of the truncated purposes of « professional associations ». Concurrently, some of the ethos-bearing functions of the man of culture are being assumed, and with some sense of responsibility, by that new strategic figure of contemporary society, the executive.

Another important change should be noticed here. With the gradual disappearance of ascribed statuses characteristic of the earlier society of estates, the status and role of the man of culture have undergone transformation. In former days the man of culture was closely associated with the court or with the upper classes. With the rise to power of the bourgeoisie and of the organized workers, class feeling has shunted the man of culture to the rank of residual status (in a fashion comparable to the changed status of the clergy). In the earlier period the man of culture was expected to play a political role because, of the ascribed status of the estate or class to which he belonged. In the subsequent period, particularly in the course of industrialization and democratization, a certain cleavage between culture and politics has ensued. For this and other reasons the man of culture must often be exhorted to recognize his responsibility with respect to the political task. In our society where a high degree of division of labor is characteristic, the man of culture is more of a specialist than formerly. In many instances he is less disposed to assume political responsibility, more disposed to remain « above the battle ».

As we have already suggested, the rise of totalitarianism and the collaboration or impotence of many men of culture have presented in an acute way the question of the political responsibility of the man of culture. Thomas Mann's change from a man of culture who renounced political responsibility to one who penitently recognized his involvement in the political process, illustrates a desire increasingly felt in some circles, the desire to participate in the processes that direcly affect decisions with respect to social policy. The resolution of this problem is by no means simple, and it will vary from country to country. What the present writer has to say obviously reflects the limited perspectives available to him from his own milieu and from his personal experience in face of the possibilities evident in that milieu.

Obviously, there are numerous ways whereby the man of culture can attempt to assume the political task. Certain subsoil work is a perennial task, and it is not readily visible to the naked eye. Here nourishment and refreshment of spirit are engendered not only for himself but also for others. Then, too, out of more direct concern for the political task the man of culture can enter into dialogue and take action with others through casual, informal contacts. But these casual, informal ways can have only a limited scope and effectiveness. More methodical and more effective are the dialogues and actions that take place in the formal associations characteristic of the democratic society. These formal associations are of peculiar significance in the shaping of public opinion and public policy.

Public opinion is a crucial factor in the democratic society. It is an important medium for the achievement of the consent of the governed. Under contemporary conditions, however, it is an elusive and even a deceptive thing. Indeed, a semblance of public opinion can appear even in a totalitarian society. But it is only a semblance, for at decisive junctures it is manipulated by the dictators. The dictators reluctantly take resistant opinion into account, but they do so primarily in order to « liquidate » it and to maintain their power. This motive impels the power élites also in the ostensibly democratic society. Accordingly, the democratic society may exhibit the *forms* of democracy while lacking the *substance*. The substance of democracy today is constantly being dissolved by a late-comer on the stage, the mass society. Typologically defined, the mass society does not possess self-conscious, critically articulated public opinion.

Professor Arnold M. Rose, an American sociologist, has suggested that the people of a mass society are not a « public » but are merely an « audience » — they think and act in similar or convergent ways simply because of a common source of stimulus. As in a cinema theatre, they have little significant contact with one another. Thus the massed stimulus moves only in one direction; the members of the « audience » do not engage in dialogue either with the source of the stimulus or with 'each other. The source of stimulus is the « propagandist » who manipulates the mass media of communication in order « to make a sale ». He uses only slogans and epithets, torsoes and fragments of ideas torn from every living context of meaning. The propagandist wants only a passive audience, a mass of people who do not engage in critical dialogue. A mass audience is not capable of « public opinion ». In the mass audience, we may say, the people fall to bits, and they achieve « consensus » only as a crowd tossed about by the winds of doctrine and brute instinct. They live in an underworld of deception.

Public opinion comes only from a « public », not from an « audience ». A public engages in multilateral discussion. Here there are elements of structure and continuity, the interplay and qualification of information and interpretation, some critical awareness of social forces and of the explanation of these forces. In order for the structure and dynamics of discussion to come into existence or to be maintained, organized groups with more or less clear purposes, with democratically selected and responsible leadership, and with recognized procedures for free dialogue and decision, are required. These are the requisites for public opinion, and for the achievement of genuine consent of the governed. Insofar as these features are absent, the dehumanization, the manipulations and dominations of the mass society ensue.

One of the characteristic, principal means for the structuring and implementation of public opinion is the political party. In a democracy a plurality of political parties is indispensable. Without a plurality of parties, political freedom is impossible: there is no effective role for discussion in face of the state and allied configurations of power, and there is no place for « loyal opposition ».

If the man of culture in the prosecution of his political task is to exercise his responsibilities with respect to the transmission, transformation, and application of ethos in the changing historical situation, he cannot on principle renounce the idea of active membership in a political party. Yet, one must recognize that such active membership is not considered to be mandatory for every citizen nor for every man of culture. Like other citizens, the man of culture may prefer to adopt means that do not operate directly within the framework of a political party, though these means may indirectly affect political parties. These means, as we have said, must include other types of formal association.

The man of culture may not properly be an island unto himself, even if this island is inhabited also by other men of culture. In order that he may fulfil his political task, the values he represents or seeks must find associational habitation in the common life. From formal associations he can best secure not only the stimulus but also the channels for the fulfilment of his practical political task. Participation in these associations is obligatory for the man of culture.

In addition to political parties, then, a decisive and characteristic instrumentality of the democratic society is the voluntary association. It is the instrumentality whereby various perspectives and needs, discussion and consensus, competent community leadership, and thus responsible public opinion come into play. Since it is argued here that participation in voluntary associations dealing with public policy is an obligation for the man of culture, we must now consider the character and the roles of these associations. After a definition and a rough classification of voluntary associations has been presented, some attention will be given to their historical development and significance, to the varieties of national tradition with respect to

them, to their social psychology and their political significance, to the dangers and perversions attendant upon voluntary associational activity, and finally to the man of culture's role in these associations.

Voluntary associations, as Max Weber has suggested, are to be contrasted with compulsory associations such as the state and the family. The definition may be formulated in terms of the contrast with associations into which one is born (the state, the family, the established church in a traditionalist society). This contrast suggests that voluntary associations appear in a social setting in which the community no longer functions as an all-inclusive social group. In the differentiation of social groups the voluntary association stands between the state and alliances of the state on the one hand and the natural community of the family on the other. It stands also between the individual and the state, and between the individual and the family. In both of these positions it can serve as an occasion for independence and freedom. From the point of view of general social structure, the association is an aspect of the shift from Gemeinschaft to Gesellschaft (Tönnies), from status to contract (Maine). Also, it is an organizational aspect of the latest phase of the development beginning with the stage of society based upon kinship, through one based on authority, towards a stage built on citizenship (Hobhouse). Or one may say that it appears in the shift from the Herrschaftlicher Verband to the Genossenschaft (Otto von Gierke). It is an association to which persons (or groups) deliberately belong and from which they may resign. Generally, then, the voluntary association has quite limited, though more or less clearly specified, purposes.

From these characterizations one might

infer that a business corporation is a voluntary association. In ordinary usage, however, the term does not apply to associations existing for the purpose of private profit, though of course many associations concern themselves with the protection or extension of « special interests » that are economic. These aspects of the voluntary association are taken into account in an apt definition set forth in the French law (1901) on associations: « L'association est la convention par laquelle deux ou plusieurs personnes mettent en commun d'une façon permanente leurs connaissances ou leur activité dans un but autre que de partager des bénéfices » (cited by Arnold).

Voluntary associations exhibit a great variety of purposes. Some exist for the sake of mere sociability or for the enjoyment of a hobby, others for the promotion of standards with respect to the arts or to general cultural or scientific purposes (the S.E.C., for example); some for the expression of interests of the members in relation to themselves (such as the securing of social status), others for influencing people outside the association, and still others for exercising influence both inward and outward. Some of these associations have an indirect, and some have a direct influence on the shaping of public policy. In all of them there tend to be specified activities, membership requirements, elective or delegated responsibilities of leadership, and specified rules of procedure. Obviously, the type of voluntary association directly concerned with public policy is of decisive significance for our consideration of the means whereby the man of culture fulfils his political task.

A brief reference to the historical development of voluntary associations will still further delineate their types and functions. For the most part, voluntary associations have appeared in urbanized and especially in democratic societies. One of course finds these associations in the cities of antiquity—the « clubs » of Greece and Rome, the « universities », and certain religious cults. In Rome Marcus Aurelius was the first to grant corporate rights to licensed *collegia*. Voluntary associations appear later in the form of Christian sects, in the early medieval gilds, in the Left Wing of the Reformation sects, in revolutionary movements, and then in philanthropic, social reform, and cooperative societies. As Max Weber has shown, the prototype of the modern voluntary association is the Protestant sect.

The thrust in the direction of voluntary association has again and again been compelled to struggle for freedom of association. In Anglo-Saxon society great sacrifices were made for the successful establishing of the right of freedom of association—by sectarian groups, by quasi-religious groups and secret societies (the Free Masons, for example), and by trade unions. Similar, if less severe, struggles have taken place in the development of modern Sweden. M. Antony Babel has given several accounts of these struggles (particularly of the workers) as they have occurred in Switzerland (see, for example, his *Freedom of Association in Switzerland*, Geneva, 1927).

In general, we may say that Nonconformity in modern religious history has made a decisive contribution to the achievement of freedom of association and thus to the development of modern democracy. In England, for example, the conception of the democratic state was probably drawn by analogy from the conception of the Free Church in which the ideas of local autonomy, of universal suffrage and the protection of the minority (an anticipation of « loyal opposition » in parliamentary democracy) were first demanded. Élie Halévy has given a masterly account of the role of Nonconformity in the development of voluntary associations and of democracy in Britain. Where Nonconformity has been suppressed or has been feeble in the modern world, both freedom of association and political democracy have been tardy in development. This is to be observed in Germany, Spain, Italy, and France. These are countries in which Roman Catholicism, and subsequently Communism, have been strong.

In France, legislation forbidding or severely limiting freedom of association has been characteristic both before and after the Revolution. Both the monarchy and the church were for long vigorous in resisting freedom of association. In contrast to the English development, the struggle of French workers for freedom of association has been largely against the government rather than against the employers, and their associations have tended to have mainly political motives and to be revolutionary in impulse. Not until 1901 was general freedom of association established by legislation, and even then important restrictions were imposed. Apart from occupational associations, few strong, independent associations have developed in France up to the present day. Many of the associations familiar in England and the United States which are concerned with philanthropy, social reform, cultural interests, and scientific research, are in France dependent upon government subsidy.

Ecclesiastical and political power in Italy has until fairly recent times prevented any significant development of freedom of association for purposes of social reform. The Movimento Comunità of Dr. Adriano Olivetti appears to represent an impressive innovation, as are also the communitarian movement in France and the development of voluntary municipal associations and of Evangelical Academies in Germany.

The United States has been called « a nation of joiners ». Perhaps no country has witnessed such a proliferation of associations. Already in 1831 De Tocqueville, following his visit to the States, observed:

« L'Amérique est le pays du monde où l'on a tiré le plus de parti de l'association, et où l'on a appliqué ce puissant moyen d'action à une plus grande diversité d'objets... » (I, 226).

Les Américains de tous les âges, de toutes les conditions, de tous les esprits, s'unissent sans cesse. Non seulement ils ont des associations commerciales et industrielles auxquelles tous prennent part; mais ils en ont encore de mille autres espèces: de religieuses, de morales, de graves, de futiles, de fort générales et de très particulières, d'immenses et de fort petites; les Américains s'associent pour donner des fêtes, fonder des séminaires, bâtir des auberges, élever des églises, répandre des livres, envoyer des missionnaires aux antipodes; ils créent de cette manière des hôpitaux, des prisons, des écoles. S'agit-il enfin de mettre en lumière une vérité, ou de développer un sentiment par l'appui d'un grand exemple: ils s'associent. Partout où, à la tête d'une entreprise nouvelle, vous voyez en France le gouvernement, et en Angleterre un grand seigneur, comptez que vous apercevrez aux Etats-Unis une association ». (II, 120) (1).

As in England, these associations have promoted universal suffrage, antislavery, better working conditions and wages for labor, temperance, public-school education, adult education, social settlement houses, slum clearance, consumers' and producers' cooperatives, foreign relief work, and a host of other « causes ». In the United States this phenomenal development of freedom of association has been the result of American individualism (promoted by Protestantism), of distrust of the government

(1) ALEXIS DE TOCQUEVILLE. *De la démocratie en Amérique*, Paris, 1850.

(originating in the colonial struggle against England), of the pioneer milieu and mentality, of the tradition of local autonomy (necessary because of the vast spaces), and of the high degree of social mobility vertical and horizontal. It should be observed, however, that labor organizations, as in most countries, were compelled to wage a prolonged struggle simply to establish freedom of association.

In the light of this account of the « organizational revolution » of the modern world we must now consider briefly the political, the social-psychological, and also the religious significance, of the data. First we shall indicate their positive significance. Thereupon, however, we shall take note of the dangers and perversions.

In the political sphere, as we have observed earlier, the voluntary associations concerned with public policy assist in the creation of a « public » and of public opinion. But more than this must be said of their political significance. These associations, in face of centralized political and economic authority, bring about the dispersion of power and responsibility. (It is clear that power and responsibility must be understood together, for responsibility is the rightful exercise of power). In this context, power is twofold. It is the capacity to exercise influence; and, as Plato suggests in the *Sophist*, it is also the capacity to be influenced. M. Campagnolo has hinted at this twofold aspect of power when he has spoken of the dialogue « qui entraîne la conscience morale et politique des interlocuteurs, les obligeant, s'il le faut, à changer leurs convictions et leurs attitudes ». The voluntary associations, alongside the political parties and in face of the state, serve to give group reality in the political sphere to what in the Protestant church tradition is called « the universal priesthood of believers ». They do this by the exercise of freedom of association. In doing so they bring about the dispersion of power and responsibility by rendering it possible for the citizenry to participate in the process of making decisions regarding public policy.

The voluntary associations provide the individual the opportunity to participate in the process of self-government and of reconceiving goals and means. That is, they offer the occasion for social inventiveness that disperses social functions and individual responsibilities into non-political as well as political agencies. As an instrument of social change the voluntary associations thus place chains upon the ever latent Leviathan, the omnicompetent state. At the same time they provide means for keeping under control the always threatening tyranny of economic collectivities (which can subvert the state to their own interest). As an instrument of social change the voluntary associations keep the society open to the recognition of the needs of all, particularly open to « minority opinion ». Through freedom of association they can prevent the necessity for violent and revolutionary change. In short, they « institutionalize revolution ».

The freedom of association has been resisted in every totalitarian régime and in ecclesiastically directed societies. Thomas Hobbes, the classical theorist of totalitarianism, entertained no doubt regarding the threat to sovereignty constituted by voluntary associations. For him, they were « worms in the entrails of the sovereign ». Nazi Germany, Soviet Russia, Fascist Italy and Spain reduced these free associations to the vanishing point.

The social-psychological significance of voluntary associations is fairly obvious. They provide the means whereby a variety of interests and needs can find social expression or recognition, and thus whereby freedom may find group structure and effectiveness through the achievement of « interpersonal competence » and consensus. They offer training in the technique of social organization and in the assumption of responsibility with respect to value orientation and to specific practical tasks related to social decisions. They make possible the training of leadership required for the articulation and implementation of these decisions. They give individuals and groups the opportunity for coming to understand social forces that impinge on their destiny, and for acquiring an interpretation of events and goals, and of needed social policies. In all of these ways, voluntary associations are a dispersed mechanism of social change and social control. In an urbanized, technologized society the smaller associations provide occasion for the increase of primary over secondary human relations, and for overcoming the debilitating and isolating effects of daily work. Sometimes they also break through the barriers of race and class. Through these associations the individual can find meaningful objets for self-identification, definitions of models of behavior, and occasions for fellowship in terms of socially significant issues and concerns. All of these features represent an antidote to the dehumanizing effects of the highly segmented mass society; they elicit the release of human energies, and they develop human talents. They give the common people a greater stake in the social system, as is illustrated in the enormous significance of the labor movement which has provided to the workers new economic security and also opportunities for social participation and control. They make of human variety a source of strength rather than of atomized impotence. In short, they are the medium for the striving towards freedom in community, a matter of supreme import in the human enterprise. In considering these functions of voluntary associations we confront as it were the ultimate issues of life. Their role in society therefore lends itself to religious interpretation, and precisely to interpretation in the spirit of the prophetic religious consciousness of which we have spoken earlier. (Accordingly, a theory of freedom of association is a crucial element in any adequate conception of the church and of religious vocation).

Voluntary associations represent a point at which « the dearest freshness deep down things » can emerge into the social conscience and into social action. Ideally they can provide the kind of social situation and organization in which the Spirit may blow where it listeth and where it may create community. In connection with the religious-social significance of these associations (including the churches) Martin Buber's words are highly pertinent: « We are created along with one another and directed to a life with one another. Creatures are placed in my way so that I, their fellow-creature, by means of them and with them find the way to God. A God reached by their exclusion would not be the God of all lives in whom all life is fulfilled ».

But not only a positive religious significance is to be seen here. Voluntary associations also give rise to perversions of human community, to the alienation of man, and of man from the God who is the ground of human community. Here we have to do with the pathology of voluntary associations. This pathology is roughly twofold, the diseases of voluntary associations in their relations to the rest of the community, and the diseases within associations themselves.

One of the major misconceptions of the

role of voluntary associations is the notion that they can in all circumstances provide viable forms of integration in the community. This view, in its extreme form, has been set forth by anarchism. A more restricted view has been held by the Liberalism which, in adherence to the theory of automatic harmony, assigns a mainly negative role to the state—the maintenance of freedom of association. Actually, this view has not been held without qualifications by the laissez-faire economists. The major crises of the past half-century, whether in international relations or in face of impending economic collapse, have demonstrated that voluntary associations are not omnicompetent alongside a « negative state ». In face of serious economic maladjustment, or of major structural social needs, the appeal for voluntary associational solution of the problem is likely to be motivated by a class ideology. The first evil then, against which we need warning is the evil of making too great claims for the competency of voluntary associations.

Other evils characteristic of voluntary associations in their relation to the community at large are not far to seek. Voluntary associations provide one of the most effective means for promoting narrow and particularist interests: the protection of special privilege for. ethnic groups, for class groups, and for economic power blocs. Accordingly, they often solicit their membership from these « special interest » groups. Whereas political parties try to mobilize majorities, pressure groups, as Schattschneider puts it, try to organize minorities. (Even voluntary associations that are not special-interest pressure groups are by no means universal in class provenance; today they still draw mainly upon the middle classes for membership). In a Nazi-like manner, the pressure groups frequently

coordinate interlocking membership for purposes of collusion. By this means they impinge upon the effectiveness of other and weaker associations, they exercise non-market controls over the « free » market, they « infiltrate » leaders into key positions in other organizations, and they impede legislation intended for the general welfare or they promote special-interest legislation. To some extent, to be sure, the conflicts between associations are countervailing. In any event, the techniques of manipulation, deception, and domination appear to be almost part and parcel of associational « freedom ». (Associations are prone to all of the evils to which flesh is heir). The principal corrective to these special-interest configurations is exposure at the hands of public opinion, that is, at the hands of other associations. The corrective is seldom promptly or substantially effective, and in many instances it is not effective at all.

Diseases in the internal structure of voluntary associations are equally frustrating and destructive. The larger an organization becomes the more readily does it become subject to the disfunctions of bureaucratization, though it is surprising how quickly a « pecking order » can develop in even a small association. Robert Michels has succinctly characterized this disease by his term, « the iron law of oligarchy ». A voluntary association, like any other, can readily come under the control of a power élite. This form of domination is aided by the default, the apathy, of the rank-and-file membership. Oftentimes the buraucracy carries out policies that are contrary to these favored by the membership; and the correction of the evil would require more energy on the part of the dissident membership than is ordinarily available. The situation is aggravated in those vocational and professional associations that are not really voluntary. In these associations membership is mandatory, and withdrawal from membership would be suicidal.

There are also other ways in which membership in an association can severely restrict freedom. Adam Smith long ago pointed out that the individual gains a certain sense of dignity by being brought within a religious sect—a dignity that comes from the discovery that others care enough about him to wish to convert him; but that at the same time the individual member, in joining the sect, may find himself in a vise that crushes his individuality and freedom. Following essentially the same pattern, some secular voluntary associations repress minority opinion within the organization. If the individual in this kind of organization hopes to be selected for leadership, he will tend to « conform » and try to gain the « confidence » of the leaders already in power. Therefore, far from being a medium for the realization of freedom, a voluntary association may be a means for its constriction. An association that lacks a permissive atmosphere may contribute to the annihilation of privacy and inner integrity. Partly with this in mind, a wit has observed that « what a man belongs to constitutes most of his life career and all of his obituary ».

But whatever the diseases to which these associations are subject, « we know », as Louis Wirth has reminded us, « that without belonging to these organizations we are paralyzed, we are impotent, we are negligible ». Moreover, without these organizations the community also is paralyzed, as the great sociologist Durkheim has pointed out (in protest against the lack of voluntary associations in France):

« Une nation ne peut se maintenir que si, entre l'Etat et les particuliers, s'intercale toute une série de groupes secondaires qui soient assez proches des individus pour les attirer fortement dans leur sphère d'action et les entraîner ainsi dans le torrent général de la vie sociale » (1).

We have seen that it is within the matrix of secondary groups that public opinion and public policy are determined. Within them consensus and social action are given shape and direction. The man of culture cannot fulfil his political task without participation in these associations.

The man of culture, in the context of voluntary associations, has perhaps a fourfold vocation to fulfil in the realization of his political task. First, to help make the general citizenry aware of the decisive importance of voluntary associations in the articulation and implementation of public opinion, contravening in this way the dehumanization brought about today by the mass society and the mass man. Second, to give himself to associations that aim directly to overcome social evils for the sake of the general welfare, in this way exerting himself especially for the sake of underprivileged groups. Third, to encourage those salutary forces which work against oligarchic tendencies within voluntary associations and within economic and political instrumentalities. And, fourth, to assume his professional and religious obligation « with a sense of infinitude » by promoting the free discussion of public issues and of fresh possibilities of policy and organization, in the name of truth and justice; in other words, to help create those social patterns that can in the ever changing historical situation transmit historic cultural values and create new values, thus transmitting, criticizing, and transforming the ethos of the

(1) EMILE DURKHEIM. *De la division du travail social.* Paris, 1932.

culture. Taken together these tasks call for the interweaving of the cultural and the political tasks of the man of culture, in a dialogue that gives social expression to the auto-theonomy of creative activity. One may add here that the participation will require careful concentration of effort if that effort is to be responsible and effective and if the fulfilment of the political task is not to demand more energy than one may reasonably expect of the man of culture or of any other finite human creature.

Public-spirited attitudes and occasional manifestoes alone are ineffectual substitutes for participation. Participation in merely cultural associations not concerned with public policy is also insufficient. Max Weber once said (of course without any intention of disparaging artistic endeavors):

« The blossoming of singing societies in Germany exercises, in my opinion, considerable effects even in fields where one would not even guess it, for example, in politics. A man who is accustomed daily to let stream from his bosom through his throat mighty feelings, without any relation to his action, without the adequate translation of these expressed powerful feelings into correspondingly powerful actions — and that is the essence of the singing - society art — that will be a man who, briefly put, will very easily become a ‘ good citizen ’ in the passive sense of the word. It is little wonder that the monarchs have such a love for such societies. ‘ Wo man singt, da lass dich ruhig nieder ’ ».

We recall that the Society has declared that today it is « plus nécessaire que jamais pour les hommes de culture d'assumer leurs responsabilités dans le domaine politique ». The man of culture who does not participate in associations concerned with the political domain remains isolated and impotent for the political task. He becomes, despite and perhaps even because of his « culture », a mass man who within the context of the community is a dominated man, like other mass men. To him the responsible citizens can say. « We fought at Arles, but you were not there ».

THE INDISPENSABLE DISCIPLINE OF SOCIAL RESPONSIBILITY

James Luther Adams

In 1927 in the city of Nuremberg, six years before the National Socialists came into power, I was watching a Sunday parade on the occasion of the annual mass rally of the Nazis. Thousands of youth, as a sign of their vigor and patriotism, had walked from various parts of Germany to attend the mass meeting of the Party. As I watched the parade which lasted for four hours and which was punctuated by trumpet and drum corps made up of hundreds of Nazis, I asked some people on the sidelines to explain to me the meaning of the swastika that decorated many of the banners. Before very long I found myself engaged in a heated argument. Suddenly someone seized me from behind and pulled me by the elbows out of the group with which I was arguing. In the firm grip of someone whom I could barely see I was forced through the crowd and propelled down a side-street and up into a dead-end alley. As this happened I assure you my palpitation rose quite perceptibly. I was beginning to feel Nazism existentially. At the end of the alley my uninvited host swung me around quickly, and he shouted at me in German, "You fool. Don't you know? In Germany today when you are watching a parade, you either keep your mouth shut or you get your head bashed in." I thought he was going to bash it in right there. But then his face changed into a friendly smile, and he said, "If you had continued that argument for five minutes longer, those fellows would have beaten you up." "Why did you decide to help me?" I asked. He replied, "I am an anti-Nazi. As I saw you there, getting into trouble, I thought of the times when in New York City as a sailor of the German merchant marine I received a wonderful hospitality. And I said to myself, 'Here is your chance to repay that hospitality.' So I grabbed you, and here we are. I am inviting you home to Sunday dinner."

This man turned out to be an unemployed worker. His home was a tenement apartment in the slums. To reach it, we climbed three flights up a staircase that was falling apart, and he ushered me into a barren room where his wife and three small children greeted their unexpected American guest in astonishment. We had the Sunday meal together, a dinner of greasy dumplings and of small beer drunk from a common jug. Within a period of two hours I learned vividly of the economic distress out of which Nazism was born. From this trade-union worker I learned also that one organization after the other that refused to bow to the Nazis was being threatened with compulsion. The totalitarian process had begun. Freedom of association was being abolished. "You keep your mouth shut, and you conform, or you get your head bashed in." A decade later in Germany I was to see at first hand the belated resistance of the churches to this attack upon freedom of speech and freedom of association.

At this juncture I had to confront a rather embarrassing question. I had to ask myself, "What in your typical behavior as an American citizen have you done that would help to prevent the rise of authoritarian government in your own country? What disciplines of democracy (except voting) have you habitually undertaken with other people which could serve in any way directly to affect public policy?" More bluntly stated: I asked myself, "What precisely is the difference between *you* and a political idiot?"

Immediately after the Second World War the Swiss theologian Karl Barth made a speaking tour in Germany, and in his talks he stressed the idea t! t every conscientious German tizen should now participate actively in voluntary associations committed to the task of making democracy work. I do not know whether Karl Barth as a professor in Germany practiced his own preaching when Nazism was on the rise. But in giving his admonition to the Germans after the war, he pointed to a characteristic feature of any democratic society, namely, freedom of association.

Every totalitarian theory rejects just this freedom. Indeed, the rejection of freedom of association, the rejection of the freedom to form groups that attempt democratically to affect public policy, can serve as the beginning of a definition of totalitarianism. We are familiar with the fulminations against freedom of association by Hobbes and Rousseau. Hobbes the totalitarian warns against "the great number of corporations which are as it were many lesser commonwealths in the body of a greater, like worms in the entrails of a natural man." The late Senator Joseph McCarthy worked in the spirit of Hobbes when he tried to smother freedom of association.

As against Hobbes the theorists of democracy have asserted that only through the exercise of freedom of association can consent of the governed become effective; only through the exercise of freedom of association can the citizen in a democracy participate in the process that gives shape to public opinion and to public policy. For this reason we may speak of the voluntary association as a distinctive and indispensable institution of democratic society.

How shall we define voluntary association? Speaking of the situation in the United States of over a hundred years ago, the Frenchman Alexis de Tocqueville observed that "in no country in the world has the principle of association been more successfully used, or applied to a greater multitude of objects, than in America. . . . Wherever, at the head of some new undertaking, you see the government in France, or a man of rank in England, in the United States you will be sure to find an association." De Tocqueville gives the classical description of the multitude of associations in the United States at that time, associations for libraries, hospitals, fire prevention, and for political and philanthropic purposes. One could sum up De Tocqueville's description of the United States at that time by saying that where two or three Americans are gathered together you may be sure that a committee is being formed. We have been "a nation of joiners."

Any healthy democratic society is a multi-group society. One finds in it business corporations, religious associations, trade unions, educational associations, recreational, philanthropic, protective and political associations, and innumerable social clubs. These associations are, or claim to be, voluntary; they presuppose freedom on the part of the individual to be or not to be a member, to join or withdraw, or to consort with others to form a new association. By way of contrast the state and the family, for example, are as associations involuntary, and in some countries the church also is virtually involuntary. Every person willy-nilly belongs to a particular state and to a particular family. It is not a matter of choice whether he will belong to these two associations. In this sense they are involuntary. There are other associations, to be sure, which it is difficult to classify under either category, voluntary or involuntary. Taken together, these associations, involuntary and voluntary, represent the institutional articulation of the pluralistic society.

The appearance of the voluntary association in Western society did not come without a struggle. The initial demand for voluntary association came from the churches of the left wing of the Reformation. These churches insisted that religion, in order to be a matter of choice, must be free from state control. Therefore they demanded the separation of church and state. This struggle for freedom of religious association continued for over two centuries. It was accompanied or followed by a struggle for freedom of economic association, for freedom to establish political parties, for freedom of workers to form unions, and for freedom to institute reforms in society. Not all voluntary associations, to be sure, are concerned with public policy. Some associations are simply social clubs, others promote hobbies, and still others are merely status groups. Considering the voluntary association that is concerned with social policy, for example, with securing civil liberties or better housing, or with overcoming racial discrimination, we may say that this sort of association stands between the individual and the state and provides the instrumentality for achieving consensus within a group, and for implementing this consensus either through political or non-political means. This sort of association provides the opportunity for discussion for assembling neglected facts, and for scrutinizing and overcoming mere propaganda.

The voluntary association at its best offers an institutional framework within which the give and take of discussion may be promoted, an institutional framework within which a given consensus may be brought under criticism and be subjected to change. It offers a means for bringing a variety of perspectives into interplay. It offers the means of breaking through old social structures in order to meet new needs. It is a means of dispersing power, in the sense that power is the capacity to participate in making social decisions. It is the training ground of the skills that are required for viable social existence in a democracy. In short, the voluntary association is a means for the institutionalizing of *gradual* revolution.

I have spoken of the fact that freedom of association was fought for by the churches of the left wing of the Reformation. Any adequate treatment of the free association demands theological interpretation. Such a treatment would show how the doctrine of the covenant in Old and New England was employed to sanction the priesthood and prophethood of all believers, and thus to express religious and social responsibility. By covenant men responded to God's community-forming power. But the prime example of the institutionalization of a doctrine of the covenant is to be found much earlier in Western history. The primitive Christian church illustrates many of the features of a voluntary association which I have mentioned. In one sense, to be sure, the primitive church was not a voluntary association as ordinarily conceived. It was believed to have come into existence through the work of God and not through the acts of men. Nor was it directly concerned with public policy as such, except that by its very existence it bespoke the demand for freedom of association. Yet the primitive church illustrates the dispersion of power and responsibility, and it illustrates also the breaking through of old social structures toward the end of creating new structures. The primitive

church broke through the bonds of the ethnic religion of Judaism: Jew, Greek, Roman and barbarian could be members. Moreover, the membership of the primitive church came from all classes of society, but especially from the lower classes (including slaves). The church also gave a new status to women. Besides all this, the primitive church gave the common man the opportunity to learn the skills required for effective social organization. The common people who were members had to learn the skills of preaching and teaching, of administration, of missionizing, and also of dispensing charity. The emergence of the primitive church represents, then, one of the great innovative movements of history, a great social revolution. Probably the recovery of the West after the Fall of Rome took place with greater speed because of the thousands of people who had been trained in skills that could be employed outside as well as inside the church organization. Here was an enormous dispersion of the capacity to participate in the making of social decision, and in response to a transcendent purpose.

By the time the church had come into its medieval form, however, a great change had taken place in its internal structure. Indeed, certain branches of the Reformation represented a protest against the monolithic, power structure of the church, and they carried through this protest by appeal to the model of the primitive church. So we see movement back and forth from one kind of social structure to another.

Thus an association originally intended to disperse power and responsibility undergoes changes moving in the opposite direction, that is, in the direction of concentration of power. In the earliest essay in America on the structure of voluntary associations William Ellery Channing, the Boston Unitarian clergyman, pointed to this danger. The voluntary association so far from serving as an instrument of freedom may end in becoming a new instrument of tyranny and conformism. Channing could speak with experience in these matters, for a number of the great reformist associations of the early nineteenth century were organized in his study.

Robert Michels, the Italian sociologist, has given a memorable account of the internal shift of power that can take place in an association. His view is that in any organization the "eager beavers" can take advantage of the indolence of the average member. By this means they gain control of the organization. This process he describes as the operation of "the iron law of oligarchy."

We can observe the iron law of oligarchy as it operates in the great pressure groups of today. A few years ago some sociologists studied the centralized bureaucracy of the American Medical Association. They found a goodly number of physicians who said that they felt that the A. M. A. through its policies was damaging the image of the physician in the United States today. On being asked why they did not do something to change the structure and the policies of the bureaucracy, some of them gave the answer, "I trained to be a doctor, and I want to practice medicine. In order to break the bureaucracy of the A. M. A., I and many of my colleagues would have to spend much more time than we can afford." It is a striking fact that the large business corporation functions by reducing the role of the shareholder. The average small shareholder surrenders his power by signing a proxy to the representative of the managers. This sort of phenomenon belongs to the pathology of associations, and we could find ample illustration of it by examining colleges and churches.

But the pathology does not end with the functioning of the iron law of oligarchy within associations. It can be observed also in the functioning of the great pressure groups as they affect public policy. Legislation regarding the pressure groups as corrected some of the evils. B the role of the special-interest pressure group today presents us with a major problem of the democratic society: the power of the pressure group is exercised through collusion with other pressure groups. The lobbyist of the wool-growers' association in face of some legislation he wishes to impede goes to the representative of the copper-producers' association and says, "I know that you are not interested pro or con in this bit of legislation, but if you will join us now, we shall give you assistance when you need it in a similar situation." In a society where the principle of freedom of association obtains, one must recognize the legitimate freedom of the pressure group. Besides this, we must recognize they do not always enter into collusion. In some

157

measure the great special-interest pressure groups function as countervailing powers that neutralize each other. This neutralization, however, does not appear when, for example, the issue has to do with the distribution of the tax burden. Here the little man gets short-changed.

This whole situation points to a major requirement for a viable and authentic democratic society. One can roughly classify the great voluntary associations concerned with public policy. The one type of association is called the special-interest group. Here the association is judged by its capacity to ring up money on the cash register of the member. These special-interest groups became very influential already at the end of the nineteenth century. Henry Demarest Lloyd pointed out this changing character of American society. Speaking of the great concentrations of business power and of the large special-interest pressure groups at the end of the century he said that the letters "USA" had come to mean "The United Syndicates of America."

The other type of association is the sort that directly aims to promote the general welfare. The member of the association does not expect to make personal gain through the association. For example, the average member of the American Civil Liberties Union seldom makes a personal gain from his participation in the organization. He spends his time and money to support the effort to re-define the nature of civil liberties in a changing society, and also to defend those whose liberties are violated

or threatened.

In some of the larger associations or pressure groups the broad constituency of the membership makes it possible for us to say that the gain of the members is a gain also for many non-members. For example, the civil-rights movement with its many associations that aim to promote the liberty of the Negro will in the long run increase the productivity of the entire nation and it will also extend the rights of other underprivileged groups. The award of the Nobel Prize to Martin Luther King served to recognize the contribution of the civil-rights organizations to the whole democratic society and even to the forces of emancipation in the world at large.

In face of these two types of association we can say that the health of democracy depends upon the capacity of general-welfare associations to function as countervailing powers against the narrower purposes of the special-interest associations.

Now, I would like to make three brief observations with regard to this demand. First, let me mention the findings of some recent studies of college graduates. These studies indicate that insofar as he is concerned with public policy the average college graduate in the United States is affiliated with special-interest groups. Besides, he gives little attention or time to participation in the organization; he simply pays his dues, and expects the bureaucracy to look after his interests. Now, a second observation. A minister in Denver has published an elaborate study of the associational behavior of the members of his middle-class church. He shows that even the associations of philanthropic character to which his church members belong serve mainly to bring together birds of a feather, that is, to bring together people possessing the same economic and political prejudices. So far from extending the range of community across ethnic and class lines, these associations serve to keep the classes and races separate. A third observation: Mirra Kamarovsky has studied the associational behavior of the residents of Manhattan. She has found that apart from membership in the church the citizens of Manhattan do not on the average belong to even ꞏ one association concerned with public policy. She asserts that we have here a good definition of the mass man. Regardless of whether he is "educated" or not, a person is a mass man who does not participate in voluntary associations concerned with the public benefit. He is only on the receiving end of the mass media of communications. In the world of public policy he is a eunuch.

The sinfulness of man expresses itself, then, in the indifference of the average citizen who is so impotent, so idiotic in the Greek sense, as not to exercise his freedom of association for the sake of the general welfare and for the sake of becoming a responsible self.

Ernst Troeltsch has made a distinction that is of prime significance here. He distinguishes between what he calls subjective and objective virtues. Subjective virtues are virtues that can be exhibited in immediate person-to-person relations. Objective virtues

require an institution for their expression. Thus, from the larger human perspective we can say that the isolated good man is a chimera. There is no such thing as a good man as such. There is only the good father or the good mother, the good physician or the good plumber, the good churchman, the good citizen. The good man of the subjective virtues, to be sure, provides the personal integrity of the individual. Without it the viable society is not possible. But from the point of view of the *institutional* commonwealth the merely good individual is good for nothing. Moreover, the narrow range of responsibility of the man who confines attention merely to his family and his job serves to dehumanize him. This narrowness of range and of responsibility is neatly symbolized in an epitaph reported from a cemetery tombstone in Scotland:

Here lies John MacDonald
Born a man
Died a grocer

At the outset I spoke of the experience in pre-Nazi Germany when a man told me, "You either keep your mouth shut, or you get your head bashed in." In the democratic society the non-participating citizen bashes his own head in. The living democratic society requires the disciplines of discussion and common action for the determination of policy. The differences between men are determined by the quality and direction of their participation. In this sense we may understand the New Testament word, "By their fruits shall you know them"; but to this word we should add the admonition, By their groups shall you know them.

VOLUNTARY ASSOCIATIONS IN SEARCH OF IDENTITY

James Luther Adams

In calling the Consultation on Voluntary Associations and Public Policy, the sponsors have recognized the need for our stepping back and taking stock of voluntary associations as a crucial feature of American society.

In his highly instructive and cogent address, Dr. Michael has placed a heavy demand upon voluntary associations, the demand for constant self-analysis, for re-examination of values and goals, and for newly relevant, innovative action in face of changing social realities both within voluntary associations and in the environing culture. This demand, as he has shown, calls for a program of systematic research, especially in turbulent times such as ours.

As I listened to his presentation, I thought of an address delivered by Max Weber exactly sixty years ago at a congress of sociologists in Frankfurt, Germany, "A Proposal for the Study of Voluntary Associations" (not yet published in English translation). "The man of today," he says, "is without doubt an association man in an awful and never dreamed of degree," and the American is the association-man par excellence. At first blush these words strike us as strange indeed: "an awful and never dreamed of degree." Weber has in mind here the large number of associations that are merely self-serving; he is thinking also of the evils as well as of the unintended consequences issuing from much associational behavior.

160

As a somewhat amusing and paradoxical example he cites the political apathy following upon "the blossoming of singing societies" all over Germany. "It is little wonder," he says, "that the monarchs have a love for such societies" which make "good" citizens (i.e., passive citizens). To be sure, he fully appreciated the artistic significance of the singing societies, but he also felt that an excessive number of them could drain off the national energies into warbling.

In this address Weber turns the attention of his colleagues in a quite new direction. He asserts that it is a fundamental task of sociology to study those voluntary structures which lie between the involuntary associations, that is, between "the politically organized or recognized powers" on the one side and "the natural community of the family" on the other.[1] In the voluntary association, individual choice is supposed to be at the maximum; by way of contrast, one does not *choose* the nation or the family into which he will be born. Taken all together, these associations, voluntary and involuntary, constitute the pluralistic shape of modern democratic society.

Alas, all too little heed was given to Weber's plea for a systematic and comparative study of voluntary associations, partly because the turbulent times of the First World War and its aftermath distracted attention from the need for self-analysis.

Dr. Michael has observed that the turbulence of the times is not the only obstruction to self-analysis and self-criticism on the part of voluntary associations. Like most institutions, these associations seem to lack the power of systematic introspection. They exhibit a built-in organizational resistance to evaluating "who they are and what they are doing." The consequence is that they tend in the long run to succeed or fail by accident. Or they start out in a burst of initiative, and they proceed to kill it. One is reminded of the gloomy gentleman who said he entered this life and he was departing it with equal enthusiasm. So people bestir themselves to form or to join an association, and then they become "good" citizens, passively succumbing in their own apathy. By this route also, they turn the association over to the oligarchy of eager beavers, thus transforming a voluntary into an involuntary association.

The main highway of the devil's toboggan slide of history, however, is down the road of accommodation—of "adjustment." Curiously enough, even organizations that initially have viewed themselves as pitted against the establishment develop their own establishment-mentality. The historian of religion is amply familiar with this reversal of goals in religious organizations. For this reason he stresses the indispensability of the prophetic function of authentic religion, the function of exercising radical criticism of social structures and radical criticism of both goals and means, of both goals and performance. Organizations, as Thoreau would say, attach themselves to "improved means with unimproved ends." Let us dwell on this point a little longer.

The sociologist of institutional behavior speaks of the reversal of purposes as "goal-displacement." To be sure, displacement can take other forms; and the occasions and reasons for it are numerous. It can appear as a consequence of routinization of procedures, of the attempt to reconcile ideological conflicts, of the effort to survive in a hostile climate, of the increasing size of the organization, of the rule of the minority. By these means an organization can become a mechanism (an "improved means") for freeing it from its ostensible purpose, that is, a mechanism for goal-displacement. They reveal what Weber speaks of as "the general 'tragedy' of every attempt to bring ideas into the world of reality."

Dr. Michael's presentation bespeaks the fact that we have reached a new phase in the study of voluntary associations, a phase in which the identification of alternative structures and possibilities (and also of the pathology of associational behavior) has become more precise than previously, or at least has found a more elaborate conceptual apparatus.[2]

With regard to the phenomenon of goal-displacement, for example, we may recall Philip Selznick's pioneering analysis of its processes and motives, set forth in his study, *TVA and the Grass Roots* (1953); or the analysis by Joseph Gusfield of opposite tendencies to be observed in the history of the Women's Christian Temperance Union, the obstinate freezing of goals and procedures in face of broad social changes taking place in society;[3] or the account of the shift of purposes when the National Foundation for Infantile Paralysis was succeeded by the National Foundation—March of Dimes;[4] or Peter Blau's delineation of changes occurring in the chronological development of the trade-unions, where a series of new goals, "a succession of goals," is to be observed.[5] These and scores of other social-scientific and philosophical studies of voluntary associations have now become available, and of course not only in the United States.

Everyone recognizes the importance of research. But an "attitude" is in itself not enough. Research within an organization is not likely to be undertaken and research findings already available will not be made use of if the task is left to chance or is only fitfully attempted. Leaving the matter to chance generally turns out to be postponement. One is reminded of Augustine's prayer, "O God, make me chaste, but not yet!"

If one looks at the history of social organizations one finds that, apart from the impact of that rare thing called "charismatic leadership," systematic self-analysis and effective self-criticism generally occur only when these processes are institutionalized and thus can function in a structural way.

Here we confront an age-old differentiation in the conduct of associations, the differentiation between those people who expect the prophetic function to be exercised in a free-wheeling, merely spontaneous fashion and those who hold that it requires an explicit organizational status. Certain types of existentialism unfortunately have perpetrated a fetish regarding the high value of spontaneity and of decisions of "the moment." Some psychologists in analogous fashion have stressed a concern for "attitudes" to the neglect of the discipline of institutionalization.

This differentiation between free-wheeling criticism and the institutionalization of criticism is to be observed typologically in the history of Protestantism. The Lutheran tradition, beginning with Luther himself, has recognized the importance of dissent. Indeed, Luther's Reformation is itself an historic example of effective, organized dissent. But once the Reformation was under way, Luther confined dissent to admonition. If the prince was in need of correction, the preacher had the obligation to protest against certain evils. If admonition had no effect, then the preacher might pray that the tyrant would mend his ways. But if the prayer was not answered, then the preacher should consider moving to another territory!

In Geneva Calvinism, on the other hand, criticism of the magistrate was given institutional status. The lower magistrates were assigned the task of criticizing and correcting the higher magistrates. In Calvin's *Institutes* (book iv, ch. xx, section 31) we read that these lower magistrates (Ephors) "have not only the right but also the duty to oppose and resist the intemperance of kings . . . for the defense of the people." The British political scientist Sir Ernest Barker asserts that this passage is "one of the seed-beds of modern liberty."[6] The British theory and practice of dissent gave rise to its institutionalization, for example, in the legitimation of political parties. The idea of "loyal opposition" actually placed dissenters on expense account (in Parliament). The earlier practice was to behead officers of state for "disloyalty."

Something analogous to this institutionalization of criticism is to be seen in the doctrine of the separation of powers articulated in the U.S. Constitution, that is, in the separation of powers between the executive, the legislative, and the judiciary branches. Moreover, the Bill of Rights with its guarantee of freedom of speech and assembly (and, by implication, of association)[7] represents an extension of the doctrine of separation of powers. The First Amendment recognizes that these freedoms belong to the citizen. The Ninth Amendment bars any construction of the Constitution which would deny to the people those rights retained by them which are not specifically enumerated in the Constitution.

Here we see, then, a kind of separation of powers between the government and the people, a recognition that the community possesses a broader jurisdiction than the state. (The state is the creature and not the creator of the community.) This constitutionally-sanctioned separation gives autonomy to voluntary associations as well as to volunteers in these associations. Indeed, voluntary associations as an arm of the community have not only the intrinsic right to exist; they may also criticize the government and attempt to affect its policies. The denial of this right is the first mark of totalitarianism.

You can readily see the bearing of the general idea of separation of powers upon the place of research in voluntary associations. Institutionalized self-analysis and re-examination of values and goals within a voluntary association is a function entitled to a special status representing separation of powers.

But how is this power to be exercised? Certainly, a research team could not properly be given the direct power to change the policy or the organizational structure of an association. Our question must be dealt with in other terms. It is to be dealt with in terms of an enterprise of mutual persuasion, especially in light of the fact that the very presence of a research team with its criticisms and proposals is likely to be viewed by the executives and the staff as a kind of threat, and thus to elicit "organizational resistance."

Certain models already exist which aim to promote mutual persuasion between the organization and the research group, in this way mollifying the sense of threat on either side. An example of this model is to be observed in a "team of evaluators" which functions in certain programs of urban renewal. The widely familiar cybernetics model provides a resource here, particularly in the conception of "feedback." Executives of voluntary associations are fully aware of the value of feedback from the constituency and from the general public. They need feedback also from a research group or department. Actually, feedback may operate in several directions. A research group looks for feedback from the executives and the staff and from the constituency. Indeed, a fully functioning "system" is one in which the executives and the staff, the Board of Directors, the constituency, and the research group are brought into the social enterprise of research and criticism, an enterprise that can be therapeutic for all who are actively involved. In some associations (including business corporations) the research group is assigned a teaching function with the understanding that members of the staff have the responsibility to enter into the learning process and thus to gain tools for self-analysis. Some such devices as these are required if the research in self-analysis is to be an integral element in the ongoing life of an association. In the end, however, no significant innovation is possible without leverage from the top executives. With this leverage even change in the life-style of an association is possible.

The discussions held at the seminar indicated that research may not properly be restricted to the methods and concerns of conventional empirical investigation. Adequate self-analysis and self-criticism include within their purview questions regarding philosophy, ethics, and history. (Generally, significant innovation involves depth-reappraisal of the past, even of a far-away past.) They include also questions regarding symbolism and the use of semantic imagination (always in short supply) and questions regarding action-strategies. Conceivably, the cybernetic procedures mentioned here can serve in some measure to cope with the built-in resistance to long-range planning referred to by Dr. Michael. They can also accomplish much to overcome the present "research gap" that obtains between decision-makers in associations and competent practitioners of social research.[8] Indeed, the consultation on Voluntary Associations and Public Policy, with its give-and-take, was a thrust in the direction of overcoming the "gap."

These procedures, you may say, are most readily feasible for large-scale organizations but scarcely for smaller associations. Conceivably, however, the research teams of a number of smaller associations might enter into cooperation with each other. Another resource should be mentioned here, the availability of the Center for a Voluntary Society and also of the Association of Voluntary Action Scholars which plans to publish not only monographs but also a quarterly journal on voluntary associations.

Like Dr. Michael, I have defined the task of self-analysis and self-criticism in very broad terms, indeed in terms that embrace the major concerns of the culture. The breadth of this definition points in a special way to the appropriate status and role of the executive of a voluntary association which deserve at least brief consideration here.

In recent decades the status of the executive in an association has more and more transcended the status of the executive in a commercial enterprise, at least as that status is generally interpreted. By virtue of the multi-dimensional character of his vocation (and of the vocation of associations) the executive in an association has taken on the status of the professional person. To be sure, the definition of the professional has undergone many changes in the past century, and this is not the place to survey those changes. Alfred North Whitehead in *Adventures of Ideas* has asserted that the emergence of the professions represents one of the most significant developments in modern society, a development that has provided a high conception of leadership and responsibility.

It must suffice here if we take into account only two of the major ingredients of the traditional definition, a definition that took shape in the Middle Ages, if not earlier. (1) The professional man was expected to have a humanistic education: He was expected to possess a disciplined familiarity with the cultural creations (of past and present) expressing the characteristic value preferences of the culture, toward the end of assuming leadership in criticizing, transforming, transmitting, and applying these perspectives in changing historical situations. We may compare this formulation to Dr. Michael's emphasis on self-analysis, reexamination of values and goals, and appropriate action-taking. (2) The professional man was expected also to possess a rational theory in terms of which he could exercise and improve his specialized skills. In both of these dimensions reflection and research are indispensable if the skills are to be related effectively and imaginatively to social realities.

166

This definition of course is not exhaustive. Alternative or additional conceptions readily spring to mind. Moreover, in the light of the feeble performance of these functions which one can see today in many quarters (particularly with respect to the first criterion) you may consider these elements of the definition proposed here to be highly idealized. Yet, in the face of the demands set forth in Dr. Michael's paper, we may say that the major premise of this seminar was the assumption that the executive of the kinds of associations represented is expected to meet some such criteria. His work is not simply the task of a foreman; it imposes broad cultural responsibilities as well as specialized organizational demands. It also requires of him that he achieve flexibility and the capacity for daring innovation in the midst of a changing world. Here the study of history and the humanities is imperative.

Permit me to quote from an address of the late Felix Frankfurter, Associate Justice of the United States Supreme Court, in which he stresses the importance of seeking the nourishment of the humanities in the midst of "the hurly-burly of life." "You will have to struggle," he says, "against falling into the slothfulness of not leaving yourself time, as so many lawyers do not, for the pursuit of the larger vistas of your profession."[9]

These cultural concerns are in the mind of the executive every day (and night) as he confronts the darker side of contemporary social reality—the widespread poverty and ignorance and unemployment, the increasing disparity between the haves and the have-nots at home and abroad, the stubborn persistence (and even increase) of racial segregation, the slick manipulation of the technology of communications, the burgeoning varieties of youth culture and of women's liberation, the gap between the rural and the urban population, the waste of human and material resources by the war, the massive loss of the nation's prestige in the world, the pervasive sense of meaninglessness.

To be sure, he can rejoice over the increase of participation in progressive voluntary associations among lower-income and ethnic-minority groups. But this change could not have come about without the assistance of the middle-income groups. Indeed, the decisive problem is that of inspiriting and activating the middle groups who have ampler resources. The civil-rights movement offers a striking example of the indispensable support from the middle classes.

But simultaneous with certain promising changes in participation, we are witnessing the reemergence of forms of repression at the hands of the government and of reactionary voluntary organizations. This repression is implicit in the 1969 legislation regarding private foundations, the impact of which is as yet only dimly seen. Recently a unit of young lawyers in the American Bar Association has reminded us of still more ominous, concerted policies of repression: the increasing role of "government by dossier," the lawlessness of government agencies in the name of law and order, the placement of informers on campuses and in activist organizations, the use of electronic and photographic surveillance—in short, the climate of opinion promoted by the Agnews and the Mitchells.[10] In many ways the government portends to become a major subversive power in the commonwealth.

In the face of these developments, the executive of the voluntary association concerned with democratic public policy is dogged by the non-participation of millions of citizens (inspired by a drive toward privatization of the meaning of life) and by the participation of many citizens, including the "professional" class, in merely self-serving associations and lobbies. The demand for "reevaluation of values and goals" turns out, then, to be something fundamental that goes to the roots of the national life, indeed to the roots of meaningful existence. From the perspective of the executive, it turns out to be a demand for an understanding of the nature of community, for an understanding of the significance of voluntary associations and of the indispensability of a separation of powers. More than that, it is the demand that this understanding shall be in wider commonalty spread through the education or reeducation of the public.

The United States of America has been called "a nation of joiners." Yet, it is rare to find a person, even an activist in voluntary associations, who possesses even a rudimentary philosophy regarding the place, the justification, the legal status, the cultural value, and the authentic role of these associations. Probably one reason for this intellectual vacuum is the prevalence of a nationalism (sometimes only half-consciously adopted) which views the state, its agencies and procedures, as the all-important as well as the unquestioned means of governance. Another reason is the seductiveness of President Nixon's proposal that the voluntary sector, on the grounds of a do-it-yourself philosophy, should leave the government alone, indeed should assume responsibilities that really belong to the government by directly attacking the problems of relieving human misery. Thus the President apparently would impose responsibility only upon private citizens who happen to have a tender conscience. In this situation a proper understanding of voluntary associations would promote the idea that one of their major functions is to get the government to do its job.[11] In this connection, however, one should not overlook the fact that a direct and well-organized criticism of abuses perpetrated by commercial corporations can effect changes in the private sector without the aid of the government, as has been demonstrated by Saul Alinsky and Nader's Raiders. In this whole sphere, as well as in the sphere of government, the need for education is a massive one.

It is a striking fact that in our schools and universities extremely little attention is given to the fundamental functions of the voluntary association. The civics textbooks, the history textbooks, the social studies, the mass media almost entirely ignore consideration of these functions. I have taken courses even in constitutional law in which they were not mentioned. For decades I have had to explain to inquirers, and even to graduate students, what a course on voluntary associations is all about. The need for explicit curriculum materials for secondary as well as for higher education is clearly evident.

We have considered the imperatives that attach to effective self-analysis and to the reexamination of values and goals in the face of changing social realities, the need for the institutionalization of self-criticism in the context of a separation of powers, certain models for institutionalized research, the broad cultural vocation of the voluntary association and its executives in the face of the demand for relevant and effective innovation, the clear and present dangers of repression at the hands of the government, and the dire need for public education respecting the significance of voluntary associations in a democratic society.

What, then, is the fundamental purpose of self-analysis and the reassessment of values and goals in a changing world? Through analogy the answer to this question was suggested by T. S. Eliot several years ago when I asked him how he came to develop his particular style of poetry.

169

In response he said that early in his career he recognized that a public was at hand for poetry in the style of Browning or Tennyson or Whitman. But if he were to speak to his own time and with his own insight, he would have to develop his own style. If he did this, however, he would be writing for a very limited public; therefore, he would have to create a new public that would accept his style. Accordingly, we may say that the fundamental purpose of self-analysis and self-criticism on the part of voluntary associations is to elicit response in a new time, to uncover and release the latent energies ever awaiting the appearance of the innovating word and the innovating strategies. The fundamental purpose is to enable men and women, young and old, black and white and red, to leap into the breach and match the time with improved means and improved ends; in short, to achieve authentic self-identity.

∽

1. For a careful definition and discussion of voluntary associations, see the article of that title by David L. Sills in the *International Encyclopedia of the Social Sciences.* An extensive bibliography is also provided.
2. A detailed account of the phases of "The Development of the Sociology of Voluntary Associations in the United States" is given by L. Sklair in *International Archives of Sociology of Cooperation and Development,* No. 24 (1968), 29-53.
3. "Social Structure and Moral Reform: A Study of the WCTU," *American Journal of Sociology,* LXI, No. 3 (November 1955), 221-232.
4. "Agency in Quest of a Cause," *Social Service Review,* 31 (March 1957), 83; David L. Sills, "Research Toward Policy Formation: A Case Study," *Public Opinion Quarterly,* 22 (Summer 1958), 170-171. See also D. L. Sills, *The Volunteers* (Glencoe, Ill.: The Free Press, 1957).
5. *Bureaucracy in Modern Society* (New York: Random House, 1956).
6. *Church, State and Education* (Ann Arbor Paperbacks, The University of Michigan Press, 1957), 84. Originally published in 1930.
7. Robert A. Horn, *Groups and the Constitution* (Stanford University Press, 1956). An outstanding study.
8. Francis X. Gannon, "Bridging the Research Gap: Cara, Response to Vatican II," *Review of Religious Research,* IX, No. 1 (Fall 1967), 3-10.
9. From "A Lawyer's Dicta on Doctors," the George W. Gay Lecture upon Medical Ethics, printed in *Harvard Medical Alumni Bulletin* (July 1958).
10. The most recent, striking evidence of resort to the hardware of repression comes from the U. S. Congress. The House Internal Security Committee has just been granted $570,000 for the coming fiscal year, the largest budget ever afforded the Committee. Representative Robert F. Drinan of Massachusetts, a member of the House Internal Security Committee who voted against the appropriation and argued that all funds should be cut off, has said that the panel maintains 754,000 card reference files on individuals and groups. Simultaneously, the Senate has approved an appropriation of $450,000 for its Committee, the amount requested by the President.
11. See "Voluntarism and the 'American Way'" by George W. Pickering, *The Journal,* Vol. 9, No. 1 (July-August 1970), 4-9.

The Voluntary Principle in the Forming
of American Religion

JAMES LUTHER ADAMS

THE DEFINITION OF VOLUNTARYISM

Several years ago at the annual meeting in Boston of the American Philosophical Association three philosophers from Russia were guest lecturers on the program. One afternoon during the conference I joined several other Americans for a closeted discussion with these Russian philosophers. Inevitably, questions regarding freedom of speech in Soviet Russia and in the United States were introduced into the discussion. The guest philosophers were quick to assert that in Russia today the citizen is allowed this freedom. Accordingly, they claimed that Soviet Russia is fundamentally democratic. At this juncture one of the Americans responded that freedom of speech is scarcely sufficient to meet the criteria of democracy, that the crucial question is whether there is freedom of association, the freedom of citizens to organize a group to promote an idea or a cause and particularly to promote a cause that may be in conflict with the policies of the establishment, in short, the freedom to organize dissent. The interpreters, however, were unable successfully to communicate this question to the guests, even though they made a persistent attempt. The Russians insisted that they could not see the significance of this question about freedom of association.

After the discussion came to an end and when we Americans were out in the corridor, a British Marxist philosopher who had served as one of the interpreters assured us that the guests from Russia simply could not afford to understand the question. Actually, the Russians might well have pointed to certain limited forms of freedom of association which obtain today in Russia. On the other hand, they could have pointed to the infringements upon freedom of association in the United States which were characteristic of the Joseph McCarthy period, and today they could point to the recent report that about three-fourths of the 1,136 people interviewed under the auspices of the Columbia Broadcasting System said that "extremist" groups should not be permitted to organize demonstrations against government policy, even if there appeared to be no clear danger of violence. In the midst of a war in which over forty thousand Americans have been killed, the government, according to this view, may draft men into a war they oppose, yet these men should not be permitted to exercise their First Amendment right to demonstrate nonviolently against such action. Here we see the disposition on the part of many Americans to limit severely the freedom of association. At the same time those Americans no doubt would claim that the United States is "the land of the free."

Why do we in entering upon a discussion of voluntaryism introduce this issue regarding freedom of association? Precisely because it impinges in a crucial way upon the definition of the term *voluntaryism*. One frequently encounters the definition of "the voluntary principle" as simply the freedom of the individual— for example, freedom of belief or of speech or of self-determination. At other times voluntaryism is defined as the rule of persuasion instead of coercion. These features, to be sure, belong to voluntaryism, but definitions of this sort fall short of grasping its essential social meaning, for they center attention too much upon the individual as an isolated entity; thus they fail to take explicitly into account the institutional ingredient, namely, the freedom to form, or to belong to, voluntary associations that can bring about innovation or criticism in the society. Voluntaryism in this institutional sense distinguishes the democratic society from any other.

Yet, as we have observed, it is by no means exempt from attack in our society. The reason is that freedom of association, viewed as a social function in the open society, represents a dynamic institutional force for social change or for resistance to it. As such, the voluntary association brings about differentiation in the community, a separation of powers.

Voluntaryism, then, involves more than an attitude in favor of freedom of choice. Many people entertain *attitudes* in favor of freedom, but socially effective freedom requires participation in associations that define or redefine freedom and that attempt to articulate or implement that freedom in a specific social milieu. Voluntaryism is an associational, institutional concept. It refers to a principal way in which the individual through association with others "gets a piece of the action." In its actual articulation it involves an exercise of power through organization. It is the means whereby the individual participates in the process of making social decisions. This process, particularly when it affects public policy, requires struggle, for in some fashion it generally entails a reshaping, and perhaps even a redistribution, of power. This means that it demands a special commitment and expenditure of directed energy in the institutional context of the society.

All of these features—the institutional articulation, the strong commitment, the expenditure of energy, the redistribution of power, the separation of powers—are to be seen in the social phenomena that belong under the rubric of voluntaryism in the modern period. These phenomena include the separation of church and state, the creation of the voluntary church, the invention of other voluntary associations for social reform or for the revitalization of the church, the missionary movement, the antislavery movement, the woman-suffrage movement, the emergence of the denomination as a new form of the church, the ecumenical movement, the demand for the welfare state and then for its reform, the civil rights movement, the struggle of the blacks for a "piece of the action," and hundreds of other group formations—

including groups to oppose such movements. The "table of contents" of the history of voluntaryism and its associations would
itself require a large volume, for the number of associations is
legion.

Obviously, the institutional dimensions of existence do not exhaust the human condition. The individual is by no means enclosed in the institutional associations. Forms of privacy remain
and play an indispensable role. In this realm of privacy the individual's inner life takes shape, as well as the intimate interpersonal relations of his daily existence. There are three dimensions
in this realm of privacy: the individual's relation to the creative
and redemptive forces available, his relation to himself (his inner
dialogue); and his immediate relations to other persons. So understood, however, the realm of privacy cannot properly be separated from the institutional associations of which we have spoken.
The inwardness and integrity of privacy affect, and are affected
by, the institutional associations.

The family is of course the most important of these associations,
particularly by reason of the nurture received by the child in in-
fancy and childhood and also by reason of the normally stabilizing
power of the family throughout life. It is therefore impossible to
separate privacy from life in the family and in the primary groups
of friendship and neighborhood. But the inwardness and integrity
of the individual impinge also upon the other associations, that is,
upon the political order and upon the various voluntary associations, including the church. Moreover, one's conception of privacy
will itself be affected by these associations in the society. From
participation in these associations the individual learns to assess
the significance of the inner life, and from this participation he
also comes to define the forms of privacy which give depth and
richness of quality to all of life. Of equal significance is the fact
that the formal associations depend for their health and integrity
upon the inwardness and independence of individual existence, in
short, upon that dynamic substance of the self which transcends
all associations. On the other hand, if privacy is itself to achieve
order and openness and creative integrity, it requires the disciplines
of the inner life which may be defined and nurtured by associa-

tions that exist for this purpose. This whole dimension of existence is presupposed by the formal associations of the political and social order. We say that it is presupposed, for only from the subsoil of privacy do the deeper motivations of human existence emerge, and from this subsoil the formal associations receive much of their vitalizing, integrating energy.

THE HISTORICAL ORIGINS OF VOLUNTARYISM

Voluntaryism did not come into history, ancient, medieval, or modern, without dust and heat. We cannot here trace this thrust into the dark backward and abysm of time. But we should observe that in the history of Christianity the first expression of voluntaryism appears in the primitive church, a voluntary association. In referring to the voluntaryism of the primitive church, however, we should not overlook the fact that the concept of voluntary association is not wholly adequate, for the Christian viewed the church in its origin and development as the work of divine grace, and thus its ultimate orientation was transcendent. Yet on the human side the church was a voluntary association. The church appealed to the individual for a voluntary decision to join the movement. It rejected civic religion, the rule of Caesar and of territoriality in the sphere of religious commitment and faith; it transcended the ethnic bonds of traditional Judaism; it gave to the individual certain responsibilities in the new organization; it was open to people of all classes and races; it gave new status to the common man, to the slave, and to women; and it soon developed forms of responsibility with respect to charity and philanthropy; it even formed credit unions. But the institutional aspects of the early church included also other features. In order to become viable this primitive church had to develop new skills of communication and of organization. Primitive Christianity, then, did not only promote new attitudes; nor is it to be understood merely in terms of its message, its kerygma. It gave institutional incarnation to a new covenant, a new commitment, a new community. Indeed, in order to continue to exist it formed an institution that could bear its message to the world—an institution that in important respects adumbrated or illustrated the meaning of

175

the message in its social consequences. Here we see one of the great innovations in the history of the West. More than that, the ethos and organization of the early church again and again served as a stimulus or model for new forms of voluntaryism.

In modern history the first crucial affirmation of voluntaryism as an institutional phenomenon appeared in the demand of the sects for the separation of church and state. In England, for example, and then later in America, the intention was to do away with direct state control of the church and also to remove official ecclesiastical influence from the political realm—toward the end of creating a voluntary church. In the voluntary church, religious faith as well as membership was to be a matter of individual choice. The individual was no longer automatically to become a member of the church simply by reason of his being born in the territory. Moreover, he could choose not to be a member of a church. Nor was rejection of the established confession any longer to be considered a political offense or to deprive the unbeliever of the civil franchise. In rejecting state control, the church (and the theological seminary) were no longer to be supported by taxation. The objection to taxation in support of the church was twofold: tax support, it was held, not only gave the state some right of control; it also represented a way of coercing the nonmember or the unbeliever to give financial support to the church. Freedom of choice for the individual brought with it another freedom, namely, the freedom to participate in the shaping of the policies of the church group of his choice. The rationale for this voluntaryism was worked out theologically by the sectarians of the sixteenth and seventeenth centuries, and more in terms of social and political theory by John Locke in the next century.

From the point of view of a theory of associations, the demand for the separation of church and state and the emergence of the voluntary church represent the end of an old era and the beginning of a new one. The earlier era had been dominated by the ideal of "Christendom," a unified structure of society in a church-state. In the new era the voluntary church, the free church, no longer supported by taxation, was to be self-sustaining; and it was to manage its own affairs. In the earlier era, kinship, caste, and restricted community groups had determined most of the interests and the forms of participation. In the new era these interests became segregated. In this respect the freedom of choice was increased. The divorce of church and state and the advent of freedom of religious association illustrate this type of increase in freedom of choice.

In accord with this new conception of religious freedom and responsibility one must view the collection plate in the church service on Sunday as a symbol of the meaning of disestablishment and of voluntaryism. The collection plate symbolizes—indeed it in part also actualizes and institutionalizes—the view that the church as a corporate body is a self-determinative group and that in giving financial support to the church the members affirm responsibility to participate in the shaping of the policies of the church. Thus the voluntary principle amounts to the principle of consent. One must add, however, that although the struggle for voluntaryism on a large scale in the church began over two hundred and fifty years ago, it was not achieved generally and officially in the United States until the nineteenth century—that is, apart from the colonies that from the beginning had had no establishment.

The thrust toward the separation of church and state could succeed only by carrying through a severe struggle for freedom of association. Initially, the authorities who opposed it asserted that the health of society was threatened by the voluntary principle. They held that uniformity of belief was a prerequisite of a viable social order. As a separation of powers, voluntaryism was viewed as a wedge for chaos. In order to defend the unrestricted sovereignty of the commonwealth, Thomas Hobbes published in 1651 *Leviathan,* the most cogent attack of the times upon the voluntary principle. In his view the church should be only an arm of the sovereign.[1] Indeed, no association of any sort was to exist apart

---

1. See "Hobbes's Theory of Associations in the Seventeenth-Century Milieu," by D. B. Robertson, in the volume edited by him, *Voluntary Associations* (Richmond: John Knox Press, 1966).

from state control. Therefore he spoke of voluntary associations, religious or secular, as "worms in the entrails of the natural man" (the integrated social whole). Analogous attacks upon the voluntary church came also from conservatives in the American colonies where establishment prevailed.

Hobbes recognized that freedom of religious association would bring in its train the demand for other freedoms of association. His fears were fully justified. Indeed, with the emergence of this multiple conception of freedom of association a new conception of society came to birth—that of the pluralistic, the multigroup, society.

THE THEORY OF ASSOCIATIONS

The pluralistic conception of society entails a modern view of the relations between the community and the state and other associations.[2] According to this view, the institutional system is made up of a complex of involuntary and voluntary associations. The state and the family are involuntary in the sense that one cannot choose whether or not he will belong to a state or to a family; nor can he ordinarily choose his state or his family. Other associations are voluntary in the sense that one may choose to belong or not to belong. Of central significance for voluntaryism within the context of these associations is the claim that the community at large is the embracing association within which the other associations live. The state is one of these associations. It is the creature and the servant of the community, not its creator. The state therefore is not omnipotent or omnicompetent. Between the individual and the involuntary associations of state and family stand the voluntary associations that provide forms of freedom which transcend both the family and the state and which may also exercise some influence upon both of these institutions. The plural-

2. A more elaborate, and more subtle, conceptual framework than the one chosen here would enable one to identify aspects of society which our scheme does not directly delineate. For example, the differentiation between communal and associational types of group, drawn from Ferdinand Tönnies, has been widely used, as in Gerhard Lenski, *The Religious Factor* (Garden City: Doubleday & Co., 1961). Each of these frameworks has its characteristic advantages and disadvantages.

ist society, then, is not a mere aggregate of individuals. It is a
group of groups that in turn are made up of individuals.

The individual is not viewed here as wholly comprehended in
the community or the state or the family or the other associations.
He possesses an integrity and freedom of his own. Luther hints
at this idea of privacy when he says that everyone must do his
own believing. For him and for other Protestants the individual
has direct access to the divine in and through and beyond all institutions and all human mediators. Yet in the developed theory
and practice of pluralism the individual's freedom is articulated
in the choices he confronts or contrives in the context of these
associations. The dependence of the individual upon these intermediary associations for freedom is succinctly stated by the
British historian J. N. Figgis: "More and more is it clear that the
mere individual's freedom against an omnipotent state may be no
better than slavery; more and more is it evident that the real
question of freedom in our day is the freedom of smaller unions
to live within the whole." [3] In this view of man and his associations, we have the rudiments of a doctrine of man and also the
framework for a philosophy of history. Man is an associational
being, and his history is the history of his associations. The history
of any open society is the history of the changing character of the
associations, and of the changing relations between the individual
and the associations, and of the changing relations between the
various associations.

In the light of this conception of man and history we may see
the historical significance of the advent of voluntaryism wherever
it appears, and especially its significance for the formation and
the expression of the religious mentality. These features became
evident in the colonies of the New World.

VOLUNTARYISM IN THE NEW WORLD

In its initial stages the development of voluntaryism in the
New World varied considerably in the different colonies, though

3. J. N. Figgis, *Churches and the Modern State*, 2d ed. (New York:
Longmans, Green & Co. 1914), p. 52.

in the course of time essentially the same dominant tendencies appeared. These tendencies exhibited voluntaryism as the burgeoning characteristic feature of the religious mentality in this part of the world.

In New England and the South the old conception of establishment had been transported from England. The colonists in the middle region, on the other hand, were committed to disestablishment. Here as well as in New England variants on covenant theory played a large role. Given the absence of any establishment in the middle colonies, the churches there could affirm and implement their voluntaryism without any significant struggle with proponents of establishment, and therefore without the necessity for compromise with establishment. From the start, then, these were voluntary, "gathered" churches; so it was unnecessary for them to carry on a struggle for freedom of association. That struggle had been ended by their leaving the Old World. So strong was the spirit of independence that for well over a century these churches held out against any strong centralized organization. This spirit of independence appeared also in the colonies where an establishment prevailed. Indeed, long before disestablishment was officially legitimated, the laity had asserted itself in the management of the congregation. Moreover, by reason of geographical factors local autonomy was practically unavoidable. Here voluntaryism and localism worked hand in hand.

But in all of the colonies a deterioration of energy—we might call it the law of entropy—served to alter the development of voluntaryism. Whereas there was a great release of energy in religious circles in early days, this energy became less readily available as the temperature of commitment diminished. Through adoption of the halfway covenant, for example, the New England churches recognized a changing identity in the succession of the generations. With the increasing number of the unchurched in all of the colonies, the problem of maintaining church commitment became all the more acute. This commitment could not be automatically transmitted from generation to generation. What initially had been a voluntary self-sustaining church gradually became a church seeking to elicit commitment and voluntary support. A new voluntaryism had to be promoted. Faced with this change, the churches in all regions found it necessary to employ the techniques of persuasion "in order to win support and gain recruits by voluntary means." [4] The Great Awakening and the subsequent revivals are to be understood in part in these terms. The law of entropy could be countered only by the attempt to activate the voluntary principle in new ways.

This attempt involved the adoption of new means and forms of communication—the itinerant preacher, the psychic excitement of revivals, the dissemination of tracts, the distribution of Bibles, and even a new rhetoric. In this effort the churches, themselves voluntary associations, began at the end of the eighteenth century to form new, specialized voluntary organizations as instrumentalities to carry out the task of persuasion. Some of these new associations were supported by several denominations in cooperation. This sort of cooperation became even more widespread in the nineteenth century. A full roster of voluntary associations founded before the end of the first quarter of the century would be long. We name only a few of them: The Missionary Society of Connecticut (1798), the Massachusetts Missionary Society (1779), the New Hampshire Missionary Society (1801), the Massachusetts Baptist Domestic Missionary Society (1802), the American Board of Commissioners of Foreign Missions (1810), the American Bible Society (1816), The American Sunday School Union (1824), the American Tract Society (1825), the American Home Mission Society (1826), and so on. By the 1830s many of these "benevolent societies" met every May in New York so that the interlocking directorates could be in ready communication with each other.

The formation of some of these missionary associations brought about severe conflict when they were autonomous and sought to raise funds outside the denominational organizations, thus avoiding accountability to these organizations. In this connection Elwyn

4. Winthrop S. Hudson. *Religion in America* (New York: Charles Scribner's Sons, 1965), pp. 16, 105.

Smith has shown that the willingness of the church groups to enter into cooperation in the formation of intergroup associations may be taken as a sign of the emergence of a new church form. The sect became a denomination, a type of association that combined "the separative and the unitive spirit of American Christianity" and which became "the fundamental church structure of the country." [5]

It should be noted here that this proliferation of associations not only provided a means for concentration upon special purposes; it also offered new definitions of vocation and even of self-identity; accordingly, it gave occasion for the release of new energies in new directions of voluntaryism.

A new stage of development is marked by the rise of non-ecclesiastical associations concerned with specific problems, social and political. In the eighteenth century these associations began to appear with variety of purpose. In the developing frontier all sorts of land development companies were formed. Later, the mounting opposition to British colonial policies gave rise to a multitude of associations both local and interprovincial. In the 1740s the Masonic Order appeared on the stage—though, to be sure, encountering continuous opposition. For a time Benjamin Franklin served as provincial grand master of the Masons. He also formed or belonged to several international societies concerned with learning and with politics. Not without knowledge of Cotton Mather's earlier proposals for the formation of associations "to do good," Franklin showed himself to be one of the major initiators of local and national voluntary organizations concerned with educational, philanthropic, and civic purposes. He also instituted the American Philosophical Society, America's oldest learned society.

After the Revolution, freewheeling political activities issued in local associations concerned with opposing views on public policy. For example, associations disseminating pro-French propaganda elicited countervailing associations. So vigorous were these associations and so intense were the disagreements that President

5. Elwyn Smith, "The Forming of a Modern American Denomination," *Church History* 31 (1962):97.

Washington in his Farewell Address warned against "all combinations and associations, under whatever plausible character, with the real design to direct, control, counteract, or awe the regular deliberation and action of the constituted authorities." This formulation approximates the kind of statement that had become familiar in the opposition to freedom of religious association. It is perhaps significant that although the First Amendment to the Constitution protects freedom of speech and assembly and rules out the establishment of religion, it makes no explicit mention of freedom of association. Nevertheless, by the end of the first quarter of the nineteenth century the country was alive with associations, religious, quasi-religious, and secular.[6] During the nineteenth century thousands of these associations were formed. Already in the 1830s religious periodicals were saying that the benevolent societies had grown beyond the most sanguine expectations of their founders; the revenues were "such as kings might envy; together they formed a benevolent empire," "a gigantic religious power . . . systematized, compact in its organization, with a polity and a government entirely its own, and independent of all control." [7] Yet most of the societies here referred to were less than ten years old.

THREE AMERICAN PROTESTANT THEORIES OF ASSOCIATION

Starting early in the nineteenth century, a Protestant literature on "the principle of association" began to appear. Testimony regarding the ways in which this voluntaryism was giving shape to American religion in its moral and social outreach is found in the writings of three of the principal theorists, Lyman Beecher, Francis Wayland, and William Ellery Channing—a Presbyterian, a Baptist, and a Unitarian—men who differed from each other as much in theology as they agreed with each other on the significance of associations.

6. A classical, compact study of this development appears in Arthur M. Schlesinger, Sr., "Biography of a Nation of Joiners," in *Paths to the Present* (New York: Macmillan Co., 1949).
7. These quotations are cited from religious journals of the 1830s. See G. H. Barnes, *The Antislavery Impulse 1830-1844* (Gloucester, Mass.: Peter Smith, 1957), p. 17.

Continuing an interest acquired in 1797 as a student under the influence of a religious revival at Yale, Beecher preached in favor of the formation of societies for the suppression of vice and "the promotion of morality." He viewed these societies as watchdogs and aides in support of the magistrates' efforts to enforce the laws. The vices mentioned for correction were swearing, drinking, gambling, playing cards, and dueling. Moreover, the laws of several of the states prohibited blasphemy, atheism, Sabbath breaking, and other gross violations of general Christian morality. The societies were to "constitute a sort of disciplined moral militia, prepared to act upon every emergency and repel every encroachment upon the liberties and morals of the state." [8] They were also to promote the careful selection of law enforcers and to lend them "support requisite to the full discharge of their official trust." [9] These efforts were calculated also to "prepare the way for the acceptance of such offices by men who will be faithful." [10] The branch societies were to scrutinize the character of schoolteachers and tavern keepers; they could also encourage boycotts of businesses run by those who violated the moral law as set forth in the Bible. In these efforts the clergy and the laity were to cooperate.

The rationale for the formation of voluntary societies Beecher coupled with a defense of the establishment (in Connecticut). Soon after disestablishment in 1818, he came to approve the fact that it "cut the churches loose from dependence on state support. It threw them wholly on their own resources and on God." [11] In 1826 he preached a sermon to praise the effectiveness of voluntary associations. "Now we are blessed," he says, "with societies to aid in the support of the Gospel at home, to extend it to the

8. Lyman Beecher, "Sermons, Delivered on Various Occasions," in *Works*, 3 vols. (Boston: John P. Jewett & Co., 1852), 2:94.
9. Lyman Beecher, *Address of the Connecticut Society for the Promotion of Good Morals to the Respective Branch Societies* (New Haven: no publisher named, 1814), p. 4.
10. Ibid.
11. Lyman Beecher, *The Autobiography of Lyman Beecher*, ed. Barbara M. Cross, 2 vols. (Cambridge, Mass.: Harvard University Press, Belknap Press, 1961), 1:253.

new settlements, and through the earth." [12] In these societies, he pointed out, the evangelicals of different types could unite in opposing rationalism and "infidelity." In association he saw strength. During his six-year pastorate in Boston, Beecher extended the range of purposes for associations by organizing or sponsoring at least a dozen societies, ranging in character and purpose from the Boston Lyceum to the Franklin Debating Society to the Young Men's Temperance Society to the Young Men's Christian Association. He supported the antislavery societies, and at the same time belonged to the American Colonization Society.

Beecher went beyond the confines of the parish and also beyond the boundaries of the "denominations," toward the end of promoting societies concerned with public policies as well as with private morals. This was, in effect, an extension of the voluntary principle to the sphere of public affairs. One can see in Beecher, however, a strong element of elitism, or what Sidney Mead has called paternalism. [13] A Federalist, he intended his voluntaryism mainly for the middle-class protectors of private and public morals rather than for underlings or "delinquents"—these were supposed to be under scrutiny and guidance. Indeed, he injected a vigorous spirit of intolerance into his crusading efforts. Beecher's attack on the Roman Catholics was probably a contributing cause for the burning of the Ursuline convent in Charleston, Massachusetts. Moreover, he apparently did not conceive of a voluntary association that could legitimately promote a cause fundamentally incompatible with his conception of Christian private or public morals. In any case, he was the head and fount of associational theory in American church life, though he did not work out a systematic theory regarding the relations between the voluntary and the involuntary associations.

The Reverend Francis Wayland (1796–1865), at one time president of Brown University, wrote extensively on associations both voluntary and involuntary. He was the author of *The Ele-*

12. Lyman Beecher, "Lectures on Political Atheism and Kindred Subjects, Together with Six Lectures on Temperance," in *Works*, 1:325.
13. Sidney E. Mead, *The Lively Experiment: The Shaping of Christianity in America* (New York: Harper & Row, 1963), pp. 97–98.

ments of Political Economy (1837), a popularization of Adam Smith's views and one of the most widely used textbooks of the period. As a Baptist, Wayland was a promoter of radically congregational polity. He opposed every kind of denominational centralization. He rejected also every attempt of the congregation to coerce the believer or the unbeliever, including any attempt of the congregation directly to regulate the behavior of members; the congregation was simply to "withdraw" from the recalcitrant deviant.

Unlike Beecher, Wayland attempted to work out a theory of associations which would relate the Christian to universal mental and moral "sensitivity" and also to natural religion. In the spirit of Bishop Joseph Butler he adopted an antiutilitarian system of conscience and duty. Natural religion and conscience, properly understood, together with Baptist voluntaryism, were viewed as conducive to the establishment of a coercion-free society. Mutual edification and education rather than compulsion, he surmised, would one day direct men's affairs. He viewed teaching as the counterpart of the church's preaching.

Wayland assigned to voluntary associations a crucial role, conceiving of them in contractual terms. The association was an instrumentality of conscience based upon contract. Just as commitment to Jesus Christ was the basis of the Christian voluntary church, and just as the autonomy of the individual believer must be protected there, so the voluntary association was a contractual arrangement, and the autonomous individual might not properly be coerced into any obligations he had not assumed freely upon entering the association. Since conscience was the basis of social order and also of authentic associations, the voluntary association was to serve to enhance individual conscience and responsibility. "Autonomy" was Wayland's watchword. Therefore voluntary associations of great size were to be viewed with skepticism and caution. They threatened always to pervert individual conscience and to dislocate responsibility.[14]

14. Francis Wayland, *The Limitations of Human Responsibility* (Boston: Gould, Kendall & Lincoln, 1838), pp. 103 ff. I am indebted for most of the citations here to a paper by Ronald M. Green on "The Social Philosophy of Francis Wayland," presented in a course at Harvard Divinity School on voluntary associations.

In the guidelines that Wayland set up for associations one can see the rudiments of a philosophy of voluntaryism which gives central place to the principle of consent. The purpose of an association and the manner of pursuing it should be clear, and they should be agreed to by all members. Moreover, they "should be perfectly and entirely innocent; that is, they must be such as are incapable of violating the rights of any human being." [15] Accordingly, he opposed abolition societies that demanded forced emancipation. He held that in face of the slaveholders the conscience-bound citizen should set an example "of the most delicate regard to their rights." Anyone "whose first act is an act of injustice" violates the dominion of right.[16]

In practice, however, the dominion of right would at times be egregiously violated not only by voluntary associations but also by "the civil society." In this situation neither passive obedience to the state nor resistance to it by force was ethically justifiable. Here the conscientious citizen might find the only recourse to be "suffering in the cause of right." Wayland's view of "righteous suffering" approximates what we today call civil disobedience; it presents, he said, "the best prospect of ultimate correction of abuse by appealing to the reason and conscience of men . . . , a more fit tribunal to which to refer moral questions than the tribunal of force." [17]

It is worth noting that whereas Beecher's theory of associations was engendered initially in the milieu and spirit of an established church and of a firm authoritarianism, Wayland's conception derived primarily from his Baptist ecclesiology and from a sectarian heritage that had suffered from persecution at the hands of the establishment. Another contrast with Beecher is to be observed in Wayland's search for a universal religious-ethical basis, a sort of doctrine of natural law, in terms of which the Christian might cooperate with the unchurched. Most noticeable, however, is Way-

---

15. Ibid., p. 109.
16. Ibid., p. 182.
17. Francis Wayland, *The Elements of Moral Science*, ed. Joseph Blau (Cambridge, Mass.: Harvard University Press, Belknap Press, 1963), p. 337. For a discussion of the significance of the voluntary association in contemporary civil disobedience, see James L. Adams, "Civil Disobedience: Its Occasions and Limits," in *Political and Legal Obligation*, eds. J. Roland Pennock and John W. Chapman (New York: Atherton Press, 1970).

land's intention to develop with complete consistency the ramifications of the voluntary principle, the principles of persuasion
and consent, not only giving special emphasis to the methods appropriate in associations but also stressing the rights and sensitivities of others in face of voluntary associations bent on persuasion.
Nothing of Beecher's paternalism is to be found here. Fearful of
the dangers of the crusading mentality, Wayland would have sym-
pathized with the aphorism that was current in England during
the period of the Restoration: "Nothing is more dangerous than
a Presbyterian just off his knees." On the other hand, with his
irenic temper he would scarcely have understood Nietzsche's
claim that some things must be loved for more than they are
worth if they are to make an impact on history. Moreover, with
his stress on autonomy, he seems to have been little aware that
autonomy is often the cloak for a hidden heteronomy. Such are
the dilemmas of voluntaryism in an imperfect world.

William Ellery Channing's "Remarks on Associations" (1830)
is the first systematic essay in American literature on voluntary
associations. For this reason it is surprising that more attention
has not been given to this treatise. By reason of his stress on freedom and autonomy, Channing stands much nearer to Wayland
than to Beecher. Likewise, he recognizes the threats to autonomy
provided by associations. Channing's essay reads very much like
a document written today. He is aware of the relation between
voluntary association and the modern technology of transportation, communications, and coalition. He even speaks of "the principle of association" as "a mighty engine."[18] "An impulse may be
given in a month to the whole country, whole states may be
deluged with tracts and other publications, and a voice like that of
many waters, be called forth from immense and widely separated
multitudes."

This essay is replete with psychological as well as sociological,
ethical, theological, and political observations and analyses. Recognizing that man is an associational being, Channing takes a view

18. William Ellery Channing, *The Works of William E. Channing* (Boston:
James Munroe & Co., 1848), 1:233.

quite different from that held, for example, by sociologist Ferdinand Tönnies, who a generation later in Germany wrote that voluntary associations represent a force of depersonalization in modern society issuing from rationalism and contractualism. "Men not only accumulate power by union, but gain warmth and earnestness. The heart is kindled," says Channing. Moreover, he sees the principle of association as a great releaser of energy. "By the feeling and interest which it arouses" union "becomes a creative principle, calls forth new forces, and gives the mind a consciousness of powers, which would otherwise have been unknown." [19]

Channing does not overestimate the significance and value of voluntary associations. He gives priority to what we have called the involuntary associations and to what he calls "those associations formed by our Creator, which spring from our very constitution, and are inseparable from our being." These associations are "the connections of family, of neighborhood, of country, and the great bond of humanity, uniting us with our whole kind." He clearly distinguishes these associations from "those of which we are now treating, which man invents for particular times and exigencies"—"missionary societies, peace societies, or charitable societies, which men have contrived."[20] He then proceeds to "illustrate the inferiority of human associations," by contrasting the pervasive and perduring benefits of the family "among the masses of men" with the limited number of people served by "asylums for children." Since he places the churches among the associations created by God he does not consider them under the rubric of the voluntary association (though he does of course favor the ecclesiology of the voluntary church—considered as established by God through Christ); and he contrasts the church with missionary societies, whose work he does not aim to discourage. The latter are not to be preferred to the church with its concern for "the common daily duties of Christians in their families, neighborhoods, and business." He notes that "the surest way of spreading Christianity is to improve Christian communities; and accordingly, he who

19. Ibid., pp. 283–84.
20. Ibid., p. 297.

frees this religion from corruption, and makes it a powerful instrument of virtue where it is already professed, is the most effectual contributor to the great work of its diffusion through the world." [21]

In the midst of the Great Awakening Jonathan Edwards wrote his *Treatise on the Religious Affections*. In an age when voluntary associations have become "a mighty engine," Channing presents in his "Remarks on Associations" a treatise on associations. Whereas Edwards deals only with individual behavior, Channing, with a moral social concern, deals also with institutional behavior. In his treatise he aims to suggest "a principle by which the claims of different associations may be estimated." In doing so, however, he gives primary status to the individual. In his explication of a criterion for the voluntary principle one finds a formulation of the essential intention of voluntaryism which Wayland could readily have approved. He states his major premise succinctly:

> The value of associations is to be measured by the energy, the freedom, the activity, the moral power, which they encourage and diffuse. In truth, the great object of all benevolence is to give power, activity, and freedom to others. We cannot, in the strict sense of the world, *make* any being happy. We can give others the *means* of happiness, together with motives to the faithful use of them; but on this faithfulness, on the free and full exercise of their own powers, their happiness depends. There is thus a fixed, impassible limit to human benevolence. It can only make men happy through themselves, through their own freedom, and energy. We go further. We believe that God has set the same limit to his own benevolence.[22]

The rest of Channing's essay is dedicated to the task of applying this criterion by examining typical associations in order to show that "associations which in any degree impair or repress the free and full action of men's powers, are thus far hurtful." He then

21. Ibid., pp. 298–302.
22. Ibid., pp. 302–3. Whereas motivations in the associational theories of Beecher and Wayland are related primarily to Congregationalist ecclesiology, we see in Channing's outlook motifs drawn in part from the Enlightenment and in part from Romanticism. For a systematic discussion of analogous changes in milieu and motif in the history of philanthropy from the colonial period to the present, see William G. McLoughlin, "Changing Patterns of Protestant Philanthropy, 1607–1969," in *The Religious Situation, 1969*, ed. Donald R. Cutler (Boston: Beacon Press, 1969).

proceeds to illustrate the ways in which certain associations repress human energy, stultify the intellect, pervert the moral powers, disseminate false information, and inflame public opinion to irrational and instinctual attitudes and behavior. Channing's warning that spurious voluntary associations will only create or entrench a sense of dependency is strikingly similar to current criticisms of undemocratically organized associations and also of the social agencies of the welfare state.

One of the principal ways in which voluntary associations "injure the free action of individuals and society" is through the accumulation of power in a few hands. There are two principal ways in which this centralization of power perverts human energies. First, voluntary associations may exercise inordinate influence on the public mind in the direction of encroaching on freedom of thought, of speech, and of the press. By artful manipulation "as cruel a persecution may be carried on in a free country as in a despotism . . . as if an inquisition were open before us." He does not spare the tract societies.

> Now, by means of Tract societies, spread over a whole community, and acting under a central body, a few individuals, perhaps not more than twenty, may determine the chief reading for a great part of the children of the community, and for a majority of the adults, and may deluge our country with worthless sectarian writings, fitted only to pervert its taste, degrade its intellect, and madden it with intolerance.[23]

Channing devotes pages to illustrating the ways in which associations can function to promote in the public at large "a servile, tame, dependent spirit" or can through internal oligarchic control exercise tyranny over the members of the association. Voluntary associations may disseminate narrow sectarianism, half-baked ideas, petty legalism, prying encroachments upon private life, and blatant chauvinism. It should be added here that Channing recurrently appeals to the example of Jesus, "that brightest manifestation of God," in order to emphasize the decisive significance of moral independence and integrity of motive for "resisting and

23. Ibid., p. 305.

191

overcoming the world." He also avers that "in no department of life has the social principle been perverted more into an instrument of intellectual thraldom, than in religion." [24]

At the same time, Channing views participation in voluntary associations as an indispensable means of exercising moral and citizenship responsibilities. He vindicates this claim by his own participation and by his voluminous writings on public issues. At least five highly significant associations were formed in his living room, including the Massachusetts Peace Society. Indeed, he ends his essay rather abruptly, saying that he had intended to "add some remarks on some other associations, particularly on the Peace Society." He then says of the "spirit of association": "We have done what we could to secure this powerful instrument against perversion." In setting forth the criteria of authentic association— or, we may say, of voluntaryism—his major presupposition, we have seen, is that "our connection with society, as it is our greatest aid, so it is our greatest peril." [25]

STRENGTHS AND WEAKNESSES OF VOLUNTARISM

If we now take a bird's-eye view of the development we have traced, we must speak of it as an organizational revolution. As such it represents the creation of space in modern society for associations, loyalties, and activities the like of which have not appeared anywhere to the same extent in previous history. These voluntary associations are significant not only in themselves but also by virtue of their influence on each other and upon the involuntary associations—for good or for ill. In the context of the present essay, however, their principal significance is their import for the shaping of American religion. As Channing suggests, the

24. Ibid., p. 295.
25. Ibid., p. 291. We have devoted these pages to the exposition of the ideas of Beecher, Wayland, and Channing, not only because one encounters in current literature only summary statements of their views, but also because their formulations provide *loci classici* of the voluntary principle. A more complete account, to be sure, would include an analysis of secular writings of the period which, like *The Federalist Papers,* set forth the dangers and values of voluntary associations. Especially instructive in these papers is the argument that pluralistic democracy would be seriously threatened if all the churches together were able to achieve one compact organization.

voluntary principle is "a creative principle." It functions as a creative principle by making way for free interaction and innovation in the spirit of community. Thus the church may remain open to influence from its members, from outside the church, and from the Holy Spirit; at the same time it assumes the responsibility of exercising influence in the community. The organizational prerequisite for this kind of interaction is the separation of powers, a separation that combines independence and interdependence and which looks toward the achievement of unity in variety. When, however, the voluntary principle is the sole principle, the question remains as to the source and character of the unity. To this question we shall return.

Not all of the churches adopted the voluntary principle without reservation. The Presbyterians and the Reformed, the Anglicans and the Lutherans in the nineteenth century rejected or severely criticized the principle insofar as it left the churches open to development in any direction that historical accident or the will of the members determined. Their resistance expressed itself in a variety of formulations. The voluntary principle, it was said, militated against any structured continuity within the rich organism of historical Christianity. For one thing, the heavy reliance, in the nineteenth century, of many of the voluntary churches on revivalism was a mixed blessing. Even where revivalism is now largely a thing of the past it has left a residue of subjectivity, erratic spontaneity, a mere sense of immediacy—with the consequence that many of these churches have shown little concern for theology or for history, for liturgical substance and form or for denominational structures.[26]

These old-line churches, however, were not alone in adversely criticizing this kind of voluntaryism. Channing, as we have already observed, criticized the bad taste, the irrationalities, the highly organized forms of ignorance, which were perpetrated by the voluntary societies set up by some of the churches. Thus one can

26. Cf. H. Shelton Smith, Robert T. Handy, and Lefferts A. Loetscher, *American Christianity: An Historical Interpretation with Representative Documents.* 2 vols. (New York: Charles Scribner's Sons, 1963), vol. 2, chap. 13.

say that the bulwark of bad taste, invincible ignorance, and wild "varieties of religious experience" is to be found in many of these voluntary churches. We shall return to this point later, in another connection.

Nevertheless, the churches that have opposed these vagaries have not been able to remain immune to the voluntary principle, as is evident especially in the similarity of the structures which obtains in the local parishes of these denominations and in those of the churches of pronounced voluntaryism. On the other hand, some of the "free churches," skeptical of the spontaneities and disruptions of revivalism, have been sensitive to the need for continuity and structure. Witness Horace Bushnell's critique a century ago of "the thunderclaps of grace" (the phrase comes from Jonathan Edwards), and his preference for "Christian nurture." Witness also his highly original analysis of language.

It would be exceedingly difficult to trace the influences back and forth in order to explain these varieties of, and changes in, religious consciousness and perception. Yet one can affirm that among the various types of churches, and in general in the pluralistic society, mutuality of influence obtains. This mutuality of influence appears not only between churches of different types but also between the churches and other associations.

The variety of voluntary associations, as we have already hinted, is almost beyond the power of unaided imagination to conceive. Their purposes have included prison reform, the prevention of cruelty to children and to animals, the establishment of schools and colleges, the conservation of natural resources, the protection of civil liberties, the attack on poverty, the improvement of race relations, the emancipation of women, church lobbies in Washington and at state capitals, the promotion of world peace, and so on. We have already mentioned the missionary societies, antislavery societies, and tract societies. Through participation in voluntary societies, members of many churches have been able to extend their perception of the social realities. Indeed, one can say that associations such as these provide the means whereby the churches achieve a knowledge of "the world." They are media through which the churches promote a vital relation between religion and culture. Like the voluntary churches, they serve also as the means for the achievement of skills of discussion and organization, and even the skills of listening. Consider, for example, the variety of knowledge and skills learned by church members, and especially by the women, in the missionary societies of the nineteenth century. In terms of skills these women might well be thought of as the spiritual ancestors of the League of Women Voters. The skills of which we speak were required initially by the men and women who were struggling for the right of freedom of association, the right to form a voluntary church. In the eighteenth century the Friends were conspicuous for their ingenuity in registering dissent and in bringing about changes in legislation.[27] These expressions of the voluntary principle have provided the occasions for the churches not only to influence other associations (including the state) but also to gain new perceptions from them, and even to gain broader conceptions of Christian responsibility.

This whole development, including the emergence of the voluntary church, probably would not have been possible without the tremendous expansion of economic resources in the modern period. Indeed, one can argue that the voluntary churches in their emergence and growth accompanied the emergence into modern history of the middle class. If we view the long historical perspective that embraces the development of the voluntary principle in Anglo-American history, however, we must see more than the emergence of the middle class. The voluntary principle was in some degree taken over into the political realm to confirm the demand for the extension of the franchise (for "government by consent") and even to promote the idea of the loyal opposition an an extension of the protection, instead of the persecution, of minority views.[28] From there the voluntary principle moved into the realm of private education; next, to the initiation of the labor

27. Norman Hunt, Exeter College, Oxford, has shown in convincing detail that the Friends in the early eighteenth century had already contrived all the essential methods we today associate with pressure groups. See his *Two Early Political Associations* (Oxford: Clarendon Press, 1961).
28. Cf. George H. Williams, "The Religious Background of the Idea of a Loyal Opposition," in Robertson, ed., *Voluntary Associations.*

movement; then, to the franchise for women, and in our day to the civil rights movement and the beginnings of a movement to promote black-empowerment. The voluntary principle has operated also in the transformation of the authoritarian family into the consensus family. All of these movements were, to be sure, opposed as well as supported by the voluntary churches.

We have spoken of the voluntary principle as the dimension in which the churches have been able with some concreteness to move in the direction of a theology of culture and to attempt to fulfill the mission of the church in a new age. This process could not take place without cooperation between church members and nonmembers. In this process the voluntary churches have learned to some degree that social order and social justice require them to cooperate even with those who do not agree with them regarding theological presuppositions or specifically Christian norms. At the same time this cooperation again and again has served to prevent the churches from making absolute claims; indeed, it has promoted the recognition that God can work through secular people and even through "infidels." Equally significant is the fact that in the twentieth century, cooperation (in voluntary associations) between Protestants and Roman Catholics became possible. Indeed, one of the documents (not yet published) of Vatican Council II proclaims it to be the responsibility of the Catholic to work with others in voluntary associations concerned with the common good. The cooperation in voluntary associations between members of different churches, Protestant and Roman Catholic, and between church members and nonmembers, is of such long standing that we may claim that it represents the oldest ecumenical movement. Possibly the existence of this sort of ecumenism explains the relative absence of significantly organized anticlerical movements in regions where the voluntary church has prevailed.

On the other hand, many of the voluntary churches and many voluntary associations as well have exhibited something less than democratic principles, not to speak of Christian perspectives. We think here not only of the Know-Nothing movement but also of the ways in which the voluntary churches have accommodated themselves to the segregations of our society—in terms of race, of class, of education, of occupation, and of neighborhood.

It is therefore reasonably fair to say that, whereas historically the voluntary churches revolted against the establishment of centralized ecclesiastical-political power, today, particularly in the middle and upper-middle classes, they represent the establishment. This observation becomes all the more pertinent if we take into account the fact that the views that obtain in the business community are almost normative for the churches.

In the light of these ambiguities in the attitudes and behavior of the churches one must conclude that the voluntary principle, taken alone, provides no guarantees with respect to the ends pursued or with regard to theological presuppositions. It does not guarantee even that there will be any interest in theology.[29] Accordingly, the spectrum of the voluntary churches reaches all the way from fundamentalism with its racism and nationalism to the churches that at least ostensibly adhere to more universal principles. The voluntary churches, however, have no monopoly on particularism and idolatry. It would be instructive to compare the performance of the voluntary churches with either that of the Old World state-churches or that of the American churches that stand in closer continuity with those state-churches with respect to theology or ecclesiology.

Actually, these ambiguities arise from the human condition itself. John Robert Godley, a British High Churchman who visited the United States in 1844, spoke to the point when he wrote regarding the American churches: "The reception by a people of any religious system will (humanly speaking) depend chiefly upon the prevalent habits of thought and feeling which exist among them; for our reason is biassed by our affections."[30] Religious

29. Cf. Robert T. Handy, "The Voluntary Principle in Religion and Religious Freedom in America," in Robertson, ed., *Voluntary Associations*.
30. John Robert Godley's essay appears in *The Voluntary Church: American Religious Life (1740–1865) Seen through the Eyes of European Visitors*, ed. Milton B. Powell (New York: Macmillan Co., 1967).

faith, as Augustine would say, is itself biased by the affections. Man becomes what he loves. And so with the church, voluntary or not.

THE REFORMATION OF REFORMATION

Since the time of its birth three or more centuries ago the voluntary church has moved more and more from nonconformity and dissent to conformity (and deformity). In the framework of associations the churches, by reason of the multiple institutional segregations of our society and by reason of the preferences nourished by these segregations, are today part and parcel of the poverty, the racism, and the nationalism of the social system. This must be said despite the large number of reformist associations that have been spawned. They simply have not been sufficient for the evil of the century. Actually, the proportion of the church membership which has participated in these associations has not been and today is not impressive. And even if the reader holds that it is so impressive as to give reason for pride, he must recognize that the racial segregation and the segregation and deprivation of the poor (of various colors) are today greater than they were two or three generations ago.

Many a churchman, to be sure, is concerned and is stricken in conscience. But we live in a society in which the most powerful associations are those which function in collusion with each other to make the involuntary association of the state serve primarily the interests of those who "have," to the detriment of those who "have not." We seem to be caught in a vise produced by the organizational and technological revolution.

In face of this situation one can bravely and rightly work for the creation of a more inclusive church,[31] and for the engendering of a piety and commitment that can serve as an effective, prophetic, nonconformist thrust. This is no mean task. It calls not only for theological reformation but also for associational reformation.

31. James M. Gustafson, "The Voluntary Church: A Moral Appraisal," in Robertson, ed., *Voluntary Associations*.

Tocqueville once suggested that a perennial temptation in a democracy, where liberty may be sought to the neglect of equality, is "lethargic somnolence." Unfortunately, the voluntary principle can serve as a sleeping pill as well as a stimulant. It may be the servant of ends and of binding attachments which in a time of somnolence are hidden assumptions.[32]

What, then, is the remedy? Certainly not the scuttling of the principle. That way lies tyranny. If the voluntary principle is to serve nourishing and prophetic purposes, the demand is for an understanding of the authentic ends of Christian piety and for the costly sacrifices that at least exhibit seriousness of commitment.

A special demand confronting the churches, then, is the demand for the reformation of reformation—the reformation of the voluntary principle. In the history of the church this function has been performed by a special kind of association, the *ecclesiola in ecclesia,* the small church in the large, which redefines Christian vocation in the changing historical situation. In the Middle Ages and also in the so-called Dark Ages monasticism functioned as an *ecclesiola.* In the modern period the *ecclesiola* has been the small group of firm dedication, which sometimes promotes the disciplines of the inner life, sometimes bends its energies to sensitize the church afflicted with ecclesiastical somnolence, sometimes cooperates with members of the latent church in the world to bring about reform in government or school or industry, or even to call for radical structural transformation.

To be sure, catastrophe can accelerate the process of reappraisal, but even then the commonwealth or the church cannot rise above the level of actual or latent spiritual integrity and power. The voluntary principle came to birth at the end of an era. In some quarters today it is held that we are approaching the end of an era. If we are, the increase in membership of the churches characteristic of our period gives little reason for encouragement, for it would appear in large part to bespeak the attractiveness of somnolence, that is, of devotion to self-serving and "religion" of privacy.

32. W. Alvin Pitcher, " 'The Politics of Mass Society': Significance for the Churches," in Robertson, ed., *Voluntary Associations.*

In any event, the voluntary principle, insofar as it pursues worthy ends, requires sharp critical judgment of the actualities and vigorous, though serene, commitments that can make freedom of association, religious or secular, the salt that has not lost its savor. These are issues that are forced upon us when we consider ways in which the voluntary spirit may contribute to an American or a Christian or a Jewish or any other kind of religion in a time of turmoil.

The Geography and Organization of Social Responsibility

James Luther Adams

"Time is of the essence" is more than a bit of conventional wisdom. It could serve as the rubric for a large corpus of philosophical and theological writing which has been produced during the last century and a half. Paul Tillich, like Ernst Troeltsch, asserted that the meaning of time (and history) is *the* problem of our period. During this period, eschatology with its "myths" of Whence and Whither has been a primary concern, both religious and secular. "Openness to the future" is the motto of existentialism, both institutional and pietistic. Futurology has almost achieved the status of an academic discipline.

It is often said that a vivid awareness of time as the channel of meaning is a mark of the modern man, beginning with Joachim of Flora and his vision of the Third Era and assuming new forms in Renaissance and Reformation. Looking further back in history, scholars distinguish between Hebraism and Hellenism in terms of the respective conceptions of time. Biblical studies have centered attention upon the theology of time and history from Abraham to the prophets to the apocalyptists to the authors of the Gospels and the Epistles.

Something important has been neglected in this centering of attention on time. Man lives also in space. He is a space-binding as well as a time-binding creature. Reflecting on the relations between time and space in ancient legend, the young Hegel said that Abraham left the abode, the space, of his fathers to move out across the spaces into time—in this fashion, he said, time conquered space. We should observe, however, that in doing so Abraham was not, like Enoch, translated to heaven. He travelled from one space to another, toward the Promised *Land*. "The Lord made a covenant with Abraham, saying, Unto thy seed have I given this land." He and his seed had to have "turf." The avowal of the granting of the land later became a central feature of the cult. Wherever we turn in even the earliest records of antiquity we find a concern for landmarks and boundaries. Every age has been a space-age.

Man has a body occupying space; he lives in community requiring space and relying upon nourishment from the land; his social relations and even his privacy require space and boundaries. Thus we hear of late about personal space, social space, shared space, communal space. Erik Erikson and R. D. Laing speak even of womb-space.

Edward T. Hall, in *The Hidden Dimension*,[1] has emphasized the crucial significance of various spaces in human relations, as affecting even national characteristics. He distinguishes, for example, between intimate distance, personal distance, social distance, and public distance. Accordingly, he shows how the spatial aspects of housing and of city-layout express or affect these forms of "distance." In varying ways these spaces impose "territorial imperatives."

These hidden dimensions of space have to do with interpersonal relations, and not ostensibly with institutional arrangements. Almost a century ago Georg Simmel, a neo-Kantian analyst of social interaction, stressed the importance of space in human institutions. He suggested that particular social forms such as the state, guilds (corporations), and churches may be interpreted in terms of spatial relationships.

The institutional articulation of the "spaces" of social participation and responsibility in a pluralistic society is the primary concern of the present essay. In stressing spatial relations, we think of spatial extensions as being expressed in relations between objects and places; temporal extensions are expressed in relations between events. Within the limits of this essay numerous important features are omitted. The question of the role of time in relation to institutional spaces would require extensive treatment. Questions of age, sex, class, psychology, and economics are scarcely dealt with. Also omitted is the systematic discussion of the norms or goals of democratic society; I presuppose a constitutional democracy with a Bill of Rights, also the unwritten covenant of a fundamentally stable political and social culture, and freedom of association—a consociational democracy. Certain of these features will appear as I proceed with my analysis of the geography of the organizations that provide the vehicles or "houses" of social participation and responsibility.

A major presupposition here is that history (or community) is not made merely through ideas and persons but through their functioning within groups and institutions. These groups and institutions occupy space, and even compete for it in a struggle for power, that is, in a struggle to participate in the shaping of social decisions. In a democratic society, social existence and participation may be understood at least in part as involving participation in a variety of organizations and as filling up space in differing ways. We shall be concerned, therefore, with a pluralistic theory of associations, political, industrial, social-reformist, and religious, and especially with associations concerned with public policy in American society today.

This presupposition regarding history and regarding man as an associational being implies that we have to do here with the ontology of the human venture in its contemporary version. In his social being man is largely what he owes to the associations, formal and informal. His participation in being appears in and between associational spaces. His participation and non-participation in associations is a mode of his being and becoming in space, of his response to the covenant of being—a depth or transcending dimension. The appropriate response is individual and corporate responsibility to work for a society of justice and mercy in which autonomous, creative individuality is cherished. The best theological grounding for this view of corporate responsibility remains the doctrines of the

1 (Garden City, New York: Doubleday, 1966).

covenant issuing from the Old and New Testaments and finding modern restatements in Neo-Calvinism.

Spaces in Association

In a pluralistic society the constituent organizations cannot function if they do not have turf. Even in order to hold meetings an organization must have a *place* of meeting and also office space. Anyone who has had experience in these matters knows that a recurrent and acute problem for many a voluntary association is the payment of the rent and the telephone bill. A "warrior" friend of mine used to say that any organization worth its salt will have to face this crisis repeatedly, the crisis of being obliged to pay the rent or "vacate." How, I wonder, has the Society for the Protection of the Foreign Born (of which Paul Lehmann for a long time has been the Chairman) been able through the years to maintain its turf?

If we expand the term *space* metaphorically, we can say that a pluralist society is one that is made up of a variety of relatively independent and interdependent "spaces." An effective organization must be able to elicit the loyalty that maintains the organization. More than that, it must be able, standing on its turf, to get a hearing if effective social criticism or innovation and new consensus with respect to social policy are to ensue. A concrete example of a struggle over a relatively simple goal of social policy will quickly identify some of the spaces within which and through which social participation and responsibility are articulated. An example is drawn from the sphere of what is today called "environmental action," specifically the struggle of over half a century to "save" the Indiana Dunes (at the southern end of Lake Michigan) from industrialization and for a national park.[2] In this whole enterprise we can identify different spaces in cooperation and conflict, the spaces and boundaries characteristic of a pluralistic society composed of relatively independent associations: citizens' groups, political parties, industrial corporations, newspapers, labor organizations, national associations for environmental action, and the official engines of public government, the government ostensibly representing the common good and consensus. In short, both public and private governments have been involved. The people in these associations are never exclusively affiliated with any one of them; indeed, they may belong to several of them.

Here, then, we see a kind of separation of powers analogous to the separation of powers obtaining within the constitutional state. Some of the associations possess the limited powers of segmental groups in the society, and they function in face of the power of the state (albeit limited) which possesses a monopoly of force and the power to make a final decision. In this congeries of associations we see the dispersion of power and group creativity characteristic in principle of a pluralistic, democratic society. The agents of the struggle described in the case of the Dunes Council represent a variety of social spaces in the commonwealth, each organization having its own locus and its limited jurisdiction, and each having its own conception of responsibility. The price of consensus is a heavy one, including the skills of organization, of fact-gathering, of analysis and propaganda, of con-

---

2 This struggle is recounted in a chapter in Senator Paul Douglas' autobiography entitled *In the Fulness of Time* (New York: Harcourt, Brace, and Jovanovich, 1972) and in an extensive report entitled "Citizens Make the Difference: Case Studies of Environmental Action," published by Citizens Advisory Council on Environmental Equality (Chairman, Laurence S. Rockefeller), 1973.

frontation, of bargaining, of compromise, of vigilant persistence—with thousands of people participating in hundreds of meetings in assigned or acquired spaces, sharing in conflict and cooperation.

If we multiply these efforts and organizations to take into account the 40,000 registered, voluntary associations in this country today, we grasp readily what is meant when our people are called "a nation of joiners" and when the society is spoken of as a "multi-group society." Max Weber has called the United States "the association-land *par excellence.*" The most frequently cited statement on this matter came from another foreign observer, Alexis de Tocqueville who in *Democracy in America* (1835) said, "In no country in the world has the principle of association been more successfully used, or applied to a greater multitude of objects, than in America . . . Wherever at the head of some new undertaking, you see the government in France, or a man of rank in England, in the United States you will be sure to find an association." Tocqueville goes on to describe the multitude of associations in the United States at that time, association for libraries, hospitals, fire prevention, and for political and philanthropic purposes. One could summarize Tocqueville's account by saying that where two or three Americans are gathered together it is likely that a committee is being formed. To be sure, not all associations of this sort work for the general welfare. One is reminded of the aphorism of Henry Mencken that where two or three Americans are together and speaking of "service," you may be sure that someone is going to get "gypped."

Voluntary associations. We must turn now to sort out the different types of voluntary organization.[3] As voluntary associations they depend upon volunteers who do not look for monetary rewards; the financial support comes from voluntary "contributions." These features distinguish voluntary associations from other private governments such as business and most labor organizations. Moreover, the member may in principle freely join an association, and he is free to withdraw from membership. As voluntary organizations concerned with public policy, they require high and sustained motivation on the part of the members for the performance of tasks.

Broadly considered, voluntary associations have a wide variety of purposes and methods. Some associations are spoken of as instrumental: they aim to influence non-members and thus to affect public policy at many levels—from the neighborhood through the municipality to the region and the country at large; some associations reach beyond the national boundaries, aiming to affect international or transnational policies. Some of these associations promote charitable, philanthropic purposes, and do not attempt to influence the public government. They may even prefer remedies that are purely voluntary.

Another type of voluntary association is called expressive. This type exists mainly to promote the interests of the members in their association with each other, such as in hobby groups, recreational groups, social clubs, self-help, educational, or cultural groups. Max Weber points out that monarchs always love these associations, for they make "good (that is, passive) citizens" by "draining off

---

3 For extensive consideration of the types and functions of associations, see the articles by David Horton Smith in the *Journal of Voluntary Action Research*, Vols. I-III (1972-1974), 1785 Massachusetts Ave., N.W., Washington, D.C. 20036.

their energies in warbling." This is not to deny the values of these associations which in certain instances may define, re-define, or protect significant privacy. Professional associations, on the other hand, combine instrumental and expressive purposes, aiming to define the occupational interests of the members (for example, in maintaining professional standards) but intending also to influence public opinion or public agencies. We may say that both instrumental and expressive purposes represent components of most ostensibly instrumental associations. In both types of association, latent as well as manifest functions obtain. For example, highly significant friendships may develop in an instrumental association concerned with promoting the general welfare without expectation of any but psychic rewards. Or, again, voluntary associations may engender leaders who later transfer to serve the public government.

Voluntary associations are generally contrasted with non-voluntary organizations, that is, with associations to which everyone in the territory belongs without choice. In principle, one has no choice as to whether he will or will not be under the political jurisdiction of the territory, no choice as to whether he will be a member of a family. In certain instances perhaps little choice obtains as to whether a worker will belong to a trades union. Although the state and the family are referred to as non-voluntary associations, they may permit or encourage certain forms of intramural voluntary action, particularly in the democratic state and in the "consensual family."

Intermediary associations. In addition to these voluntary and non-voluntary associations there is another type in which membership is more or less voluntary, but the purpose is to make a profit, as in business or industry or finance. Large associations of this type, besides providing goods or services, sometimes form pressure groups to affect public government policy. Labor unions in the main belong to this class, although (like business corporations) they may promote enterprises of general cultural benefit to the community apart from the benefits to members of the corporation or the union. The union members constitute such a large segment of the population that what benefits them, for example, as consumers, will be to the interest of all consumers. If the unions achieve the upgrading of women and blacks, these minority groups in general begin to enjoy new status and privilege. Women's liberation and black liberation were promoted by the unions long before the civil rights movement and the current movement for women's liberation. Taken together, these economic associations in a technological society increasingly represent the most powerful sector of the territory. Although they are private governments, these associations are not usually classed as voluntary, for they are not associations of volunteers.

And then there are the churches. Since the time of separation of church and state they have been classified as voluntary associations: they depend in principle upon voluntary membership and voluntary contributions. The collection plate in the Sunday Service is sometimes objected to for aesthetic reasons, but it is an earnest, indeed a symbol, of the voluntary character of the association; and it should be interpreted in this fashion. It is a way of saying to the community, "This is our voluntary, independent enterprise, and under God's mercy we who believe in it will support it. We do not for its support appeal to the coercive power of the state."

By reason of adapting a usage initiated by Montesquieu, voluntary associations are spoken of as intermediary associations standing between the individual and the state and in some instances even between the individual and the family. If we contrast these intermediary associations with the corporations of the Middle Ages, we observe that these associations have served to break the kinship pattern that dominates in a traditionalist society. We see an anticipation of this break with kinship patterns in the early Christian churches. More than this, however, was brought about in early Christianity. The authoritarian civil religion of Rome was also broken by the primitive church. Whitehead has put the matter pithily. Commenting on the maxim, "Render unto Ceaesar the things that are Caesar's and unto God the things that are God's," he says that "very quickly God was conceived as a principle of social organization in complete disjunction from Caesar.[4]

The Freedom of Association

Anglo-American historians have given little systematic attention to the history of voluntary associations. It is noteworthy that intermediary associations of modern vintage may be traced back in part to the heresies of the late Middle Ages. Heretical religious organizations or movements by their very existence flaunted the societal pattern of authority represented by the church-state Establishment of the Middle Ages, and thus they created a new space. The social-organizational significance of the sects of the Radical Reformation is crucial here. Max Weber held that the sect is the prototype of all voluntary associations. More than that, the sects were the principal midwife of a pluralistic society.

As with the early Christian churches, these sectarian groups were considered "illicit," to use the term from Roman law. This view was the legal basis for the persecution of the early Christian churches. Roman law is generally characterized as rooted in a special kind of individualism; that is, from the point of view of Roman law only the individual freeman possessed intrinsic legal status. Intermediary associations were licit or legal only if they were under the control of the state. At the beginning of the modern period, this issue came to the fore again. It is sometimes said that the appearance of the sectarian groups represented a violation of the concessive theory of associations (probably wrongly) attributed to Innocent III. According to this theory of concession, every association's legitimation depends entirely upon the church-state Establishment. The sectarian movements in principle rejected the theory of concession. In effect, they claimed the right of freedom of association, and they claimed it by appeal to the New Testament ("Render unto God the things that are God's"). Many of the sects viewed themselves as promoting the restoration of the church from its "fallen" state. According to this view, the church of the first period provided a model of independence and of martyrdom for the sake of independence. The church "fell" when under Constantine it received the exclusive sanction and support of the state. According to this view, the church of the first period provided a model of independence.

In claiming the right to freedom of association the Reformation sects were demanding social space for freedom to interpret the gospel according to their own choice. Semantic studies of the word *heresy* in the sixteenth century confirm this

4 *Adventures of Ideas* (New York: Macmillan, 1933), p. 69.

view. A widespread meaning of the word *heresy* was the literal meaning of the word taken from the Greek, namely, *I choose*. From the point of view of the Establishment this claim to make one's own choice in matters of faith was blasphemous and also destructive of social order, blasphemous because it presumed to reject established authority sanctioned by the apostolic succession, and destructive of social order because it tore the seamless robe of a unified society.

Religious freedom and the notion of democracy. The demand for the freedom of religious association gradually was extended to the demand for freedom of voluntary association in general. On the Continent, in France and Germany and Spain, the sectarians were successfully liquidated through murder and inquisition. Thousands upon thousands of sectarians were slaughtered. As a consequence, the principle of freedom of association was suppressed, thus delaying the development of a pluralistic, democratic society. In England, and subsequently in the American colonies, the persecution was less systematic. Underwood, in his *History of the Baptists,* recounts the growth not only of the Baptist churches; he also points out that many Baptists, in exercise of the claimed right of freedom of association, took special delight in the forming of new associations outside the church. Indeed, the effect of the heady wine of the new conception of freedom of association is to be seen in the disposition of these Baptists to form new associations, to join such an association and then to withdraw in order to form or join a new association. Out of this milieu was born what is called "the gathered church" and congregational polity, a polity that attached to non-ecclesiastical as well as to ecclesiastical associations. Congregational polity was the principle in terms of which these sectarians sought new social space in the commonwealth. The Presbyterian Independents pursued the same course.

With the claim of the Quakers for freedom of religious association came also the claim of the right of the minority view to be heard and protected within the religious community. In effect, the Friends asserted that if the Holy Spirit is to give utterance, it is likely to be through a minority speaking to the majority in the church meeting. Thereby the Quakers and also some of the so-called Independents fought for personal space for the individual as well as for social space for the gathered community of believers. This radical demand of course presupposed that by voluntary means, significant consensus would emerge, a theory of pre-established harmony which was likewise adopted in economic theory.

In the secular realm equally important developments are to be observed. The Levellers, for example, especially through John Lilburne, sought for a new social space in governmental jurisdiction. They demanded an extension of the suffrage, they insisted that the monarch should be made subject to the law of the land, that there should be regular elections, and even that a written constitution was required. In some quarters, the conception of a democratic church was extended to the demand for a democratic state. Toward this end John Lilburne ('good old John,' as he was called) invented a continuing, rational technique of agitation. When he was whipped as a criminal through the streets of London, he seized the occasion to address the admiring multitude whenever the official whippers paused to take a breath. The use of this deliberate technique of agitation in season and out, we may say, brought onto the horizon of history what came to be called 'public opinion.'

207

Already in seventeenth-century England the principle of freedom of association gave rise to a wilding variety of associations pursuing a wilding variety of purposes. The mention of the Ranters, the Seekers, the Familists, and the Diggers, is sufficient to show the wildness of the variety. Rufus Jones says that in some of these sects there were plain lunatics. John Dennis early in the eighteenth century said of them that for one who was inspired ten thousand were demented.

Yet despite fanaticism, the central thrust of these sects gave rise to democracy as we know it. Roger Williams who exercised considerable influence in England called for a strictly civil "covenant," which explicitly used the word "democratical" and provided for majority rule, government by consent, and due process of law.

In face of the wilding growth Thomas Hobbes had a traumatic experience and wrote *Leviathan* to show that chaos results if freedom of association is permitted; he called for a total centralization of power, all associations including the Established Church to be under the exclusive rule of the territorial sovereign. He spoke of voluntary associations as "worms in the entrails of the natural man," the crippled sovereign. This book, *Leviathan,* is probably the most influential book on political theory published in English, for in succeeding generations almost every systematic proponent of democracy felt obliged to give answer to it in favor of personal and social space, that is, in favor of a pluralistic society.[5]

The state as one association.   The answers to Hobbes have repeatedly set forth arguments against totally centralized power and against Hobbes's "statism." According to this pluralistic view, the state is only one association among many. The state is not the creator of the community, it is its creature, as are other associations. The community is therefore the source of a plurality of covenants or social contracts; the state is accountable to the community as are other associations. The term "we the people" in the Preamble to the American Constitution asserts the embracing jurisdiction of the community over the state with its delegated powers and over other associations. These other associations are *sui generis*, and (more than that) they may legitimately criticize the state and under certain circumstances may engage in organized dissent. The best example of an association that is clearly not the creature of the state is the church; moreover, the Christian church lays claim to a transcendent reference in face of which all associations, including the state and the church, stand under judgment. If we may use a spatial metaphor here we may say that in the multi-group conception of society we have a picture of the architectonics of the community of associations.

It has been customary to interpret this conception of associations in terms of

---

5 A pertinent definition of totalitarianism is implied here. It is a society in which no voluntary associations concerned with public policy are permitted. They become desolate windswept spaces. From a constitutional point of view the struggle against Nazism was a struggle for freedom of association. The current appeal of Rudolf Bultmann to the German people to remember the lesson of the Nazi terror by taking an interest in public affairs has a hollow sound apart from an appeal for participation in associations concerned with public policy. For an earlier discussion of the issue in post-war Germany see Karl Barth, *The Only Way* (New York: Philosophical Library, 1947): "Instead of sitting under a weeping willow they should join this Movement [for a Free Germany], make it their own, help to make it strong.... Start taking part of your own free will right now" (p. 59).

social contract, and accordingly to say that the emergence of the theory and practice of voluntary associations is an aspect of modern contractualism. Sir Henry Maine over a century ago in his book entitled *Ancient Law* suggested that modern in contrast to pre-modern society is the result of movement from status to contract. This topic of contract and social contract we cannot discuss further here; in this connection an adequate treatment of it should take into account also the concept of covenant.[6]

I want to call attention to an aspect of association theory which has been widely neglected. F. W. Maitland, the eminent English jurist and historian of law, in an impressive study entitled "Trust and Corporation" (1904) shows that the trust which was originally a legal act by which a landowner contrived to release some of his property and to vest it in trustees, became the legal instrument for the protection of associations. A trust can be used and in innumerable instances has been used to set up a property, perhaps issuing from subscriptions by members of a society, a property that enables a society (or voluntary association) to achieve a common purpose through time. The society does not even need incorporation. Thus, according to Maitland the trust has "all the generality, all the elasticity of Contract," and for several centuries now it has served as a dominant factor in the history of our social morphology, a great "instrument of social experimentation." Even judges who were themselves stout adherents of the state church have had to uphold as "charitable," trusts that involved the maintenance of Catholicism, Presbyterianism, Judaism, or "some queer sect."

The Influence of Association

The concern for voluntary-association theory in the United States antedates Tocqueville's treatment which I have mentioned. The names of Cotton Mather and Benjamin Franklin belong in the roster. Already 140 years ago William Ellery Channing, a Unitarian divine, wrote the first systematic treatise in America on voluntary organizations ("Remarks on Associations"). Significant writings on the subject came also from the pens of the Congregationalist Lyman Beecher and the Baptist Francis Wayland—a literature that comes down to John Dewey's *The Public and Its Problems*. The systematic literature on associations of course goes back through *The Federalist Papers* to John Locke and the Calvinist Althusius to Aristotle.

In both theory and practice the status and role of voluntary associations must be understood, as already suggested, in the relation to the non-voluntary associations, the state and the family. We must give a little further attention to this matter here. From the Continental point of view Anglo-American society has never promoted an adequate conception of the state in its full *imperium* and *majestas*. Again and again, beginning with Magna Carta, forceful limitations have been imposed upon the state. These limitations are best illustrated by the claim of the right of dissent. Here we must make a distinction that is of primary significance in this whole problem-area, the distinction between attitudes of dissent and the institutionalization of dissent. Attitudes do not become effective in public life until they find an institutional instrument. In the history of Protestant-

6 Of special interest here is an essay by H. Richard Niebuhr, "The Idea of Covenant and American Democracy," *Church History*, XXIII (1954), 126-35.

ism the institutionalization of dissent, as we have seen, has Calvinist and Ana-
baptist roots. This is what Puritanism was all about (in both church and state).
Sir Ernest Barker, commenting on these religious sources, says that "one of the
seed-beds of modern liberty" is that section of Calvin's *Institutes* (Book IV, chapter xx, section 31) where dissent is given institutional status: the lower magistrates have the delegated obligation to scrutinize and check the upper magistrates.[7] One sees this sort of institutionalization also in the old Calvinist churches
where the elders sat around the pulpit as representatives of the congregation, to
scrutinize and peradventure to correct the preacher of the Word. In the period in
England after the Presbyterians failed to take over the Establishment, the Neo-Calvinists (who, as Troeltsch observed, "had a genius for forming associations") institutionalized dissent through the use of voluntary associations. By means of
these associations the "Nonconformist conscience" directed its dissent not only against the church Establishment but also against the state. It is true that Nonconformity found an ally in economic groups wishing to free themselves from
state control. In the long run, however, the voluntary associations became a gathering point for non-church people along with church members. This kind of cooperation probably represents the oldest form of effective ecumenism, the oldest
ecumenical movement of coalition, bringing together not only people from the
religious groups but also the "unbelievers." Dissent in the outcome was not only
negative in its thrust, it also took the positive form of demanding and working for
social change. In some instances, the voluntary associations tried to find remedies
in voluntary action and organizations, that is, in private governments. In the
course of time, however, the members of voluntary associations became convinced that with regard to fundamental social evils the responsibility rests upon
the entire community and not only upon those of tender conscience. They therefore sought remedies at the hands of the public government rather than of merely
private governments. Sometimes the dissent took the form of creating utopian
communities which introduced innovations that at first were considered lunatic
but which then eventually were adopted in some fashion by the community at
large. In these various ways voluntary associations have affected public opinion
and public-government policy.[8] (To be sure, certain associations have opposed
these changes; indeed, they have again and again promoted merely class interests
and even racist interests. In the present essay we have not by any means given
them the attention they deserve.) In addition to the fulfillment of citizenship responsibilities through voluntary associations the individual of course may participate in the activities of political parties, a matter of no small moment. But here
again voluntary associations play a significant role in the combat with "the machine."

The relations between voluntary associations and the family are equally significant. Members of the family, singly or the parental couple together, may be-

---

7 "A Hugenot Theory of Politics," in *Church, State, and Study* (London: Methuen & Company,
   1930), p. 84.

8 In his famous study, *The Protestant Ethic and the Spirit of Capitalism* (1904), Max Weber, by
   reason of centering his attention on economic behavior, failed to note these aspects of Nonconformist performance. See the present author's analysis in " 'The Protestant Ethic' with Fewer
   Tears," *In the Name of Life,* Essays in Honor of Erich Fromm (New York: Holt, Rinehart and
   Winston, 1971).

long to instrumental associations concerned with community and public-govern-
mental policy, or to business associations, or to expressive associations. The husband and the wife in belonging to different associations achieve a certain independence from each other. Of special significance in the present century are the
youth associations. Youth organizations have their own behavior-patterns, dress-
patterns, even language-patterns. In a society where individual autonomy is a
substantial ingredient of the ethos, the youth organization provides the young
person with the opportunity to achieve a certain independence, sometimes in
hostile tension with the family. The proliferation of these youth associations, formal and informal, and of the multitude of other associations, provides new difficulties
for the family in its search for meaningful integrity and continuity. Ideally, the fulfillment of social responsibility within the family is related to the recognition of responsibility in the other associations, voluntary and non-voluntary. It
would be comforting if we could say that the contemporary church provides an
effective integrating orientation that gives ballast to the family in face of the over-
lapping spaces and responsibilities.

Competing influences. One aspect of the competition of the associations for the
attention of the individual deserves at least passing reference. A major study of
"mass political apathy" in the United States by Bernard Barber argues that the
decline of participation in politics and in politically oriented voluntary associations is due to the pressures coming from the family and from occupational demands.[9] Recognizing that the family shares the improved or unimproved status
of the head of the family, the latter eschews associations that might interfere with
the improvement of his economic status. One is reminded here of the view of
Plato that the family is the enemy of justice, that is, it may be the occasion for
the entire distraction of attention from the concerns and responsibilities of citizenship.

This problem of competing responsibilities is compounded if we now consider only two aspects of one of the most important associations (which we have
scarcely mentioned), the association within which one earns his livelihood. First to
be noted is the characteristic feature of urban society, the separation of the place
of work from the place of residence, and the separation of these from the places of
recreation and from the places of instrumental associations. Fragmentation of
existence is the inevitable consequence of this spatialization of life. This observation gives weight to the definition of secularism as fragmentation and incoher-
ence of meaning. This leads to the consideration of the major, largely hidden
source of "integration" (or is it disintegration?). In a technological society, in rural as well as in urban setting, the major corporations largely determine the patterns of authority, the definitions of success, the form and content of the mass
media of communications, and even the perduring policies of public government. We can look here only briefly at this last-mentioned phenomenon.

Ernst Fraenkel, a political scientist at the Free University in Berlin, in his widely used book on *Die Amerikanische Regierung* has defined the American Congress

9 Dr. Barber's Harvard doctoral dissertation is partly summarized in "Participation and Mass Apathy in Associations," Alvin W. Gouldner, ed., *Studies in Leadership* (New York: Harper &
Bros., 1950).

as in the main a clearing-house of the great pressure groups. Former Senator Paul Douglas in a study of these pressure groups has shown the geography of these associations—the cotton interests are rooted in the South, the lumber interests in the Northwest, the copper interests in the Rockies, the dairy and grain interests in the Middle West, the steel interests in Pittsburgh and Gary, and so on. The Ervin Committee has recently been attempting to expose the ways in which major financial interests support party politics. Class legislation promoted by these special-interest groups has become readily visible to the naked eye under the present Administration, particularly by reason of the energy crisis and the current revelation of the hidden subsidies.

The coordinated power of the major corporations enables them to maintain affluent pressure groups at all levels of government, and these pressure groups exercise their power by means of coalition (or better called collusion). The lobbyist for the cotton interests at a particular juncture says to the lobbyist for the copper interests, "I know you are not at all interested in promoting or stopping this particular piece of legislation, but if you will assist me now, I shall repay you when you need similar support." Because of this feature of contemporary society our economy is called "interest-group democracy." The private economic governments, including the multinationals and some of the professional societies, have become stronger than the public governments. One is reminded of James Madison's warning that a principal threat to democratic public government would be the inordinate power of a single faction. This warning represents one of the oldest arguments of democratic socialism against capitalism. In any event, the relation between voluntary and non-voluntary associations encounters acute crisis here. In the halls of public government the major conflict is between the voluntary associations concerned for the general welfare and the lobbies of the major economic power groups which aim to promote or protect "special interests." Considering the massive concentration of economic-political cultural power, we may say that our condition today is not unlike that which obtained at the beginning of the modern period. Max Weber called it a cage.

Associations to Combat Governmental Disease

Considering the wide range and the effectiveness of the activities and lawsuits being promoted by Ralph Nader and his associates, we may expect that in the coming years policy-oriented voluntary associations will give increasing attention to the behavior of the major industrial corporations. Whereas in the past, organized dissent—the only kind that is ordinarily effective—has been directed against the state, in the future, the associations promoting dissent will be more and more directed at both the state and the economy. In addition to exposing the dubious relationships between private and public governments, these associations will increasingly scrutinize the internal structures of the corporations and also the policies of deception in advertising and marketing. With regard to the internal structures, it will be recalled, Ralph Nader and his associates have been demanding that protection be afforded employees who with integrity expose deception and other anti-social policies promoted by the employing corporation. This issue, as we have seen, was long ago faced in the Radical Reformation, when the protection of minority opinion was required by some of the church groups. This sort of protection for the individual citizen has been sanctioned by the Bill of Rights in the U.S.

Constitution. An analogous protection is now demanded for the individual in private governments. In this whole problem-area, we encounter what we might call the diseases that can appear in associations, public and private. Over a century ago, Channing set forth a pathology, pointing out that the very associations that promise new freedoms can become also the occasion for new tyrannies.

Taken together, these demands presuppose that effective accountability on the part of the economic sector requires more than the kinds of correction promised by free-market theory and practice. In "the Protestant Era," this sort of accountability has been late in coming on the agenda. This belatedness is due partly to the inordinate independence accorded to the economic sector, as R. H. Tawney documented long ago as beginning with the Puritan Reformation. But more than this must be said. The achievement of the integrity of public government requires the expansion of accountability to the private sector. The absence of this accountability is a major cause of the current, widespread skepticism that obtains regarding the effectiveness of citizenship participation in politics. The lack of accountability, it is seen, has made possible the erosion of the moral limits to the legitimate power of private governments.

Ultimately, moreover, the vindication of the claims made for the pluralist society as the free and open society requires the flank attack upon the private governments that exercise inordinate and hidden power in politics and in the society at large. The bloating of this power is a major ingredient in the now heralded "decline of pluralism." Today some of the drive among the youth in the direction of privatization (and "copping out") has been rooted in the awareness of this decline.

As we look at the developing Third World, we see analogous issues coming to the fore in face of centralized political and economic power and in face of the multinational organizations that elicit obsequious obedience at the hands of local political authorities. Pluralistic democracy in the Third World is encountering in a shortened time-span the paradoxes and impediments exhibited in the West over a much longer period of time. The free spaces, rare enough in a traditional society, are not to be achieved in the Third World without dust and heat, if at all.[10]

In order to check the diseases of government (public and private), new forms of coalition have been emerging. We have noted the composite constituency of many voluntary associations of the past century, amounting to a sort of ecumenism of church persons and non-church persons. In the present century collaboration has appeared in a different form, a coalition between church and nonchurch agencies. The earlier form brought *individuals* of differing orientations together. The new form effects collaboration between *associations,* religious and secular. A generation ago furtive efforts were made to bring into cooperation the churches and burgeoning labor organizations, a collaboration that began much earlier in England. Local, regional, and denominational church committees, serving as agencies of the churches, though not necessarily as official representatives, have been operating in this way. In Illinois, for example, a coalition calling for the impeachment of the

10 Constance Parvey has outlined the problem-areas in this respect for the Third World, in "The Role of Voluntary Association in the Third World," *Journal of Voluntary Action Research,* Vol. II, No. 2 (April, 1972), 2-7. This article issued from a Seminar on voluntary associations co-conducted by Miss Parvey at Harvard Divinity School, a Seminar supported by the Center for a Voluntary Society.

President of the U.S. has been active throughout the State. Another coalition, the Alliance to End Repression, has been centering attention on police and jail practices, even training "visitors" to serve on panels investigating deaths in jails and prisons. The Clergy and Laity Concerned have elicited cooperation in the effort to challenge industrial production of weapons for chemical warfare. The American Friends Service Committee and the Unitarian Universalist Service Committee, collaborating with the League of Women Voters and the American Civil Liberties Union, have been promoting "court watching" and the training of "court watchers" to promote greater fairness in the criminal-justice process.[11] Other similar coalitions could be mentioned, especially those promoted by state and municipal federations of churches. Coalitions of this sort will presumably develop to "attack" other areas of performance in public and private governments.[12]

The agenda is a heavy one, for example, in the areas of education, health, care for the aged, the eradication of poverty, civil rights, the conservation of the nation's natural resources and beauties, and race relations. To contemplate the death and dying compressed in the failure to work vigorously on these agenda staggers the imagination.

Here, then, we come to the pragmatic test. How well has this nation used its associations, its governments, private and public? What have been the consequences? The dark answer to these questions is the major reason for the heralded "decline of pluralism." Ernst Troeltsch fifty years ago had already predicted that the Western democracies before the end of the century would encounter disenchantment, that an increasing number of people would lose their enthusiasm for the promise of one man/one vote. As I understand Troeltsch's view, political democracy can remain viable only if it assumes responsibility for economic realities.

These considerations pose the question also as to whether the voluntary association has shown itself capable of eliciting sufficient social responsibility to correct the political and economic institutions. One may rightly say that the middle class initially was born in modern history largely by means of the voluntary association, that many workingmen's organizations found their niche in the society through the innovations of the voluntary association, that ethnic minorities have made their climb in similar fashion. But millions are still left out, and the cruelty and disease and deprivation are appalling, as are the bombings, kidnappings and shootings. The spaces available to the deprived are simply too cramped. Is this the reason Paul Lehmann's next book deals with revolution?[13]

It may be that it is unrealistic to expect that a top-heavy civilization such as ours can solve its problems through deliberate thought and action. It may be that a wider measure of social and economic justice can come only after the advent of national or international crisis of mammoth proportions.

11 "Judging the Judges," *Wall Street Journal*, March 7, 1974.
12 William Simpson in his article entitled, "The New Left, the Churches, and Some Old Questions," *Journal of Current Social Issues*, (Winter 1972-73), indicates in some detail desirable methods of coalition between the churches' agencies for social ministry and other "public-regarding associations." In this kind of coalition he envisages the cooperative mobilization of "the conscience constituency" for the sake of "large-scale social change," that is, for "healthy associational action."
13 Nothing said here should be taken to imply that the remedy is some blueprint-socialism. Tawney and Crossland, long ago offering proposals for the British Labor Party, dismissed public ownership as "irrelevant."

Conclusion

So far, we have been considering the geography of social responsibility in terms of institutional spaces. We should observe, however, that important aspects of social responsibility have to do with the single individual, that is, with the geography of the self. Two of these may be mentioned here.

Of first importance is the recognition of a distinction between what Ernst Troeltsch has called subjective and objective obligations:

> With regard to moral experience, we distinguish the duties that proceed purely from the relations of the subject to itself and to other subjects (courage, prudence, truthfulness, on the one hand, and good will, justice, piety, on the other) and the obligation to esteem and strive after objective values of the family, the state, the society, science, art and religion. . . . Only with the two together can we show the relationship to experience of the moral idea that is necessary in itself.[14]

In other words, personal and interpersonal obligations must be accompanied by trans-personal obligations that impinge upon institutional behavior; personal, social, and communal spaces belong together in tension.[15] It has been the characteristically false assumption of pietism, whether religious or secular, to suppose that if personal and interpersonal obligations are met, the institutional arrangements will take care of themselves. This pietism, in confining itself to personal and interpersonal obligations, fails to observe collective responsibility for the character of the society (the insight of Old Testament prophetism). But this pietism seldom actually confines itself to the personal and interpersonal spheres. Willy-nilly it brings preferences regarding public policy in through the back door, and thus it incurs the responsibility of morally justifying these preferences. The ample geography of the self will include both dimensions of responsibility, the personal and the institutional. If the pietist were consistent in confining himself to personal and interpersonal obligations, he would turn out to be what the ancient Greeks called an "idiot," one who is not concerned with public policy. This is the irresponsible path of privatization.

A second aspect of the geography of the self is closely related to the first. What is at stake is the concept of vocation. In wide circles, even in Christian circles, one finds the doctrine of vocation interpreted simply in terms of the obligations of the occupation—doing one's job well. As with pietism, the assumption here is that if everyone does his job well, social benefits will be spread in the widest commonalty. The ample geography of the self includes a second vocation, the vocation to participate in the social processes that aim to determine public policy.

The geography of social responsibility, then, is a geography of the "spaces," of the objective institutional vehicles through which social responsibility is exercised. It

---

14 "Grundprobleme der Ethik," *Ges. Schriften*, III (Tübingen: J. C. B. Mohr, 1913), p. 618.

15 It is noteworthy that Troeltsch's essay quoted here is a critique of Wilhelm Herrmann's *Ethik* for its neglect of the sphere of social institutions and values. Roger Johnson, in his Harvard doctoral dissertation, has shown the similarity between Bultmann's neo-pietist ethics and Herrmann's. Both scholars were (successively) professors at Marburg. (See note 6, *supra*.) The opposite lopsidedness is characteristic of "vulgar Marxism."

presupposes what we have called the geographv of the self—the duality and the dynamic interrelationship of the interior and interpersonal responsibilities on the one hand and the institutional responsibilities on the other. This geography of the self involves also the dual vocation of the individual's occupational vocation and his vocation to participate in the common enterprise of promoting a society of justice and mercy.

Whitehead asserted that man is what he does with his solitariness (an aphorism that has been misinterpreted). We might alter the axiom to read, man is what he does with his spaces. In our pluralistic society, the crucial spaces of social responsibility are the governments, private and public, religious and secular, in tension and interplay. What man does with these spaces is a matter of the organization of power—the organization of the capacity to participate in making social decisions.

Mediating Structures and the Separation of Powers

James Luther Adams

Nothing makes one long for water more than to be without it in a desert. The loss of the mediating structures that exist between the individual and the state creates such a desert, one that was experienced by millions of people in Nazi Germany. One of the first things Adolf Hitler did after seizing power was to abolish, or attempt to abolish, all organizations that would not submit to control. The middle organizations—for example, the universities, the churches, and voluntary associations—were so lacking in political concern that they created a space into which a powerful charismatic leader could march with his Brown Shirts. Paradoxically, in taking the way left open to him, Hitler developed a mediating organization himself. By the use of mass persuasion, psychic violence, blackmail, and terror his organization practically wiped out the others as if they were tottering ninepins. He persuaded his followers to abandon freedom for absolute unity under a *Führer*. This toboggan slide into totalitarianism was accelerated by the compliance of governmental structures, provincial and local, including the secondary school system. Considering this broad range of compliance, we may define the totalitarian society as one lacking effective mediating structures that protect the self-determination of individuals and groups.

The suffering and death brought on by Nazism—in Germany as a nation, in the holocaust for the Jews, and throughout the world—staggers the imagination. The whole story, to be sure, is a complicated one that can easily be oversimplified, especially if we ignore the complicity by default of the Western allies after Hitler came to power. And when the allies did turn to resistance they surrounded us with the shades of Dresden and Hiroshima and Nagasaki. As Wilfred Owen said, our feet should be sore as we walk "in the alleys cobbled" with our fellows who died in the struggle.

I have mentioned the Nazi tyranny here at the outset not only because of its intrinsic significance. I have mentioned it also because of my months of witnessing at first hand the struggles and strategies of the Protestant churches in the anti-Nazi underground. My oldest friend in Germany, a pastor and university instructor who after the collapse of Nazism became a professor of theology at Heidelberg, was a leader in this resistance. For several months he was a prisoner in Dachau concentration camp, having been taken forcibly from his parish. The network of the underground was so efficient that his associates outside knew in advance the very day on which he would be released. Immediately after his release he returned to his activity in the resistance movement, where I joined him and in turn myself came into the grasp of the Gestapo. It was my association with him and his fellow resisters that brought to me a vivid and enduring awareness of the significance and function of mediating structures in making the consent of the governed into an effective, and often dissenting, power. These mediating structures I came to see as the indispensable separation of powers in a democratic society.

The term "mediating structures" has been given currency in some circles today by a small book by Peter L. Berger and Richard John Neuhaus.[1] These authors define mediating structures as those existing between the individual and the state. In this book they center attention upon the neighborhood, the family, the church, and the voluntary association, structures rooted in the private sector. We should note that, in contrast to the usage adopted by these authors, the literature of political science has tended to identify the middle structures as those existing in both the governmental and the private sector. This usage can be traced at least as far back as the seventeenth century to the writings of Johannes Althusius, the "father" of modern systematic discussion of our subject. Althusius includes among the middle organizations the lower tiers of government, such as the provinces (or states) and the local governments, along with the family and other associations not under the direction of the central political order. Another distinction that must be taken into account is that between voluntary associations, which one may choose to join or not to join, and involuntary ones, in which such a choice is excluded. According to this conceptualization, the state and the family have been seen as involuntary, for one may not choose whether or not to belong to a political order or to a family. Membership is "given" and inescapable. In modern democratic society the church is viewed as a voluntary association. However, be-

[1] *To Empower People: The Role of Mediating Structures in Public Policy* (Washington, D.C.: American Enterprise Institute, 1977), 45 pp. This serves as an introduction to the basic ideas of an extensive project sponsored by the institute and partially funded by the National Endowment for the Humanities.

cause it is frequently tied closely to the family, it in some respects possesses involuntary elements.

In the context of these distinctions we see that Berger and Neuhaus have included under the rubric of mediating structures both voluntary and involuntary groupings. Moreover, they have given attention to the state (and its mediating structures) only insofar as its policies relate directly to the internal concerns of the neighborhood, the family, the church, and the voluntary association. They have not dealt with the state in other respects, especially in order to center attention upon the need for participation and self-determination in the mediating structures selected, a need of crucial significance in our kind of welfare state.[2] In the present essay, however, I have taken the broader definition of mediating structures as obtaining in the public as well as in the private sector.

The democratic society, then, is an association of associations. This web includes a plethora of groupings, commercial, industrial, educational, artistic, professional, recreational, and philanthropic. To be sure, the individual is not absorbed without remainder in these groupings. Members, at least in principle, retain their independence, their own rights and responsibilities. In this connection a perennial problem emerges, that of combining unity and liberty within and between the mediating structures. The criterion here is more an aesthetic than a moral one, the maintenance of unity in the midst of variety. As we have seen, Nazi Germany succumbed to suffocating unity.

In order to achieve their purposes, the various associations elicit commitments. The life-blood that flows through this pluralistic network of arteries and veins is an ever-renewing vitality in the face of reappearing enervations, impediments, and distortions. The vitality depends upon bondings and compacts engendered and nourished by mutual confidence in the midst of a diversity of interests, perspectives, and ideals. It is precisely in order to prevent self-enclosed, that is, idolatrous, commitments hostile to mutual confidence and uncoerced participation that a principle of separation of powers is required. This conception of the division of powers, it should be noted, is more embracing than the division of powers familiar to us in the American Constitution, the division in government between the executive, the legislative, and the judicial powers. It is more embracing because it allows for the continuous growth of new channels of participation and

---

[2] For a critical and extensive discussion of this and other related studies by Berger and Neuhaus, see the articles by Theodore M. Kerrine, Jay Mechling, and David Price (and rejoinders by Berger and Neuhaus) in *Soundings*, vol. 62, no. 4 (1979), pp. 331–416.

decision making. At the same time, it allows room for the relative independence of the associations while rendering them accessible to mutual criticism and influence.

Without participation in these spaces that function as wedges preventing overweening powers from presenting a united front against criticism—without participation in the separation of powers under law —the citizen can become impotent, thus opening the way to domination, even if he or she feels free. The individual can become a torso of a human being; or, as the poet Christoph Morgenstern would say, the person can become only "a knee that hobbles through the world." In changing historical situations freedom depends upon these associations for its redefinition as well as for its achievement or preservation. Considering the importance of people's participation or failure to participate in these groups, we may say, By their groups shall you know them.

Participation, however, requires power.

The Nature of Power

Power is to be distinguished from force, although force must be viewed as a form of power. In its most general sense, power is the ability to exercise influence—active power. As Plato observed, however, it is also the passive capacity to be influenced by and the capacity to resist other powers. Power includes, then, the ability to make decisions affecting the values of others.

What, then, is social power of the sort required for the functioning of mediating structures? The answer to this question reveals a variety of ingredients. Social power depends upon the creation and maintenance (and also the recurrent transformation) of an efficacious social will in a more or less unified enterprise. I say "more or less unified," for if coercion is not to be resorted to, the sought-for unity must make a space for openness and variety through mutual interchange. It is within this ethos that the individual in freedom comes to identify with the enterprise and the organization.

This kind of social will, then, is a complex thing. It includes the capacity of the group to engender leadership, to elicit a supporting, consenting constituency that can tolerate a reasonable amount of dissent. Creative dissent is not only necessary for growth in the organization but also for the maintenance of the integrity of the individual. The leadership and the constituency require experience that produces the skills of organization, procedure, and strategy, a division of labor—in short, the skills that belong to governance by discussion. All of these skills and sensitivities are invaluable for the society as a whole; the

220

skills may be transferred to other enterprises. They presuppose the articulation of common goals undergirded by mutual trust, a quality that can persist in the face of changing situations. In moments of stress nothing less than seasoned friendship will suffice. These are not the moments for new-hatched, unfledged comrades.

Social will depends, then, upon latent as well as upon manifest functions. The manifest function of an organization may be the particular policies or goals promoted. The latent function will be the friendships, the growth of the individual in interpersonal competence and in the skills acquired, and also an improved capacity to communicate effectively with others. Social power is a complex exercise in communication, in the process of influencing and being influenced.

The incentives for participation in voluntary organizations, of course, vary greatly. One view is that the individual in working in an organization is merely seeking recognition, and that he is therefore only interested in personal psychic rewards. Max Weber in his essay on voluntary associations holds that the principal motive is the search for the opportunity "to put oneself over" or to gain prestige. He asserts that in belonging to a church the individual may aim in part to enhance his credit-rating.[3] One wonders whether Weber would be content to attribute only these motives to his membership in the community of scholarship.

These self-regarding motives appear commonly in human affairs. But, surely, one need not adopt the ascetic view that the only authentic motive for participation is complete self-denial—in earlier days this view took the form of the question, Would you be willing to be damned for the glory of God?

With respect to the claim that only subjective psychic rewards are sought for, we must recognize that the civic-minded citizen involved in a voluntary association concerned with public policy does not expect or hope for rewards accruing only to his own private benefit. Nor does he center attention on the psychic rewards. On the contrary, this citizen expects to spend time and money in a common cause that will issue in the general benefit. This fact becomes especially clear if one considers the citizen who in pursuing an unpopular cause may not only face controversy but may also earn obloquy—for example, in the promotion of the rights of blacks or of women or of gays or of the poor. Moreover, sociological studies amply demonstrate that avoidance of

---

[3] Max Weber, "Proposal for the Sociological Study of Voluntary Associations," *Journal of Voluntary Action Research*, vol. 1, no. 1 (Winter 1972), pp. 20–23. From "Geschäftsbericht," *Verhandlungen des ersten deutschen Soziologentages von 19–22 Oktober, 1910*, in Frankfurt a.M. (Tübingen, 1911), pp. 52–60.

participation in controversial voluntary associations is often motivated by the intention to allow nothing to get in the way of personal success in one's business or profession. The associations dealt with by Berger and Neuhaus are associations characteristically concerned with community values (where controversy is almost inevitable).

Mediating Structures and the Religious Dimension

We have noted some of the social and psychological functions of the structures mediating between the individual and the state. I turn now to a brief and very broad theological interpretation.

The structures we have been considering exist on the horizontal level (if we may employ a spatial metaphor). The religious consciousness, however, is concerned also with structures that obtain in a vertical dimension and which in both positive and negative ways relate the whole human enterprise (and nature) to a deeper, or higher, reality that transcends and qualifies all activities on the horizontal level. This mediation is quite different from that which is ordinarily associated with the mediating organizations.

Strikingly enough, in the context of our discussion, those who have pointed in decisive ways to the vertical dimension have been called "intermediaries."[4] The important intermediaries referred to here include a founder of a new religious movement and his disciples, a prophet, a mystic, and a charismatic personality. Figures such as these speak *de profundis* in the name of the holy, they speak of both its distance from and its nearness to all human concerns, of the creative and fearful powers that work from the depth of being, bringing both fulfillment and judgment. These intermediaries point to the divine host that must be reckoned with.

Characteristic in Judaism and Christianity is a concern for history and also a communal concern that looks toward social salvation in community and not toward the escape of the individual from history into the suprahistorical. The intermediaries give rise to institutions that provide identity and direction to a community with a goal in and beyond history. They give rise to what we have called social will, the social power of the group formations that spell out history. The intermediaries disclose the divine reality as offering both a gift and a corresponding duty, a gift and a task, the task being to strive for justice and mercy in society, to engage in a struggle between justice and injustice. One may

---

[4] Robert R. Wilson, *Prophecy and Society in Ancient Israel* (Philadelphia: Fortress Press, 1980).

characterize this divine reality as a creative, sustaining, judging, trans-forming, community-forming power working within history.

In this connection we must observe more closely the ways in which the intermediaries render this orientation historically relevant, and observe also the types of authority entailed.

Within the religious community the intermediaries point to para-digmatic events such as the Exodus from oppression, the message and suffering of the social prophets, the proclamation by Jesus in word and deed of a coming kingdom of righteousness and peace, the calling of the disciples, the activity of the Holy Spirit at Pentecost. These and similar events are termed "acts of God," the working of divine grace calling for dedicated response. From a theological perspective these are mediating events, and they presuppose a covenant that gives to the community and its members a vocation. Here the ideas of covenant and vocation are mediating concepts. Hence, one can speak of the vocation of Israel or of the Christian community and its members. In the Chris-tian community each of the members, according to St. Paul, is by grace endowed with special gifts (*charismata*). None of these gifts is in the possession of the believer, yet they impose the obligation of stewardship relating them to the unity or common good of the community.

We do not need to enter here into a discussion of the distinction between common grace and grace sufficient for salvation. But we must take into account the question of authority. Here the distinctions (sug-gested by Ernst Troeltsch and Paul Tillich) between heteronomous, autonomous, and theonomous authority are crucial for the interpreta-tion of the ground of meaning. Heteronomous authority demands sub-mission to a tangible, fixated "other" (*heteros*) that claims to be absolute and thus to be exempt from radical criticism. In contrast, autonomous authority validates meaning by appealing to the inde-pendent (or socialized) self (*autos*) that in principle renounces absolute claims. Autonomous authority, to be sure, can become empty and degenerate into what amounts to heteronomous submission. Theonomy rejects as idolatrous and demonic the identification of any finite author-ity with the infinite, of the relative with the absolute. It recognizes a divine reality beyond the self and beyond every fixation imposed by the "other." This orientation aims to fulfill (rather than abrogate) the intrinsic humanity of autonomy, and yet acknowledges dependence upon a transcending, creative, divine power that supports inclusive meaning and also holds everything finite under judgment. It aims to respect the divine command, "Thou shalt have no other gods before me."

This command is one that is all too seldom respected, as the his-tory of culture and religion amply demonstrates. Human beings, especially in groups, search for (false) security and are driven to attach themselves in polytheistic fashion to particular "spaces"—a book, a social system, a church, a human faculty (reason or feeling), or a nation (blood and soil). For this reason nationalism has been called "modern man's other religion." Perhaps the natural religion of humanity is polytheism, as David Hume suggested—heteronomous polytheism. Yet, under prophetic challenge heteronomy may be drawn toward theonomy. Or a regnant heteronomy may give rise to the protests of autonomy. But autonomy may carry heteronomous elements within it or may seek its way toward theonomy. We see, then, that these distinctions obtain not only in the area of the explicitly religious; they may obtain in all spheres of meaningful existence.

In the face of these options and the demand for theonomous authority, we can now indicate the different levels or aspects of vocation. It is exercised not only in the immediate relationship of the soul to God and in the interpersonal relations with other human beings but also in the search for viable institutional structures. The prophet repeatedly points to contemporary heteronomous or autonomous violations of vocation and calls the community to "turn" to renewal of covenant and to faithfulness to it. In the spirit of the demand for timeliness religious leaders have spoken of the obligation to interpret the signs of the time in order to achieve new relevance and meaning in response to the judging and creative powers of the divine.

In this connection the Jewish and Christian communities provide mediating ceremonies manifesting the presence of the divine with its gift and its task. In Christian practice these are called sacraments—means of grace. Matrimony and the formation of the family is one of them; baptism and confirmation are others. Considering the broader social vocation, one might with boldness interpret responsible involvement in the continuing reformation of mediating structures to be a means of grace, sacramental in the sense of being a spiritual bond of sacred significance. Here we may see an aspect of the vocation of the lay apostolate.

A multitude of obstacles to the exercise of vocation is always present. The term "institutionalism" suggests the perennial danger of centering attention on the institution as an end in itself. That way lies idolatry, the distortion of the vertical dimension. Toward the correction of this ossification, pietistic movements emerge, but they can narrow the vocation by confining it to the interpersonal level and eliminating the concern for broader institutional analysis and obligation. Similarly, we should observe a possible narrowing of scope through exclusive attention to the internal concerns of organizations to the neglect of the macrocosmic sphere of the embracing political and economic order.

The danger is also always present that a mediating structure will ✓ be used as a means of increasing only the power to dominate or to restrict the authentic rights of others. As with the Ku Klux Klan, this can lead to a self-serving, demonic attempt to play God. We see again the indispensability of the dispersion, the separation, of powers.

This outline of a theology of history, of a "public theology," is, of course, highly selective, covering (and concealing) wide stretches of history. Its presupposition is that history is made by groups exercising power—the power of influence and the power of being influenced. Its presupposition is also that power must be both distributed and shared if tyranny or domination is to be held in check. The outline can provide some guidelines for interpreting a variety of examples of the dispersion of power brought about by social will rooted in religious impulse. The description of these examples must also be highly selective, each example serving as an ideal historical type similar to Max Weber's ideal type of the Protestant ethic.

Some High Points in the Historical Development of the Separation of Powers

Probably the oldest example on record of a structured dispersion of power comes from the period of prehistory, the fourth millennium B.C. in Mesopotamia before the advent of autocratic rule. The historian Thorkild Jacobsen has found plausible evidence in that time for what he calls "primitive democracy." According to the mythology of that early period, the gods and goddesses assembled in a council that had established the rule of arriving at decision only after discussion—the gods "asking one another" in order to clarify the issues until agreement could be reached. One might say that here the sign of an authentic god or goddess was its willingness to hear what the others wished to say. Jacobsen infers that this heavenly assembly was a projection of earthly councils of the time when the ruler was obliged to secure the consent of representative citizens in assembly. This assembly possessed the authority to grant kingship, and it could even rescind this kingship. A *separation* of powers did not obtain in this "primitive democracy"; yet, there was at least a collegial dispersion of power throughout the assembly.[5]

---

[5] Thorkild Jacobsen, "Primitive Democracy in Ancient Mesopotamia," *Journal of Near Eastern Studies*, vol. 2, no. 3 (July 1943), pp. 159–72.

More nearly approaching a separation of powers is the independent status assumed by the Hebrew prophets. As charismatic intermediaries, they in the name of a covenant proclaimed, "Thus saith the Lord"—to (and against) the king and the people. The definition and exercise of this independent role of intervention is a remarkable and singular cultural creation, not achieved without dust and heat. From this came the classical definition of the prophet in our tradition.

The "prophets" in countries adjacent to Israel were not independent; they were attached to the court—on expense account, as it were. The Hebrew prophets condemned as false prophets those who simply served the king. The singularity of the Hebrew conception of the liberty of prophesying—a separation of powers—must be understood in terms of the historical context of the time.

There is a fundamental difference between Israel and the neighboring kingdoms. It may be characterized as the contrast between a historical and an ahistorical orientation. In Babylon and Egypt a static, stratified social order was sanctioned by a timeless, suprahistorical cosmic model: the established order of society had been defined once and for all in this model. Accordingly, an impregnable space of heteronomous authority dominated time. One might call this a spatialized religion. In Israel, on the other hand, an event in time, the emancipation of the people from slavery in Egypt, had liberated them from a cramped, oppressive space, drawing them into a time-orientation. As Hegel suggested, time and its promise would be viewed as superior to any fixated space of a regnant social order. The memory of this event and of a covenant from Yahweh, "acts of God," became the sanction for a continuing struggle for freedom against tyranny, and thus for independent prophetic criticism or intervention. In the light of these "acts of God" the meaning of existence was found in the struggle for a righteous community of the future, the promise and demand of the covenant. Here, then, we encounter an eschatological orientation, a historical religion, time overcoming space. The individual and the community were held responsible for the character of the society, and especially for the protection of the deprived and the poor at the gate. Before their liberation from Egypt, had not the children of Israel been strangers and deprived of freedom?

Since the covenant and its law were in this and other ways applied and broadened, we may speak of the authority here as theonomous in contrast with the heteronomous authority respected in Babylon and Egypt. To be sure, one can discern "the birth of conscience" in one short period in the history of Egypt. So much for the contrast between a historical and an ahistorical orientation as it relates to the separation or nonseparation of powers.

In Israel the bifurcation of powers, that between the prince and the prophet, began to appear as early as the time of Samuel. Increasingly, the prophet became the relentless proponent of freedom, equality, and justice.[6] In general, we may say that a tension obtained between law, order, and security, on the one side, and reform, on the other. The covenant was thereby interpreted as inimical to special privilege, whether for the dominant class or for the nation as a whole. The separation of powers opened the way for radical criticism in the name of the covenant. It opened the way for institutionalized dissent. Understandably, Max Weber spoke of Hebrew prophetism as an anticipation of the power of the free press in modern society.

Early Christianity

The Hebrew prophets apparently acted singly. They did not form a continuing organization as a mediating structure, though there were "schools of the prophets" (about which little is known). The members of the primitive Christian churches, however, did form an enduring organization. Jesus, like the prophets, appeared as an intermediary between the God of the covenant and the people of Israel. The "world" in its actual state he viewed in radically pessimistic terms full of warning. In defiance of regnant demonic powers holding individuals and society in their grip, he announced the advent of the kingdom of God. This message engendered a new community imbued with acute eschatological urgency and tension. With theonomous appeal he came into conflict with rigid interpretations of the Jewish law, offering a new freedom. He came into conflict also with questionable practices such as those of the money-changers in the temple and of the rich grinding the poor.

The early community came into conflict also with the Roman state. Under St. Paul the community recognized Roman law as the protector of civil rights and as a punisher of evil-doing. Yet, by its very existence the community violated Roman law. The issue at stake was one that has aroused recurrent controversy in the West, the question of freedom of association. According to Roman law—the concession theory—associations required permission from the Emperor in order to become "licit." Otherwise, they were "illicit." One of the reasons

---

[6] For some of these formulations, I am indebted to conversations with my colleague Paul D. Hanson and to his article, "Prophets and Kings," *Humanitas*, vol. 15, no. 3 (November 1979), pp. 287–303.

for the persecution of the Christians was this legal ground. Another reason was the Christians' refusal to pour libations in worship of Caesar.

In defense of their status the churches could point to the saying attributed to Jesus when he was confronted with the question of paying the tribute money to Rome: "Render therefore unto Caesar the things which are Caesar's; and unto God the things which are God's." This division of responsibilities was again and again confirmed by the claim that one must obey God rather than man. It is clear, however, that the Christians believed the state to have an authentic role. Therefore they could complain that Pilate failed in his duty by permitting an innocent man to go to the cross. At the same time, by claiming the independence of the church as an association they demanded a separation of powers.

Alfred North Whitehead, commenting on the admonition of Jesus about rendering unto God that which is God's, was wont to say that "however limited may be the original intention of the saying, very quickly God was conceived as a principle of organization in complete disjunction from Caesar."[7] This principle of organization had shocking consequences, for it meant that not everything belonged to Caesar. Here we observe a claim analogous to that of the prophets: the church assumed the status of an intermediary between the transcendent and the individual, between the transcendent and the Israelite society, and between the transcendent and the Roman civil religion.

In this separation of powers the early Christians broke not only with Rome but also with the theocratic conception of the Jewish state. More than that, they broke the connection between religion and ethnic heritage; they also broke the bond between religion and family, in the sense that the individual might join the church in independence of the family. Yet, none of these institutions of the world was in their view consigned to outer darkness. In accord with their eschatological orientation, they held that with the fulfillment of the kingdom of God, when God will be all in all, social institutions as well as individuals (and even nature) will be redeemed. Hence, the message of the prophets was confirmed. According to Father George Tyrrell, the Christian eschatology moved from immediate pessimism to ultimate optimism. The divisions of power were to be overcome through the power of God. Hope became an evangelical virtue.

---

[7] *Adventures of Ideas* (New York: The Macmillan Co., 1933), p. 69. Whitehead here speaks of "complete disjunction from Caesar," because the Christians "had no responsibility for the maintenance of the complex system" of the Roman Empire (p. 20).

The theonomous character of the authority for the intermediary role was attested by the belief in the rule of the Holy Spirit. This emphasis led the jurist Rudolf Sohm to speak of the *ecclesia* as a *pneumato*cracy. In this view, the church had no legal constitution, nor was it a democracy. The members of the church under the inspiration of the Spirit sought for consensus in all important matters, including consensus regarding the authenticity of the charismatic leadership.[8]

The latent sociological function of the early churches is worthy of special note. As a consequence of the spread of the churches in the Mediterranean basin, hundreds of people were given vocations in the maintenance and expansion of the organization, vocations requiring a great variety of skills. But with the growth of the churches after the periods of persecution, Constantine altered their status by making Christianity the official religion.

For reasons of space we cannot trace the changes and conflicts of power which punctuated the developments of the ensuing millennium. Viewing these developments, the church historian Leopold von Ranke went so far as to assert that the meaning of history in the West is to be seen in the struggle between the church and the state. Since the time of Charlemagne, a great variety of middle structures have appeared, including monastic orders, guilds, universities, and also deviant heretical movements. A major struggle occurred between the monarchical and the conciliar principals, between absolutism and constitutionalism. The latter in the name of a division of powers attempted to impose limits on government (on the pontiff and the emperor). The conflict was again rooted in what Whitehead called opposing conceptions of "God . . . as a principle of organization."

Conciliarism shifted the center of authority from the papacy to the bishops and the priests, a dispersion of power. Insofar as this impulse appealed to lay support we may see here an anticipation of the principle of subsidiarity set forth by the nineteenth-century Jesuit Heinrich Pesch. This conception was to gain favor in Roman Catholic circles in the twentieth century.

---

[8] The later bureaucratization of the developing episcopacy tended to replace charismatic leadership with officials possessing essentially legal permanence of tenure. Under the influence of Rudolf Sohm, Max Weber spoke of this development as the "routinization of charisma." Moreover, going beyond Sohm's distinction between charismatic and legal-rational authority, Weber added traditional authority as a third type. On the basis of this threefold typology Weber developed a philosophy of history, describing charismatic authority as the dynamic element transcending the other types of authority and opening the way to radical criticism and innovation. See James L. Adams, *On Being Human Religiously* (Boston: Beacon Press, 1976), chap. 13 (on Rudolf Sohm).

In the late Middle Ages still another factor came into play in favor of the dispersion of power. The rise of the cities created a new space for a lay civilization to develop independently of the declining support for ecclesiastical power. This dispersion of power was to appear in at least two ways: first, through the mobility of the lay population and, second, through sectarian movements that could flourish in the new space.

The Radical Reformation

The division of powers crucial for modern history came with the Reformation, and especially with the aggressive sects in its Puritan left wing (also called the Radical Reformation). This movement appeared in the sixteenth and seventeenth centuries. In England in the first half of the seventeenth century the conflict was connected with the struggle against king and parliament which led to the Civil War.

The aggressive sects are to be seen in contrast with the withdrawing sects (a Troeltschean distinction). The latter withdrew from the "fallen" church and society to form enclaves "unspotted from the world" of ceaseless compromise. Living apart from this world ruled by the principalities and powers of evil, they did not form mediating structures, except in the sense of mediating between God and the individual soul. The aggressive sects, on the other hand, remained "in the world" to serve as a leaven to transform it. In this respect they may be compared with the prophetic intermediaries and interveners of ancient Judaism, bringing about a division of powers *within* society—in this case, intervening with a social organization demanding freedom of association. In making this demand they rejected the prevailing view of "Christendom" that uniformity of faith is an absolute prerequisite for a stable society. Those who held to this traditional conviction found in it the religious sanction to harry the heretics out of the land.

The Baptists, the Independents, and the Quakers regarded their congregations as "gathered" churches, in contrast with a territorial church, where membership was tantamount to being born in a particular jurisdiction and was therefore involuntary. They were a gathered church of voluntary believers who had experienced regeneration and who strove for an explicit faith in place of the implicit faith found in the hierarchical territorial church, the church of the masses. These left-wing congregations considered themselves to be under the immediate headship of Christ and the guidance of the Holy Spirit, committed to a way of living set forth in the Bible. They aimed to be "free churches," liberated from bondage in "Egypt," that is, from a monolithic, standing order.[9]

Even before the Civil War this same opposition appeared in New England, where the seceders from the theocracy of the Massachusetts Bay Colony launched out to form independent commonwealths of freedom. In the Fundamental Orders of Connecticut (1639) both religious and property qualifications on the franchise were abolished. Here began the challenge to all restrictive covenants, a struggle that is still with us. Under Roger Williams in Rhode Island, a strictly civil "covenant" (called "democratical") was adopted, providing for majority rule, government by consent, "due process of law,"[10] and freedom of association. But the doctrine of the free church was central here, as in old England.

In the demand for freedom of association the left-wing congregations generally appealed to the independence and structure of the early Christian churches as the model. In doing this they aimed to recover the idea of the church as the covenanted people of God (and, as we have seen, Roger Williams extended the concept to that of a civil covenant). They set themselves in opposition to the coordination of the hierarchical political-ecclesiastical hierarchies, the church-state establishment. In short, they broke away from the Constantinian order: they called for a separation of church and state and for a church of congregational polity.

Under congregational polity these churches aimed to be self-governing, self-supporting groups in which every member had the right and responsibility to participate in the shaping of policy—a radical dispersion of power. They therefore rejected the coercive taxation that supported the established church. Believers alone were depended upon for the financial support. One might say that the passing of the collection plate became almost a sacrament, as did the reading of the Bible in public and private. It has often been observed that this latter practice brought about a high degree of literacy.

Accordingly, this whole movement is often referred to as "radical laicism." In this spirit one of my professors in theological school used to remind us "that Jesus was not a parson." In these congregational churches the covenant was "personalized" by placing responsibility upon

---

[9] For a discussion of the major motifs of this movement see Michael Novak, "The Meaning of 'Church' in Anabaptism and Roman Catholicism: Past and Present," in D. B. Robertson, ed., *Voluntary Associations: A Study of Groups in Free Societies* (Richmond, Va.: John Knox Press, 1966), pp. 91–108.

[10] See James Hastings Nichols, *Democracy and the Churches* (Philadelphia: The Westminster Press, 1951), chap. 1.

the individual conscience and by affirming the priesthood of all believers. In accord with this view, congregational polity incorporated the principle of separation of powers into the structure of the congregation. The clergy were ordained by the congregation and, of course, were not under the aegis of apostolic succession; they were given restricted powers, other powers being reserved for the laity (in the church meeting). Among the Quakers the congregation had the obligation to protect and listen to minorities within the congregation, an anticipation of the idea of loyal opposition in government.

This demand for respect for minorities was related to a general characteristic of these independent congregations, the rule of Scripture as known through the witness of the Holy Spirit. They held that Christ demanded of them a church in which the Spirit is "free to blow where it listeth and make all things new." Hence, the term "radical laicism" is scarcely adequate as a description. Here again we encounter an intermediary factor, a church in which the authority is pneumatocratic. In principle the authority was theonomous and charismatic, though one readily finds also a biblicist literalism. To be sure, some of the groups to the left of the independent congregations gave rise to wilding growths. John Dennis, a critic in the eighteenth century commenting on the "enthusiasts" in these groups, said, "Where one is inspired, ten thousand will be demented." The basic conviction in the independent congregations, however, was that the Holy Spirit, properly listened to, engenders consensus.

Another feature of congregational polity should be noted here. The dispersion of power was so radical and the authority of the local congregation was so much stressed that one may speak of the protest against the centralization of power as a drive toward localism, the geographical localism of scattered independent congregations. The question as to the relationship between congregations was soon raised, and gave rise to attempts at nonhierarchical "connectionalism," a search for a broad, if loose, unity in the midst of variety.

It is a striking fact that this move toward localism found a parallel in the concurrent protest of small businessmen against the concentration of power and against special privileges in the chartered monopolies granted by the crown. Indeed, it is likely that some members of the independent congregations were also small businessmen. Nonconformity was to become the haven of the emerging middle class.

A similar parallel can be found with the emergence of democratic political thought in these circles. Some historians have suggested that the idea of political democracy was born in part as a consequence of analogy drawn from congregational polity. This transfer becomes partly evident in the Leveller movement. John Lilburne, its leader, in his later years became a Quaker. But the Levellers were influenced also by legal theories and by a conception of natural rights which took root in some of the aggressive sects. The doctrine of separation of powers was spelled out in the Leveller *Agreements of the People*, among the first written democratic constitutions. In Lilburne's view, separation of and competition among the powers was not sufficient. The powers, including the king, had to be subject to the rule of law, to some concept of justice.

Of special importance was the development of voluntary associations. Among the left-wing Puritans, associations were initially formed to disseminate their ideas among the church-members of the establishment. Presently, independent associations flourished. In fact, the heady wine of freedom of association gave rise to such a goodly number of groups that members moved readily from one to another, or to the formation of a new one. John Lilburne in the context of these associations developed dramatic agitation as a technique for arousing public opinion. Because of "good olde John" public opinion began to play a new and crucial role, another dimension of the division of powers. Thomas Hobbes in *Leviathan* was so fearful of threatening chaos that he described these associations, including the sects, as "worms in the entrails of the natural sovereign."[11]

During the century after the 1640s we see the appearance of many associations concerned with influencing public opinion on public policy and also with social reform. In *Two Early Political Associations* Norman Hunt has shown that in the first quarter of the eighteenth century the Quakers developed the major techniques we associate with the modern pressure group: disseminating information, raising public consciousness, collecting signatures, and bringing influence upon various agencies of the government—including the legislature and members of the royal family. Here again we see the institutionalizing of dissent.

One of the most significant advances in the eighteenth century was the rise of the independent Nonconformist academies for education, the Dissenting Academies—another division of power. Some scholars in the field have argued that the creation of free academies that could promote higher education without submission to the ecclesiastical rules and the creedal demands of, say, Cambridge and Oxford, constituted a major revolution.

---

[11] See D. B. Robertson, "Hobbes's Theory of Associations in the Seventeenth-Century Milieu," in Robertson, *Voluntary Associations*, pp. 109–28. See also his book, *The Religious Foundations of Leveller Democracy* (New York: King's Crown Press, 1951).

233

The British political scientist and historian A. D. Lindsay, following Sidney and Beatrice Webb's suggestion in *Industrial Democracy*, has stressed the importance of Nonconformity in the development of trade unionism in the early nineteenth century. His characterization of this influence deserves quotation here at length.

> Where Nonconformity was strong trade unionism was strong, and where it was weak trade unionism was weak. It was the Nonconformist chapels which supplied democratic experience and the leadership of industrial democracy, whether in trade unionism or in cooperation. The British labour movement inherited from this source its intense democracy, its belief in government by persuasion and consent rather than by force, or, more exactly, its preference for negotiation and discussion and argument rather than compulsion, its idealism and its inclination to pacifism. It inherited also from Nonconformity its experience of the power for leadership inherent in the most apparently ordinary people, its concern with and care of what it calls the "rank and file."[12]

We are indebted to Max Weber for his contributions in this area of scholarship. I should mention in passing, however, a criticism of the characterization of the Protestant ethic presented in *The Protestant Ethic and the Spirit of Capitalism*. Weber asserted repeatedly in that work that he intended to confine his attention exclusively to economic behavior. Initially, he planned to produce a second volume on Protestant political behavior, but he later changed his mind. The result is that his conception of the Protestant ethic is lopsided. He gives no attention to the development of voluntary associations concerned with public policy or to the democratic internal structure of the small congregations. He presents none of the evidence of that aspect of the Protestant ethic. These Protestants were not peas in a pod, to use Emerson's phrase; they were vigorous, if not always consistent, proponents of the separation of powers and of a pluralistic society.

Likewise, Weber's treatment of Cotton Mather and Benjamin Franklin overlooks the fact that these two figures were prototypical in their formation of mediating structures. Franklin himself formed six or eight of the most important voluntary associations of that time, and he expressed indebtedness to Mather, who a century before had urged church members to form associations for philanthropic purposes.[13]

---

[12] "The Philosophy of the British Labour Government," in F. S. C. Northrop, ed., *Ideological Differences and World Order* (New Haven: Yale University Press, 1949), pp. 250–68.

[13] See James L. Adams, *Being Human*, chap. 12 (on Weber).

I am not aware of any attempt on Franklin's part to set forth a theoretical analysis of the nature and purposes of mediating structures. During the next two generations, however, that attempt was made by three eminent religious leaders: Lyman Beecher, a New Haven Congregationalist; Francis Wayland, a Baptist and the president of Brown University; and William Ellery Channing, a Unitarian in Boston.[14] Much of this writing preceded that of de Tocqueville on democracy in America.

It is a curious fact that relatively little attention has been given to the experience of the seventeenth-century independent congregations as a background for understanding the conceptions of the division of powers set forth by the founding fathers of the American Constitution. The attention has been given, rather, to the writings of, for example, Montesquieu and John Locke—who himself cannot properly be understood apart from that background.

I turn now to a consideration of a political view of the division of powers as set forth by James Madison in *The Federalist* and in his other writings. Here we shall inevitably encounter certain motifs that have come to the fore in our historical survey.

James Madison's Views on Mediating Structures

For Madison the separation of powers is the touchstone of a democratic society. Only through this division can freedom be achieved or preserved. Separation should therefore appear at the different levels in society, from the federal government to the various mediating structures in the public as well as in the private sector. Madison favored a government powerful enough to preserve order, an order balanced by a society with liberty enough to prevent tyranny. The major "desideratum," he says, is order and freedom.[15]

Presupposed, however, is a separation qualifying all levels, the basic separation between the society and the government. In a fashion somewhat similar to that of John Locke, Madison adopted the theory of a double-compact. According to this view, the people first formed themselves into a community, and then as a society formed a government. The government is not the creator of the society. Rather, it is the creature and the servant of the society to which it is accountable. The authority of the government issues from the society and its public opin-

---

[14] See my article, "The Voluntary Principle in the Forming of American Religion," in Elwyn A. Smith, ed., *The Religion of the Republic* (Philadelphia: Fortress Press, 1971).

[15] *Writings of James Madison*, ed. Gaileard Hunt, 9 vols. (New York, 1900–1910), vol. 6, pp. 85, 96.

ion, which place limits on the government. This public opinion comes from the minorities as well as from the majority, for both the majority and the minorities constitute society as a whole.

The separation of powers belongs in turn to all agencies of governance. In the federal government, partitions obtain between the executive, the legislative, and the judicial powers, and the legislature is repartitioned into different houses. Madison also recognized the need for different levels of government. In this connection he spoke of "the intermediate existence of State government." The states and their subordinate levels represent a separation of powers supplementing the partitions in the federal government.[16] They are mediating structures between the federal government and the society. (He felt, however, that the abuse of rights was a greater danger in state governments than in the federal.)

The society, however, is not an abstract entity; it is composed of a large number of groups functioning independently of the government and serving as mediating structures in addition to those within the government. In identifying the mediating structures in the society, Madison used a variety of terms, often synonymously: parties, factions, interests, classes, sects, and institutions. In *Federalist*, No. 51, he gave special attention to noneconomic and religious groups. In *Federalist*, No. 10, he dealt with economic groups, stating that these groups are formed according to whether people do or do not enjoy wealth. An association might be created by either haves or have-nots: creditors or debtors, rich or poor, propertied or nonpropertied. Madison also listed occupational groups that cut across distinctions of wealth. He mentioned "regular branches of manufacturing and mechanical industry," as well as "civil professions of more elevated pretensions, the merchant, the lawyer, the physician, the philosopher and the divine."

Misconceptions have arisen regarding Madison's view of mediating structures because of his somewhat pejorative definition of factions in *Federalist*, No. 10. "By a faction," he says, "I understand a number of citizens, whether amounting to a majority or a minority of the whole, who are activated by some impulse of passion, of interest, adverse to the rights of other citizens, or to the permanent aggregate interests of the community." But Madison also saw in factions a salutary dispersion of power, "a protection for freedom in society against potentially tyrannical intentions of the majority." Viewing the mediating structures all together, he said in *Federalist*, No. 51, that by this means "the society itself will be broken into so many parts, interests and classes of

---

[16] Ibid., p. 91.

citizens, that the rights of individuals, or of the minority, will be in little danger from interested combinations of the majority." This view is not dissimilar to the outlook of the independent congregations of the previous century.

Madison's position regarding the separation of church and state is well known and fits into this pattern. Of great importance here is his insistence on freedom of conscience and on "the free exercise of religion"—his phrase in the First Amendment. (We have noted already that this separation of powers stems in part from primitive Christianity.) Madison did not, in this connection, however, refer to theological or ecclesiastical doctrines.[17] He did not consider himself to be a deist. He was a practicing Presbyterian, having all his life maintained connections with leaders in this denomination. Mrs. Madison had once been a Quaker and was known to continue to defend this group. In the main he appealed for justification of his religious ideas to the common experience of mankind. He was attracted to the common-sense philosophy of the Scottish Enlightenment—Ferguson, Hutchison, and others.

In this connection Roy Branson, in a recent article, reminds us that Madison's concept of factions rests on a doctrine of human nature which in his formulations indicates no theological orientation. By reason of its succinctness, I quote here a passage from Branson's article:

> [Factions] arise from liberty being granted to the diverse aspects of man's nature. In addition to deplorable self-love, factions reflect man's reason arriving at opinions. Man tries to make his views more pervasive and potent by creating groups to inculcate and propagate them. Man's nature includes certain "faculties" or talents which lead him to possess certain interests. Again, man creates groups to achieve these interests. Madison never applauded self-love, but expression of opinion and exercise of talents were considered by him to be legitimate aspects of man's activity. The right to hold and communicate opinions is a basic right, and in this same essay, Federalist #10, Madison indicated how important he considered the right to exercise one's talents when he said that "the protection of these faculties is the first object of government."[18]

---

[17] In a letter he expressed his conviction that "the belief in a God, all powerful, wise and good is essential to the moral order of the world and to the happiness of mankind." *Letters and Other Writings of James Madison*, 4 vols. (Philadelphia, Penn.: 1865), vol. 3, p. 503.

[18] *Journal of the History of Ideas*, vol. 40, no. 2 (April–June 1979), pp. 246–47. For many of the citations in the above paragraphs, I am indebted to Branson's Harvard doctoral dissertation, "Theories of Religious Pluralism and the American Founding Fathers" (1967).

Here we see ingredients of the classical humanist tradition. Reason has an interest in the realization of human capacities; *logos* can disclose a *telos* toward which human life strives, and which judges the quality of that life. In sum, then, Madison believed that the separation of powers is necessary for the achievement of popular sovereignty, enabling the appearance of innovation and of evolutionary social change and reform, in adherence to the law of the Constitution. If we view his system of the separation of powers as a whole, we see that he favored a pyramid of separated powers, reaching from the bottom to the top, rather than a hierarchical order, from the top to the bottom. For this system of "order and freedom of government and society," these lines from Shakespeare are pertinent:

> So we grew together,
> Like to a double cherry, seeming parted
> But yet an union in partition.

The Separation of Powers Today

Madison's conception of the separation of powers was set forth in a small preindustrial society, when the federal and the state governments were in swaddling clothes and when these governments—the so-called "negative state"—aimed to serve as umpire in the face of mediating structures. Moreover, wide expanses of frontier remained to be explored and inhabited.

Today, however, we live in a welfare state, a social-service state, an industrial state, and a garrison state. The government is no longer merely a negative state serving as umpire. It has become a positive state with an enormous bureaucracy and regulatory agencies in the face of powerful corporations. The scope of the problems has enormously increased the functions of the federal government. The garrison state depends upon giant corporations, and its policies reach across the planet. Moreover, the welfare state and the social-service state give substantial support to the states for the maintenance of a bureaucracy. The corporations in turn require millions of workers and an extensive technology. In short, the separation of powers in our time takes on larger dimensions and a much broader scope than a century ago, especially in the garrison state. The world situation confronts us with a unique problem in connection with the separation of powers. The size of the world powers, the United States and Russia, renders them almost impervious to the influence of mediating structures in the society and, in the United States, beyond the control of Congress in crucial moments. One thing is

238

clear: Whereas a century ago domestic policy could claim priority, it cannot today be divorced from foreign policy.

For this reason especially, the centering of attention in the Berger-Neuhaus book on the internal concerns of the local mediating structures must be recognized as a limited enterprise, as the authors would also affirm. On the other hand, this concentration of attention is highly pertinent, for these authors point to an imbalance that obtains in the welfare state, where the policies are controlled mainly from the top down, leaving little room for self-determination on the part of the ostensible beneficiaries. Consequently, people in the mediating structures in this area are placed in the position of exercising only the passive power of adjustment to authority in precisely those matters that concern them most. Here one encounters in many quarters a mass apathy. This condition shows the perennial relevance of the localism evident in the seventeenth-century independent congregations. In the end, however, the achievement of localism in these earlier groups moved towards affecting state policies and thereby their own lives also.

But the prevalence of passive power is not confined to those who are on welfare. Mass apathy is readily evident today in the area of political concerns. In the last century the proportion of eligible voters who have participated in presidential elections has diminished by over 30 percent. One reason for this, it is said, is what one might call a lamentable form of localism, the relatively exclusive devotion to the concerns of the family. This trend has been explained as an aspect of our "achievement society." The heads of the family, conscious of the fact that all members of the family share in the prestige accruing from economic success, give their energy to enhancing that prestige. Political and community responsibilities are therefore given little attention. One is reminded of Plato's view that the family is the enemy of justice in the state. A society in which so much energy is directed to personal success cannot be rightly thought of as inhibited by apathy.

The individual is reduced to passive power also in other areas. One of the most important of the middle structures in our society is the mass media. Here again the individual usually exercises the passive power of listening, which is not accompanied by talk-back or by active participation. Before the radio or the television set no division of powers exists, except in the sense that the consumer may refuse to listen and turn off the apparatus. It is true, however, that the participation of the consumer in other mediating structures can provide him with reference groups that may serve to engender his critical judgment and to provide criteria for exercising judgment.

The prevalence of passive power appears at the place of work perhaps more than anywhere else. This condition results from the hierarchical structure of the corporation. This structure is institutionalized in the bureaucracy necessary in any large undertaking. But institutionalized dissent is lacking. In some quarters corporations and labor organizations have made attempts at improvement. But always heteronomy tends to smother autonomy. Moreover, the heteronomy of passive power engendered by large organizations in industry cannot help spilling over into the political sphere, thereby becoming an impediment to political democracy.[19] In many ways society today finds itself in a situation comparable to that in which modern political democracy came to birth as a protest demanding the dispersion and separation of powers. We have noted this situation in the seventeenth century. The struggle was, of course, to continue. In the economic sphere Adam Smith, in the next century, aimed to diffuse power by resort to the market mechanism. It has been generally overlooked, however, that he extolled this mechanism as a countervailing power to the authority and the special privileges of the great landed estates. The market mechanism was to give freedom, with the opportunity for initiative and rewards to the businessman and to the corporation—that is, to the small corporation of the time. What actually happened was the unanticipated rise of the giant corporations. An analogous process is to be seen in a development appearing in Adam Smith's time. Somewhere in *The Wealth of Nations* he speaks of the evangelical movement that gave to the miner a new sense of dignity by convincing him that he has an eternal soul, but soon after he joined a sect he found himself in a tight vise of moral control. So it is that the modern corporation has helped to bring about a higher standard of living and, in a period of increasing population, has given the opportunity for employment, and yet has also promoted a division of labor without a corresponding division of powers. At the same time the modern corporate community has produced units of disproportionate power in the commonwealth. In this respect Madison's description of the separation of powers has become obsolete. The imbalance is evident in the well-organized lobbies with their affluent expense accounts, a power that has been spoken of as greater than that of the government.

For the correction of the internal hierarchical structure of the large corporation, Germany has contrived what is called "codetermination" (*Mitbestimmung*). It is now legally required that the large corporation shall have representatives of labor on the board of directors.

[19] See Robert A. Dahl, "On Removing Certain Impediments to Democracy in the United States," *Dissent* (Summer 1978), pp. 310–24.

The labor unions are even training their representatives for these positions. Premier Helmut Schmidt has asserted that this development represents contemporary Germany's major contribution to democracy. It is perhaps premature to assess the significance of this dispersion of power. In my conversations with German business executives, however, I have been told that they find the practice of codetermination tedious, yet worth the effort by reason of the change in spirit. Alternative ways of bringing about the dispersion of power in the American corporation are described in a publication by David Ewing of the Harvard Business School.[20] More fundamental is Douglas Sturm's penetrating analysis, "Corporations, Constitutions, and Covenants,"[21] beginning with the question regarding the corporation in its current forms and proceeding to the proposal that the corporation adopt the procedures of constitutionalism (with its broad consensus in the population) and the qualities of covenant.

In discussing the imbalance in the division of powers we have given attention to that resulting from the inordinate size and power of the great corporations. An adequate treatment of the subject would, of course, include a consideration of the imbalance due to those who live in poverty and unemployment. It would also include a consideration of the imbalance due to the size and structure of the trade unions, and also that due to the enormous bureaucracies in the executive branch of the federal government. Just as Adam Smith could not foresee the size of the corporations of the future, so Madison could not foresee the size and virtual intractability of these bureaucracies and their powers, especially evident in the State Department and the Pentagon, in the administration of the welfare state and in the regulatory agencies.[22]

What we have been discussing is the theory and development of modern federalism. The word "federal" is derived from the Latin *foedus*—treaty, compact, covenant. This term illustrates Robert Louis Stevenson's aphorism, "Man does not live by bread alone but also by metaphors." Indeed, one could survey Western history in terms of the root metaphors, beginning with the domestic metaphor of a patriarchal society—in the Bible one finds such metaphors as God the Father and

---

[20] *Freedom Inside the Organization* (New York: E. P. Dutton, 1977).

[21] Article of that title in *Journal of the American Academy of Religion*, vol. 41, no. 3 (September 1973), pp. 331–53.

[22] For a seasoned analysis of the expansion of the federal government, see the writings of Arthur Miller, especially his articles, "Private Governments and the Constitution" (Santa Barbara, Calif.: Center for the Study of Democratic Institutions, Fund for the Republic Occasional Paper, 1959), and "Separation of Powers—Does It Still Work?" *Political Quarterly*, vol. 48 (1977), pp. 54–64.

the church as the Bride of Christ. The organic metaphor has been perhaps the ruling one. For Plato the state is the individual organism writ large. For St. Paul the church is the Body of Christ; believers are members of this Body. These organic metaphors have served in the main as a sanction for a hierarchical structure of organization with authority emanating from the head down. (Contemporary exegesis, however, has shown that the Pauline model is a coarchy and not a hierarchy.) Otto von Gierke, a major historian in this matter, has traced the development of the organic metaphor in medieval thought until its transformation into federalism—the combination of unity *and* liberty. This transformation moved toward a structure in which corporate decision making depended upon the constituent groups from below. In the sixteenth and seventeenth centuries the metaphor of mechanism played a leading role. In this same period, as we have seen, the idea of covenant, which had been used in ancient times, was revived.

I have surveyed the history of the idea of covenant with special reference to the separation of powers and to the role of mediating structures in relation to this separation in a pluralistic society. In this survey we have observed some of the signs of the decline of pluralism as a consequence of an imbalance in the division of powers as conceived by James Madison. Without attempting here to spell out further remedies for this decline, I would like to conclude by considering some of the theological perspectives mentioned earlier, but in a different context.

The idea of covenant is a political metaphor, drawn initially from the sphere of international affairs in the ancient Near East. It seems to be modeled on the kind of treaty made between a superior power and subordinate powers, with promises made on both sides. Through the Hebrew prophets the concept was given a new vertical as well as a new horizontal dimension. The vertical dimension related the human enterprise to a cosmic power requiring commitment in freedom to work for a righteous society.

We should pause here, however, to observe that a wide spectrum of structures has been sanctioned by the idea of covenant. This spectrum reaches all the way from authoritarian theocracy to spiritual anarchism. In this spectrum two motifs appear—reliance upon a cosmically oriented institutional structure of unity and reliance upon the divinely given dignity and spontaneity of the individual. A variety of ways of combining the two motifs has appeared in history.

As a political metaphor the idea of covenant rejects the notion that faithfulness to it is possible for the individual alone; the jurisdiction of the covenant covers, as it were, the whole territory and entails collective responsibility. Responsibility attaches to institutional as well

242

as to individual behavior. This view of responsibility rejects, on the one hand, a tight collectivism and, on the other, a merely atomistic individualism. In short, this conception of covenant calls for mediating structures to protect and nourish the individual and to relate the individual in responsibility to embracing structures. From a theological perspective, both immediate and mediate relationships are defined in the context of a cosmic orientation. Covenant reaches from the immediate and intimate to the ultimate. Dr. Daniel Elazar has pointed out that the covenant relationship is to social and political life what Martin Buber's I-thou relationship is to personal life.

The intimate and the ultimate—indeed, all parts of the interrelated world—the individual, the middle structures, the government, the society, and the divine creative ground of meaning—are held together by covenant. The bonding and binding quality of covenant, the ordering principle, is promises. God is the promise-making, promise-keeping reality upon which we ultimately depend as the reliable, creative, sustaining, judging, community-forming, and community-transforming power. Wherever these powers are working, the divine is working. Accordingly, to be human is to be able to make a commitment in response to the divine promise. But human promises all too often turn out to be fickle. The human being is a promise-making, promise-keeping, but also a promise-breaking creature. The divine reality, however, makes new beginnings possible, and thus is the promise-renewing power in life. This power is manifest not only in interpersonal relations; it can appear also in institutional behavior, even if only ambiguously and incompletely. The separation of powers in society makes possible intervention in the name of the promises, intended to prevent bondage to any finite power. It is the necessary, if not a sufficient, condition for avoiding the idolatry of domination or tyranny. It may even serve to reduce the violation of the divine command, "Thou shalt have no other gods before me."

The secular-minded person who is alienated by the churches or the theologians, or who for some other reason is not (in Weber's phrase) "religiously musical," may find unacceptable any theological formulation. Yet, this promise-making, promise-renewing power is the flywheel of meaningful human existence.

Edmund Burke expressed this conviction in covenantal terms in his memorable statement:

> Society is indeed a contract. Subordinate contracts for objects of mere occasional interest may be dissolved at pleasure —but the state ought not to be considered as nothing better

than a partnership agreement in a trade of pepper and coffee, calico or tobacco, or some other such low concern, to be taken up for a little temporary interest, and to be dissolved by the fancy of the parties. It is to be looked on with other reverence; because it is not a partnership in things subservient only to the gross animal existence of a temporary and perishable nature. It is a partnership in all science; a partnership in all art; a partnership in every virtue, and in all perfection. As the ends of such a partnership cannot be obtained in many generations, it becomes a partnership not only between those who are living, but between those who are dead, and those who are to be born. Each contract of each particular state is but a clause in the great primeval contract of eternal society, linking the lower with the higher natures, connecting the visible and invisible world, according to a fixed compact sanctioned by the inviolable oath which holds all physical and all moral natures, each in their appointed place.[23]

Here is an awareness of vocation which appeals to the fundamentally human promise-making and promise-keeping obligations, vocation which calls for both humility and resoluteness.

---

[23] E. Burke, *Works* (1861), vol. 2, p. 368.

Discussion

QUESTION: You made reference in passing to the civil disobedience practiced by the early Christians, and you mentioned the saying of Jesus, "Therefore render unto Caesar that which is Caesar's, and unto God that which is God's." I think it is possible to interpret this passage in quite a different way. The Christians can be interpreted as saying, "We will do whatever we must in order to render unto God that which is His, but we will not challenge the government." They did not intend civil disobedience.

PROFESSOR ADAMS: Thank you for this question. It gives me the opportunity to offer some clarification. Let me say at the outset that the variety of interpretations provided by scholars reminds one of what the Mad Hatter said to Alice in Wonderland: "Here, you see, everyone gets prizes."

Some scholars have stressed the idea that for Jesus his kingdom was not of this world and that he did not wish to clash with Rome; more important matters were on his agenda. Other scholars (quite recently again) have claimed that Jesus was a zealot bent on the overthrow of Rome. Others have argued that Jesus believed in passive resistance and that he was a pacifist—though he did not condemn military service.

In any event, it is clear that the Christians refused to pour libations in worship of Caesar. Moreover, from the perspective of Roman law, they formed an association without imperial license. As a consequence, the church was an "illicit" association.

Yet, I would not be inclined to attribute civil disobedience to the early Christians. It is true that, like St. Paul, many of them in loyalty to Christ were willing to suffer imprisonment or martyrdom at the hands of the state. But apparently they did not believe in civil disobedience as we understand it today. They were not engaged in a general struggle for freedom of association. They did not demand freedom such as their own for other groups.

I referred to the passage in question in order to say that although the early Christians favored the payment of tribute money to the emperor, they did not hold that everything belongs to him. For our discussion of the separation of powers, the crucial element is found in Whitehead's observation (which I have mentioned earlier) that here one sees that God has become a principle of organization. Christianity was rejecting the civil religion of Rome and its institutions, and it was affirming the need for a separate organization to promote the worship of God beyond Caesar. This separation of powers endured for several centuries, and the theory reappeared in later history.

QUESTION: You mentioned in passing that it is difficult to find institutionalized dissent in the executive branch of government, probably more difficult to find than in business. Herbert Simon's books on organization deal with this problem of decision making in both types of organization. He indicates that a vast number of decisions are involved in every decision. Now, that may be institutionalized dissent. Or is it?

You mentioned also that unions in Britain took a cue from the independent churches of the seventeenth century, becoming an arrow of dissent against both business and the government. But, unfortunately, there is a common characteristic of all human beings, including professors just as much as businessmen: as soon as they rise to the point where they see the trade union can capture the state or the party, and really become the dominant factor, they then forget others who do not have power. Consequently, you have the trade union movement that is now in Britain. I think we need to remember that power is what is at stake in most associations.

PROFESSOR ADAMS: In dealing with the development of the separation of powers I attempted to give a sketch of the historical background, showing that in the seventeenth century the independent churches were opposed to the church-state establishment, and that early in the nineteenth century the trade unions encountered an analogous opposition. At this point, according to A. D. Lindsay, motifs from the earlier church struggle reappeared. In the nineteenth century in the United States, Massachusetts, especially in the courts, was the most die-hard in its opposition to organizations seeking to disperse power protected by the establishment. Here the opposition to collective bargaining was severe. Much of the same sort of struggle seen in the seventeenth century had to be fought again.

As you say, the moment a group acquires new power it will tend to forget its own earlier claims in favor of freedom. One reason is that within the organization itself a power struggle ensues, certain groups angle for control. The Italian sociologist Robert Michels called this "the iron law of oligarchy," the tendency of the eager-beavers to take control. I once heard Arnold Toynbee say that the trade-union leaders divided their energies, devoting half of these energies to the goals of the organization and giving the other half to preventing other people from climbing the ladder to power in the organization.

The trend toward oligarchy in an organization is supported by the indifference of the average member. Everyone knows that in almost every organization it is extremely difficult to maintain the interest and working support of all the members. Some years ago a team of American sociologists studied the trade union in Britain that was supposed to be the most democratic. They found that roughly 13 percent were interested enough to participate in decision making. On this problem I once heard this aphorism: "Every member has his own contribution to make, the problem is to get him to make it." The democratization of any organization is a perennial problem.

When I speak of the need for institutionalized dissent, I have in mind the fact that if the individual must *de novo* organize dissent, the advantage rests almost entirely with the established powers in the organization or the society. If, on the other hand, a generally recognized (that is, legitimized) channel of dissent exists, the individual not only knows how to proceed, he can also be recognized as doing something that the organization has made room for in its constitution. The alternative is for the individual to be attacked as disloyal or subversive.

An early example of institutionalized dissent (and separation of powers) is to be seen in the appearance of political parties. Before the formation of parties, significant dissenters were beheaded; after the formation of parties, they occupied opposition benches—on expense account. It is worth noting here that one of the larger trade unions in the United States has a two-party system. I have already mentioned the practice of codetermination in large German corporations, where labor representatives are legally required to serve on the boards of directors—a dispersion of power. Premier Helmut Schmidt has said that this practice is contemporary Germany's best contribution to democracy. Business executives from Germany with whom I have talked say that they find the discussions with labor representatives on the board to be tedious, but they add that the change in spirit makes the venture worthwhile. The trade unions, for their part, are attempting to reduce the tedium by sending their representatives to training courses. They want to become vigorous participants in board discussions.

Curiously enough, one of the effective means of dissent today is the independent research group employed by the organization. Such a research group is frequently in the government, in business, and also in the churches.

QUESTION: I wonder if sometimes we do not see too much in the model of economic activity when we apply it to other fields, such as to religion. I am sure that Madison had no use for the idea that in politics one works for one's own self-interest. That is the reason he defined factions the way he did. He hoped that factions would be neutralized, so that the politician could seek the public interest. It seems to me to be dangerous to extrapolate from the economic model to other areas. For example, we do not need to make analogies between contracts and the religious commitment of covenant. Does this sort of analogy trouble you?

PROFESSOR ADAMS: I quite agree with your objection to this analogy. A contract is made between two parties for a specific, limited purpose, and an equitable contract is one that in principle is between equals. In a religious covenant such as one finds in the Old Testament, the goal is the fulfillment of the meaning of life, the aspiration for a society in which righteousness and peace will prevail—the eschatological dimension. In the second place, a covenant between God and the people is not between equals. Moreover, in a contract each party attempts to achieve an agreement that will serve his own interest. It is an enterprise in bargaining and an attempt to make it legally binding. The basis of covenant in the Old Testament, however, is not legality or mere self-interest. The basis, as I have said earlier, is gratitude and affection on the part of those receiving the covenant and its vocation. Violation of the covenant is violation of law, but it is more than that; it is a violation of abiding affection and abiding loyalty.

One of the most deplorable things in the history of the idea of covenant is its deterioration into an idea of contract. In this view, the believer has made a contract with God, who promises, "If you do my will, I shall give you the reward of success in all things." The Book of Job is a protest against this idea of covenant as contract. In the face of disaster Job nevertheless says, "I know that my Redeemer liveth." Thereby he affirms the mystery of covenant.

Another aspect of covenant should be emphasized here in connection with the view that the basis of covenant is affection and loyalty. Hosea stresses this idea when he presents Yahweh as going in pursuit of the faithless bride, Israel, and as saying, "I know you have been faithless, but I want you to come back to me. Don't you know, I love you?" In other words, a new beginning is possible. Here the ethos is utterly different from that of contract. One can also see here a contrast with the Greek idea of Nemesis, where new beginnings are futile, for the vengeance of the gods is ceaseless and relentless.

Still another aspect of covenant should be mentioned. A contract, I have said, is between two parties for a specific, limited purpose, and a covenant is holistic. The Old Testament covenant (and also that of the New Testament) impinges upon institutional existence as well as upon the individual. In his essay fifty years ago on the Old Testament prophets, Ernst Troeltsch noted that if you examine the sins identified by them, you will find that they are not primarily sins of individual but of institutional behavior (to be sure, involving individual responsibility and participation). In this connection Troeltsch reminds us that some of the prophets were protesting against the impersonality of the life developing in the cities and in the money economy. In protesting against urbanism they were radically conservative in their idealizing of the previous, simpler life of the quasinomadic society. For example, in the adjudication of conflict the elder transcended the mere legalism of contract. He knew everybody in the families on both sides, and he knew their situation. Therefore, he could view the conflict in its multidimensional character.

Troeltsch goes on to say that in this respect the prophetic message was irrelevant for urban existence. The city is here to stay, and this aspect of the message is permanently irrelevant. Instead of this, one should say that the personalism of the prophetic message is permanently relevant.

Let me add something here about the difference we have been discussing, the difference between a contract and a covenant. Something of the ethos of covenant, it seems to me, lies behind the Burkean conception of social covenant, to which I referred at the end of my paper. Moreover, since our major theme here is the relation between the separation of powers and mediating structures, we should recall that Edmund Burke held that "platoons" of civic-minded citizens are the means whereby they can introduce criticism and innovation for the public good. They represent a separation of powers.

Voluntary Associations

Voluntary associations are generally said to be of two types. If the association is concerned with the immediate satisfactions of leisure-time activities of the participants, it is spoken of as an *expressive association,* e.g., for the improvement of gardens or photography, the enjoyment of literature and the arts, the cultivation of hobbies. If the association is concerned to affect nonmembers as well as members for public goals with satisfactions immediate or deferred, it is called an *instrumental association;* usually, the intention is to engender or affect public opinion as a social force, and thus to resist or promote social change. Neither kind of association exists for the making of monetary profits. Both kinds of association are voluntary in the sense that a member is free to join or to sever membership. Although a church as a voluntary organization shares some of the characteristics of these associations, its self-understanding is different, especially because of its transcendent orientation, its sense of being called of God.

In federalist theory instrumental associations are to be understood in terms of a separation of powers, separation in that these associations provide intermediary "spaces," middle structures, between the relatively involuntary associations, the family* and the state*. These associations claim the constitutional right to freedom of association, a freedom that has had to be fought for, not without dust and heat. They provide the opportunity for the dispersion of power, the freedom of the individual or the group to participate in the making of social decisions affecting public policy. The voluntary and involuntary associations interact with each other in conflict or cooperation; when in conflict the voluntary association amounts to the institutionalization of dissent—in contrast to merely individual (relatively ineffective) dissent*. The open society is not willing to say, "*L'État c'est moi!*" The *moi* is larger. The voluntary association is not the creature of the state; moreover, the state itself is the creature of the community, which in turn is limited by a bill of rights preventing the sovereignty of the majority; democracy is *not* the rule of the majority.

The separation of powers may be traced far back in history. Max Weber observed that the Hebrew prophets by reason of their independence anticipated the modern free press. These prophets found sanction for dissent in numinous, charismatic authority. Likewise, the primitive Christian churches were associations independent of the establishment. The maxim "Render therefore to Caesar the things that are Caesar's, and to God the things that are God's" expresses this independence. Alfred North Whitehead speaks of it as a new principle of social organization. In Roman law the young churches were in principle outlawed.

In the Middle Ages heretical groups were conspicuous dissenting associations. Taking the primitive church as its model, the covenanted "voluntary church" of left-wing Puritanism had to struggle through exile for its freedom of association, an important element of "the Protestant ethic" (overlooked by Weber). For Thomas Hobbes free associations were "worms in the entrails of the sovereign," necessarily to be "wormed." The demand for freedom of religious association opened the way for the demand for freedom of other associations to be actively concerned with public affairs. The demand for freedom of religious association brought about the separation of church and state; the voluntary church, the church of believers, thus relied upon voluntary financial support and not upon coercive taxation at the hands of the state. The collection plate almost became a sacrament. But more than independence was at stake. By the middle of the 18th century sectarians like the Quakers had devised the major strategies of the modern pressure group.

Already, then, the modern "organizational revolution" was taking place, manifest in the changing structure of the state, the separation of powers. With this revolution came also the antislavery movements, the organization of dissenting minorities, ethnic groups and women, neighborhood associations, scientific and professional societies, missionary societies, communitarian groups proposing models of an alternative society, socialists looking toward fundamental structural change, the promotion of civil rights or civil disobedience, or of liberation theology, private academies, libraries, and so on.

Church members have formed or have participated in these groups, and thereby have entered into association with members of other denominations and with nonchurch people. Vatican Council II promoted voluntary associations for the lay apostolate. In this way new conceptions of social responsibility, new types of leadership, new skills of organization appear, expanding the concept of the consent of the governed.

The voluntary association has become the characteristic and indispensable institution of a democratic, pluralistic polity—in contrast to an authoritarian or overintegrated (totalitarian) polity. Inevitably, associations compete with each other for support. Moreover, racist and other "antisocial" or antidemocratic groups enter into the competition. The availability of a variety of voluntary associations makes it possible for an individual to cooperate in concert with others of similar mind on a particular issue, and yet to participate also in other associations bringing together people quite unwilling to support the particular concern of the former group. This is the organizational meaning of pluralism*. Thus individuals do not need to agree on everything in a differentiated society where they presuppose a basic principle of freedom and order and at the same time agree to disagree on penultimate issues. Here we see the multiple relatedness of the individual in an open society.

At times the citizenry can find itself in the situation where voluntary-association theory becomes an ideology* for reducing the responsibilities of the state in face of the deprived. Voluntary associations often serve as watchdogs exposing the government as a violator of the law (also as refusing to enforce the law). They also attempt to expose lobbies and coalitions of lobbies supported by ample expense accounts from major economic "special interests" and geographical groupings, cotton, dairy products, lumber, corn and wheat, etc. Because of these coalitions the legislature has been called the "clearinghouse" for the lobbies. Of peculiar significance in the present era of nuclear weaponry is the opposition of increasingly international voluntary associations to the industrial-military-university complex.

See **Democracy; Ecclesiology and Ethics; Freedom; Pluralism; Politics; Society; State; Totalitarian State.**

J. L. Adams, "Mediating Structures and the Separation of Powers," *Democracy and Mediating Structures: A Theological Inquiry,* ed. M. Novak, 1980; F. I. Gamwell, *Beyond Preference: Liberal Theories of Independent Associations,* 1985; D. B. Robertson (ed.), *Voluntary Associations: A Study of Groups in Free Societies,* 1966; C. Smith and A. Freedman, *Voluntary Associations,* 1972.

JAMES LUTHER ADAMS

NOTES ON THE STUDY OF GOULD FARM

By James Luther Adams
The Meadville Theological School
The University of Chicago

"Fellowship is life; lack of fellowship is death". This is a line from a contemporary "psalm." It states the religious principle in the name of which Gould Farm has labored since the time of its founding. It expresses the insight of the founder, William Gould, who lost his life fighting a forest fire on the Farm but whose spirit still informs the way of life pursued there. For William Gould, his associates, and his successors the meaning and fullness of life are to be realized in responsiveness to the divine power that gives birth to fellowship, to fellowship in freedom. For them the substance of religion is not only communion between the individual soul and God. It is also a horizontal relation between man and man under God in a covenanted community: in principle religious commitment must issue in an appropriate pattern of social life and institution. In a world of extreme complexity where the personal element of "I and Thou" is constantly threatened, Gould Farm aims to be that pattern—a pattern of fellowship in worship, in work, in play, and in healing.

For over forty years Gould Farm has been that unique thing which today is called an "intentional community"; it is a deliberately formed community in which people live together sharing, receiving, and incarnating religious vision. In the world today there are numerous intentional communities. But Gould Farm is a unique species of this unique genus. Most intentional communities are short-lived; they are proud if they can survive for a decade. Gould Farm is now in its forty-second year. The uniqueness of the Farm is to be discerned not only in its survival power. With its extended, old New England farmhouse surrounded by numerous attractive cottages nestling in the fair Berkshire hills near Great Barrington, Massachusetts, Gould Farm, imbued by the quality of its purpose, has what is called "the spirit of a place." This spirit combines the outlook of an intentional community with the simplicity, the frugality, and the individualism of rural New England.

Gould Farm is a fellowship not only for the inner "family" of members who maintain the community. It is open to "outsiders," to people who in distress of mind or spirit wish for a time to participate in a community of affection that gives renewed meaning and depth to life. Gould Farm, in short, is a therapeutic community. It does not live merely for itself, as many intentional communities have done. It is a "self-transcending" community. To all sorts of people it offers healing, the healing that can only emerge, as William Gould believed and showed, in the atmosphere of harmony and mutual aid which characterizes the true family. The Farm has been a haven not only for those who in sickness of spirit desperately needed the fellowship that is new life but also for those who, like the many refugees from Europe of the past two decades, needed a place in which to get new bearings and a new start in a strange land. Many have come with nothing or little in hand to pay for shelter. For others the maximum weekly fee is a very modest one.

The extent of the fellowship that has been brought to birth through Gould Farm is in part evident from the fact that in 1954, for example, a total of 601 different individuals whose periods of stay gave a daily average of 71 people lived at the Farm. A good many of these people return from time to time to the Farm for the major holidays, Thanksgiving and Christmas, or for brief vacation visits. This fact bespeaks the feeling of at-homeness they enjoy there. The continuing, more permanent community is made up of about thirty people of various gifts and of great devotion, most of whom have cast their lot entirely with the community and its labor of love.

An intentional community that achieves its purposes must have more than housing and food, more than atmosphere, more even than spontaneous kindliness and mutuality. Gould Farm, besides possessing these things, has of course a structure of organization, a division of labor, various subgroups for special interests and needs, and withal a way of life where society and solitude, responsibility and relaxation, counseling and being counseled obtain together. Thus it aims to provide something like what is now called "group therapy." Long before this name was invented by the psychologists, Gould Farm had a special and intentional version of the thing itself. Gould Farm is not a psychiatric institution. Its "group therapy" is in certain ways formalized, but it is unprofessional. Underlying all of these factors is the "intention" of the community to achieve quiet, enduring fellowship in responsiveness to the love of God.

Through the years hundreds have entered into this fellowship, each in his own way—there is no "orthodox" pattern demanding conformity. Many of the people who have lived at the Farm are among the leaders in various walks of life—artists, writers, clergymen, lawyers, businessmen, scholars. Some of the workers have been theological students undertaking an informal internship. Others have come because of an initial interest in intentional communities as such. Let me speak personally here. Students as well as faculty from my own school at the University of Chicago have been coming to the Farm now for over a generation. One of my former students, the Rev. Donald Harrington, now minister of Community Church in New York City, in the summer of 1936 took a group of underprivileged boys from Chicago to the Farm in order to give them the advantages of community life. As for myself, a visitor who for almost a decade has lived at the Farm for periods up to three months at a time, I have come to know the life of the community in a measure "from the inside"—assigned as I was to dish-washing, to giving an occasional sermon, and to participating in a music-appreciation group.

At the Farm one meets people who have been hospitalized and who require a half-way station on the road to complete recovery. Or one meets the young man or woman whose doctor believes he requires the social contacts he has been avoiding, the person who has had a shattering experience of bereavement, the woman who on becoming blind must learn to read Braille, the mother who needs temporary relief from overheavy responsibility, the person impeded by physical handicap, the taxi-

---

[1] See Henrik F. Infield. "The American Intentional Communities". New Jersey, 1956, Glen Gardner Community Press.

driver recovering from alcoholism, the gifted young Negro musician who has been suffering from the indignities of segregation. At first blush most of these people appear to be like normal folk anywhere. Only after closer acquaintance does one become aware of the special need. Some of these people come only seeking help, and soon they find that they are needed by others. And then, too, one meets the people who look upon their stay at the Farm as an unusual opportunity for service to others. Over the years I have witnessed the benison gathered from the fellowship by its permanent members as well as by those guests who have come in search of healing and have found it. Inevitably, to be sure, some have gone away without fully satisfying benefit. This brings us to an important finding gained from a recent study.

In a brief comparative study of intentional communities[*] Dr. Henrik Infield has brought into bold relief the uniqueness of Gould Farm which has made it a veritable "second home" for many a seeker for fellowship. This is the first formal sociological study that has been made of Gould Farm.

A community of this sort cannot grow in wisdom and stature without taking inventory from time to time. Gould Farm is aware of this fact. Its acceptance of Dr. Infield's offer to make a sociological analysis of the structure and functioning of the community is evidence of that. Its agreeing to the publication of his findings is itself a sign of its desire to invite others to participate in the process of new seeking. There are few of such communities, if any, in this country. More of them should be established. As Dr. Infield says, the example of Gould Farm makes this task easier.

In his outlook at the end of his book, Dr. Infield gives some consideration to the future of Communities in America, conjecturing as to how they can hope to reach firmer ground and begin to start a stronger impact on the American scene. He sees two possible ways in which this might happen—a breakdown of the American economy or the use of community to tackle the spread of mental illness through the curative effect of the group itself as "group therapy"—not in artificial groups as now generally familiar, but in natural community groups. Dr. Infield rules out the possibility of the first, the "artificial" way, and goes on to say, "The only solution would seem to lie in a step forward to the genuine, naturally grown group, the therapeutic community, a community that, in order to be able to offer therapy as a service and not for profit, will have to be cooperative in function if not in name".

Dr. Infield's findings have done much to make the Gould Farm members and the guests alike newly aware of the unique significance and mission of Gould Farm (of which I have spoken earlier). They have revealed elements of strength in the community and, as might have been expected, also elements of weakness, symptoms of frustrated purpose. The strengths of the community which Dr. Infield discloses will not surprise and will gratify all friends of Gould Farm. The weaknesses revealed provide occasion for taking new soundings and new directions. It is apparent, for example, that some new, youthful members must be recruited for the permanent therapeutic community; new structures and dispersions of authority and cooperation must be sought. Perhaps new opportunities for group decisions and for the distribution of the work must be devised.

New means for old purposes are already being tried at the Farm. To say this is to say that Gould Farm is a living community. The community recognizes that a living fellowship must be a fellowship of renewal. Gould Farm, unlike those intentional communities that have not survived, is relearning this law of life. Dr. Infield's studies and proposals have already become an important part of this relearning venture. Indeed, since the study was made, some new people with qualities of leadership have become working members of the community.

The old friends of Gould Farm and the new ones (now increasing in number) will take heart. In the Gould Farm of the future there will be, as in the past, new treasures as well as old. Indeed, without new treasures the old ones are themselves likely to disappear. This fact calls for a risking faith. Gould Farm cherishes its past, but it also moves venturingly into the burgeoning present. Its faith is in a *living* God. Fellowship with Him is life —New Life.

SOME NOTES ON THE MINISTRY
OF THE CLERGY AND THE LAITY —James Luther Adams

The late William Wallace Fenn, Dean of the Harvard Divinity School, was fond of reminding his students that Jesus was not a parson. In making this assertion Dean Fenn was not only concerned to disparage professionalism in the ministry but also to emphasize the decisive importance of the laity (and particularly in the liberal church). Is it not correct for us to say that one of the best ways to test a church is by the quality and participation of the laity?

Our Universalist-Unitarian heritage from the beginning has been committed to "radical laicism." This heritage we may trace back to the earliest phases of the tradition of Nonconformity. The term "Nonconformity" had its origin in the protest against the Established Church, the state church. Accordingly, Nonconformity implies first of all the separation of church and state, the attempt to eliminate political influence from the church and ecclesiastical influence from the state. Already we see here a thrust in the direction of the dispersion of power, the assumption of autonomous responsibility on the part of the churches themselves. But more than this must be said in order to characterize the Nonconformist heritage of our liberal churches. The term "radical laicism" suggests other important ingredients of our heritage. Four of these ingredients are of special significance: the priesthood of all believers, the prophethood of all believers, the demand for "explicit faith," the protection of minorities, and congregational polity.

The priesthood of all believers in the tradition of radical laicism implied that every member of the church has the obligation to share in the work of reconciliation and healing which belongs to the mission of the church; it implied also that every member of the church has the privilege and the obligation of participating in the shaping of the policies of the church. In the earliest days the doctrine stood in opposition to the control exercised by the clergy and especially by the bishops. In England, James I, recognizing the radically democratic implications of the doctrine said, Today they are attacking the bishops, tomorrow they will attack

James Luther Adams is the Edward Mallinckrodt, Jr. Professor of Divinity, Harvard Divinity School. He comes to this post following distinguished service for a score of years at Meadville Theological School and the Federated Theological faculty of the University of Chicago. Dr. Adams is known throughout the literate theological world as one of its most probing and incisive minds.

the monarchy. His prediction came true. From the demand for a democratic church came the demand for a democratic state.

The prophethood of all believers implied that every member of the church must share with the clergy the obligation of directing prophetic criticism at both the church and the society. This view repudiated the notion that the clergy may properly possess a monopoly on prophetic criticism. Looked at in another way, it meant that the clergy and the laity owe to each other mutual support in the "liberty of prophesying."

Taken together these two doctrines, the priesthood and the prophethood, of all believers, represent the essential features of a radical Protestantism. Here we should see the "collection plate," the offertory, as a symbol of radical laicism. Charles Peguy, the French Catholic writer of a generation ago, aptly contrasted the Protestant and the Catholic by saying that in Roman Catholicism the priests prepare the meal according to established recipes and then present the food to the "faithful" who are expected humbly to eat with gratitude and without criticism; and that in radical Protestantism both the clergy *and* the laity go to the kitchen and prepare the food and then together take it to the table for the common meal.

Related to these doctrines is what has been called the demand for "explicit faith." Here again a contrast with Roman Catholicism is instructive. In Roman Catholicism, according to Thomas Aquinas, God in his graciousness makes salvation available to

259

all people who in good faith accept the doctrines and disciplines of the church at the hands of the clergy, whether or not these people fully understand these doctrines and disciplines. According to Aquinas, many of these people do not have the competence or the leisure to achieve an "explicit" faith"; hence, they are permitted "implicit faith" which is sufficient for salvation. Radical laicism in our heritage has stressed the idea that every man must do his own believing and that he is responsible for this believing: he may not as it were believe vicariously. Explicit faith requires religious literacy for both the laity and the clergy.

Bound up with these Nonconformist conceptions of the true church was the view that the fellowship of faith is a fellowship in freedom. Uniformity of belief is not required for the achievement of fellowship. In other words, the churches of the liberal heritage in principle demand the protection of minority convictions within the fellowship. In the seventeenth century this conception presupposed that only when minorities are encouraged and protected can the church avail itself of the promptings of the Holy Spirit. Conformity can lead to deformity.

Finally, this radical laicism demanded congregational polity, the autonomy of the local church. What a radical dispersion of power all of these ingredients involved—power here being defined as the capacity to participate in the shaping of decision. But what a heavy burden of responsibility this radical laicism places upon both clergy and laity.

The burden is particularly demanding in our mass society with its many norms, with its personalization, with its engines of propaganda, and with its pressure for conformity. The mass society of our day in many quarters threatens to bring about what we may call the Catholization of the Protestant churches (including the liberal churches). Even Roman Catholicism has recognized the dissipation of Catholic faith that has ensued in the mass society. Consequently, Roman Catholicism today stresses more and more the *lay* apostolate. In many of the Protestant countries a new emphasis is being placed today on the role of the laity. In England and Scotland the "house church" has appeared as a social invention that appeals for sanction to the New Testament period when Christians gathered in homes rather than in church edifices. In the countries of the Continent "centers of new life" have sprung up, centers (outside the conventional spheres of church life) which provide the occasion for the laity to nourish their imagination for the prosecution of the priesthood and prophethood of all believers. In Germany, particularly through the Evangelical Academies, the laity are assuming new roles, and the clergy are finding new ways to achieve closer contact with "the world." In these Academies the clergy are not to the fore, they exhibit their sense of obligation to "listen" and thus to discover new ways of achieving relevance in their own special work. In the United States the "cell group" movement represents a thrust in the direction of recovering radical laicism. Other lay group movements could be mentioned.

The vitality and effectiveness of our churches has always depended and continues to depend upon the quality of the laity as well as of the clergy. This is particularly true among us, for we know that the health of the church is displayed not only when the laity is gathered on Sunday but also when they are "scattered" in their various walks of life and in the cadres of community life. The fulfillment of the responsibilities implicit here obviously requires form and skill and discipline.

How shall we judge of our churches if we apply the tests suggested by the elements of radical laicism? And how shall we evaluate our work as ministers? Must we not as clergy emphatically include the test of our capacity to elicit radical laicism? The test bears upon the ministry of the clergy and the laity not only in church life but also in the democratic society. Ultimately, the test is a group test. "By their groups shall ye know them."

THE SOCIAL IMPORT OF THE PROFESSIONS

JAMES LUTHER ADAMS

In the Middle Ages one of the most celebrated and influential treatises on the Liberal Arts was *The Marriage of Mercury and Philology*, attributed to Martianus Capella, an African grammarian of the fifth century. In this treatise, Capella, wishing to wed the rigor of the learned disciplines to the beauty and grace of the imagination, introduces his manual with a romance. He imagines that Mercury, having decided to take unto himself a wife, asks the hand of Philology. In order to fetch home his bride, Mercury appears on the wedding-day with a retinue of the Seven Arts. He presents in turn each of these paranymphs, and in the presence of the god each gives a discourse on the art she represents.

To modern taste the machinery of allegory employed by Capella is as artificial as a Sunday School pageant. But the artists and theorists of the Middle Ages were dazzled by Capella's "great figures of radiant women, superhuman as Byzantine mosaics," figures that represented the seven Liberal Arts. No monastery or cathedral library was deemed to be complete without a copy of this text-book. Capella's personification of each of the arts re-appears in the treatises, the poetry, and the plastic arts of the Middle Ages—on the facades of Chartres and Laon, in the frescoes of Botticelli, and even in the Elizabethan drama.[1]

Two things captured the medieval imagination in this whole conception presented by Capella. First, the Liberal Arts were held to be in the service of a god, either Philology or Philosophy. Stuart Pratt Sherman's phrase offers an Americanized formulation of this aspect of the medieval conception. The arts, he says, have "a heart full of service." Second, each of the arts found its proper place in relation to the god and to each other only by virtue of a clearly defined character of its own. Martianus Capella accomplished what greater creative artists came short of. His figures became

---

1. Émile Mâle, *Religious Art in France: XIII Century*, tr. Dora Mussey, London, 1913, pp. 76ff.

permanent types, all of them together constituting the pictorial representation of the Trivium and the Quadrivium, the seven paths of human activity leading man to what is possible apart from revelation. Yet, they were also servants of revelation. Indeed, they were held to be indispensable for the understanding of the Scriptures and for the service of God even in the church. Moses, it was said, knew something more than the divine law received directly from on high. According to Cassiodorus, he "possessed a complete knowledge of the Liberal Arts; the pagans did but steal a few tatters of his learning." Augustine, earlier than Cassiodorus, thought of compiling a manual of the Seven Arts. But it was Capella who adumbrated the symbols which came to be associated with the indelible character of the arts. In his finely wrought definitions each of the disciplines found its soul.

Capella's imaginative conception is not without significance for our understanding of the social import of the professions. Indeed, the first full-fledged conception of the professions was taking shape during the period when t'. definitions of the Liberal Arts were being worked out. Moreover, like the process of defining the arts, the process of defining the professions took place within the universities. This fact, as we shall see, is of significance not only because it indicates the inextricable relationship between the professions and the universities. It is of significance also because of its bearing upon the developing conceptions of leadership. Like the delineation of the Liberal Arts and of the Trivium and the Quadrivium, the definitions of professional leadership acquired crucial significance for that society and also for the subsequent culture of the West. Moreover, the professions, like the arts, were understood to possess a divinely sanctioned vocation.

The crucial significance of this process of defining the professions must be taken as axiomatic for the discussion of our theme. One of the most revealing ways of grasping the character of any civilization is precisely through discerning the ultimate orientation and the types of leadership which that civilization adopts. The forms of authority determine or express distinguishing features of the ethos of a society. They determine in part also the ways in which these elements of the ethos are transmitted and are transformed in the changing historical situation. The esteemed types of leadership thus provide the cultural forms through which the society achieves an awareness of its own identity. Moreover, they supply important means whereby certain men of ability and training make their functional contribution and at the same time elicit recognition in the society.

The crucial significance of the definitions of leadership can be readily illustrated if we recall the concept of the prophet in ancient Israel. This concept is itself a religious-cultural creation of the highest order, highest because it is a conception that presupposes the very source and meaning of the life of the individual and of the covenanted community. Something comparable is to be observed in the creation and influence of the concept of the mahatma in India. Each of these cultural forms expresses and elicits certain basic attitudes or evaluations characteristic of a religious culture. When a person appears in the social group who approximates the model of the prophet or of the mahatma, his status is immediately enhanced, and he tends to confirm and also probably to transform the awareness of basic value preferences and commitments. These callings are not professional, but they illustrate very well the decisive significance of the forms of leadership in a culture.

Taking into account the facets of social existence we have been mentioning, we can recognize the enormous import of the concept of the professions as a cultural creation defining a type of leadership. Alfred North Whitehead, with some degree of oversimplification, asserts .that "ancient civilizations were dominated by crafts. Modern life ever to a greater extent is grouping itself into professions. Thus ancient society was a coordination of crafts for the instinctive purposes of communal life, whereas modern society is a coordination of professions."[2] Actually, certain of the professions, such as law and medicine, trace their lineage to ancient times. Moreover, the modern professions as well as the crafts descended from the guilds of the late medieval period. In any event, this cultural creation, the concept of the professions, represents a primary expression of decisive elements in the ethos of modern Western culture. This fact becomes immediately evident when we consider the ingredients of the definition of the professions.

In our dynamic, post-traditionalist society, however, a

---

2. A. N. Whitehead, *Adventures of Ideas*, New York, 1933, p. 73.

variety of definitions is available; and, besides, the definitions undergo change, altering the emphasis placed on this or that element. No authoritative or pervasive set of criteria obtains whereby we can distinguish professions from other occupations. Writers on the professions today include among them a wide range of vocations, such as law, theology, medicine, teaching, nursing, physiotherapy, physics, dentistry, optometry, engineering, architecture, veterinary science, business and public administration, war, accountancy, journalism, brokerage, midwifery.[3] Carr-Saunders and Wilson, in one of the standard volumes on the professions, exclude from consideration the church and the army. "The former is left out," we are told, "because all those functions related to the ordinary business of life, education among them, which used to fall to the Church, have been taken over by other vocations. The functions remaining to the Church are spiritual, and we are only concerned with the professions in their relation to the ordinary business of life. The Army is omitted, because the service which soldiers are trained to render is one which it is hoped they will never be called upon to perform."[4] Even churchmen who renounce the claim to be professional men will understandably protest against the reason given here for the omission of the clergy. And as for the Army, the increasing role of military bureaucracy in our world and also of the military man as diplomat and as government executive would seem to me to justify its inclusion in a study so broadly conceived as that of Carr-Saunders and Wilson. Moreover, one could add other vocations that today claim professional status, for example, psychiatry, social work, public relations. It is clear that the concept of the professions is in flux, some of the older professions taking on new functions, others losing certain functions and even declining in rank, while still other, new vocations are emerging upon the scene and claiming a place in the sun. In this situation it is not possible to come upon a fixed definition of the term "profession."

It is doubtful, however, that we should accept R. H. Tawney's definition. "A profession," he says, "may be defined, most simply as a trade which is organized incom-

---

3. See R. W. H. Hawken, *The University and the Professions*, Brisbane, 1947; A. M. Carr-Saunders and P. A. Wilson, *The Professions*, Oxford, 1933.

4. Carr-Saunders and Wilson, *op. cit.*, p. 3.

pletely, no doubt, but genuinely, for the performance of function."[5] This definition is scarcely adequate if it is to retain any substantial vestige of what the professions have represented historically; it appears to include all vocations except those which are unorganized. Historically, the professions have been concerned not merely with a set of techniques for doing some useful work, but also with some fundamental aspect of life in society. The work done by a profession is "a matter of broad public concern."[6]

In face of the welter of definitions available today, one who ventures to set forth a definitive formulation enters a No-Man's Land where he is likely to encounter cross-fire. But we must adopt for our purpose a general, if loose, definition. Accordingly, let us say that a profession includes these features: it performs a unique and essential social service; it requires a long period of general and specialized training, usually in connection with a university; it presupposes skills that are subjected to rational analysis;[7] service to the community rather than economic gain is supposed to be a dominant motive; standards of competence are defined by a comprehensive self-governing organization of practitioners; a high degree of autonomy is presupposed for the individual practitioner and for the professional group as a whole; some code of ethics is adumbrated by the professional group for the performance of its service.[8]

At least these characteristics should be taken into account in any adequate appraisal of the social import of the professions. One should also indicate outstanding changes that have been taking place in the professions, and one should consider the ways in which some of the self-styled professions fail to measure up to the criteria proposed. In the present brief discussion, however, we shall have to confine attention to certain broad considerations. We can do no more than refer rather casually and loosely to historical aspects of the theme. We shall be concerned particularly

---

5. R. H. Tawney, *The Acquisitive Society*, New York, 1920, p. 92.

6. Everett C. Hughes, "The Making of a Physician," *Human Organization*, XIV (1956), p. 21.

7. Cf. A. N. Whitehead, *op. cit.*, 72: "Here the term Profession means an avocation whose activities are subjected to theoretical analysis, and are modified by theoretical conclusions derived from that analysis." Again, the university orientation is involved.

8. Cf. Talcott Parsons, *Essays in Sociological Theory Pure and Applied*, Glencoe, Ill., 1949, Chap. VIII; Myron Lieberman, *Education as a Profession*, Englewood Cliffs, N. J., 1956, Chap. I.

with the social import of the professions as self-governing
bodies and also as related to the universities; with the general social responsibilities implicit in the leadership assigned
to the professions; and with the ways in which the specialist
functions and the bureaucratization of the professions con-
spire against the fulfillment of the general responsibility.
We shall be concerned also with the principal means by
which the professional man, like any other leader, may meet
his general social responsibility with respect to the shaping
of the social policies of the community. In the course of the
discussion, we shall consider briefly the social import of the
ministry as a profession and a calling, in comparison and
contrast with other professions.

* * *

Capella's exalted mythological device for setting forth the
character and significance of the Liberal Arts may appear to
be a rather grandiose way of suggesting by analogy the
social import of the professions. Actually, however, the
advent of the professions, viewed in historical perspective,
typific and enhances a feature of social organization which
is of marked significance for Western culture, and particularly in the democratic societies. In doing so, the professions
express a decisive element in the ethos of these societies of
the West. And they do this in terms of one of the most
symbolically powerful conceptions, the concept of vocation.[9]
Perhaps, then, Capella's device is peculiarly appropriate.

We are accustomed to hearing it said that the democratic
ethos presupposes a Judeo-Christian evaluation of the individual person as a child of God possessing an integrity and
freedom that are inviolable. This is true, and other similar
things could be added respecting the relation between the
democratic ethos and the Judeo-Christian doctrine of man.
But this relationship should not be interpreted merely ab-
stractly. An important feature of any society (and of leadership in that society) is the way in which power is socially
organized. The power may be centralized, for example, in
the state; or it may be dispersed so that certain groups
enjoy autonomy in face of the state and other groupings.
The social organization of the democratic society is of the

9. For an impressive account of medieval and early modern concep-
tions of vocation see the German historian Karl Holl's essay, "Die
Geschichte des Worts Beruf," *Aufsaetze zur Kirchengeschichte*, Vol.
III, Tübingen, 1928.

latter type. This type of organization itself presupposes a view that may be traced at least in part to Christian sources.

In the early period of the Christian era, the churches, rendering to God that which is God's and to Caesar that which is Caesar's, claimed independence of the state and of the culture. This constituted an unprecedented dispersion of power. In its early form this independence on the part of the churches may be viewed as an anticipation of modern multi-group society. The medieval universities and guilds in their turn represent an emerging dispersion of power independent of political organizations. By this time, however, the church had extended its power far beyond its earlier status. In the Middle Ages, as Whitehead observes, "the church so towered above other institutions that it out-rivaled the state itself. Accordingly, its analogy to secular guilds and to other professional institutions such as the universities was obscured by its greatness."[10] From these dispersions of power in face of church and state has come the modern institution, the voluntary association, the organization that stands between the individual and the state and that (without political control) provides the opportunity for the individual to achieve freedom and consensus with his fellows on matters of common concern. We should observe in this connection that a long struggle had to be carried on for the achievement of freedom of *religious* association. This was the struggle of the sects of the Radical Reformation.

Wherever a monolithic authority has existed or has newly appeared, it has rejected the principle of voluntary association. Thomas Hobbes, defender of absolute state sovereignty, spoke of voluntary associations as worms in the entrails of the sovereign. He feared the autonomous associations, religious and secular, which had emerged with such vigor in his own time. This hostility to voluntary associations has reappeared again and again in anti-democratic movements—for example, in the aftermath of the French Revolution, in Hitlerism, and in Stalinism. What is at stake here is not merely individual freedom but also the freedom of groups.

Now it was precisely the professions that helped to give rise to this new form of liberty, liberty not only for the

---

10. Whitehead, *op. cit.*, p. 74.

individual in the fulfillment of his vocation, but liberty also for the self-governing professional organizations. This process is to be observed in the development of non-vocational as well as of professional groups. The autonomous freedom of the professional group is best exemplified by the venerable institution of the lawyers in England, the Inns of Court. F. W. Maitland, in his famous Introduction to Gierke, has cited the Inns of Court as the classic example and model of the voluntary association—a corporation existing in its own right and not dependent on concession from the state. The university has in many instances exhibited a more ambiguous status in face of church and state.

In promoting the drive towards group freedom in modern society, the professional group has provided an instrument making for innovation. But as a self-governing organization it has promoted disciplined freedom and innovation, as against merely sporadic and arbitrary spontaneity. It has done this especially in defining or redefining standards of professional performance and also in defining a code of ethics. Here the relation between the professions and the universities is of signal importa: :e. The university has been the repository of a basic featuı e of the ethos of modern Western culture, freedom of inquiry conjoined with the ideal of rationality. This aspect of the university (and of the professions) has been significant in the development and the maintenance of a universality that transcends local religious or nationalist tradition, though of course the ideal has all too often been compromised. All of the elements we have mentioned must be taken into account as aspects of the character and significance of the freedom of the self-governing professional organizations.[11]

Still another important aspect of the professions deserves

11. An additional aspect of freedom promoted by the professions should be mentioned. Ideally, the professional groups have made possible a certain freedom for the recipients of professional services. The skills of the professional man are supposed to be available to all men, even if these men are not in every instance able to pay for the services. This availability of professional services is connected with the historic idea that a professional man does not work primarily for economic success but for the general welfare. On the other hand, professional groups in many instances have also unduly restricted admission to the professions. This restriction of freedom by professional groups calls to mind the restrictions imposed within the groups themselves through the operation of "the iron law of oligarchy." For a detailed account of this kind of restriction in one of the professions see Oliver Garceau, *The Politics of the American Medical Association*, Cambridge, Mass., 1941.

emphasis, a characteristic arising from the fact that the professions in their orientation and training are associated with the university. Here again we encounter justification for the high conception of the professions which we have assimilated to the mythological allegory coming from Martianus Capella. In the German language the professional man may be called an *Akademiker*. In all countries the professional man historically has been expected to secure a higher education before entering upon his specialist training. Accordingly, the professional man possesses an academic gown. This prerequisite of the professional man determines in part the definition of his type of leadership and responsibility in society. It serves also in part as the basis for the prestige he is supposed to enjoy.

What are the implications of the academic gown? If we answer this question, we come upon an aspect of the professions which today threatens to derogate their social import in the life of the culture. As a university man the professional is expected to have acquired critical familiarity with the characteristic lore of the culture, in the sciences and the arts. The wearing of the academic gown presupposes that the bearer accepts some responsibility for transmitting, criticizing, transforming, and applying the characteristic ethos of the culture in face of the changing historical situation. Accordingly, the professional man is expected to exercise a leadership that impinges upon the determination of general public policy.

This presupposition was made evident in the analyses and evaluations of medical and legal education given to us in the present conference by Dean Lippard and Professor Sutherland. These scholars stressed the fact that the training of the physician and the lawyer aims to enable these professional men to concern themselves critically and imaginatively with the subsurface issues of life which impinge upon their performance of their tasks. This conception of professional training reminds us that the history of medicine is intertwined with the whole history of the culture and with the changing forms of sensitivity characteristic of the culture. The history of the law as a profession is likewise interrelated with the history of the basic theological and philosophical lore and with the history of the conceptions of right relations between men and between institutions. These facts stand out prominently, for example, in Henry E.

269

Sigerist's *A History of Medicine* and in Dean Roscoe Pound's account of *The Lawyer from Antiquity to Modern Times.* The learning of the great physicians and of the great jurists of modern times is not the learning of mere specialists, it is the learning appropriate for the responsible transmission, criticism, transformation, and application of ethical and religious value preferences. Dean Pound's *The Spirit of the Common Law* shows how, in the past century, court decisions and legal thinking generally have responded to a major shift of outlook from what he calls Puritan individualism to the revival of "the feudal element" in law, the stress on responsibility for the social consequences of legislation.

The professional man willy nilly deals with fundamental issues of life. As a leader in the society, as a man of higher education, he is expected to be a decisive bearer and critic of the culture. This is a part of his community service, and in the long run his prestige depends upon his performance in this respect as well as in his more narrowly specialized services. Indeed the general and the specialist responsibilities are bound together, though they are also in many instances distinguishable. At this point the professional man who is also a Christian faces always the necessity of newly interpreting his tasks.

A principal threat to the continuance of the broad cultural character and responsibility of the professions in the present century has been the outlook of the mere specialist, a view that is to be contrasted with the ethos of the humanist in the traditional conception of the university. The tension between the humanist and the specialist is to be observed already in the Renaissance. The threat to the continuance of the professional man as a bearer and critic of culture has appeared as a consequence not only of the dissolution of traditional values and not only of the utilitarian *embourgeoisement* and trivialization of the higher learning. It has appeared also as a consequence of the pressing demands made upon the professional man to specialize. In the course of this trend towards specialization the generalized functions of the professions have declined in favor of "specificity of function." This emphasis on specificity of function, to be sure, represents a definitely legitimate professional responsibility, a limitation of claim to expertness in face of the client. It belongs to the impersonality and impartiality

270

of "professional service." But in many quarters today the service is so highly specialized that the professional man tends to deal only with a segment of the human person or of the human institution. Accordingly, he fails to see his specialist responsibilities within the context of the total fabric of life. In this process the specialist himself may become in his work only a segment of a person. One is reminded of the epitaph which the late Dean Sperry of Harvard Divinity School reported encountering in Scotland.

> Here lies John MacDonald
> Born a man
> Died a grocer.

The wide-ranging human concerns of the old-fashioned grocer scarcely illustrate the reduction I am suggesting. We should rather speak of a wrapping clerk in a supermarket.

* * *

This whole matter of the tension between the generalized and the specialist functions of the professional man gives us occasion at this point to observe the character of the ministry as a profession. First, however, we should note that the concept of the profession by no means fits neatly upon the clergy. We say this not only because many of the American clergy have had something less than a higher education, not to speak of their lack of professional education. The concept of the professional man is inadequate for characterizing the minister also because the minister of a Christian church is something more than, or other than, a professional man. Kierkegaard's distinction between the apostle and the genius is useful here to bring into relief a non-professional ingredient in the vocation of the ministry. The minister's calling is "not of this world."

Properly understood, he is not a spokesman for a cultural tradition. Within the context of a community of faith he shares the vocation of bringing culture under judgment in the name of that which stands over and beyond culture. He has the vocation of preaching the Gospel not only to the culture, but especially to the almost equally difficult mission field, the actual church. In the fulfillment of this vocation in its amplitude, he relies upon the working of the Holy Spirit. This dimension of the vocation of the minister, viewed particularly in its impingement upon new situations, is sometimes referred to as charismatic, a witnessing to that which rejects self-sufficient culture and to that which alone can profoundly transform church and culture under the great Taskmaster's eye. We should add, however, that there is no necessary opposition between *charisma* and *logos*, between *charisma* and professional responsibility.

But apart from these considerations, we can see that, in contrast to the emphasis on specificity of function characteristic of the typical specialist today, the minister is usually concerned with the total human person; he performs diffuse or generalized functions. The minister's status depends in part upon technical competence of the sort represented by the theological disciplines, theoretical and practical; but his status in the church and the community requires of him also that he maintain a generalized responsibility which is not so clearly based upon strictly professional skills. His vocation as such has the task of probing to that which lies behind and criticizes all vocations. Moreover, he ideally must fulfill his responsibility directly in face of a wide range of configurations — the family and the encompassing institutions of church and society. Certain other qualifications should be noted here. In contrast to what obtains in other professions, the minister's clientele, so to speak, is primarily made up of the members of the organized group of which he is the leader. His clientele is itself an organized fellowship. The members of his congregation "share" him as leader, priest, pastor, preacher, religious educator, friend. The minister, moreover, is comparable to the business executive in the sense that he has the responsibility for maintaining morale in an organization, he represents his organization in face of the community, and he has responsibilities with respect to the denomination within which he works. Verily, his role is diffuse. Moreover, it is subject to considerable variety of definition. In the main, nevertheless, it performs an integrative function in the society.

In face of the more specialized professions, the minister's status has suffered decline just because of the diffused, generalized character of his responsibilities. In response, some ministers have emphasized or resumed authoritarian claims —in some instances possibly as a compensation for the frustrations incident to residual status. Others have been developing new types of specialization. In the larger churches, we are witnessing a division of labor that is somewhat analogous to that of the specialized professions. One can

272

see, for example, the emergence today of the minister who is the preacher, or the pastoral counselor, assisted by the minister who is an executive director or a religious educator. The Niebuhr-Williams-Gustafson report on *The Purpose of the Church and Its Ministry* envisages the dominance in our time of the pastoral director, a generalized function which will probably be subjected to more refined division of labor.

What should be emphasized, however, is the fact that today the generalized character of ministerial responsibility stands in marked contrast to the highly specialized work of many of the other professions. This role of the minister assumes special significance in the situation. His diffused responsibility is all the more needed at a time when other professions have increasingly surrendered their generalized cultural functions.[12] On the other hand, one can observe minor shifts taking place within other major professions in order to recapture something of the generalized function of the professional man as historically understood. One hears today of a new stress upon the holistic approach for the physician. Some medical schools are also attem. .ing to encourage the reappearance of the family doctor. Among lawyers in general practice, I am told, there is a marked tendency to increase the amount of effort given to a sort of pastoral counseling of the client. A lawyer friend of mine complains that his legal training did not fit him for the large amount of personal counseling he has to provide. He has turned to psychiatrist and ministerial friends for counsel. The appearance of the psychiatrist is itself a sign of the demand for professional men who are capable of a wider competence than is suggested by the term "specificity of function." One may, by the way, question whether the average psychiatrist has the professional training that fits him for his dealing with the basic questions of ethos having to do with the very meaning of life itself.

* * *

We must now in conclusion return to consider certain implications and consequences of the major tendency in the

---

12. Perhaps taking the initial suggestion from Talcott Parsons, Rabbi Robert J. Marx, in his Yale Ph.D. dissertation, "Changing Patterns of Leadership in the American Reform Rabbinate," stresses the mediating role of the clergy, speaking of it as interactional or interstitial. Cf. also Kaspar Naegele, "Clergymen, Teachers, and Psychiatrists: A Study in Roles and Socia''zation," *Canadian Journal of Economics and Political Science*, XXII (1956), 46-62.

professions to neglect generalized functions and broad cultural responsibilities. We have already suggested that if the professional man is to be worthy of the prestige that accrues to him because of his higher education, if he is actually to rate as a bearer and critic of culture, he must perform functions in the community at large which have to do with general public policy. One of the major obstacles at this point arises from the bureaucratization of professional life.

Let it be noted without delay that the minister is not exempt from the hazards of bureaucratization; his work is bound up with the life of a denomination and of a local church. Consequently, the minister can find in himself a greater diversity of role-conflict than any other vocation: he can combine within himself the tension between the professional, the bureaucratic, and the charismatic roles. In many churches the minister faces a sort of Vatican of authority in his Board of Trustees, an authority that can speak very firmly in favor of special class or race interests. As a consequence, his vocation as a critic of culture, either from a charismatic or a professional perspective, is frustrated. The pressure to conform is heavy. Of the most subservient of the clerical bureaucrats the epitaph might well read:

> Here lies John MacDonald
> Born a man
> Died a trimmer.

The art of trimming and thus of betraying the trust placed in the professions is to be seen wherever rigid bureaucracy has encircled its tentacles. To be sure, a critical attitude towards the status quo can be smothered by the desire to get customers, whether the professional man works as an individual or within the confines of a bureaucracy. But the pressures from a bureaucracy are particularly importunate. The lawyer working for a large firm is often timid about taking a public stand on controversial issues respecting general social policy. Not long ago I encountered a lawyer who was reproached by his firm because he belonged to a church that was promoting desegregation of the Negro. His employer told him that clients in the neighborhood had complained about his being a member of this church. In indignation this lawyer asked in reply if the firm proposed to tell him what church he should or should not belong to.

Presently thereafter he resigned from the firm. We are all familiar with the pressures a physician can receive from his professional association if he defends socialized medicine, albeit in the name of the democracy of health. Bureaucratization can mean routinization, and this in turn can mean the studied acquisition of profitable insensitivities and irresponsibilities. Warning against such dangers of the routinization of insensitivity, Supreme Court Justice Felix Frankfurter in his recent Gay Lecture at the Harvard Medical School defined the profession of medicine as a dynamic concern for the health of men and women, and in order to illustrate his conception he set forth extensive biographical accounts of four physicians of the past century who broke loose from professionalism and probed into hitherto unexplored areas of research and public service. At the time several of these men were considered by their colleagues to be "cranks."

Many of the trained social scientists of our day are marketing their wares to large commercial bureaucracies in which they are obliged to accept meekly the ends already established. Thoreau offered a cryptic description of this situation in his phrase, "Improved means with unimproved ends." Even if White's book on *The Organization Man* may be criticized for its oversimplifications, the pejorative connotations of the term "organization man" are largely justified, and that for most of the professions.[13]

This compromising of professional integrity or independence sometimes takes place under political motivation. Recently this fact was brought out for me very forcibly in a description of many lawyers in the United States during the period of the McCarthyite hysteria. To an eminent jurist the claim was made in my hearing that if ever there was a time when the lawyers as a profession had the obligation to speak out for the sake of democratic values and for a vital legal tradition, it was during the period when Senator Joseph McCarthy was swinging his axe. In response, the jurist said that he thought the clergy had established a better record at that time than the lawyers. Indeed, he went on to say that at that time in the backrooms of the Bar Association meetings one could hear lawyers of rank say

---

13. Cf. Graham Hutton, "Professionalism and Bureaucracy," *British Medical Journal*, May 25, 1957. Already in 1829 William Ellery Channing warned against the repressions available at the hands of "voluntary" associations. See his "Remarks on Associations."

that of course basic human rights were being violated by Senator McCarthy and his cohorts, but that the end being served had to take precedence, namely, that a certain political party should be categorized as soft towards the Communists. It was admitted that reputations and rights were being destroyed, but it was said that later on when the right political party had regained power, the lawyers could take up the sag and restore human rights. Meanwhile, a few innocent people might have to suffer for the greater glory of economic interests.

The professional man has the opportunity and the responsibility to perform a generalized cultural function in the course of his daily work, and it goes without saying that many professional men do yeoman work in this respect at many levels of their professional performance. It remains now to indicate one of the principal ways in which professional leadership in the democratic society may fulfill its larger vocation with respect to cultural values and with respect to the criticism and transformation of culture. We have asserted that a decisive and characteristic institution of the democratic society is the voluntary association. Indeed, we have found that the self-governing professional organizations represent a major example of the voluntary association, even if some of these organizations, like the earlier medieval guilds, have degenerated into well-nigh involuntary associations.

The cultural leadership incumbent upon the professions cannot be effectively carried out without the participation of professional men in the non-professional voluntary associations that provide the opportunity for the sifting of facts about public policy, and for the achievement of tentative consensus and of implementation of that consensus through political and non-political means. As De Tocqueville and Lord Bryce pointed out long ago, the health of the democratic society depends upon the vitality of voluntary associations concerned with public policy. These voluntary associations provide the occasion for the exercise of the decisive liberty of the democratic citizen, the liberty of association for the sake of the general welfare. If the professional man confines his participation in voluntary associations to his professional association, he cannot escape promoting merely class and narrow professional interests. It is at this point that the clergy as well as the other professions quite generally show themselves to be impotent and unconcerned. An important test of the quality of responsibility assumed by the clergyman or the member of other professions is the degree to which he participates vitally in associations that are concerned with the controversial issues of public policy, and with the maintenance and extension of human rights, indeed with the redefinition of these rights in face of the changing historical situation. The professonal man is adept at finding alibis for non-participation. He may say that his specialty requires his whole energy; he may say that he works at the level of subsurfaces more important than the strategies of external organizations. But in this fashion he simply finds rationalizations for remaining a eunuch in the bosom of the body politic. The professional man (like any other citizen) must face the responsibility for the consequences of inaction as well as of action.

Nathaniel Hawthorne in his story *Lady Eleanor's Mantle* deftly sets before us the alternatives. He tells of an aristocratic lady from the old world who disliked to be seen on occasions where the commoners congregated. Lady Eleanor wore a beautiful scarf, a sign of her aristocratic breeding. With his characteristically pungent symbolism Hawthorne presents a commoner who approaches Lady Eleanor and begs that she will drink from a communal chalice as a recognition of her identification with the common lot. The Lady declines the offer. A few days after she had refused to drink from the proferred common chalice, an infectious disease broke out in the colony. In the end it was discovered that the initial germ of the disease had been carried by Lady Eleanor's scarf. Willy nilly she was a part of the total community.

The social import of the professions historically has been bound up with responsibility for the pervasive concerns and needs of the commonwealth. The prestige of the professions has depended upon generalized as well as specialized competence. Only where both of these dimensions of responsibility of leadership are promoted is the vindication of the university and the church tradition possible. The legend that has apostrophized the professions is *Noblesse oblige.* Better stated in Christian terms, the legend should read, God is sovereign over the whole of life.

The Place of Discipline in Christian Ethics

By James Luther Adams

I. *Introduction*

PROFESSOR KARL JASPERS in 1936 asserted in a conversation, "Religious liberalism today has no positive significance because as a corporate movement it has no stamina and no discipline. I would counsel any young religious liberal training for the Protestant ministry to adopt the most orthodox form of his religious heritage. Orthodoxy alone has shown effective resistance to Nazi nihilism."

In our time the lack of resistance and discipline in religious circles has been crucially evident not only in face of a Nazi nihilism. Sociological observers of our military forces in the Second World War report that the men and women possessing a dogmatic and even a narrow faith showed the clearest resistance to moral and spiritual relaxation. For some of the fundamentalists (and others) this resistance was barely distinguishable from rejection of normal contacts. The history of monasticism and of the sects of withdrawal exemplifies this same rejection on the part of groups intent on maintaining purity of doctrine and moral life. The problem is a perennial one.

Historically, discipline in the Christian church appeared as an effort of the Christian community to keep itself unspotted from the world, to secure the spiritual well-being of its members, and to impose sanctions upon offenders against its constitution and teachings. The question concerning the place of discipline in Christian ethics is the question regarding the practical means by which a Christian group maintains its character and resists accommodation.

278

II. *The Creation and Fall of Discipline*

From a modern Protestant point of view, church discipline, as it has been understood and practiced in wide stretches of Christian history, is unethical and has no place in Christian ethics. In both ancient and modern, especially in medieval history, church discipline has employed all manners of coercion and penalty. Perhaps the first rule of discipline in the New Testament is given in Matt. 18: 15-17: "If thy brother shall trespass against thee, go and tell him his fault between thee and him alone: if he shall hear thee, thou hast gained thy brother. But if he will not hear thee, then take with thee one or two more, that in the mouth of two or three witnesses every word may be established. And if he shall neglect to hear them, tell it unto the church; but if he neglect to hear the church, let him be unto thee as a heathen man and a publican." Here the *aims* are the reformation of the offender; and, failing that, the purification of the church. The *method* is that the offended person takes the first step, and, that failing, a small church committee acts; and, in case of their failure, the church is called in and the obstinate offender is cut off from fellowship.

The *apostolic* discipline is illustrated by Paul's treatment of the incestuous person, namely, excommunication "in the name of our Lord Jesus Christ." Paul implies that the "judgment" lies with the church, "Do not ye judge them that are within?" (I Cor. 5:12) To be sure, expulsion could be remedied by the repentance of the offender; Paul exhorts the church to "forgive and comfort him," and restore him to fellowship (II Cor. 2:7). The whole elaborate system of Christian discipline is anticipated in the apostolic church — excommunication, deprivation of the benefits of external communion, penance, in short the exercise of the power of the keys, of the power to bind and loose. It would be wrong, however, to suppose that the church in the early centuries conceived of the high demands of Christianity as a yoke placed on the believer. As Holl remarks, they were considered a gift, indeed a sign of the redemptive working of God. The essential victory had been won already in Christ; evil no longer had real power[1].

In the Canon Law, sanctions were termed either medicinal *(poena medicinales)* or strictly penal *(poena vindicative)*. Discipline in these senses has included reproof, penitential regulations, book-burning, economic sanctions, inquisition, torture, and capital punishment. Generally, these disciplines were administered with

---

1. Karl Holl, "Die Missionsmethode der alten und die mittelalterlichen Kirche," *Gesammelte Aufsätze zur Kirchengeschichte,* III, 122.

the aid of the secular arm, except in the heritage of the Left Wing of the Reformation. In Catholicism and in the Right Wing of the Reformation, these penal disciplines were usually controlled by the clergy or a consistory; in the Left Wing by the congregation. On the whole the church types of religious organization have imposed coercive disciplines in the name of a compulsory association for the administration of grace, (though it should be added that Luther wished the people's church to be voluntary). The sects exercised discipline in the name of a voluntary association of religiously qualified persons.[2]

The motive for these sanctions is given characteristic expression in John Knox's *Order of Excommunication* where it is stated "that, as it would be a work both uncharitable and cruel to join together in one bed persons infected with pestilent and other contagious and infectious sores, with tender children or such as were sound, so it is no less cruelty to suffer amongst the flock of Christ such obstinate rebels . . . for a little leaven corrupteth the whole mass."[3] Analogous motivation is appealed to by Thomas Aquinas, though with him there is also the presupposition that the stability of society requires uniformity of faith.

In the Wesleyan movement, the motive for the exercise of penal discipline was the maintenance of the purity of the group bent on perfection. Here the occasions for expulsion and for other penalties were legion. At the Society in Newcastle, Wesley in 1743, after reading the rules to the members, excluded sixty-four; "two for cursing and swearing, two for habitual Sabbath-breaking, seventeen for drunkenness, two for retailing spiritous liquors, three for quarelling and brawling, one for beating his wife, three for habitual willful lying, four for railing and evil speaking, one for idleness and laziness, and nine and twenty for lightness and carelessness"[4]. Many other forms of "deviation" were deemed ground for expulsion. Wesley even compelled his followers to give proof of their allegiance to the Crown. Information regarding the wayward was gleaned at the band meetings and at class meetings, where attendance was compulsory, and where such questions as these were posed: "Do you desire to be told of all your faults? Do you desire that everyone of us should tell you, from time to time, whatsoever is in his heart concerning you? Do you desire we should tell you whatso-

2. See Max Weber's extensive discussion, "The Protestant Sects and the Spirit of Capitalism," in H. H. Gerth and C. Wright Mills, eds., *From Max Weber: Essays in Sociology* (New York, 1946), pp. 302-322.
3. John Knox, "Order of Excommunication," Ch. iii.
4. John Wesley, *Journal*, March 12, 1743.

ever we think, whatsoever we fear, whatsoever we hear concerning you? What known sins have you committeed since our last meeting? What temptations have you met with? How were you delivered? What have you thought, said, or done, of which you doubt whether it be sin or not?"[5]

One may with almost equal plausibility explain "success" of the Methodist (and similar) practices on the ground that in the face of widespread moral degradation firm discipline was essential "if the Societies were to enjoy health and strength" (Wearmouth) or on the ground that the worth of socially repressed strata in society was "guaranteed or constituted by an ethical imperative,or by their own functional achievement" (Weber).

The modern rejection of church discipline has been due not only to the modern distaste for coercion in religion and to the disposition to assign this sort of sanction to civil law and authority. It has been due also to an increasing awareness of the self-righteous legalism and the irreligious moralism of the disciplinarians. The spiritual ill-health incident upon these types of legalism and moralism has become evident again in our time in the organized production of neurosis at the hands of the Buchmanites. Moreover, the triviality of some of the occasions for discipline (smoking, dancing, card-playing, attending the theatre) have given rise to the evangelical objection that the religious virtuosos tithe mint and anise and cummin, and have left undone the weightier matters of the law, justice, and mercy and faith. Daniel Jenkins has put the case against this picayune moralism in telling words: "Everything had to be in black and white. Drinking, gambling, sexual irregularity, sectarian education — these were all clear-cut issues, and all who supported our views on these matters were angels of light and all who did not were the beast from the abyss. The result was that we forgot that few things are wholly black or wholly white in this fallen world, and conscience was not sharpened but blunted. In thundering about these issues men became more and more pharisaical and complacent, imagining that all was well with them before God because they took 'the party line'; while the real spiritual needs of their age were increasingly lost sight of."[6]

However justified may be the revolt against church discipline in modern Protestantism, the total result is little more gratifying than that of the old ways of discipline. In some quarters the relaxations of individualism and freedom of conscience have conspired to

5. *Works*, VIII, 273. Quoted by R. F. Wearmouth, *Methodism and the Common People of the Eighteenth Century* (London, 1945), pp. 241-242.
6. Daniel Jenkins, *The Church Meeting and Democracy* (London, 1944), pp. 51-52.

make "the Christian life" become more synonymous with general affability, or good breeding, or submission to the disciplines of class and nation. The nadir of church discipline is intimated in a contemporary American parish's application for membership which reads: "I wish to join the . . . Church to share its free fellowship and to advance its purposes of liberal worship and service. I understand that, by this act, I am not in any way limiting my freedom either of thought, or conscience, nor am I surrendering ideals, convictions, or ways of living which I now value . . ." Probably the formulations employed in this statement say less than was intended; in any event, this blurring of the character of church membership in favor of "freedom" represents the extreme opposite of the spirit revealed by Calvin's assertion that any minister who "knowingly and intentionally admits an unworthy person (to the Lord's supper) whom he might justly reject, is as guilty of sacrilege as if he were to give the Lord's body to dogs."

III. Theological Principles

The widespread disappearance of traditional church discipline, as we have observed, is not to be explained only in terms of relaxation. It has been supported by positive religious motives. On the theological level, perhaps the most instructive rival evaluations of the place of discipline in Christi : ethics are to be discerned in certain characteristic differences between Calvin and Luther. These differences, to be sure, do not constitute mutually exclusive contrasts; they are rather differences in emphasis.

John Calvin in his treatment of discipline observes that "some have such a hatred of discipline as to abhor the very name." To them Calvin replies, "that if no society, and even no home, though containing only a small family, can be preserved in a proper state without discipline, this is far more necessary in the church, the state of which ought to be the most orderly of all. As the saving doctrine of Christ is the soul of the Church, so discipline forms the ligaments which connect the members together, and keep each in its proper place. Whoever, therefore, either desire the abolition of all discipline, or obstruct its restoration, whether they act from design or inadvertency, they certainly promote the entire dissolution of the church."[7] Whereas the Roman Church had demanded only ecclesiastical obedience, Calvin would not tolerate deviation within the church. In effect he regarded the Gospel as a new law designed to be embodied in new life, social as well as individual. The old

---

7. John Calvin, *Institutes of the Christian Religion*, Book IV, Chapter 12.

church had made a decisive demand mainly with respect to confession of belief. The new church, under the hand of Calvin, demanded confession of life; and the state had the obligation to preserve the true doctrine, to regulate life in a manner requisite for the social welfare. Offences against the church became offences against the state, or vice versa, and deserved punishment.

Luther, on the other hand, had seen enough of coercive discipline and legalism, and he sought a completely new basis for the Christian life. For him, Law and Gospel "are the two opposite halves of one whole and cannot operate side by side. Where Christ is present, there the Law must not rule the conscience, but must retreat and must give the bed to Christ alone . . . . He alone must have the right and rule in justice, assurance, joy and life, so that the conscience may joyfully go to sleep in Jesus, unconscious of Law, without fear of death."[8] The principle of the priesthood of all believers demanded that the Evangelical Christian stand directly before God. The power of the keys, the exercise of secular power in the church, excommunication, auricular confession, formalized corrective disciplines in the church were rejected (though some of these sanctions with modification reappeared later under consistorial authority). Luther was by no means unwilling to rebuke and admonish, but for discipline he in general turned to the state. In his view government rules in the told of law, for the law is the work of man, as faith is the work of God. The church was to be a community informed by faith and living in Christ — a *Gemeindeleben;* it was not to be a state within the state. Her power is not the power of law but the power of the Word of grace and forgiveness eliciting repentance and the liberty of the Christian man. Indeed, if all men were genuine Christians, he believed, the state itself and its disciplines would be unnecessary. Actually, however, genuine Christians are "rare birds." This fact gives to the state its divine mission. But even though the church is a communion of sinners, legalism and works of merit there could only minimize faith. Discipline may have its limited place, but it does not give shape and sinew to the church. Luther did resort to discipline within the church, but he worked out no clear theory or system.

In the light of Luther's emphasis on the power of the Word, we must understand the claim made by Rudolf Sohm that genuine Lutheranism, in contrast to Calvinism, rejects discipline in the traditional sense. According to Sohm, natural man is born a Catholic, who wants his religious as well as his civil life to be regulated

---

8. H. H. Borcherdt, *Martin Luther: Ausgewählte Werke*, II, 170.

by law. "The church is man's life with God, the world is man's life with man. This life in the world requires law, compulsion. Social life is not possible without laws and regulations. But in the kingdom of God, the (invisible) church proper, *gratia* and *fides* rule; in the world *lex* and *ratio*."[9] For Sohm, as for Weber (who adopted much of his analysis of types of authority and of religious associations), the decisive power and authority of the church are neither traditional nor rational, but charismatic. Sohm deplores the routinization of charisma. It issues in bondage to reason, law, and the past. It represents a form of idolatry, a despair of the divine, redemptive, renewing power. The church has only to follow the Word of God which is recognized not by any formal criterion, but by its inherent power and by free inward consent. The Christian community is no order in which diversities of gifts unfold. "But all of these work that one and same spirit, dividing to every man severally as he will."[10] To make law the guide of the Christian life or of the ordering of the church is to domesticate and frustrate the Holy Spirit. The visible church is a tentative manifestation of the divine community created by the power of God in Christ; it is the arena within which charismatic gifts in all their variety appear and are tested by the power of the spirit.

It is not possible here to evaluate Sohm's idealization of charismatic community (if indeed one grants that his view has been accurately adumbrated here). It must be admitted that Sohm leaves something to be desired with respect to the conception of the structure of the Christian community. He has not shown how it is possible to have a church and an organized religious fellowship without some kind of law for church and order.[11] Taken in contrast to Calvin's emphasis, however, his view does serve to bring into relief the crucial question concerning the proper character of discipline in Christian ethics.

In his theory of discipline Calvin is concerned primarily with giving tangible ligaments to the Christian community. Sohm, on the other hand, is primarily concerned with the productive power that creates, informs, and transforms the historical community. To be sure, Calvin is concerned with the *communio sanctorum*, but his

---

9. J. O. Evjen, "Rudolf Sohm," *Crede Ecclesiam*, I, No. 1, April 1, 1935, 5. (Rudolf Sohm, the Lutheran jurist and historian, 1841-1917, regarded the introduction of law as the moment of the "fall" of the church. See Sohm, *Outlines of Church History*, with Introduction by James Luther Adams, Boston, 1958.)
10. I Cor. 12:11.
11. Ernst Troeltsch, *The Social Teaching of the Christian Churches*, I (London, 1931), p. 98.

doctrine of predestination and his biblicism cause him to view the Word and Will of God as promulgated law. Consequently, discipline is interpreted as the complex of sanctions whereby the moral purity of the community of the elect is protected. Sohm turns the attention from *disciplines* understood as the application of a set of rules, to *charisma* understood as a response to the divine community-forming power. Sohm would perhaps say to Calvin, The letter killeth, the spirit giveth life. But, in reply, Calvin could say, The spirit killeth, the letter giveth life.

Somewhere between these two attitudes we must find the place of discipline in Christian ethics. Accordingly, we should shift the attention from disciplines understood as penal and remedial to the process in community out of which the gifts and fruits of the spirit are engendered. Disciplines may then be understood as the means that open the way for this process to take place. This is the meaning of discipline in certain modern Protestant groups, for example, in the Society of Friends.

The place of disciplines in Christian ethics is the place at which the dialogue between spirit and law occurs for the creation and re-creation of community. Spirit is subjective, inward, personal; law is objective, external impersonal. Spirit is original, vividly present, transcendent; law is derivative, a precipitate from the past, a conditioned form. The dialogue between spirit and law, between spirit and spirit, between law and law can alone give both tangible character ("ligaments") and power of renewal to the Christian community. Spirit molds Christian life and community, but in turn is affected by the created forms which "make channels for the streams of love." There are, then, two dimensions within the life of the individual Christian and of the Christian community: inwardness of spirit which gives new depth and concern and life, and the objective forms of church ordinance and discipline which give tangibility, order, and direction. Both *lex* and *gratia,* both *ratio* and *fides,* belong within the dialogue of Christian community.

Where the one dimension of law has been emphasized to the neglect of the other, we find the patterns of domination in church and state, rigid immobility, functional specificity and bureaucracy, the sanctification of the established powers, or the drive towards a re-formed rigidity. This is the dimension of conservatism. Where the other dimension prevails, we find the patterns of independency, mobility, diffusion of function and radical laicism, the sanctification of the demanded. This is the dimension of pneumatocracy or mystical democracy. Neither pattern alone possesses validity.[12]

The root metaphors of Christian theology tend to emphasize the one or the other dimension. Law and Gospel, the covenant of obedience and the Kingdom of God, the visible church and the invisible church: each of these doctrines needs its corollary. In the one the objective forces that are the vessels of spirit are stressed, in the other the inwardness of spirit is emphasized. Together, these dimensions constitute the structure of the Christian life, the structure that at the same time gives Christian nurture and is open to new tides of the spirit. The proper place of discipline in Christian ethics is not in a police department of the church, it is at the juncture of these two dimensions of the working of the divine power.

IV. *Social-Pychological Principles*

"Be not conformed to this world: but be ye transformed by the renewing of your mind." Discipline in the Christian community serves the same general purpose as in any other directioned community, namely, to elicit and maintain integrity. The disciplines of Calvinist Geneva, the disciplines of early Methodism, the disciplines of the Communist party, the disciplines of the Confessional church — all of these are to be understood as the means for the opposition to the disciplines of the adversary, whether the adversary be Roman Catholicism, the moral degradation of the disinherited, capitalism, or Naziism.

For the early Christians, conformity to the world was conformity to its disciplines. For them the "world" was not merely the flat-surfaced phenomena of state and cultus; it was under the control of the adversary, the principalities and powers of evil. Out of this sense of tension came a great variety of transforming nonconformities. To lapse from the holy community was to resume the disciplines of the "world", it was to render obedience to demonic powers.

Modern Protestantism surrendered disciplines not only because of the perversions and legalisms of orthodoxy. The surrender came also as a consequence of the relaxation of struggle with the adversary. This relaxation was to be sure accompanied by a "pathos" for individual responsibility. But this "pathos" found its sanction in a new and false conception of the world and man, the conception

---

12. For an analogous interpretation of two similar motifs — inwardness and objective spirit — as they apply to political theory, see Ernst Troeltsch, *Politische Ethik and Christentum*, 1904.

of preestablished harmony and the belief in original virtue (instead of original sin). Spontaneity, detachment from tradition, agreement to disagree, the free market of ideas, could be trusted (it was believed) because the outcome of the free enterprise would be ever richer harmony and progress. The Hegelian concept of synthesis symbolizes this non-tragic view of history and community, a view that sees the conflicts as a dialectic between complementary "goods" moving towards resolution, enrichment, sublation. This concept is almost the direct opposite of what is expressed in the early church's view of the "world" as the adversary.

The outcome has been surprisingly different from the expectations. It exemplifies the maxim that nothing fails like success. The patterns of independency so characteristic of the individual stages of the "progress" have given way to new patterns of rigid conformity and to new penal disciplines. Increasingly, radical criticism has been muffled, models of behavior have been established by the centrally controlled engines of mass communication, these models have heads stuffed with straw, and the bourgeoisie has become a lumpen-bourgeoisie. However one may characterize the ethos of the lumpen-bourgeoisie, not to speak of that of the lumpen-petty-bourgeoisie, this ethos has permeated the church community — and the adversary has made conquest. The disciplines of nation, class, and race are the effective disciplines that form "community". This has been the modern "pilgrim's regress" towards a mass society in which all too many church members have an "implicit" Christian faith which operates within a constricted area and an "explicit" faith which is derived from the "world" of popular culture.

A holy community must be a militant community with its own explicit faith; and this explicit faith cannot be engendered without disciplines that shape the ethos of the group and that issue in the criticism of the society and of the "religious" community itself.

In face of the popular culture of a mass society these disciplines cannot emerge and be effective except in a primary group of person-to-person relations. In the primary group alone can faith become at the same time explicit and interiorized. In the primary group alone can the counter-models against the models of the world be defined and made effective. The function of discipline, then, is to provide the conditions under which the judging, transforming power of God may be released.

To say that such discipline must appear in a primary group is to say that the divine community-forming power works primarily and decisively in the *ecclesiola in ecclesia*. Accordingly, the larger church is the initial point of contact with the "world." For this reason cell groups possessing an "intentional discipline" believe it to be their mission to prepare for the conversion of the church. This does not mean that the city of earth and the city of God are necessarily viewed as black and white. God's grace is not bound to the *ecclesiola in ecclesia;* nor is the only *ecclesiola* to be found within the ecclesiastical institution. But the *ecclesiola* cannot even achieve its own self-consciousness without "separation," that is, without the disciplines that express a recognition of the "call" to come out from the world and to be a peculiar people. It is precisely at the point of defining this "peculiarity" that the decisive dialogue between law and Gospel, between form and spirit, between *lex* and *gratia,* between *ratio* and *fides,* must take place.

The *ecclesiola* is the place par excellence for "intentional disciplines," because the primary group is the place where the vitalities of the "sect" (in contrast to the "church") may become manifest in ethos and in social invention: What are these vitalities? Intimate "pneumatic" fellowship in word and sacrament, explicit faith, the identification of the adversary, achievement of consensus, the protection of the freedom of the spirit, the definition of models (for example, the model of the Protestant man), the expression of "concerns" about church and society, the practice of self-criticism of the group, the disciplined application of norms to the personal life, fami , work, politics, and business — in short, the joining of the prie....ood and the prophethood of all believers. In such a group penal and remedial disciplines may appear. But, ideally, they should be informal and self-imposed. For such a group it will not be a very urgent problem how to deal with the false and insincere members. The group should have little attraction for such members.

The place of discipline in the sense here proposed certainly cannot be the great church. The appearance of such a place within the *ecclesiola* is itself much to expect. Only if it appears there, can it appear elsewhere. First of the *ecclesiola* and then of the *ecclesia* may one say with R.H. Tawney: "Either a church is a society or it is nothing. But if a society is to exist, it must possess a corporate mind and will. And if the church which is a Christian society is to exist, its mind and will must be set upon that type of conduct which is specifically Christian."[13]

---

13. R. H. Tawney, *The Acquisitive Society* (London, 1921).

CIVIL DISOBEDIENCE:
ITS OCCASIONS AND LIMITS

JAMES LUTHER ADAMS

In a day when an increasing number of people, especially students and blacks, are speaking of the present "transition from dissent to resistance" as the advent of the second American Revolution, there could scarcely be a more timely subject for discussion than civil disobedience. As a sanction for this dissent and resistance an appeal is made to the first American Revolution, to Jefferson and Locke, and also to Thoreau and Gandhi.

To a theologian, civil disobedience suggests the names of figures from an earlier period, for example, John Knox, John Lilburne, or George Fox. Even these names, however, come from a late period in the history of Christianity. From its very beginning Christianity was an outlaw religion committed to disobedience to the "world." The slogan "Christianity is illegal" may be

Reprinted by Permission of the Publishers, Hebrew Publishing Company, Copyright © 1970. All rights reserved.

traced back to the second-century figure Tertullian, a lawyer by training. By the time of the second century something like civil disobedience was already an old story, for the Christian group had long been considered an "illicit" religious association in the Roman empire; its transcendental and transpolitical orientation had brought the Christians into radical conflict with civic religion. Early Christian martyrdom was occasioned in the main by this rejection of civic religion. A sanction for this disobedience was found in the familiar axioms of the New Testament, "Render unto Caesar that which is Caesar's and unto God that which is God's" and "Man must obey God rather than men." Similar disobedience appears in the prophetic tradition of the Old Testament and is symbolized by the narrative in the Book of Daniel about Shadrach, Meshach, and Abednego, who were cast into the fiery furnace by Nebuchadnezzar. In Judaism and Christianity much of the history of the theory of disobedience to civic authorities could be documented by examining in succession through the centuries the sermons and commentaries on the Book of Daniel. On the other hand, there has been a much more influential and opposing tradition of obedience stemming from Jewish respect for law and from the Pauline admonition of Romans 13, "Let every person be subject to the governing authorities. For there is no authority except from God, and those that exist have been instituted by God."

It must be recognized, moreover, that insofar as disobedience was sanctioned or practiced by Christians in the New Testament period and in early Christianity it was scarcely in accord with modern conceptions of civil disobedience. We can confirm this judgment only if we have in mind a clear definition of the modern phenomenon.

A synoptic view of modern civil disobedience yields some such definition as the following. Civil disobedience is (1) a nonviolent, (2) public violation (3) of a specific law or set of laws, or of a policy of government having the effect of law, (4) which expresses a sense of justice in a civil society of cooperation among equals and (5) which is generally undertaken in the name of a presumed higher authority than the law in question (6) as a last resort (7) for the purpose of changing the law and (8) with the intention of accepting the penalty which the prevailing law imposes. Here we have a conception of disobedience considerably broader in range and purpose than that found in early Christianity.[1]

Certain features that are implicit in this definition should be mentioned at the outset. Civil disobedience is occasioned by a major grievance that calls for immediate protest in the name of justice. In a democratic society it reflects the indisposition to wait upon the slow processes of the ballot box and other political procedures that bring about change in the law; at the same time the civil disobedient is willing to be subject to legal police action and he respects just court procedures. In general, then, civil disobedience presupposes a general acceptance of legal authority, due process, and the legitimacy of the legal system as a whole. That is, it aims to function within the framework of a legal system. Yet, it expresses a sense of moral obligation to disobey a specific law for the sake of conscience and of improving the law and thus of serving the public good. In this sense it is conscientious disobedience. The law against which it protests may or may not be deemed constitutional. In many instances civil disobedience aims to test the constitutionality of the constitutional assumptions of a law or policy. In this respect it belongs to a large class of litigation and thus approaches the character of normal procedure.

There is, however, another type of civil disobedience, that which obtains when an individual or group violates a valid law with which it has no quarrel but does so in order to call attention to and to protest against some other law or policy which may or may not be related to the law which is being violated. In a loose way this kind of disobedience is sometimes called indirect civil disobedience. A major purpose of this indirect disobedience is to gain effective publicity for the protest. This motive usually attaches also to direct, civil disobedience. In this respect there is

[1] According to the definition given here, the disobedience of the early Christians was civil disobedience only in a narrow sense. Although they did refuse to pay religious homage with incense and wine to Caesar's image, the purpose of their disobedience was not to improve the law; they thought the end of the age was at hand. Nor did they attempt to promote the freedom of other religious associations. Yet, they did express a nonviolent protest against a demonic state and against a civic religion. At the same time the means were not available to them to undertake to change the law. Only in restricted ways, then, can early Christian disobedience be considered civil disobedience as the latter is understood today.

generally a dramatic or melodramatic element in all civil disobedience. If it is to affect public opinion and to change the law it must be able to rivet attention on the evil that is under attack.

Another aspect of civil disobedience deserves to be stressed. Ordinarily, civil disobedience expresses a sense of justice in a civil society of cooperation among equals. Two important presuppositions or implications attach to this view. First, the principle of reversibility: the civil disobedient presupposes that his demand for justice possesses a universal validity and therefore holds that it would be appropriate for other citizens or associations to undertake similar civil disobedience. Second, civil disobedience presupposes the right to protest and the right to participate in the shaping of public policy. In this respect it is an appeal to the principle of the consent of the governed.

On the other hand, we should recognize that a certain religious type of civil disobedient is not primarily concerned with the purpose and motives we have mentioned. He is concerned rather to "bear witness" to a set of values which he holds to be quite incompatible with the ways of the world. He may be willing to undergo severe suffering for the sake of his faith, but he does not expect to improve the law. In his view the world is under the control of the principalities and powers of evil. Accordingly, his disobedience is almost "systemic," but it is not the sort of disobedience that looks toward the creation of a better society. Nor does he appeal to the state to achieve its essential character and purpose or to overcome the inconsistencies between its best and its worst laws. A member of Jehovah's Witnesses, for example, in refusing to salute the flag, has no hope for a better world or for improvement of the state under the present dispensation. He looks for a new dispensation to be inaugurated by the apocalyptic action of God. In general, we may say that this kind of disobedience has been characteristic of groups which Ernst Troeltsch has called "withdrawing sects."

In certain instances, what appears to be civil disobedience in one legal context may be viewed as civil obedience in a different legal context. In the civil-rights movement in the United States disobedience was often undertaken in protest against a municipal ordinance or a state statute. But this ordinance or statute was itself held to be in contradiction to the basic law of the land, that is, to federal legislation or to decisions of the Supreme Court. Therefore this type of disobedience is ambiguous in character, for it claims to be also a form of obedience to law.[2]

Our definition of civil disobedience may be clarified if we further indicate what it is not. It does not resort to force. It is not clandestine evasion of the law, as is ordinary crime. It does not conceal the evidence but offers it to the authorities. Nor does it employ the strategy of evasion which deliberately attempts to postpone the application of the law. Civil disobedience, moreover, is not a "systemic" disobedience, a total rejection of the legal system; nor does it aim to promote general lawlessness; nor is it anarchy or conspiracy (as ordinarily understood). It is not infidelity to law, for it willingly accepts punishment at the hands of the law, and it is not merely an expression of individual frustration, for it aims to change the law and to contribute to the good of the society. Motivated by a sense of justice, it is not undertaken for merely personal advantage or privilege.

It may be useful to "place" civil disobedience as defined here on a spectrum of disobedience. It may be distinguished from resistance (*Widerstand*) which may be in part clandestine; this form of resistance appears in a totalitarian society where no legal or open organizational means for securing change in the law exists. Civil disobedience is ordinarily distinguished from military disobedience (though a change in definition appears to be taking place today in this respect); from insurrection, the use of collective violence for a specific end; from rebellion, the forceful attempt to overthrow the social or legal order; from anarchism, a "systemic" rejection of all government as evil; and from dissent, a protest that does not entail disobedience. And in the United States today it is to be distinguished from religious conscientious objection to all war, an objection that was previously a form of civil disobedience but which is now legally defined as permissible. To be sure, the definition is still being contested, toward the end of broadening the concept of the "religious" grounds of conscience.

[2]For a discussion of this form of nonobservance and of related issues see Charles L. Black, "The Problem of the Compatibility of Civil Disobedience with American Institutions of Government," 43 *Texas Law Review*, 492–506. It should be pointed out here that although Martin Luther King's civil disobedience in general fits the description in the text, he did disobey also in defiance of a state court injunction.

These distinctions, if sound, are not in widest commonality familiar. Apart from technical legal writings, the pertinence of making them is of fairly recent vintage, though to be sure the distinctions have been recognized in previous periods. It is a striking fact that in one of the most widely used books in Protestant circles, John C. Bennett's *Christians and the State,* published in 1958, civil disobedience is not discussed.[3] Within the next few years, however, the whole question rapidly came to the fore in connection with the civil-rights movement. In 1964 a National Study Conference on Church and State met to formulate "Advice to the National Council of Churches and Its Member Denominations," and in its report it articulated the essential ingredients of civil disobedience in the following statement:

> In a state in which redress for wrong exists, and legal and organizational means for change are normally available, the Christian may nevertheless find certain laws and customs intolerably unjust. When the governmental processes are not realistically adequate to correct them, resistance [or, more precisely, we should say *disobedience*] to civil authority is a valid course for Christians to take. Such action includes the willingness to accept the consequences. While affirming his responsibility to obey civil authority generally, a Christian may well serve justice by disobeying a particular unjust law. Disobedience to civil authority in this context is intended to serve the government, to serve the good it has accomplished, and to move it another step toward becoming a more just institution.

It should be added here that 13 out of 245 delegates to this conference recorded their dissent to the whole section of the report from which the above paragraph is quoted.

An important issue that is not taken into account in this report or in my definition above is the question of whether the law that is disobeyed in civil disobedience is considered to be formally valid or is considered to be invalid because it is unjust. The latter view was held by Thomas Aquinas. For him, the law must be just and in harmony with the common good; otherwise,

---

[3] See, however, Prof. Bennett's article, "The Place of Civil Disobedience," *Christianity and Crisis,* XXVII, No. 22 (December 25, 1967), 299–302.

it is devoid of the nature of law. If the former issue is raised, that is, if the claim is made that the law in question is not formally valid, we encounter civil disobedience of a somewhat different sort. Some of the citizens who today engage in civil disobedience in the face of the administration's policy in Vietnam claim that the policy is not formally valid, in the sense that it is a violation of treaties or that it has not received proper approval by the Senate.[4]

A more fundamental question than that of the legal or moral validity or invalidity of the law must also be taken into account. In some quarters all civil disobedience as such is rejected in principle, as serving no conceivable public good. Here the authority to which civil disobedience makes appeal—for example, a higher law or conscience—is radically called in question. The civil disobedient is contemned even though he declares his willingness to accept punishment at the hands of the law.

A different formulation of the objection to civil disobedience as such is the charge that it is nothing but lawlessness. For example, Judge Charles E. Wyzanski, Jr., in an article discussing civil disobedience to the draft, asserts: "Every time that a law is disobeyed by even a man whose motive is solely ethical, in the sense that it is responsive to deep moral conviction, there are unfortunate consequences. He himself becomes more prone to disobey laws for which he has no profound repugnance. He sets an example for others who may not have his pure motives. He weakens the fabric of society."[5] Here Judge Wyzanski says that he agrees with G. E. Moore, who in *Principia Ethica* concludes that "in most instances civil disobedience is immoral," and he goes on to say that a dramatic precursor of Moore was Socrates, who "swallowed hemlock . . . rather than refuse obedience to the laws of the city-state which had formed and protected him."

These formulations are no doubt intended to stress the obligation to obey the law, but they leave much to be desired insofar as they imply an absolute and unqualified obligation to obey even

---

[4] For a discussion of civil disobedience in protest against a law or policy that is allegedly unconstitutional, for example, the draft law and the war in Vietnam, and also for a discussion pro and con of government policy with respect to this type of disobedience, see Ronald Dworkin, "On Not Prosecuting Civil Disobedience," *New York Review of Books*, June 6, 1968.

[5] Charles E. Wyzanski, Jr., "On Civil Disobedience," *Atlantic*, 221, No. 2 (February 1968), 59.

in the face of tyranny. The formulations raise other questions, too. Why, for example, should one point only to the possibility that civil disobedience may lead to other forms of disobedience which are irresponsible? Why not assume also the likelihood that the high moral seriousness of authentic civil disobedience as a public protest will enhance elements of moral seriousness in the community? The civil disobedient's acceptance of legal punishment by reason of his conscientious disobedience might be expected to enhance rather than to erode moral seriousness in the community. This consequence is by no means a weakening of the "fabric of society." Of course there are no guarantees in these matters, no more than with respect to the use and abuse of a razor.

These considerations lead to other questions about Judge Wyzanski's formulations regarding the weakening of the "fabric of society." A danger not taken into account by his argument is the danger that the fabric of society at a given time may actually be too tightly woven as a consequence of demonic repression or the apathetic routinization of conscience. In this kind of situation the civil disobedient holds that his protest is a public and not a secret protest against *one* law or policy and that by his remaining law-abiding in other regards and by his accepting punishment for his disobedience he shows his respect for law and helps to maintain the fabric, and yet that as a last resort his disobedience aims to improve the law and to rectify the fabric of society. The civil disobedient, and anyone else for that matter, may also rightly claim that what obtains under the rubric of law in the society often turns out to be only camouflage for egregious class or race interest or for jingoistic and destructive patriotism. He may also claim that, far from weakening the fabric of society, authentic civil disobedience is a means of reducing the demand for rebellious and violent protest against the law. Actually, the term "fabric of society" is somewhat misleading insofar as it implies that the complex of law and obligation in any society is a neat, readily identifiable package.[6]

Probably none of these arguments will influence the radical critic of civil disobedience unless he recognizes the bludgeonings of conscience in a patently intolerable situation that demonstrates for a protracted period that it cannot be effectively challenged by normal political procedures. It would be instructive for grasping the full force of the critic's argument if one could know whether he holds that John Lilburne or George Fox or Gandhi or Martin Luther King, Jr., should never have practiced civil disobedience—that is, whether these civil disobedients may be properly characterized as only having weakened the "fabric of society."

The claim that civil disobedience constitutes mere lawlessness and the subversion of legitimate authority sometimes takes the form of simply identifying it with crime. For example, United States Senator Sam Ervin, protesting against a statement on civil disobedience by the Methodist General Conference (1964), declared that it was prompted more by "impatience than reason," and then he went on to say: "I make an affirmation which is subject to no exception or modification. The right of clergymen and civil rights agitators to disobey laws they deem unjust is exactly the same as the right of the arsonist, the burglar, the murderer, the rapist and the thief to disobey the laws forbidding arson, burglary, murder, rape and theft." It is sufficient to indicate the indiscriminate character of this declaration if we observe the occasions that have called forth civil disobedience.

The occasions for civil disobedience have been numerous. They include opposition to slavery, to suffrage restricted by race or sex, to prohibition of alcoholic beverages, to compulsory school attendance, to vaccination, to military conscription, to taxation for war purposes, to war and the preparations for nuclear and biological warfare, to laws against collective bargaining, to race discrimination in education, housing, and employment, and to conscription for a particular war. These occasions for civil disobedience are obviously of a quite different character from arson, murder, and rape. For one thing, the latter are not acts of conscience.

A similar variety may be observed if we consider the specific sanctions and the scope of these different occasions for civil disobedience. In some instances the civil disobedient appeals to a sanction of morals beyond (or "higher" than) the law or to "the best elements in the American tradition." In other instances the sanction appealed to is explicitly theological; in yet others it is religious in a broader, humanistic sense. With respect to scope: in some instances the civil disobedient seeks to change a law that directly affects people in all classes; in others he is concerned to correct injustices that obtain for particular groups or classes—in our day especially for deprived groups such as the blacks and other ethnic minorities.

Another kind of classification is worth noting. If we consider the ethical issues that have given rise to the forms of civil disobedience listed above, we find that the specific goals of protest are few in number. It is true that in most of these forms of disobedience the protection of human dignity and the promotion of self-determination are involved, but the social and personal values may be reduced to five, namely, equality, due process, the rejection of certain types of violence authorized by the state, the protection of private morality, and certain eccentric religious sensitivities. In the main, however, the issues at stake have been the values of equality and nonviolence. As against the present war in Vietnam, civil disobedience seeks to restore peace and also the honor of the nation. Civil disobedience in protest against slavery or race discrimination is undertaken in the name of equality and due process, as is civil disobedience for the sake of a broader suffrage or for the sake of collective bargaining. Here the demand for equality is in large measure a demand for power in the sense of capacity to participate in the making of decisions regarding public policy. The protest against the prohibition of alcoholic beverages, however, is motivated by the desire to protect private morality against legal enforcement. Opposition to vaccination and school attendance rests upon unique religious presuppositions. But conscientious objection to military conscription and to participation in a particular war represents a protest against what is considered to be mass violence at the hands of the state.

CIVIL DISOBEDIENCE AND THE DOCTRINE OF THE JUST WAR

The references to violence point to a striking feature of civil disobedience in general, indeed to a somewhat surprising feature that has not been noticed hitherto. If we ask for the tests by which authentic civil disobedience is to be measured, we find that some of the most pertinent tests are similar to those employed in the doctrine of the just war. The tests are pertinent for our purpose despite the fact that in many quarters the doctrine of the just war is emphatically held to be outmoded.

It is not surprising that the similarity has not been noted, for we encounter here a curious paradox. The tests of the just war relate to the norms for the use of violence; at the same time they can serve as the norms of authentic civil disobedience, even though civil disobedience often represents a protest against violence. How is one to explain this paradox? Perhaps the answer is that both war and civil disobedience deviate from the normal procedures that prevail between states or between the individual and the state.

The norms traditionally employed in just-war doctrine have been the following: (1) The cause must be just. (2) War must be the last resort. (3) War must be made by a lawful public authority. (4) There must be a reasonable hope of victory. (5) The intention of the government engaging in war must be free from mere hatred, greed, cruelty, or glee. (6) There must be due proportion between the good probably to be accomplished and the probable evil effect. (7) The war must be rightly conducted through the use of right means.

In the definition of civil disobedience set forth at the beginning of this paper some of these norms have been mentioned. Here we shall consider these and other features insofar as they are analogous to the norms of just war. This consideration will bring to the fore certain aspects of the question regarding proper authority and of the question regarding the circumstances under which or the limits within which civil disobedience is justifiable.

First, the cause must be just. In authentic civil disobedience the citizen appeals in the name of justice (fairness, equality, self-determination, due process). This is true not only in the sense that he attempts to correct an injustice but also in the sense that in some instances he hopes to bring about the redefinition of the content of justice. He does this by claiming to appeal from the less-informed conscience to a better-informed conscience. His appeal is ostensibly an appeal in the name of a universal value. Therefore, the authentic civil disobedient recognizes that others besides himself are in normal circumstances entitled to do what he himself is doing. Indeed, he hopes that others will lend support to his challenge to injustice.

It must be admitted that the conscientious objector will often appear to be arbitrary in his claims. He may even elicit the charge that he is pathologically conditioned to be a mere publicity-seeker. But in these respects the civil disobedient is not unique. Anyone who turns to normal political procedures to effect change may have to face similar charges. In the long run public opinion and due process must be relied upon to determine the issue in an open society.

The second criterion of the just war is the claim that war is the last resort, other means of securing justice and peace having failed. In both military policy and civil disobedience the concept of "last resort" is a weasel concept. The appeal to it is therefore always subject to vigorous disagreement. Here the difference between war and civil disobedience is of crucial significance. The civil disobedient can be brought to book by legal agencies (and generally the warring state cannot). Indeed, he stands ready to accept punishment at the hands of these agencies. But this fact does not clarify the application of the concept.

In support of the claim of "last resort" the civil disobedient should be able to point to evidence of the fact that the slower political processes are egregiously ineffective or that immediacy of decision is necessary. Here the timing of the civil disobedience becomes important in several ways. The clearest example of the demand for immediacy of decision is in civil disobedience that opposes military conscription. In the area of race discrimination the claim of "last resort" can point to the intolerable delay that has attended the correction of the evil. Here the civil disobedient can claim that his disobedience and that of others may help to accelerate political processes that bring about change in the law or in the enforcement of the law. Who can deny that the civil disobedience attending the civil-rights movement has actually served in many instances to affect legislation regarding civil rights, or has served to bring about more quickly the enforcement of law that is supposed to protect civil rights? To this consideration one may add the argument that delay in these matters could be a stimulus to violence as a last resort. In the face of this contingency the civil disobedient can claim that in the long run his disobedience may serve to strengthen confidence in the legal system by stimulating it to achieve its true ends; in short, he may claim that it is a nonviolent protest calculated to reduce violence and to increase lawfulness.

One further consideration regarding the claim to "last resort" should be taken into account here. As we have observed, civil disobedience as a last resort presupposes that normal procedures have been tried and have been found to be seriously in default. The civil disobedient is not entitled, however, to make this presupposition if he has not himself participated vigorously in these processes. But even if he has made this effort, he can claim, for example, that the outcome of balloting has been ambiguous and thus has fallen short of presenting a clear mandate. Or he can claim that governmental authorities have refused to obey a mandate or have failed to enforce the law. Or he may be able to assert that normal political processes are not available to him by reason of his not yet being of voting age, yet that the law or policy in question directly affects him. And does not the black likewise the more understandably engage in civil disobedience as a last resort if by law or custom he has not been permitted to participate in the political processes that determine law or policy? And is not the citizen belonging to an ethnic minority to be expected in an open society to turn to civil disobedience as a last resort if majority rule normally ignores or violates his rights? Here the principle of the consent of the governed is at stake.[7] Nothing said here, however, can properly eliminate nonviolence from the criteria of civil disobedience.

The third criterion of the just war is that it must be made by a lawful authority. At first blush this criterion may appear not to be pertinent for testing authentic civil disobedience. Actually, however, it has been the occasion for struggle over a long period of time. Think how horrified the general public was when civil disobedience was first practiced by people claiming the right to

[7] For a somewhat broader interpretation than that which is suggested here see Ralph Conant, "Rioting, Insurrection and Civil Disobedience," *The American Scholar*, XXXVII, No. 3 (Summer 1968). Prof. Conant states that civil disobedience is justified (1) when an oppressed group is deprived of lawful channels for remedying its condition; (2) when government takes or condones actions that are inconsistant with values on which the society and the political system are built; and (3) when a change in law or policy is demanded by social or economic need in the community and the normal procedures of law and politics are inadequate, obstructed, or held captive by antilegal forces.

freedom of religious association or by workers claiming the right to bargain collectively. Civil disobedience in protest against war is still considered in many quarters to be a sign of treason or at least of absence of patriotism, especially when many citizens are risking or giving their lives in war effort. A whole complex of moral and political issues is involved in the examples just cited. But criticism and change in these areas, and also individual responsibility, are impaired if individual conscience must be suppressed. In this context the presupposition that the individual is a legitimate "authority," entitled to demand the consent of the governed, is axiomatic in modern society. Open conflict between perspectives is essential for the maintenance of integrity in the society and in its members. My colleague Professor George Hunston Williams, Hollis Professor of Divinity at Harvard, in an unpublished letter to Pope Paul VI elucidates this view when, in referring to selective rejection of military conscription, he says, "In the present crisis of conscience it is not the Christian Emperor, nor the Christian King, nor even the Christian knight with his consecrated sword but the individual democratic citizen who is ultimately accountable for what constitutes just war." Today, as we shall see, the freedom of association is also at stake. In a democracy the citizen with a conscience is a lawful authority for exercising civil disobedience under the conditions we have been considering. But he must leave it to the legal agencies to determine whether he has misconceived or abused his authority. In doing so he stands ready to be punished.

Reasonable hope for victory, the fourth criterion of the just war, is not easy to apply to either war or civil disobedience. In its initial formulation the criterion intended, among other things, to preclude suicidal war. If we were to apply this aspect of the criterion directly and literally to civil disobedience, the application would not be without pertinence, for suicide has sometimes been resorted to as a desperate measure to register conscientious objection and to draw attention to the evil being protested.

But apart from this application, is the criterion pertinent for assessing civil disobedience? What is the positive meaning of "victory" with respect to civil disobedience? Here we may refer back to the major purpose of civil disobedience. Reasonable hope for victory, then, would mean reasonable hope to change a particular law or policy. If, however, we view the history of civil disobedience in retrospect, we must acknowledge that such a hope must be a long-range hope. In the light of this fact, we should perhaps alter the formulation "reasonable hope for victory" in order to take into account a long process that occurs by stages. The process is one that first requires a change of public opinion. In this process civil disobedience may engender new sensitivities, new prickings of conscience, in the public domain, new sensitivities that move the community in the direction of a more ample sense of justice. Obviously, the translation of a new attitude into new law or new policy generally requires the tedious process of normal political processes. The question, then, regarding reasonable hope for victory, is the question regarding the proper efficacy of civil disobedience. And the answer to the question is that civil disobedience is efficacious when it contributes to the process we have just described.

To be sure, the actual change in the law or the policy may not be precisely what the civil disobedient had hoped for. Yet the change in the climate of opinion which brings about an unpredictable, though relatively desirable, change can properly be assessed as a sign of the efficacy (the victory) of civil disobedience. Presently we shall return to these considerations in another context.

Another important aspect of civil disobedience should be mentioned in connection with this criterion of "reasonable hope for victory." The civil disobedient will often assert that regardless of whether or not his action is to issue in the change of a law or policy, he nevertheless will disobey for conscience' sake. Here we encounter an aspect of the "ethics of conscience" in contrast to the "ethics of consequences." In the present context the civil disobedient motivated by the "ethics of conscience" asserts that loyalty to conscience is an end in itself, and that the possible consequence of change in the law or policy is a "plus" that is not decisive in determining his action. We must acknowledge that this kind of civil disobedience in a measure qualifies the definition we have proposed at the outset. Under the "ethics of conscience" the essential purpose of civil disobedience is not change in the law but maintenance of personal integrity under all circumstances. To be sure, this conception of integrity and of fidelity to conscience can become a form of irresponsibility, particularly if the civil disobedient in the name of conscience asserts that he is in no way concerned with consequences, whatever they may be. This view of conscience is a narrow conception indeed. The truly conscientious man should be willing to consider himself at least in part responsible for reasonably foreseeable, destructive consequences of his action. This sense of responsibility for consequences as well as for purity of motive belongs under the rubric of conscience when the latter is properly understood.

The fifth criterion of just-war doctrine is that the war action should be just in the sense of being free from vindictive hatred, greed, cruelty, or glee. So also authentic civil disobedience is not a search for revenge or an attempt to injure others or to ventilate frustration. Nor is it a free-wheeling activity designed merely to bring about obstruction or annoyance; nor is it teen-age sport indulged in order to see what the authorities will do. In human affairs, whether in war or in civil disobedience, the criterion of freedom from hatred or from desire for revenge is obviously difficult to satisfy. To ask for complete absence of these motives is utopian, especially in connection with racial tensions and even opposition to war.

The sixth criterion is that there must be due proportion between the good probably to be accomplished and the probable evil effects of the war. In many quarters today this criterion is held to be an anachronism. The probable evil effect of all-out war, it is said, could be nuclear and bacteriological genocide on the one side and national suicide on the other. Even apart from this consideration, however, the criterion is still applicable to the situation in Vietnam, and even among people who know little about just-war doctrine as such it figures largely in the continuing criticism of the American military effort there. In any event, the criterion is pertinent for application to civil disobedience.

As in its application to military matters, however, the use of this criterion in assessing civil disobedience is fraught with difficulty. How, for example, does one determine due proportion between the good probably to be accomplished and the probable evil effects? Only in the instance of obvious disproportion between the good and the evil does the criterion seem to yield clear guidance. But even to identify the situation that clearly precludes civil disobedience is sometimes difficult. If, for example, the protest is against the Vietnam war, the civil disobedient quite plausibly says that the very occasion for the protest is the already evident evil in the Vietnam venture, the great loss of life among combatants and noncombatants, the use of napalm, the destruction of villages and crops, the dwindling hope for victory, the support of the Van Thieu regime, the ineffectiveness of the pacification program, and the unlikelihood of successful remedy of this policy.[8] The civil disobedient in resolving to protest asserts that little he can do can remotely approach on the domestic scene the evils perpetrated in Vietnam. Due proportion between the good probably to be accomplished and the probable evil effects, he says, is relatively easy for him to establish. We need not rehearse here the rejoinders given by the supporters of current Vietnam policy. For quite different reasons they hold that the greater good is probably to be accomplished by somehow maintaining the essential policy in Vietnam, and they warn against the probable evil effects of discontinuing it; and they view civil disobedience accordingly. Indeed, they envisage as intolerable any success enjoyed by the civil disobedients in promoting draft resistance and in influencing public opinion. Meanwhile, the government enjoys an immediate advantage over the disobedients by reason of possessing more effective access to public opinion and by reason of its control over the agencies of the law. We shall presently return to this matter when we consider the Spock case.

At the moment we should pause to observe that the fact that quite opposite evaluations are derived from applying the criteria of just-war doctrine (for example, that the war must be just and the means just) demonstrates that the criteria are inadequate. The inadequacy, it is held, issues from the abstract character of the criteria; that is, these criteria do not carry with them an explicit definition of justice. Accordingly, the opposite evaluations presuppose or emphasize different ingredients of a theory of justice, and they also emphasize different aspects and interpretations of the situation.

This observation gives occasion for us to emphasize that, though in our presentation here we have referred again and again to conceptions and ingredients of justice appealed to by civil disobedients, we have defined the efficacy of civil disobedi-

[8] For a brief discussion of just-war doctrine in relation to the Vietnam war see Ralph B. Potter, *War and Moral Discourse* (Richmond, Va.: John Knox Press, 1969), ch. 5.

ence as the capacity to raise or reformulate the ethical issues in such a way as to contribute to the process whereby public opinion reexamines them with reference to a particular law or policy. And, as we have already indicated, from the point of view of authentic civil disobedience the outcome of the process hoped for is the change of the law or policy.

This question of efficacy gives special significance to the last of the criteria of just-war doctrine as applied to civil disobedience, namely, that the means must be just. As we have indicated, civil disobedience, viewed in terms of its major purpose, is more a strategy of persuasion than an occasion for merely announcing or registering a concern of conscience. The concern of conscience and its appeal for a more ample conception of justice is the nerve of the strategy of persuasion. Therefore the adoption of unjust means not only calls in question the conscientiousness of the civil disobedient; as a consequence, it also frustrates the efficacy of the strategy of persuasion. Moreover, besides violating the obligation to use just means, it reduces or nullifies the likelihood of due proportion obtaining between the good probably to be accomplished and the probable evil effects.

We have stressed the view that authentic civil disobedience is nonviolent. But one should recognize that violence is not easy to fend off when civil disobedience functions as a group activity. In a tense situation what starts out to be nonviolent can degenerate into producing chaos or near-chaos. We recall that resistance to the draft in 1863, accompanied by cries of "the rich man's money and the poor man's blood," gave rise to serious disturbances in New York City when rioters seized City Hall and invoked a reign of terror which took more than a thousand lives. With respect to draft-resistance the situation appears to have become less volatile today. In World War I there were over 300,000 draft delinquents, but the number of draft-resisters today is relatively small. Nevertheless, radical criticism of the war in Vietnam is widespread, and the situation is sufficiently volatile.

Likewise, in the sphere of race relations the civil disobedient cannot today properly disregard warnings, not when he recalls that ours is the only industrialized democracy in which one has come to expect riots every summer, and that some people are shouting that violence is an old American tradition and that in Vietnam it provides an example for violence at home.

Somewhat in this vein, perversion of civil disobedience appears in the group burning of draft cards, in the slogan "Clog for peace—the streets are yours," and in the plea for "nonviolent, creative disruption" or for "a Christmas mill-in—a merry disruption." Many of the civil disobedients and demonstrators assert that they march "unarmed, with no intention of violence." Others assert, however, that "it is irresponsible to say that all we can use against this terrible evil are the traditional forms of protest—picketing and marching." Accordingly, they go on to say, "We don't think there will be any change in the Government's policy unless we can raise the cost of war in terms of political harassment, social disruption and real money costs."[9] Generally, these kinds of harassment get out of control, whether according to plan or not. None of these tactics, however, justifies police harassment or brutality, or inordinate detention or sentence. Perversion does not justify perversion, even though it elicits it. On the other hand, just means do not exclude the deliberate use of dramatic group confrontation, though the civil disobedients might be expected, precisely for the sake of efficacy, to select time and place with prudence.

This consideration suggests that group tactics should be related to a general strategy calculated to avoid violence and to respond to it with nonviolence. Not that there is any violence-proof strategy. Gandhi, it will be recalled, despite all his admonitions against violence, was not able to prevent his supporters from resorting to it (whereupon he would undertake a fast in protest and penitence). Actually, the more a strictly nonviolent strategy is successful in eliciting public sympathy, the more likely it is to encounter lunatic-fringe violence. One can say here that the ethical demands ideally should guide the civil disobedient into the mean between feckless timidity and reckless courage.

One could go on devising formulations of this sort with the intention of refining them so as to take care of every contingency. As with most ethical formulations dealing with complex and volatile situations, however, they are nets to catch the wind. The sum of them would probably embrace and fill in all the crannies of Pascal's axiom, practice opposite virtues and occupy all the distance in between.

---

9 *New York Times*, November 22 and December 24, 1967.

DELAYED CIVIL DISOBEDIENCE

In the light of the hazards of civil disobedience for the commonweal and with a very restricted conception of it, Judge Wyzanski counsels what he calls "delayed civil disobedience." He advises the civil disobedient "to await at the very least an induction order before resisting. Indeed, since, when inducted, one does not know if he will be sent to Vietnam or if sent, will be called upon directly to do what he regards as an immoral act, it may well be that resistance at the moment of induction is premature."[10] Earlier in this article he says that "no one can tell whether, as the resisters hope, they . . . by provoking the responsive passions of the belligerent, would set the stage for a revival of virulent McCarthyism, an administrative system of impressment into the armed forces, and the establishment of a despotic tyranny bent on impairing traditional civil liberties and civic rights."[11] Group action, then, runs the special danger of arousing a virulent backlash.

Judge Wyzanski acknowledges that during the winter of 1860–61 Oliver Wendell Holmes, Jr., the future Justice, "joined the small group of Abolitionists who made themselves responsible for securing the physical safety of Wendell Phillips against the threats of Boston mobs, a protection which the Boston police seemed unlikely to provide,"[12] and he adds that "if it was morally right to break the laws supporting slavery even when it cost the nation its unity and helped to precipitate what, despite W. H. Seward may not have been an 'irrepressible conflict,' one cannot be so certain that it is morally wrong to resist the war in Vietnam if one deeply believes its purposes or methods are wicked." Yet, he holds that "each of us may bide his time until he personally is faced with an order requiring him as an individual to do a wrongful act." In support of this view he cites the

---

[10] *Op. cit.*, p. 60. It should be noted here that not all of those who turn in their draft cards are directly resisting military service. Some have turned in their cards in order to protest alleged injustices in the selective-service system; others seek confrontation on the constitutionality of the law requiring the physical possession of a draft card. As a consequence of civil disobedience for these purposes some of the theological students have been punished by their draft boards: they have been reclassified 1-A, and have been called for induction.

[11] *Ibid.*, p. 59.

[12] *Ibid.*, p. 59.

example of Sir Thomas More, who did not rush to protest the Act of Henry VIII's Parliament. "Only when attempt was made to force him to subscribe to [the Oath of Supremacy] did he resist." Judge Wyzanski concludes the article with a note of caution: "Those who look upon Sir Thomas More as one of the noblest exemplars of the human spirit reflecting the impact of the love of God may find a delayed civil disobedience the response most likely to give peace of mind and to evidence moral courage."[13]

Before proceeding to consider further the concept of delayed civil disobedience we should note in passing two related issues posed by Judge Wyzanski in this connection. "There are situations," he says, "when it seems plainly moral for a man to disobey an evil law promulgated by a government which is entirely lacking in ethical character. If a man has lost confidence in the integrity of his society . . . then there is much justification for his disobedience." This statement is not intended by the judge to qualify his preference for delayed civil disobedience. But we should observe something else here. He refers to civil disobedience, but strictly speaking the statement has little to do with civil disobedience properly defined. In authentic civil disobedience, as we have already observed, the civil disobedient has not "lost confidence in the integrity of his society"; nor does he hold the government to be "entirely lacking in ethical character." For this reason he aims to disobey within a legal framework, in order to improve a specific law or policy. With confidence in the integrity of his society and its government he invites legal agencies to deal with him, even to punish him, and he expects them to deal with him fairly. Complete loss of confidence in the society, as described by the judge, would seem to call for "systemic" disobedience from morally conscientious men; that is, it would call for rebellion and not for civil disobedience.

In order to fortify the definition of civil disobedience set forth in this paper I would like to raise a second question about Judge Wyzanski's conception. As we have noted, he says in recommending delayed civil disobedience, "Each of us may bide his time until he personally is faced with an order requiring him as an individual to do a wrongful act." Here again the nature and

[13] *Ibid.*, p. 60.

purpose of civil disobedience are overlooked. The authentic civil disobedient is not motivated merely by the desire to escape personal complicity in the performing of wrongful acts. He is concerned to make a public protest and to bring about the change of a law or policy. He is not acting merely for the sake of keeping his conscience clean; he intends to act as a citizen, fulfilling the responsibilities of conscientious citizenship.

In the light of this purpose of civil disobedience I am inclined to say that Judge Wyzanski's conception of delayed civil disobedience, restricted as it is to isolated, individual, and delayed action, would seem in practice to have the effect of reducing to a minimum the social efficacy of the disobedience. It reduces almost to a vanishing point the publicity that might move public opinion. Is it not asking a great deal of civilly disobedient draft-resisters to go one after the other silently and meekly to jail to join the thousand other resisters already there and thus to be unnoticed or forgotten by the general public? Indeed, is it not asking them to nullify a basic purpose of their disobedience? These considerations are pertinent not only for assessing protest against war; they obtain also for civil disobedience in other areas, as for example in the sphere of the civil-rights movement.

One should emphasize, however, that Judge Wyzanski's cautions deserve heeding. Civil disobedience, especially in dramatic, group form, can bring into play a social law of action and reaction; that is, it can give rise to irrational and violent response. Having said this, we should add that the dangers latent in a tense situation are aggravated the more when backlash reaction is allowed free rein as a consequence of the massive inertia of comfortable and indifferent "citizens." Plenty of evidence exists of the "law" of action and reaction in stormy bursts of the winds of doctrine. Judge Wyzanski speaks of the danger of a "revival of virulent McCarthyism." The present rash of proposed legislation in various states which combines the worst features of the old Smith Act and the McCarran Act confirms this warning.

It is clear that civil disobedience should not be entered into lightly or unadvisedly but discreetly and soberly. Nevertheless, risks must be taken. It would be futile, and also immoral, at the present time to ask civil disobedients to desist for the sake of the public safety. Only a clear and present danger to the stability of the social and legal order could justify such counsel.

THE RESPONSIBILITIES OF THE GOVERNMENT

We have considered at length the responsibilities and dangers attaching to civil disobedience, but we have by no means completed the reckoning. The heavier weight of responsibility and of possible danger appears on the other side of the scale. Therefore, we must now consider the hazards encountered by the civil disobedient in his attempt to vindicate his action in the face of and within the legal system. Here the crucial responsibility belongs to the agencies of government and to the general public. Indeed, the agencies of government can seriously fall short of their responsibility to the citizen who in the name of justice and conscience challenges a law or policy. This means that in their performance here they can also fall short of their responsibility to society in general and to the constitution in particular. Judge Wyzanski, speaking of the intemperatre response of the government and the public to civil disobedience, warns against the possibility of the "establishment of . despotic tyranny bent on impairing traditional civil liberties and civic rights. We have mentioned already the current attempts of certain legislators to revitalize the Smith Act and the McCarran Act. More familiar is intemperate and brutal police action. The civil disobedient in an immediate way provides the occasion for the appearance of these forms of restriction, but he is not primarily responsible for them. The primary and direct responsibility rests more squarely upon the general public and upon the government. Again and again in the history of the United States the agencies of government have permitted or promoted the violation of civil liberties—freedom of speech and of association. They have done this through the perversion of due process and through other repressive policies. It is striking and scandalous that only recently (August 1969) has a court ordered the trial of a suit to test the constitutionality of the House Internal Security Committee. It is to the credit of the U.S. Court of Appeals (Seventh Circuit) that it has ordered this trial. Professor Arthur Kinoy of the Rutgers Law School, one of the seven lawyers for the plaintiffs, on hearing of the Circuit

Court's ordering of the trial, said, "What that means is that we will finally have the right to prove in a court of law that the committee has conducted a 30-year witch hunt in violation of the Constitution and the rights of citizens."[14] The examples of the failure of government to protect the First-Amendment rights of citizens, including civil disobedients, are legion and may be traced far back in American (and European) history.

In the face of civil disobedience the agencies of the state are immediately and inescapably brought into action, either to enforce the law or to maintain and protect the government policy under challenge. In a government of separation of powers, the functioning of the state to deal with civil disobedience entails a division of labor. Thus the police and the legislative and judicial functions involve different agencies. If the rights of civil disobedients are to be protected adequately, the integrity and efficacy of public opinion and nongovernmental agencies of the community are extremely important. If these agencies are not alert and critical, the agencies of the state are the more likely to overreach themselves. A large number of these nongovernmental agencies function in any vital democracy, agencies representing the general welfare and also special interests. In the sphere of civil disobedience today one of the most significant nongovernmental agencies is the American Civil Liberties Union. We should also mention here the Legal Defense Fund of the National Association for the Advancement of Colored People. Both these agencies have been active in attempting to keep the public properly informed regarding both fact and law and in bringing or supporting court action.

This kind of function performed by nongovernmental agencies is succinctly formulated in the "Statement on Civil Disobedience" (February 1, 1969) of the American Civil Liberties Union. Here the ACLU defines its purpose as that of attempting to promote equal protection of the laws and also due process of law in the community's or the state's treatment of civil disobedients, particularly in terms of the First and the Fourteenth Amendments of the Constitution. In pursuing these purposes the ACLU

[14] *New York Times*, August 10, 1969.

of course does not attempt to protect the civil disobedient from all punishment as a consequence of his disobedience. In this connection, the Statement asserts: "The right to counsel must be provided, the trial held in an atmosphere that is not prejudicial to the rights of the accused, and the sentence imposed not more severe than would be imposed on another person who violated the same law." It is not difficult to cite cases in which atmosphere prejudicial to the rights of the accused has prevailed. Moreover, state courts have sometimes employed excessive bail determination not only to detain and punish but also to prejudice the fairness of trial of individuals or groups that hold allegedly antisocial beliefs or are too poor to pay for their release. Thus the "bail system" can serve to violate the equal-protection guaranteed by the Fourteenth Amendment. Sometimes the government prejudices fairness of trial in the definition of the "crime," and with the same effect as a prejudicial determination of bail. These devices can influence the jury and the public to assess the "crime" of civil disobedience as fearful and horrendous. Fortunately, these devices can win reversal from a higher court.

In the judgment of many the U.S. government in its concern during recent years to maintain and enforce its war policy and the military-draft law has come close to perverting due process and to impairing both freedom of speech and freedom of association. This tendency has been detected in the government's handling of the Spock case, particularly in its decision to indict for conspiracy and in the misguidance of the jury. This case has won such wide publicity that we do well to give attention here to aspects of it which exemplify fundamental problems to be encountered by civil disobedients in face of the government and the community.

THE SPOCK CASE

The issues involved in the Spock case are complex, and this complexity has been compounded by reason of the decision of the First District Court of Appeals (Nos. 7205-08, July 11, 1969) to acquit two of the four defendants, Dr. Benjamin Spock and Michael Ferber, and to order a new trial for the Rev. William S.

Coffin, Jr., and Mitchell Goodman. At the time of this writing the government has not yet decided what action to take with respect to the new trial.

In the context of the present essay three aspects of the Spock case deserve our notice. First we should observe an aspect of every legal system. Often we hear it said that ours is a government of laws and not of men. But this cliché conceals the fact that important areas of discretion obtain within the legal system. These areas of discretion are pertinent for any discussion of cases dealing with civil disobedience. An important preliminary decision must be made by the law-enforcement agency of the government. The government may exercise discretion, indeed it cannot avoid exercising it, in the decision *whether* and *when* to indict. Moreover, if indictment is to be sought, the prosecutor has the freedom or discretion to formulate the terms of the indictment. And then the grand jury and the court in turn exercise judgment in the decision to accept or reject the definition provided by the prosecutor. And, finally, the trial jury is in principle free to accept or reject the definition.

Professor Joseph L. Sax of the University of Michigan has made very cogent comment on the discretion belonging to the prosecutor. His comment deserves extensive quotation here:

> Through the miracle of prosecutorial discretion—a device central to the operation of the legal system, but widely ignored in discussions of civil disobedience—criminality can be, and is, produced or ignored virtually at will by law-enforcement officials. Businessmen know that if the building and fire laws were fully implemented they could be in court virtually every day.
>
> Justice Jackson once said that "a prosecutor has more control over our life, liberty, and reputation than any other person in America . . . he can choose his defendant . . . a prosecutor stands a fair chance of finding at least a technical violation of some act on the part of almost anyone."
>
> The law is so vast in its technical coverage and so open-ended in its possible interpretation by police officers, prosecutors, and judges that it becomes almost meaningless to talk about civil disobedience as if there were conduct which "the law"—as some external force—declared illegal.
>
> In fact, no society could operate if it did not tolerate a great deal of technically or arguably illegal conduct on the

ground that certain laws were absolute and others unwise as written or as applied to particular situations.[15]

These observations have considerable bearing upon our previous discussion of the "fabric of society" in its legal aspects. This fabric is a good deal more ambiguous and flexible than Judge Wyzanski's argument (cited earlier in this paper) suggests when he asks for delayed civil disobedience.

The comments of Professor Sax have equal bearing upon the "prosecutorial discretion" exercised in the Spock case. The crucial discretion exercised by the government in this case is manifest in the Attorney General's and the prosecutor's decision to define the "crime" not merely as counseling, aiding, and abetting refusal and evasion of the draft (section 12 of the Military Selective Service Act of 1967) but also as conspiracy to counsel and aid (here the Court appealed not to legislation but rather to alleged precedents).

It is difficult enough to define precisely the meaning of the charge of counseling and aiding the commission of a crime. In this case the defendants had proclaimed far and wide their view that the war in Vietnam is immoral and illegal. Is it possible to do this without in effect counseling and abetting refusal of the draft? If not, does the legislation abridge free speech? But it is even more difficult to define authoritatively the crime of conspiracy.

In making the charge of conspiracy the government imported a vague and amorphous concept, indeed one that has served again and again in history to repress freedom of speech and of association, not to speak of violating due process. It was employed a century and a half ago to indict trade unions as criminal conspiracies, and also more recently in the Joseph McCarthy era in extrajudicial efforts to subvert the protections of the First and Fourteenth Amendments.

Despite the protest of Mr. Justice Harlan in the Grunewald case (353 US 91) that "every conspiracy is by its nature secret," the decision of the Court of Appeals asserts that the element of secrecy is not essential. Thus conspiracy in this case, according to the Court decision, consisted of an "agreement" that was legal insofar as it entailed opposition to the war and the draft (an

[15] Joseph L. Sax, "Civil Disobedience: The Law Is Never Blind," *Saturday Review*, September 28, 1968, p. 22.

exercise of the right of free speech) but which was illegal in "that the means or intermediate objectives encompassed both legal and illegal activity without any clear indication, initially, as to who intended what." This conspiracy, be it noted, was not secret; it was loudly and publicly proclaimed. Moreover, the illegal action of others—refusal of the draft on the part of young men—occurred later.

In noting the gap between the counseling and the acts of disobedience of the young men Judge Frank M. Coffin in his dissenting opinion calls the Court's view "a delayed fuse approach." Arguing also that the use of the conspiracy charge represents a dubious extension of precedents, he raises the question whether "reason and authority" compel the application of the charge of conspiracy "to a wholly open, amorphous and shifting association, having a broad focus of interest in changing public policy, and encompassing a wide spectrum of purposes, legal and illegal." In his dissent from the order for a new trial for the Rev. Mr. Coffin and Mitchell Goodman, Judge Coffin says that "such diverse groups as Clergy Concerned, a consumers' boycott of California grapes, a parents' group for so-called 'freedom of choice' plans within a Southern school district might find themselves facing a conspiracy indictment." He therefore asks whether "the ation's well-being and security cannot be as well served in less repressive ways," and he suggests that the broad interpretation placed by the court upon conspiracy will have a "chilling effect" on the exercise of freedom of speech and association. "Even if the Court's safeguards were rigorously applied," he says, "the ranks of individuals enlisted in a controversial public cause would visibly shrink if they knew that the jury could find them to be members of a conspiracy." In the main, then, Judge Coffin's dissent is based on the view that applying the doctrine of conspiracy in these cases is "not consistent with the First Amendment." And in this connection he adds, "It would be small comfort to be told that one could still be vindicated via the appellate process after an expenditure of time and money in substantial amounts."

Judge Coffin concludes this remarkable dissenting opinion with words of salutary warning:

> This is a landmark case and no one, I take it, supposes that this will be the last attempt by the government to use the

conspiracy weapon. The government has cast a wide net and caught only two fish. My objection is not that more were not caught but that the government can try again on another day in another court and the court's rationale provides no meaningful basis for predicting who will find themselves within the net. Finally, there is the greater danger that the casting of the net has scared away many whom the government had no right to catch.

Judge Coffin's objections to the court's acceptance of the indictment for conspiracy reminds one of the statement of Mr. Justice Jackson in which he called conspiracy "that elastic, sprawling and pervasive offense . . . so vague that it almost defies definition . . . the looseness and pliability of the doctrine present inherent dangers which should be in the background of judicial thought wherever it is sought to extend the doctrine to meet the exigencies of a particular case" (concurring opinion, *Krulewitch* v. *United States,* 336 US 446, 449). This citation is given in the *amicus curiae* brief of the Unitarian Universalist Association.

This brief submitted by the Unitarian Universalist Association analyzes in considerable detail the incompatibility between the government's charge of conspiracy and its obligation to protect the right of the citizen to criticize government policy and to enter into association with others for the purpose.

This brings us to the third consideration which is of special significance in the Spock case, the relation between civil disobedience and freedom of association. Citing precedents, the brief emphasizes the idea that "persons acting in association do not lose their first-amendment rights even if on other occasions or on the same occasion they engage in separate, illegal conduct." But how did the government attempt to proceed in the Spock case? The brief asserts that "as the case was submitted, the jury may well have believed that *any group* criticism of the government alone permitted an inference of an illegal conspiracy."[16]

We need not discuss here the reasons for the Court's acquittal of Dr. Spock and Michael Ferber or the reasons for the ordering

[16] For a lively, sharp treatment of earlier phases and consequences of the litigation and also for an analysis of the strikingly inadequate reporting and interpretation of the case by the press (including James Reston of the *New York Times*), see Jessica Mitford, "Guilty as Charged by the Judge," *Atlantic,* August 1969.

of a new trial. It suffices to say that the two defendants were cleared of the conspiracy charge and that the retrial of the remaining two defendants was ordered on account of the misconduct of the previous trial.

We have given extensive attention to the Spock case and the related cases because they provide examples not only of the large role of discretion belonging to the government in civil disobedience cases but also of the ways in which the government may undertake to impair the freedom of speech and the freedom of association. The relevance and legal status of the conspiracy charge in these cases has not yet been settled. It is significant that there is no evidence that members of the jury considered this question.[17] And for that matter, if the Coffin and Goodman cases are finally appealed to the U.S. Supreme Court, it is possible that the Court will not give a ruling on the conspiracy charge. It may not be necessary for it to do so (though it has done so in the past), for already in the District Court's decision one can see that the crucial issue may turn out to be a distinction between freedom of *expression* and affirmative aiding and abetting of violations of the draft statutes. Moreover, in a previous case before the Supreme Court, when the conspiracy charge had been made against Communists, the Court ruled only against the suppression of free speech and did not rule on the conspiracy charge.

In any event, the government in the Spock-case indictment, far from protecting the rights of speech and of association, used its discretion to bring an indictment for conspiracy. As a consequence it has administered what Judge Coffin has called a "chilling effect" to many citizens who might have been disposed to criticize, or to enter into association to criticize, government policy in Vietnam. The "chilling effect" was probably intended also for any young men who might have been considering undertaking civil disobedience in protest against this policy or against the draft statutes. It matters not that Dr. Spock and Michael Ferber have been acquitted "via the appellate process after the expenditure of time and money in substantial amounts" (again

[17] Prof. Sax, writing about Judge Francis Ford, who presided over the first conviction of the defendants, says that "another judge could have found a dozen cogent reasons, all supported by precedent and good legal logic, to have dismissed the indictment before the trial ever began" (*op. cit.*, p. 24).

the words of the dissenting opinion). It matters not that in the remaining cases the conspiracy charge may drop out of sight. The "chilling effect" may already have served one of the purposes of the government, regardless of the final disposition to be made of the cases by the courts, indeed regardless of whether or not the government ever expected the conspiracy charge to be vindicated.

We have been discussing the Spock case as an illustration of civil disobedience and of government discretion in the face of civil disobedience. According to our definition of civil disobedience, however, the defendants should have been expected to plead guilty and to accept the penalty. But in actuality they decided to challenge the indictment. The reason for their doing this was made quite clear by the Rev. Mr. Coffin soon after the announcement of the indictment for conspiracy. "I was persuaded," he said, "that fighting this indictment would be the best support we could offer to those who are resisting the draft." He elaborated this statement by saying, "Unchallenged, the precedent it would set might make it much too easy for the Government to indict anybody for conspiracy, and this would diminish the possibilities of dissent and the exercise of the rights of conscience."[18] What was at stake, then, was the maintenance of the rights of freedom of speech and of association, and also the right of conscience to criticize government policy or to undertake civil disobedience without incurring the charge of conspiracy.[19]

[18] Fred C. Shapiro, "God and That Man at Yale," *New York Times Magazine*, March 3, 1968, p. 62.

[19] Before leaving this section of the paper on the responsibilities of government in civil disobedience matters I would like to call attention to a highly instructive and suggestive discussion of the topic by Ronald Dworkin in the article referred to earlier here, *New York Review of Books*, June 8, 1968. In this article the author considers, among other things, the responsibility of government to recognize the contributions of civil disobedients to the clarification of public issues and of the meaning of civil rights in a changing social and legal situation. For example, the civil disobedient challenges laws and policies which are of dubious moral and legal character, stimulating the public and the courts to scrutinize anew these laws and policies; he may expose violations of due process and of the right to equal protection of the law; he may also bring to the attention of the public and Congress the need for the amendment of laws that are unclear or repressive.

Specifically, civil disobedience in our day has brought to sharper focus many questions regarding the compromised rights of ethnic minorities, regarding the validity of the military draft laws, and regarding immoral and

CIVIL DISOBEDIENCE AND
FREEDOM OF ASSOCIATION

In the previous section we have seen that the Spock litigation illustrates the large role of "prosecutorial discretion" in civil disobedience cases. In the previous paragraph we have observed another important aspect of our subject: generally, civil disobedience is not merely the act of a single individual alone; it usually turns out to be the exercise of freedom of association.

In the "Advice to the National Council of Churches," cited above, appears the statement that even when the civil disobedient "is alone in his disobedience, he acts as one who is a member of a fellowship committed to obedience to God." A sense of fellowship or of common commitment among civil disobedients is strikingly evident in the history of democracy—in social reform movements that have employed civil disobedience,[20] and before that in the left-wing, aggressive Protestant sects. Initially democracy itself was conceived in civil disobedience and first became incarnate in freedom of association, that is, in voluntary associations formal and informal. Indeed, the voluntary association has become a characteristic and indispensable organ of the democratic polity, a principal medium of group commitment and fellowship. Indeed, it has been voluntary organizations which

---

illegal aspects of the Vietnam war, and this at a time when government policy is being increasingly questioned by the public. In this connection the author asserts that society can tolerate some disobedience (especially in the light of the considerations just mentioned) and that the prosecutor, in the face of certain types of disobedience, may and should, as in other types of cases, decide not to press charges. Society suffers a special loss, he says, if it punishes a group that includes its most thoughtful and loyal citizens. In this whole complex of law and circumstance the government has a special responsibility to recognize the social value of the development and testing of law and policy through experimentation by citizens and through the adversary process. All in all, one can infer from these views that the government and the public have the responsibility to recognize the subtle and even illegal ways in which enlivened conscience can give new meaning to both the law and the spirit of the law. One is reminded here of the famous statement of Judge Learned Hand in which he urged that justices 'be aware of the changing social tensions in every society which make it an organism [and] which will disrupt it, if rigidly confined."

[20] After the present writing was completed the author's attention was drawn to the essay on the sense of mutual obligation that develops among civil disobedients, by Michael Walzer, "The Obligation to Disobey," in David Spitz (ed.), *Political Theory and Social Change* (New York: Atherton Press, 1967), pp. 185–202.

have impressed upon the community and the state the demands for democratic rights. One sees this most clearly in the activities of the Puritans in dissent and in civil disobedience. The history of civil disobedience is thus closely bound up with the history of political democracy, with the interplay between voluntary associations and the state, an involuntary association in its distinctive features.[21]

The voluntary association is an old institution. It was given new thrust in early modern history by civil disobedients who protested against the monolithic principles of the involuntary political and ecclesiastical Establishment. At the beginning of the struggle, civil disobedience and the idea of freedom of association were viewed by the Establishment as a radical threat to the stability of society. Thomas Hobbes, in opposing these free associations, asserted that they were completely incompatible with the sovereignty of the ruler. Voluntary associations, he said, "are worms in the entrails of the natural man." And in his view they of course should be wormed.

These associations included not only the independent churches and social reform associations but also scientific and professional societies like the one that has brought us together here today. Along with universities, labor unions, and pressure groups they have come to represent the organizational ingredients of modern pluralistic society.

It was partly from associations such as these that the principle of loyal opposition entered into modern democratic theory and practice. The late A. D. Lindsay of Balliol College, Oxford, has pointed out that this principle came into the modern state especially from the independent churches of the seventeenth century which insisted not only upon their rights as minorities but also upon the protection of the minorities within their own churches. Only through this sort of organization, they held, could the Spirit blow where it listeth.[22]

---

[21] A wide range of these phenomena is dealt with in D. B. Robertson (ed.), *Voluntary Associations* (Richmond, Va.: John Knox Press, 1966); and in J. Roland Pennock and John W. Chapman (eds.), *Voluntary Associations, Nomos XI* (New York: Atherton Press, 1969).

[22] For a well-documented account of "The Origins of the Idea of Loyal Opposition," see the chapter by George H. Williams in D. B. Robertson, *op. cit.*

In the democratic state's adoption of the idea of loyal opposition a principle of nongovernmental associations was taken over into the government. The birth of political parties was related to this development. If we observe that this development followed upon the appearance of the claim for freedom of religious association, we may say that pluralism (or nonconformity) in religion was followed by pluralism within the state itself. (Compare the theory of checks and balances.)

An analogous prototypical development in earlier Western civilization came in part from the doctrine that the Christian must render unto Caesar that which is Caesar's and unto God that which is God's. Speaking of this New Testament axiom, Alfred North Whitehead was wont to say that there appeared here a new principle of social organization.[23] The state was not only placed within limits and under criticism, but this criticism was to be supported by an association independent of the state. This independent religious association in no way considered itself the creature of the state. Quite the contrary. That would have made the church merely a function of the state, that is, of civic religion. It is striking to observe, however, how short a time this pluralistic conception was able to maintain itself and survive. By the fifth century Christianity had almost acquired the status of a civic religion.

In the modern period the idea of freedom of association gave rise to a pluralistic conception of the relation between the community and the state. Here the state is viewed not as the creator but as an organ of the community, and it is only one of these organs. The state as an involuntary association has its particular, changing functions, but properly understood it operates in cybernetic interplay with other associations in the community. Both the state and the voluntary associations are expressions of and within the embracing, open community. To be sure, many of these cells represent "special interests" rather than universal concern for the general welfare. On the other hand, the church claims a transcendent reference beyond the community and even beyond itself. Indeed, individual conscience may make an analogous claim.

[23] Alfred North Whitehead, *Adventures of Ideas* (New York: Macmillan Co., 1933), p. 69.

These voluntary associations serve as mediators of sensitivity, of expanding conceptions of justice and mercy, of new prickings of conscience, which are transmitted from minority groups to the community at large. Already by the end of the first quarter of the eighteenth century the Friends, veterans of civil disobedience, had devised the major technique of the modern pressure group, as an extension of their strategy of persuasion, in the transition from dissent to politics.[24]

The mediating institutions, however, are not confined to non-governmental instruments. The jury, for example, can serve as a mediating instrumentality between the community and the state, transmitting to the legal process new sensitivities (or old prejudices), so much so that it has often been remarked that in effect the jury offers modification of the law. Accordingly, Sir Edward Coke asserted that "the jurors are chancellors."[25] The prerequisite of the jury as a mediating instrument is of course the ethically sensitive juror. In civil disobedience cases the advocate for the defendant looks for the juror who can respond to burgeoning moral demands.[26] The prosecutor on the other hand tends to look for the juror who seems to be a "right-thinking" citizen who believes in "law and order" as defined by a government bent on enforcing (that is, forcing) its policy. All too often a jury does not represent a full cross-section of the community; it represents instead the "microcosm of the system and the central prejudices of the community." It is not easy to find jurors of the sort that will be patient of civil disobedience. Nor for that matter is it easy to find a judge who will carefully and completely instruct the jury regarding its prerogatives. The consequence oftentimes is that the jurors suppress or even pervert their own function as a mediating agency.

The voluntary associations that develop in connection with

24 Norman Hunt, *Two Early Political Associations* (New York: Oxford University Press, 1965).

25 Cf. Charles E. Wyzanski, Jr., *Whereas—A Judge's Prem. ses* (Boston: Atlantic-Little Brown, 1965), p. 12; also Patrick Devlin, *The Enforcement of Morals* (New York: Oxford University Press, 1965), chaps. I and V.

26 Philip J. Hirschkop, Washington civil-rights trial lawyer, gives a striking, colloquial description of the juror sought for in civil-rights cases. "We look," he says, "for guys who are in conflict with themselves. The only chance we stand, in many instances, is to get a man who will delve into his own conscience. . . . Forget about the straight-shooter—the guy who is very sure of himself." *Washington Post*, Potomac section, January 28, 1968.

civil disobedience are likewise mediating agencies between the community and the state. Of course, the enterprise is not always efficacious; it may even turn out to be an expression of egregiously distorted conscience. When properly effective, however, it expresses a burgeoning modification of consensus within the community. As such it stirs the apathy of the citizen from its dead center, reminding him that his routine conscience may have missed something. It brings about new alignments and new creative tensions.[27] In this way civil disobedience expresses and impinges upon the consciousness of the whole community and ultimately upon the processes of government. It does this within the framework of a legal system, modifying precedents out of the past and making new precedents for the future. Without this disturbance the legal system and the social order can become a stagnant haven of injustice, a harbinger of violence or of revolutionary action. When other checks and balances in the society and the government do not function adequately, civil disobedience can step into the breach and promote the fundamental values of a just democratic society. That it has done this in the current situation at least in some measure is to be observed in recent court decisions expanding the legal freedom of citizens to use certain public facilities for sit-in demonstrations and for the distribution of literature of protest; and accomplishments besides these have been indicated elsewhere in the present paper.

Why, one may ask, cannot this disturbance be engendered and channeled through normal political processes? And does not the disturbance through civil disobedience weaken "the basic fabric of society"? The answer is that:

> those who think resisters are tearing the fabric of the

[27] This process is indicated in a genial way by Yale's Dean E. F. Thompson in his comment on the influence of the indictment (for conspiracy) of the Rev. William S. Coffin, Jr., Chaplain of Yale University: "I'm very fond of Bill; I argue with him all along. But now I have to look at my own position and see if there isn't something basically wrong with our society if an intelligent man who has given a lot of thought to it finds himself forced to disobey the law." Quoted by Fred C. Shapiro, *op. cit.*, p. 56. Compare the comment of Yale President Kingman Brewster: after stating that he is constrained to "disagree with the chaplain's position on draft resistance, and in this instance deplore his style," he says that "thanks in large part to his personal verve and social action . . . the rebellious instinct, which elsewhere expresses itself in sour withdrawal, cynical nihilism and disruption, is here [at Yale] more often than not both affirmative and constructive, thanks in considerable measure to the chaplain's influence" (*Ibid.*, p. 56).

society might wish to consider the possibility that a society is best able to survive if it permits a means for taking an issue back to the public over the heads of public official-dom; when it recognizes that a government may have so implicated itself in a wretched policy that it needs to be extricated by popular repudiation in a forum more imme-diately available—and less politically compromised—than the ballot box.[28]

This consideration becomes the more pertinent in a time when (especially in the area of race relations) society is being reor-dered, but when an increasing number of blacks are questioning the ability of the established political system to meet their desire in the name of consent of the governed to share the benefits of the most productive society on earth, and when a Walter Lippmann can question the ability of Congress to deal in proper time with the maladjustments.

In a time like this the process of disturbance does not become efficacious through the action of individuals alone. It requires the crystallizing of sentiment, the establishment of morale among the dissidents, and a certain mobilization for action. These goals are possible of achievement only throu;.1 association. This is the reason freedom of speech tends to stand or fall with freedom of association. Darnell Rucker is correct when he says that "civil disobedience is the last bastion of the individual against his society,"[29] but it would be more accurate to say that the last bastion is freedom of association, for without this freedom civil disobedience is not likely to be efficacious. Here again we see the significance of the Spock case and the threat to democratic principles in the government's charge of conspiracy in that case.

By reason of the character of disturbance at the hands of the civil disobedients the demands upon the community and the legal system are of paradoxical order. If the process is to promote an open and viable legal order, courage will be required of the trustees of the law as well as of the civil disobedients, of the Creons as well as of the Antigones.[30]

[28] Joseph L. Sax, "Conscience and Anarchy: The Prosecution of War Resisters," *Yale Review*, LVII, No. 4 (June 1968), 494.

[29] Darnell Rucker, "The Moral Grounds of Civil Disobedience," *Ethics*, LXXVI, No. 2 (January 1966), 142.

[30] Harry W. Jones, "Civil Disobedience," *Proceedings of the American Philosophical Society*, 111, No. 4 (August 1967), 198.

In a concluding word, how shall we assess the significance of authentic civil disobedience? We have tried to indicate something of its character, its hazards, its dangers, its accomplishments, its possibilities, its limits. But at the end here we must recognize its built-in limitation, a limitation of which many a civil disobedient is aware.

Civil disobedience, obviously, is not adequate to cope with the basic problems of positive construction required in a mass, technological society. It offers essentially a criticism and a correction from the margin. Because of this character and limitation there are many civil disobedients today who undertake their disobedience out of despair and not in reasonable hope of victory. They do this by reason of the feeble results of their efforts. Some of them engage in civil disobedience really as an act of withdrawal. They sometimes suspect that civil disobedience is a strategy that enables a society to evade the fundamental problems of social transformation: it enables evasion precisely because it does not compel widespread fundamental rethinking and positive action. As for war and poverty and discrimination in employment and education, many a civil disobedient recognizes that progress has been intolerably slow and ambiguous in these spheres. The black leader LeRoi Jones, in despair by re on of the inefficacy of nonviolence and civil disobedience, even argues that nonviolence is a device that by default serves primarily to leave the status quo undisturbed. "Nonviolence in the American context," he says, "means, at its most honest evocation, a proposed immersion into the mainstream of a bankrupt American culture, and that's all. . . . Even the proposition is, finally, a fake. No such immersion is even possible. It is much too late."[31]

It is the limitation of civil disobedience that it cannot make broad, frontal constructive attack on these problems. In short, it cannot replace normal political procedures. Indeed, this should never be its intention. But normal political procedures will not make frontal attack in any moment short of crisis. At its best, then, civil disobedience makes its contribution only in a long-range timespan that covers decades. In the immediate situation its principal contribution is to offer the challenge of quickened

[31] *Home: Social Essays* (New York: William Morrow & Co., 1966), p. 149.

conscience and, along with other forces, to elicit that sense of crisis which from time to time bestirs a people into concerted action. The alternative to these slow processes is revoltuion. Civil disobedience by its strategy repeatedly reminds the nation of the wisdom articulated by Walter Bagehot: "Strong beliefs win strong men and make them stronger."

SOCIAL ETHICS AND PASTORAL CARE

James Luther Adams

Person and institution, law and liberty, individual and community are realities that are generally viewed as somehow standing in opposition to, or at least in tension with, each other. The same must be said of social ethics and psychotherapy, and also of social ethics and pastoral care. So much is the distance between them taken for granted that one seldom finds in the literature any substantial reference to their relationship, except to be sure that psychological and interpersonal aspects of social ethics receive consideration. But such discussions conspicuously ignore institutional questions.

The writer on Christian ethics usually does not concern himself with the social-ethical or institutional aspects of the conduct of pastoral care. On the other hand, the literature of pastoral care for its part largely ignores the problems presented by economic and political institutions, though to be sure the family as an institution, and perhaps also the school, receive attention. Then, too, one may encounter passing reference to economic institutions if the writer on psychotherapy or pastoral care comments on the inadequacy of the therapy of mere adjustment.

By way of justification for this virtual segregation, one could say that each discipline demands increasing specialization if it is to take seriously its own characteristic problems. This claim must be granted, but serious questions abide. Does not pastoral care relate to the prophetic aspect of the church's mission? Does not authentic therapy bring the restored person to participation in the normal institutional obligations of the churchman as citizen or of the church as a corporate body? Corresponding questions can be directed to the Christian (or secular) ethicist with respect to the impingement of pastoral care upon his discipline and its institutional concerns. These are among the searching questions that Carl Wennerstrom's dissertation poses. And certainly no one will claim that the answers are ready to hand.

It is Wennerstrom's thesis that social prophetism, bent on institutional reform, and a correspondingly rationalistic perspective on human personality, have promoted the neglect of pastoral care on the part of the liberal clergy; more than that, they tend to make the religious liberal shy away from the individual who has suffered personal catastrophe or is in some other way distressed in body, mind, or estate. Moreover, Wennerstrom views these lopsided emphases as contributing to an overdramatic conception of problem solving, and finally to a depersonalizing social distance between the pastoral counselor and the parishioner in distress. These impediments to authentic pastoral care Wennerstrom identifies under the names of rationalism, reformism, dramatics, and social distance. Moreover, he makes so bold as to speak of them as characteristic features of religious liberalism.

Wennerstrom's view of these dimensions of religious

liberalism, we should observe, is not simply a negative evaluation. Rather, he takes an ambivalent attitude. Indeed, as I read him, I find that he adopts a tragic view; religious liberalism has had noble intentions (he seems to say), but by reason of demonic lopsidedness it has engendered *hubris*. We might put it this way: the drive of liberalism has been to liberate the individual from authoritarianism and to open the way for autonomy and rationality. This drive has focused the energy of the liberal upon a militant reformism and rationalism, it has given him an overclear and overdramatic conception of his ability to solve problems, and it has reduced the desire or the capacity for intimate relationships. The liberal minister of this sort cannot "feel" or does not want to feel the other person as person, particularly if the other is in emotional distress.

Religious liberalism, in this view, has served as a sort of avalanche that has almost snowed under the liberal minister's capacity to perceive what does not fit into or support his highly selective, tailor-made thought structure. He maintains a social distance from the actual sufferer. Considering this outcome, Wennerstrom says of the major motifs of religious liberalism: Nothing fails like success. The situation is the more tragic insofar as the liberal minister, fired with reformism and rationalism, is unaware of this reality test. Pastoral care cannot become authentic until this kind of religious liberalism can be corrected. The correction will require an altered conception of man himself. In this connection John F. Hayward, in his chapter of this volume, looks beyond the stance of the minister and pungently sets forth the implications of Wennerstrom's outlook for a revision of the liberal-religious doctrine of man.

At first blush Wennerstrom's characterization of the ingredients of religious liberalism may appear to some readers to be merely a caricature. This impression of caricature could readily be gained from the elliptic summary I have given here. Actually, Wennerstrom's presentation exhibits more of the subtlety and paradox that attach to the reality.

We should observe immediately, however, that religious liberalism has no monopoly on the features Wennerstrom assigns to it. There are surprising similarities between religious liberalism and other religious movements of the modern period. For example, the first and the last features in Wennerstrom's list, rationalism and social distance, one could assign also to confessional orthodoxy as it has appeared since the seventeenth and eighteenth centuries. Indeed, even more of the four features are to be found in the Enlightenment. Both religious liberalism and confessional orthodoxy (with its rationalism in the formulation of "pure" doctrine) took on their special qualities during the period of the Enlightenment.

A more striking similarity than these, however, is to be remarked. In reading Wennerstrom's description of the features of religious liberalism one could readily substitute for religious liberalism the term "modern man," and the description would be almost equally cogent and pertinent. The four features adumbrated by Wennerstrom, when taken together, closely approximate what in many quarters have been summed up under the term "modernity." These four features, in one formulation or another, appear prominently in the typological writings of such analysts of modern man as Max Weber, Ernst Troeltsch, Paul Tillich, Karl Jaspers, Lewis Mumford, or Talcott Parsons. This observation of the similarity between Wennerstrom's description of the religious liberal and the regnant characterizations of modern man should not be at all surprising. Religious liberalism has taken its shape in part as an aspect of modernity. Indeed, this has been the proud claim of religious liberalism.

"Modern Man" as the Framework

What are the characteristic features of modernity? A comprehensive answer to this question would entail our comparing and contrasting "the modern" with "the medieval" and "the ancient." We need not enter here into such an elaborate analysis. It will suffice for our present purpose if we center attention directly upon what is meant by the terms "modern man" and "modernity."

At the outset we should observe that the concepts "modernity" and "modernization" possess a certain ambiguity. They can be viewed as connoting a value judgment; that is, they can be used as synonymous with good or desirable. At the same time they can express the intention to be merely descriptive. In either case, these concepts, like all concepts, are constructions. In this respect they necessarily select or emphasize certain features of the outlook or experience of modern man. Nuclear weapons, bacteriological warfare, fascism and communism, right-wing and left-wing movements, secularism and religious revivals, the social sciences and depth psychology, must be included among modern man's accomplishments or endeavors. One can readily see that there must be some discrepancy between modernity as a descriptive term and modernity as a term implying a positive value judgment.[1] From what has already been said about Wennerstrom's characterization of religious liberalism

[1] For a penetrating analysis of these ambiguities see Wilfred Cantwell Smith, *Modernisation of a Traditional Society* (New York: Asia Publishing House, 1965). See also Robert N. Bellah, ed., *Religion and Progress in Modern Asia* (New York: The Free Press, 1965). See especially the "epilogue" of the latter.

it becomes evident that he combines description and evaluation in his use of the term.

Let us now outline the framework within which we may
consider our theme, Social Ethics and Pastoral Care among
Liberals, toward the end of relating it to Wennerstrom's
conception of pastoral care as it is conducted (or distorted)
in the liberal churches.

It has been characteristic of modern man to rebel in
the name of God or reason or freedom against authoritarianism, in the economic and political spheres as well as in the
religious sphere. Similar religious motifs, or secularized versions of them, have played a central role also with respect
to the idea of the person and with respect to conceptions
of social organization. In turning away from authoritarianism the liberal has striven for the freedom and autonomy
of the individual, for freedom of conscience, and freedom
of choice. He has also made the claim to universality, bringing particular religious and cultural traditions under criticism. For example, he has claimed to discern and to represent a "natural religion" or a universal religiousness around
the world. But especially has he believed that nature and
history are amenable to human understanding and control,
that man can be master of his fate, that reason, imagination,
and will can give a new shape to human nature and the
world. This world-shaping will has had its roots in the
ethos of this-worldliness (as against otherworldliness). Moreover, old social ties of origin were to be dissolved. Pure
and applied science have been viewed as allies in this venture. Religious liberalism, accordingly, attempted to end the
warfare between religion and science.

All of these things were involved when modern man lost
his confidence in merely traditional authorities. Thus he
adopted what has been called substantial reason and techni-

cal reason, substantial in the sense of exercising freedom to consider and choose regarding the ends of life, and technical in the sense of seeking new means to achieve these ends. Everything was to be brought under the aegis of "one increasing purpose." This mentality, beginning with the Renaissance and especially with Francis Bacon, was supported and enhanced by the idea of progress, a dramatic interpretation of history which assumed both religious and secular formulation. What Wennerstrom calls rationalism gave rise also, then, to reformism. Modern man, with his faith in rationality, has believed that it is possible for him to define and solve problems anew if autonomy is allowed free rein. This whole process brought about a crisis in identity, not only because of the consequent acceleration of social change, but also because of the criticism directed at mere traditionalism in religion. This crisis in identity inevitably placed a heavy responsibility upon the psyche in face of a religious symbolism that was brought under question and also in face of a bewildering variety of emerging symbolism or reinterpreted symbolism.

We have spoken of individualism as an ingredient of liberalism. Strictly speaking, however, we may not say that liberalism is to be equated with atomistic individualism. Modern man has promoted the features of modernity we have mentioned by forming a multitude of associations, industrial, philanthropic, educational, professional, reformist, and religious. He has even created the modern state (in part a product of rational construction), an institution that did not exist in the Middle Ages. In the early modern period the state was assigned the function of protecting the rights of the individual, toward the end of liberating religious and economic institutions from political control.

In Anglo-American society, Calvinism and the common law, in collaboration, have given support here.

Of major significance was the proliferation of associations concerned with public policy (indispensable for the development of that uniquely modern phenomenon, public opinion) and of professional associations to promote rationality of skill and high standards of education and performance. The outcome of these associational efforts has been what we call the pluralistic society wherein freedom of choice is supposed to be given institutional configuration through freedom of association. At the same time modern man within and between these associations has attempted to promote freedom of individual thought and action. In large part this kind of society has been the product of rationalism and reformism, though of course with all sorts of residues from previous periods.

This whole movement in its Gestalt of concerns—freedom of conscience, individual responsibility, critique of traditional institutions and authorities, differentiation and independence of associations, cooperation between religion and science as well as mutual criticism, extension of the franchise, openness to social change—is something unique as well as fairly recent in history. This uniqueness becomes fully evident if one recalls that, in the main, historic religion, both West and East, has not favored pluralism, nor even the patterns of this-worldly change. Instead, it has promoted the authority of an elite that maintained a "divinely established," rigid pattern of society, and which inculcated the "virtue" of obedient humility. Only in the modern period has a dynamic conception of history become widely prevalent.

It is not accurate, therefore, to say that modernity in the West is the product of technology. Modernization has emerged from an internalized vision of history and responsibility which ventured to change history in order to bring man to his "maturity." Think, for example, of Immanuel Kant's conception of Enlightenment as the cutting of the apron strings of "minority." In the light of the worldview and the scope of this modernity one can scarcely accept Cyril Black's definition: "Modernization may be defined as the totality of the influence of the unprecedented increase in man's knowledge and control over his environment that has taken place in recent centuries." [2] This definition falls short of expressing the *ethos* of modernity, its vision of history, its boldness of innovation, its spirit of inquiry, its voluntarism of effort. At the same time, the definition does point to an important aspect of modernity, the technical rationalism and the relentless drive toward efficiency. This, too, was a goal of liberalism's "reformism," a reformism that eventually would itself require reform.

At this point we should observe a major psychological aspect of this whole development. One must be cautious about generalizations of this sort, particularly when they are applied to a whole period of historical development. Yet, it does seem plausible to say that, compared to the traditional medieval society, the modern rational, reforming, differentiating (pluralist) society draws much more upon the cognitive and voluntarist elements in the psyche than upon affective elements.[3] Likewise, the struggle of religious

[2] Quoted by Bellah, *Religion and Progress*, p. 170.
[3] One of the most suggestive treatments of these three aspects of the human psyche which I have encountered is by the Danish philosopher Harald Höffding, *Outlines of Psychology*, trans. Mary E. Lowndes (London: The Macmillan Co. 1892). It is a striking fact that this tripartite division into cognition, feeling, and will replaced in the eighteenth and nineteenth centuries the bipartite division into cognition and will which had been followed from the time of Aristotle. Rousseau

liberalism against traditionalist authoritarianism placed heavy demands upon the cognitive "faculties." In the modern period one does find, to be sure, certain conspicuous expressions of the affective side of personality. For example, the idea of romantic love did much to break through the old patterns that prevented courtship and marriage outside the boundaries of ascribed status. Moreover, in Protestant circles the conception of love set forth in the Gospels has been much stressed; but in the urbanized, competitive society this ethic of love has served in large measure as a compensatory ethic. To be sure, philanthropy, even highly organized philanthropy, has also been characteristic of modernity; but it gave expression more to cognition and will than to the affective (and affectional) faculties. It maintained its social distance. I shall not attempt in the present essay to pursue this motif about cognitive and affective faculties. Yet some aspects of modernity will become readily evident if we look at the evolution of liberalism, and especially if we look at its rationalism and reformism.

In the earlier modern period, rationalism and reformism gave rise to the economy of free enterprise. The means of production were geared to produce the maximum amount of goods at the maximum rate of speed and at the minimum cost. These goods were delivered to a free and anonymous authority, the market, a mechanism that was to promote competition and efficiency, and which in turn was supposed to issue in an automatic, ecological balance or harmony. Likewise, the innovation and testing of ideas were to be

---

and Kant exercised decisive influence here. My attribution of cognitive and voluntarist qualities to liberalism does not come from Höffding. William Dilthey, it will be recalled, formulated his typology of world views in terms of the tripartite psychology, discerning respectively three major world views, those oriented to reason, to will, and to feeling.

promoted by "free trade in ideas." Efficiency became a moral demand, a demand that was not previously made by Christianity. By the nineteenth century the ideal of efficiency had become practically a religious demand.

In order to initiate these changes a vigorous social reform had to be carried through, particularly for the sake of freeing business and the church from the restrictions of special privilege or of political control. This reform has been characterized by Henry Maine as the movement from status to contract. Under the aegis of these demands all sorts of new organizations came to birth. Insofar as these organizations were "instrumental" associations they continued vigorously to promote rationality and efficiency. Indeed, these values seem to have taken precedence over concern for the individual person as such. Impersonality was required if the free trade in goods and ideas was to be effective.

Here we see a striking paradox: the requirements of impersonality in the social system and the need for aggressive personality in the personality system if the social system was to be effective in reaching its goals. The Friends in their history combined these elements, on the one hand (for example), demanding that price tags take the place of dickering, and on the other hand setting a high value on the I-Thou relation, yet moving steadily from the meetinghouse to the countinghouse. But the emphasis on personhood and individualism was largely a class phenomenon; it brought the middle class onto the stage of history, but at the same time it moved the lower classes into a more depressed style of living than was characteristic of the earlier period. Social distance was by no means diminished, either between the old aristocracy and the new bourgeoisie or between the middle and the lower classes, or even within the middle class. Moreover, freedom rather than justice was the dominant ideal. Justice was to be taken care of by means of the automatic harmony.

Rationality and reformism in time, however, found themselves confronted by new demands. Laissez-faire came into crisis. The old liberalism was not able, after all, to enter into the promised land of automatic harmony. Instead, structural maladjustment became the disorder of the day, imbalance between production and consumption, cyclical unemployment. Millions of people became victims of the automatic disharmony. Presently, a new liberalism appeared on the horizon, demanding that private rights be qualified by communal responsibilities and that the community as a whole assume responsibility to achieve greater economic stability. Consequently, a more positive conception of the state came to birth. The new situation demanded a revision of the old ideas of rationality and reform, precisely in order to protect or elevate some of the people who had been forgotten. In short, rationality and efficiency were required to bring the welfare state into being (and religious liberalism played a positive as well as a negative role here). At the same time they did not alter the ethos of social distance.

The sense of success, however, was short-lived. Within the period of a generation this new ordering of institutions in its turn brought new frustrations. The people who were to be recovered for the enjoyment of the benefits of the welfare state now protested against the status of dependency induced by the system. The demand of historic liberalism expresses itself here, the demand for autonomy. The recipients of the welfare would prefer to be given employment rather than largesse, and also to have some share in the enjoyment of self-determination.[4]

[4] James Luther Adams, "Exiles Trapped in the Welfare State," *The Unitarian Christian* 22 (Winter, 1967), 3-9.

In this situation the Black Power Movement has intensified the demands and the tensions; and its leaders have accused the liberals of being both ineffectual and hypocritical. During the past forty or fifty years, we should add, the tensions have been augmented by the world-embracing ideological and international conflicts between capitalism, socialism, fascism, and communism. Meanwhile, the churches have been compelled to reassess their own self-image and their mission. Taken together, these tensions and demands have induced in wide circles a whole series of identity crises. Indeed, they have given rise to the very concept of identity crisis.

It is no accident that during the past two generations psychotherapy and pastoral counseling have taken on a new significance. Indeed, it was during this period that they acquired the status of special disciplines, partly as a consequence of the tremendous stimulus provided by advances in the study of psychology and especially of depth psychology. As Seward Hiltner shows in his chapter in the present volume, the religious liberals have provided much of the significant leadership in the development of the new discipline of pastoral psychology. From Wennerstrom's point of view, however, the *hubris* of the old religious liberalism has by no means played itself out. Moreover, the social-distance characteristic of the liberal-religious mentality continues to function as an impediment to the effective practice of pastoral counseling among religious liberals.

We have now traced in barest outline the morphology of liberalism adumbrated by Wennerstrom when he speaks of rationalism, reformism, dramatics, and social distance. From this survey it should become clear that Wennerstrom's description and critique of religious liberalism, if it is understood in historical context, is actually a description and criticism of much that goes under the name modernity. But even as an outline the account is a truncated one. There is more to the story.

Tension as Modernity Emerged

Did not eighteenth-century liberalism attempt to correct the distortions of the human psyche brought about by rationalism? Did not the Enlightenment itself turn against rationalism by stressing the role of benevolence, sympathy, feeling, and the like? And did not Romanticism also turn against the rationalism of the Enlightenment by extolling spontaneity of feeling, and also by stressing the preciousness and integrity of the individual, and even by appealing to a mystical sense of transcendence, the sense of the brooding presence of the Whole, or of the Infinite, in every part? Did not these movements attempt to correct the overemphasis upon the cognitive and voluntarist elements in human nature by appealing to something deeper and more fraternal or affectional in man? And did not the evangelical Awakenings profoundly alter the Anglo-American religious mentality?

It is true that from Romanticism an organic, neo-medieval social theory did emerge which promoted a Catholic revival, but there is little evidence to show that either the eighteenth-century benevolence theory or Romanticism gave new impetus or content to pastoral care. Nor did the evangelistic revivals significantly correct the element of social distance in interpersonal relations. The Great Awakening of the eighteenth century called the individual out of his loneliness and into the enjoyment of a seemingly total commitment of heart and soul. Also the Methodist class-meeting developed a certain intimacy of personal relations, but it developed rigid moralistic tests of the authenticity of conversion.

Adam Smith pointed out that revivalism brought the lonely and forgotten man out of isolation and gave him a new dignity by convincing him that he had an eternal soul worth saving, but that he soon found himself caught in a vise of moralistic conformity. At the outset, then, this revivalism made appeal against rationalism in favor of affective elements, but in the end impersonal and cognitive and voluntarist elements prevailed. The individuality of the person was submerged by means of a concocted identity forced on the convert by social coercion.

The Second Awakening of the early decades of the nineteenth century was likewise a turn away from rationalism (the emphasis on clarity of cognition), but increasingly it took on a communal and even nationalistic character. It aimed to regenerate "communities en bloc," and in the end it sought to justify itself in face of criticism at the hands of the religious liberals by claiming to contribute to national health and religious self-identity, in short, to patriotism. In connection with this thrust the revivals brought into play a kind of technological rationalism. In 1835 Charles Finney argued that the forces that were "unfriendly to religion" appealed to "the great political and other worldly excitements," and that the cause of religion was to be promoted only through "the counterexcitements," "the religious excitements," of revivalism. Finney in this vein spelled out the techniques for saving souls.[5]

In some measure the revivalism of the nineteenth and

---

[5] For this analysis and evaluation of the revivalism of the early nineteenth century and its contribution to a sense of national destiny see Perry Miller, *The Life of the Mind in America* (New York: Harcourt, Brace & World, 1965), especially chapter 1.

the early twentieth centuries in America can be viewed also as an evasive and atavistic reaction to threatening social change or maladjustment. Instead of attacking the new social problems of the receding frontier through rational analysis and reformism, it offered (somewhat in the manner of Billy Graham today) the deceptive remedy of individual "regeneration" and of return to "the good old ways" of conventional moralism in the private sphere. On the whole, though not entirely, revivalism has been the haven of political conservatism, and it has been hostile to reformism. Even if one holds that revivalism was the soil out of which social reform was to grow, nevertheless one cannot argue that it overcame the social distance of which Wennerstrom speaks. It did not promote concern for the pastoral care of individual souls; through the stereotyping of the conversion experience it tended to treat them all alike, as brands to be snatched from the burning.

In the nineteenth century a more personal approach is to be observed among the religious liberals who criticized and opposed the revivals. Characteristic for this tradition are the views of Henry Ware, Jr., professor of pulpit eloquence and pastoral care at Harvard Divinity School in the 1830's and 1840's, and formerly minister of the Second Church in Boston. It is significant that Ware was conscious of the tension between the prophetic role and the pastoral role of the minister. Indeed, he warned against reformism as prone to underestimate the importance and uniqueness of the pastoral role, and especially to militate against the personal quality required for that role. "We are too ready," he says, "to regard Christianity as designed to operate on society, and accomplish a great work for the progress and information of the world." Even if we look at a single parish, he continues, "we are too apt to see it in this general view, and address it as a community, rather than as a collection of individuals." [6]

It would be difficult to find in the nineteenth century in America a more painstaking elaboration of the nature of the pastoral office than that of Ware. The flavor of his conception can be indicated by two or three quotations. Speaking of the concern of the true pastor for the individual member of the flock, he asserts:

The man who is familiar with the situation, trials and wants of those whom he addresses; who goes up to the pulpit from their firesides and chambers—full of interest in their characters, and sympathy with their condition—feels that he is not meeting a congregation in the abstract but men and women whom he knows and cares for, and who are waiting to catch from him something which will suit their necessities, and be for them guidance and improvement.[7]

The preacher's lack of close personal association with members of his flock, according to Ware, is the principal source of the spurious, inflated rhetoric of the pulpit:

I know no cure for false rhetoric like this. And whenever I witness the grandiloquence of the sophomore in the pulpit,— when I hear there the flashy commonplaces of flowers, and rivers, and clouds, and rainbows, and dews—when I listen to the empty music of periods which are rounded only to be harmonious, and the tricks of speech which perform no office for the sense; then I say that all this miserable foppery—as false to good taste as it is to the souls of men and the truth

---

[6] Henry Ware, Jr., *The Connexion Between the Duties of the Pulpit and the Pastoral Office: An Introductory Address Delivered to the Members of the Theological School in Cambridge, October 18 and 25, 1830* (Cambridge: Williams and Brown, 1830), p. 7.

[7] *Ibid.*, p. 9.

of God—could never have been committed by a man who walked faithfully among his people, caring for their actual wants, and anxious to feed them with knowledge and understanding.[8]

Ware is so convinced of the indispensability of the personal relation between the pastor and the parishioner that he frowns upon the clerical practice of exchanging pulpits: "However sleepers may be sometimes most effectually awakened by the warning cry of a stranger, the whole flock is best watched and fed by regular and stated shepherds." [9]

It will be noted in these passages, however, that Ware stresses "knowledge and understanding" (cognitive awareness) as the contribution of the pastor. It is possible that Ware in his practice as a pastoral counselor amply exhibited the affective as well as the cognitive quality, in short, that his practice was better than his theory. In the main, however, his theory apparently conformed to the tradition within Protestantism which was moralistic and was lacking in the empathy and sympathy that Wennerstrom desiderates.

Modern Development of the Professions

Now, from what source did Carl Wennerstrom get this criterion of the authentic stance of the pastoral counselor? Clearly, it did not originate in merely individual hunch or insight. Actually, the criterion was the outcome of a kind of rationalism, a cognition, which has been promoted in recent years by professional students on the basis of empirical observation of pastoral counseling. Seward Hiltner in one of his essays has given an account of these developments (up to 1951) in the dialogue between pastoral

[8] *Ibid.*, p. 13.
[9] *Ibid.*, p. 19.

theology and secular psychology.[10] So far from promoting social distance in pastoral care and in psychotherapy this analytical or rational empiricism has actually made us aware of the nature of social distance and of the impediment it can create for the pastoral counselor.[11]

Here we should observe a highly significant aspect of the relation between pastoral psychology and psychotherapy, namely, the development of a professional outlook or mentality. This observation has so many ramifications for the theme of the present chapter that I must dwell at some length on the nature and implications of this professional outlook.

It must be granted that professionalism can become the occasion for the frustration of the work of the pastoral counselor, for example, by inducing him to consider the parishioner who is in distress as a "case." In all of the professions the disease of professionalism appears especially in the rigidities that belong to orthodoxy or to bureaucratization. But the professional attitude of course should not be

[10] Seward Hiltner, "Pastoral Theology and Psychology," in Arnold S. Nash, ed., *Protestant Thought in the Twentieth Century* (New York: The Macmillan Co., 1951), pp. 181-98.

[11] One of the earliest definitions of "social distance" appears in the article by the Chicago sociologist Robert E. Park, entitled "The Concept of Social Distance," *Journal of Applied Sociology* VIII (July-August, 1924), 339-344. Here he contrasts the "impulse that leads us to enter imaginatively into the other persons' minds, to share their experience and sympathize with their pains and pleasures, joys and sorrows, hopes and fears," with the sense of social distance which bespeaks self-consciousness and reserve and which appears in such group phenomena as race consciousness or class consciousness. Emory S. Bogardus during the same decade (and later) wrote extensively on the concept, and contrived devices for the measurement of social distance. Sociometry later on developed similarly precise means for measuring social distance. The concept of social distance appears frequently in the literature of race relations and of pastoral psychology.

equated with professionalism in these senses. Indeed, the authentic professional attitude recognizes these and other dangers of professionalism.

The concept of the professions is by no means a strictly modern one, though it has been developed in elaborate ways in the modern period. It can be traced back to antiquity, particularly in the practice of law and medicine. Moreover, already by the second century the Christian churches began (under pagan influence) to consider the work of the priest as in part a professional task: the idea became current that it is not enough for the man of God to know the tradition—the sacred literature, the liturgy, the administration of the sacraments. It was held that he should study rhetoric in order to become familiar with the literature of the humanities and also in order to become a proficient teacher and preacher. (Augustine tells us that he was first attracted to Christianity by the "rhetorical" skill of Bishop Ambrose, rhetorical in the broad cultural sense just indicated.) Eventually, the preparation of the minister came to require systematic theological education with its various disciplines. Even the care of souls acquired a certain professional quality, for example, in the systematic study of cases of conscience. Here one should mention also the venerable tradition of "spiritual direction." The spiritual director became a highly specialized figure. Indeed, in the Roman Catholic Church a variety of "schools" of spiritual direction developed. Previous to this, however, the medieval universities exercised a decisive influence in the shaping of the disciplines of the professions. As Whitehead (*Adventures of Ideas*) and other historians have observed, the development of the definition and the ideals of the professions represents one of the major elements in the history of modernity in the West.

During the past generation or two both psychotherapy

and pastoral counseling in differing degrees have taken on a professional character. What is meant by the term *profession* in this context? A professional man is one who possesses a higher education in the humanities and the sciences: he has been exposed to the disciplines that familiarize him with the characteristic values of the cultural tradition; he has the task of criticizing, transmitting, and applying these value preferences; he understands and improves his special skills in terms of a rational theory; he acquires his skills and his theory in relation to the disciplines of the university; and, generally, he belongs to a professional association that articulates a consensus with respect to professional ethics and with respect to the standards of the performance of his skills.[12]

This list of criteria is not exhaustive; nor is it once-for-all "established." Indeed, in a rapidly changing society with rapidly expanding knowledge considerable disagreement develops in face of the claims of newly emerging professions. We should add here that the clergyman is not to be brought completely under the rubric of the professions. He stands also in the tradition of a religious community, a community of faith. Moreover, some of his skills, for example, the skill of pastoral counseling, may be viewed as quasi-professional.

In the area of pastoral care the past generation has witnessed the appearance of professional associations and of learned journals concerned not only with pastoral counseling but also with psychotherapy. Seward Hiltner in his chapter in the present volume has outlined the development of pastoral counseling as a discipline, contributed to in primary ways, though not exclusively, by religious liberals.

[12] James Luther Adams, "The Social Import of the Professions," *American Association of Theological Schools Bulletin* 23 (June, 1958), 152-68.

This whole development is an aspect of the rationality that attaches to modernity. Moreover, the advance of the discipline of training in pastoral counseling has required a vigorous reformism in the ministry, in theological education, and in the relation between theology and the behavioral sciences, areas in which much unfinished business remains to be undertaken. One consequence of these developments has been the appearance of a new awareness of ethical dimensions of pastoral counseling which were previously of simpler perception, particularly with regard to guilt, anxiety, autonomy, conscience, and identity. A whole range of new conceptualization has been the result. The appearance of this new discipline has had considerable effect in turn upon the study of the older disciplines of theology and ethics; and it has uncovered psychological and sociological dimensions of religion which were previously much less appreciated.

The "professional" element in this development is to be seen also in the awareness of the limitations of the pastoral counselor. Even the least instructed minister today recognizes that ours is a world of professionals. Indeed, even the man who considers himself omnicompetent by reason of his ordination as "a man of God" is aware of his responsibility to recognize his limitations by knowing when he should refer the troubled person to a specialist. On the other hand, the better instructed pastor will be aware also of the existence of various "schools" or types of psychotherapy.

The perceptive minister in face of the variety of these types will also be aware of the conflicting "images of man" presented by these types, images that bespeak rival philosophical or theological conceptions of man. Almost at random I select an example here, the shift in Freud's thinking from his earlier to his later period, a shift, according to

Erik Erikson, from an epicurean to a stoic conception.[13] We should mention here also the profound change in the conception of human nature which has resulted from the adoption of the theory of the unconscious.

Pastoral Care and Personal Ethics

These changes and variations have shed new light on the problems of personal ethics. New implications of historic theological-ethical doctrines have thus been disclosed. For example, the pastoral counselor who is a religious liberal seeks new formulation of the old doctrine of autonomy. He sees it to be his ethical responsibility not to try to *impose* an ethical standard but rather to enable the parishioner to achieve freedom of choice; at the same time he acknowledges that he must try to assist him to overcome obsession with self. Wennerstrom, to his credit, recognized that in this whole area of personal ethics special problems appear because of the inadequacy of the ingredients of religious liberalism. For example, the parishioner will very likely need to overcome the rationalism that looks for a clear and definitive solution to his problem; he may need to be content with something less than a dramatic solution. Indeed, something other than a merely ethical issue may be at stake; the question of facing tragedy and of going "beyond tragedy." (Here the pastoral counselor is confronted by theological problems that the secular psychotherapist may evade.) The same thing must be said regarding problems of conscience, of guilt, and anxiety. The advantage enjoyed by both the counselor and the parishioner is not only their common membership in a religious community but also the sense of

[13] Erik H. Erikson, *Young Man Luther* (New York: W. W. Norton and Co., 1958), p. 253.

the availability of more than human resources. In our day, however, when old symbols have lost much of their meaning, the task of the counselor is profoundly difficult. Again, a professional skill is almost required not only to venture new formulations but also to do so in face of a particular individual who possesses his own special semantic habits and frustrations.

One other professional aspect of the work of the counselor should be mentioned here. We can say that Carl Wennerstrom's critical characterization of the ingredients of religious liberalism in relation to pastoral care is itself a manifestation of professional analysis. He made the analysis in his pursuit of the professional, doctoral degree, and toward the end of improving the theory and practice of pastoral counseling. The conceptual apparatus that he employs he adapted from social psychology and psychotherapy. Moreover, his view that the pastoral counselor, instead of resorting to rationalism, should overcome social distance and "feel with" the person in distress, is a view that is characteristic of the emphasis of certain schools of psychotherapy. In this connection he would have recognized that the parishioner who seeks pastoral counsel wants more than sympathy and empathy. Not everyone can give him the empathy he cherishes. The pastoral counselor who offers sympathy or empathy, the parishioner knows, is something more than a mere sympathizer or empathizer. He is expected to offer counsel on the basis of experience and reflection in these matters, and toward the end of therapy or healing. Here again rationality plays a significant role. Indeed, a modicum of social distance or detachment will be required if the therapy is to achieve its purpose. Talcott Parsons speaks of this sort of detachment as "affective neutrality."

I have spoken only briefly and in general terms of the concern of the pastoral counselor for personal ethics. This concern generally, and for obvious reasons, takes priority. A major problem appears in the struggle against regressive, constrictive forms of moral control. The concern for personal ethics cannot be separated from reflection upon the basic issues of life and tragedy and death—the meaning of life itself, the meaning also of forgiveness and reconciliation and fellowship. Here the counselor and the parishioner are led to the boundary situation where one becomes newly aware of the ultimate resources upon which man depends and in which he places his trust. Carl Wennerstrom in this connection speaks of the presence of the Holy Spirit, thus pointing to a reality that transcends both the counselor and the parishioner.

It must be recognized that typical pastoral counseling (and also the training for pastoral counseling) gives major attention to personal ethics. But the matter cannot be left here. The work of the counselor is not the only task of the minister. He is a teacher, a preacher, an executive director, a man in the community. None of these roles can be divorced from his task as pastoral counselor. In all of these roles the openness, the sympathy, the tragic sense of life must inform his activity. At the same time the social-ethical demands upon the church as a corporate body and upon the individual member make their claims; and these claims impinge upon the work of the counselor.

Objective and Subjective Value

How, then, are we to conceive of the relation between pastoral counseling and these social-ethical demands? This question brings us to recognize a curious anomaly. For the sake of healing, the counselor is constrained to give at least initial priority to the personal problems of the troubled person. Yet, these personal problems cannot be resolved apart from the context of the corporate responsibilities of the church and the individual with respect to social and institutional problems. Every personal problem is a social problem, and every social problem is a personal problem. Wennerstrom's presentation of social action (reformism) in contrast to pastoral care could make it appear that social-ethical problems and demands—and particularly institutional aspects of social change—must be put on the side for the sake of the intimate personal relation that is requisite for authentic counseling. But I doubt that in the last analysis Wennerstrom would accept this interpretation.

In this connection it is pertinent to recall a distinction that has been given currency by Ernst Troeltsch, the distinction between subjective and objective values.[14] This distinction has to do with the difference between the values that attach to private life and those that belong to the public order. The subjective values spring entirely from the individual's relation as an individual to God, his direct relation to other persons, and his internal dialogue in the striving for integrity. Here truthfulness, honesty in self-awareness, thoughtfulness, openness, benevolence, and loyalty are the characteristic values. The objective values, on the other hand, are the ethical claims that inform or guide men in the realm of "history"—the sphere of group life which demands institutional expression. Objective values require in-

[14] Ernst Troeltsch, "Fundamental Problems of Ethics," the translation of a portion of which appears in Warren F. Groff and Donald E. Miller, The Shaping of Modern Christian Thought, trans. Donald E. Miller (Cleveland: World Publishing Company, 1968), pp. 23-35. See also Friedrich von Hügel, Essays and Addresses, First Series (London: J. M. Dent, 1929), pp. 153-54.

stitutional participation for their manifestation. They attach to the structures of society, the family (especially in its relation to other spheres), the state, the community, property and production, education, science, art, and "organized" religion. The moral life, than, comprises both subjective and objective values, in each case individual and social. It is not appropriate to interpret the distinction in such a way as to make it cognate with that between inner and outer or between interiorization and institutionalization. Nor is it appropriate to promote a dualism between subjective and objective values. Each ultimately requires the other.

Now, it is understandable (as we have said) if psychotherapy and pastoral counseling give primary, if not exclusive, attention to subjective values. The difficulties of the troubled individual present themselves for the most part as interpersonal. They do not ordinarily arise out of conflicts or frustrations the individual has encountered as a consequence of his attempting to change institutions. Moreover, the therapeutic process promoted by the counselor cannot take place directly in the context of the larger institutional structures. It appears, at least initially, in the I-Thou encounter between the counselor and the parishioner, or in a small group, or in the family. This factor, the ostensibly interpersonal character of both the problem and the therapy, has the effect of drawing attention to subjective rather than to objective values.

The concentration of attention upon subjective values tends to appear also in the preaching of the minister who deals with personal problems he encounters directly in the parish. The minister who allows the strictly interpersonal problems encountered in his work as counselor to determine his preaching will tend to select sermon topics such as "How to Overcome Your Worries," or "The War Between the Generations," or "Peace of Mind," or "Peace of Soul," or "What We Must Learn from Freud." He will seldom choose controversial topics regarding public policy.

The reference here to Freud possesses a special pertinence. In the main, Freud's experience was that of the clinical worker and not of the citizen concerned with public policy; in this clinical concern he dealt with the disturbed state of the individual and not with any systematic analysis of institutional problems. Moreover, when he concerned himself with the problems of "civilization and its discontents" he did so through a psychological approach which interpreted the major problem of civilization as that of the coercion of the individual and the major problem of the individual as that of the renunciation (or sublimation) of instinct. Equally important is the fact that he attempted to understand the fundamental facts and problems of human nature in terms of inner-family relationships. Thus his basic conceptual apparatus was drawn in part from the observation of the individual (repression, anxiety, projection), and in part from the observation of the family. Insofar as his basic concepts were oriented to the family his vocabulary was domestic; it presupposed a familial model, providing a paradigm of family relationships—between child and mother, child and father, child and siblings. Domestic metaphors rather than political dominate in his writings, and subjective values rather than objective. His major tendency was to subordinate cultural and broadly sociological and political factors to biological and psychological factors, that is, to the private man. His contributions to understanding and to therapy should not be minimized. Yet, his neglect of sociology and the other social sciences continues to be evident in his influence, despite the efforts of Karen Horney, Harry Stack Sullivan, Erich Fromm, and others. Freud supplied a sanction for indifference to politics. Moreover, he viewed the state as mainly an engine for the protection of society against anarchy. In this respect his outlook is much more similar to that of Lutheranism and erotic Jewish mysticism than to that of the Jewish tradition where the positive demand for social righteousness informs the life of a covenanted people.

A similar restriction of interest and perception is to be observed in the psychology of religion as generally conceived. We may take William James as an example here. In *The Varieties of Religious Experience* one finds almost exclusive presentation of the individual in his relation to subjective values. Conversion, the once-born and the twice-born man, the reorientation of values, are not dealt with in the context of institutional behavior, but rather as inner-personal and interpersonal phenomena. James's interpretation of pragmatism led him to look for the influence of religion as almost entirely in the personal sphere. "By their fruits ye shall know them" was in the main interpreted in terms of personal ethics and not in terms of institutional analysis or consequences.

Max Weber states that "James's pragmatic valuation of the significance of religious ideas according to their influence on life is . . . a true child of the world of ideas of the Puritan home of that eminent scholar." [15] This characterization can be quite misleading if it is taken to mean that James's perception of the pragmatic meaning of Christian conversion

[15] Max Weber, *The Protestant Ethic and the Spirit of Capitalism*, trans. Talcott Parsons (Paperback ed.; New York: Charles Scribner's Sons, 1958), pp. 232-33. For a critique of Weber's presentation of Puritanism and his distorted conception of "the Protestant ethic" see James L. Adams, "Theokratie, Kapitalismus und Demokratie," *Zeitschrift für Evangelishe Ethik* 12 (July-September, 1968), pp. 247-67.

was a Puritan perception. Puritanism, and the Calvinism in which it was rooted, strove not only to engender the twice-born man, but also to promote a new order of society. Its characteristic metaphors are not psychological or domestic but political (for example, covenant and kingdom of God). It promoted social as well as individual salvation. In line with its doctrine of sanctification Puritanism threw much of its energy into forming associations that provided not only a social discipline but also a means of reforming society. William James was personally "unmusical" in this area of the practical import of religion (and of Calvinism), as is to be observed not only in *The Varieties* . . . but also in his own life-style. When, for example, Francis Greenwood Peabody urged James to join him and other Harvard colleagues in an attempt to influence the Massachusetts legislature, James in effect replied, "Leave me out of that sort of thing." He was much more interested in the psychology of the individual than in institutional behavior, in subjective than in objective values. In his presentation the prophetic dimension of religion was reduced to the vanishing point. In this respect he was more similar to the pietist than to the Puritan. In short, the diversity of experience presented in his work is so limited that the title *The Varieties of Religious Experience* is scarcely justified.

This limitation of interest and perception on the part of William James has often been observed by the sociologists. It has been sharply criticized also by Roman Catholics. Recently I have encountered a typical Roman Catholic criticism that is worth mentioning here. In going through a volume from William James's private library, now in Widener Library at Harvard, I found a handwritten letter of May 10, 1909, from Baron Friedrich von Hügel to James, commenting on the latter's *Varieties* (which James had sent to him). After expressing grateful indebtedness to James in this letter, von Hügel goes on to speak of his "dissatisfactions." "I continue to feel," he says, that "your taking of the religious experience as separable from its institutional, historical occasions and environment. . .to be schematic, a priori, not what your method, so concrete and a posteriori, seems to demand." Von Hügel concludes by saying that if James in *The Varieties* had presented this broader, institutional dimension of religion, "The result, I think, would have been of greater permanent value and instructiveness."

In response to this criticism James might have repeated what he says in his first lecture on *The Varieties*, that his standpoint was that of psychology, "the only branch of learning in which I am particularly versed." Moreover, he could point to an emphasis in his interpretation of religion which is of primary significance to the pastoral counselor as Wennestrom presents him:

The recesses of feeling, the darker, blinder strata of character, are the only places in the world in which we catch real fact in the making, and directly perceive events happen, and how work is actually done. Compared with this world of individualized feelings, the world of generalized objects which the intellect contemplates is without solidity or life. As in stereoscopic or kinoscopic pictures seen outside the instrument, the third dimension, the movement, the vital element, are not there.[16]

In this vein James speaks eloquently to the pastoral counselor when he says that to attempt to describe the world while leaving out "the various feelings of the individual

[16] William James, *The Varieties of Religious Experience* (New York: Longmans, Green, 1902), pp. 501-2.

pinch of destiny, all the various spiritual attitudes," is to leave the world a hollow and abstract affair. "What keeps religion going," he says, "is something else than abstract definitions and systems of concatenated adjectives, and something different from faculties of theology and their professors." [17]

James's emphasis upon the "feelings of the individual pinch of destiny" brings him into close affinity with the existentialists. Here again the primary concern is with the subjective values. Kierkegaard has exercised a decisive influence on both theological and secular writers among the existentialists, for example, Bultmann and Heidegger. He was so passionately concerned with subjective values and *Innerlichkeit* that his concern for objective values found expression only in his criticism of the bourgeois church and of the mass society. He showed little interest in a positive doctrine of the church or of society. His type of pietism helped to create the vacuum into which Marxism rushed with resentful fervor. Kierkegaard himself preferred old-fashioned monarchy to stave off mobocracy.

In general, however, pietism and Marxism exhibit opposite forms of lopsidedness, the former being concerned with subjective and the latter with objective values. One is reminded of Sainte Beuve's word that nothing is so much like a swelling as a hole. In view of the fact that Freud's restriction of perception is formally analogous to that of existentialism it is understandable that Erich Fromm has attempted to persuade the Freudians to study Marx, and the Marxists to study Freud. Fromm, to be sure, prefers the ideas of the young Marx before Marx became a Marxist.

[17] *Ibid.*, p. 447.

The existentialist ethic represents an individualist bias; the individual is admonished to liberate himself from the routinized, banal, and technologized society toward the end of achieving a new responsibility; but the conception of responsibility does not carry with it a positive institutional articulation.

We have noted the similarity between pietism and existentialism, particularly in the primary concern for subjective values. It should be added, however, that pietism sometimes promotes the concern for objective values in the sense that it favors philanthropic endeavor that aims to ameliorate social evils. This social outreach of pietism, however, does not go so far as to include social-structural analysis or basic institutional transformation. Conversion is for individuals; according to the gospel of Billy Graham, institutions will change if the individuals are "converted." Here one should observe the contrast with prophetism of the sort stemming from the Old Testament which exhibits concern for both objective and subjective values. We think here of Isaiah, Jeremiah, and the Psalms, or of the Puritans and the Friends.

The contrast between the emphasis on subjective and the emphasis on objective values is to be seen in the contrast between Lutheranism and Calvinism. The Lutherans have tended, on the basis of their interpretation of the New Testament, to emphasize *Innerlichkeit* and the world of subjective values as the salient sphere of religion, and to leave the world of objective values (beyond the realm of the family) to the magistrates under God. This division of labor into the Two Kingdoms assigns to the individual the vocation of doing his own thing in private life and the obligation of obedience to the magistrates in the public sphere. Hence, the vocation of citizenship was alien to Luther.[18] (In contemporary Lutheranism this conception of the two kingdoms has been considerably revised.)

The Calvinist, on the other hand, emphasized a general as well as a specialized conception of vocation, the general responsibility to work for the establishment of a community of justice as well as the more specialized responsibility to perform one's own daily work. Out of the performance of the generalized vocation the Puritans and their descendants formed the many associations to which reference has been made earlier. Max Weber's conception of "the Protestant ethic" completely ignores this generalized conception of vocation (which stems from theocratic Calvinism and which, we should add, often issues in a conspiratorial conception of history as a struggle between the righteous and the damned, the saints and the sinners). He excludes from the record the reformist associations that struggled to correct what he calls the Protestant ethic. Weber does, to be sure, note the legalist mentality of Calvinism which stands in contrast with the Lutheran mentality. Some of these con-

[18] The lopsidedness in Lutheranism with respect to the emphasis on subjective values and the doctrine of vocation has militated in the public order in Germany against the Lutherans' coming to terms positively and creatively with the reformist element in modernity. Hans Kohn has recently pointed out the detrimental consequences for Germany. "Fascism," he says, "was the 'philosophy' of politically and socially retarded nations faced by the challenge of modernity. . . . There is today no grass-roots democracy, as there was none in Weimar; there is only a party hierarchy and a bureaucracy planning in secrecy behind a parliamentary spirit, or perhaps any spirit. . . . A world of 'highly individual values has emerged, which puts the experienced happiness of the individual in first place and increasingly lets the so-called whole slip from sight.' . . . human values are mostly those of the private individual." Review of *The Future of Germany* by Karl Jaspers and of *Society and Democracy in Germany* by Ralf Dahrendorf, in *Psychiatry and Social Science Review* II (June, 1968), 22-23.

trasts between Calvinism and Lutheranism appear in the differences between the corresponding conceptions of pastoral care. We shall presently return to this theme.

But first we should note a striking similarity that obtains between the various outlooks that stress subjective rather than objective values. We have seen that Freudianism, James's interpretation of religion, existentialism, pietism, and revivalism turn out to belong to the same family. Strange bedfellows! Freud, James, Kierkegaard, Bultmann, and Billy Graham!

Sociology and Pastoral Care

The question now arises: Does pastoral care belong to this family? This is a crucial question for the consideration of the relations between pastoral care and social or institutional ethics. It would seem that it does belong to this family if its concern is mainly with subjective values.

Our question then becomes: Can pastoral care be equated with pastoral psychology? That is, can pastoral psychology get along without pastoral sociology? Can psychotherapy get along without sociotherapy? These are questions that have been coming increasingly to the fore during the past decade, though it must be remembered that already thirty years ago social scientists attempted (with little success) to raise these issues. These questions imply the necessity of examining the training of the psychotherapist and the pastoral counselor. In some theological schools the proportion of the number of staff members and courses in the area of pastoral care is much larger than that in social ethics, sociology, and sociotherapy. Moreover, clinical training is widely interpreted in such a way as largely to exclude clinical training in community organization and in agencies concerned with public policy.

Wennerstrom's unfinished dissertation does not explicitly deal with these questions. He appears mainly to say that certain features of religious liberalism, which we have seen to be the features also of modernity, militate against the conduct of authentic pastoral care. But his solution was not to liquidate modernity. Instead, he wished to protect pastoral care from the ravages of a demonic modernity.

Obviously, the limitations of space here do not permit our dealing with these questions in an adequate way. We must confine our discussion to two major aspects of the subject: first, the role of sociology in the understanding of pastoral care (and mental health), specifically with respect to social ethics; and, second, the place of objective values in the practice of pastoral care.

At this late date it is not necessary to belabor the claim that the pastoral counselor (and the psychotherapist) requires the assistance of the social sciences if he is to achieve self-understanding with regard to his role. Leaving aside for the moment the consideration of the peculiarly religious aspects of pastoral counseling, we may say that the task of the pastoral counselor, like that of the psychotherapist, is conditioned in decisive ways not only by the social system within which he finds himself, but also by the strains within that system at a given period.

In simplest terms this means that the troubled person must be understood in relation to social class, occupation, local community integration or disintegration, the oversocialization of the middle class and the undersocialization of the lower-income groups, the training available within the society for achieving a sense of identity, differentiations in modal personalities, economic power and powerlessness,

majority-group or minority-group status, the viability or decay of a symbol system, and the existence of a variety of
norms.

An enormous literature is accumulating regarding these
phenomena and relationships. Obviously, the pastoral counselor who is even quasi-professional cannot be innocent of
these relationships or of this literature. Seward Hiltner's
Alden-Tuthill Lectures of 1966 may be taken as typical
of the (all-too-few) studies relating pastoral counseling to
the sociological factors mentioned here. In those lectures
Hiltner gives an instructive description of the social matrix
of the American suburb which largely determines the type
of mental illness and suffering in this milieu: the limited
perspectives and perceptions of the population, the "anonymous conformism," the (unwarranted) predisposition to regard practically all difficulties except physical illness as
family problems; and the anachronism of suburbia in the
developing city. He shows especially "what these peculiar
pressures do to and about suffering." [19]

None of the studies of this sort presupposes that the
pastoral counselor may substitute sociological analysis for
awareness of the unique person before him or for personal
confrontation and sympathy. But they do presuppose that
it is insufficient for the pastoral counselor merely to exhibit
sympathy with the troubled person. He is expected to recognize and deal with the parishioner in his total milieu. With
the increase today of juvenile delinquency in suburbia, for
example, the pastoral counselor becomes aware of deviant
behavior as "a property of groups."

The pastoral counselor or the psychotherapist can readily
be discouraged in face of the heavy demands upon his

[19] Seward Hiltner, "Troubled People in a Troubled World,"
Princeton Seminary Bulletin LIX (June, 1966), 54-78.

energy if the resources of the social sciences are to be exploited in any systematic fashion. It may be that more attention should be directed towards living, interdisciplinary dialogue. In this connection I mention here the Boston Marriage Study Association, a small organization of which I was a member some years ago. This group was initially formed by Prof. Carleton Beals of the Harvard Law School, and was made up of representatives of the professions concerned with the family—psychiatrists, lawyers, judges, social workers, professors, and clergymen. At the regular meetings of this group we discussed the basic literature which we had agreed to survey. The group also arrived at a consensus regarding matters which a clergyman should discuss in premarital counseling. We even drew up printed forms for the purpose of reporting "findings" gathered by the clerical members from specific counseling sessions.

Through these meetings it was possible for us all to achieve an understanding of each other's roles and perspectives, and also in emergency to call upon each other for assistance. Only through some such interplay of perspectives can the rationalism that Wennerstrom criticizes be corrected, or rationality and adequate sensitivity in the practice of pastoral care be approximated. By this means also one can make available the constant reminder that every personal problem is a social problem, and that every social problem is a personal problem.

Social Ethical Norms and Pastoral Care

We turn now, finally, to a still broader context of pastoral care in its relation to social ethics, consideration of the ethical norms that give structure to subjective and objective values.

Earlier in this chapter the nature of the professions has been adumbrated. The first criterion of a profession, we noted, is the obligation to transmit, criticize, transform, and apply the values that inhere in a cultural tradition. Historically, this element of the professional role has been symbolized by the academic gown, the sign that the professional man has been exposed to the disciplines of the humanities, the *litterae humaniores*, the study that aims to make one more human. Many of the professions today have reduced this obligation almost to the vanishing point. This reduction is the hazard of specialization. Neither the pastoral counselor nor the secular psychotherapist can properly escape this cultural obligation. Here "culture is another name for a design of motives directing the self outward toward those communal purposes in which alone the self can be realized and satisfied." [20] This design of motives necessarily comprises both the subjective and the objective values.

A marked tendency in pastoral care as well as in psychotherapy, alas, has been to concentrate attention upon the subjective values. This tendency is readily evident in definitions of mental health. Almost at random I select this definition from a professional manual: "A healthy person's response to life is without strain; his ambitions are within the scope of practical realization; he has a shrewd appreciation of his own strengths and weaknesses; he can be helpful, but can also accept aid. He is resilient in failure and level-headed in success. . . . His pattern of behavior has consistency so that he is 'true to himself.' " And so on. Generally speaking, I would say that this definition clearly belongs under the rubric of only subjective values—of (secular)

[20] Philip Rieff, *The Triumph of the Therapeutic: Uses of Faith After Freud* (New York: Harper & Row, 1966), p. 4.

pietism. The orientation is completely noninstitutional. The conception of therapy here presupposed is apparently the notion that the therapist will assist the client to gain "the confidence needed to go forward to meet whatever the future has in store for him." [21] But for the client (and for the therapist) the future is bound to have more in store than merely personal problems.

The psychotherapist who fulfills his cultural obligation cannot confine himself to the task of promoting mental health as defined above. As a professional man he is the representative of the culture and of the critical stance in face of the culture. The culture includes the institutions and a criticism of them. Mental health includes the capacity to challenge the prevailing standards and to participate in their transformation. If this is not presupposed, then the above-quoted definition of mental health can become merely the recipe for "adjustment." For lack of space and at the risk of sounding quite dogmatic I venture to say that if a reasonable degree of maturity is the goal of therapy, the psychotherapist should look toward bringing the client into creative and critical participation in those social processes and in those institutions that constitute the public domain. He should aim to prepare the client to help change the society from which he comes and to which he returns. Any lesser aim can lead to social irresponsibility.

If we think of politics in this connection, can we not say that the old-fashioned system that places the client on the

[21] Barbara Wootton, *Social Science and Social Pathology* (London: George Allen and Unwin, 1959), p. 331. Lady Wootton's whole book is devoted to a discussion of the inadequacy of concern merely for the subjective values. She points out the undesirable consequences that follow from "reluctance to examine the imperfections of our institutions as thoroughly as we examine the faults, failings or misfortunes of individuals" (p. 330).

couch is in the end unsatisfactory? Ultimately, the client expects to see in the therapist an example of maturity in the democratic society. If the therapist is himself a political eunuch, if he is "not involved" in the processes that somehow affect public policy, he is himself an alienated person, immature, or mentally deficient (if not ill). And if the client is simply put back on the road to which he is accustomed, he may simply be restored to peace of mind in an organized form of alienation. From his therapy he may have secured only the analogue of what he would get if a revivalist were his therapist. Actually, he may not have gained the confidence needed to go forward to meet whatever the future has in store for him. The future might require, for example, that he come to terms with black power or with class-bound demands for law and order or with war.

The condition of the inadequate psychotherapist today is similar to that of the practitioner of medicine who is cut off from the rest of society. In face of this condition Oliver Cope, professor of surgery at Harvard Medical School, has recently argued for the inclusion of psychiatry and the behavioral sciences, anthropology and sociology, as important parts of medical education. He holds that the doctor today who is ignorant in these areas is not only intellectually (and probably emotionally as well) cut off from the world around him, but also ignorant in the practice of his own healing profession.[22] What is demanded here of the physi-

---

[22] Eliot Fremont-Smith. Review of Oliver Cope, *Man, Mind and Medicine* (Philadelphia: J. B. Lippincott, 1968), in *The New York Times*, August 9, 1968, p. 37. A similar view with respect to psychotherapy is set forth in Matthew P. Dumont, *The Absurd Healer: Perspectives of a Community Psychiatrist* (New York: Science House, 1968). See also the new magazine *Psychiatry and Social Science Review*.

cian is even more pertinent for the psychotherapist because of the scope of his therapy. The alienation of the psychotherapist from society not only distorts the intentioned therapy which he offers. It also induces alienation by reason of the unintentional, poor example he as a human being and a citizen provides for his client. A sophisticated existentialism should find in this truncated psychotherapy new material for "the literature of the absurd." Freud, with a different purpose in mind, has bequeathed the appropriate title: *The Future of an Illusion.*

One must acknowledge, however, that the traditional demand upon the professions to combine the general cultural function with the specialized theory and skill is a heavy one. The relative disappearance of the first of these functions in part reflects the conviction that it is too heavy. Few people would claim to know the solution to the problem. A hopeful sign, however, is to be seen in the reforms now taking place or being demanded in professional education; in medicine, business administration, pedagogy, and law. These reforms bespeak recognition of what Felix Frankfurter of the Supreme Court was wont to say, that the great professional men of the past century, for example, in law and medicine, were men who broke the mold. Wennerstrom's plea was itself a plea to the liberal clergy to break its regnant mold.

The reduction of the vocations of medicine and of psychotherapy gives us the paradigm of a widespread alienation promoted by the elimination of the first criterion of a profession, responsibility with respect to the basic cultural values. The reduction is in part the consequence of rationalism in the sense employed by Wennerstrom: addiction to thought-structures that are separated from reality. The drive towards rationality has produced a whole congeries of specializations that advance man's knowledge and yet in the process reduce the specialist to a torso. Max Weber has suggested that at the beginning of the modern era the adoption of a vocation was intended to be like the donning of a cloak. "But fate has decreed that the cloak should become an iron cage." [23] It would be appropriate to say also that in the professions the cage has been much reduced in size.

It may be said that the psychotherapist deals with mental illness of such acute quality that he can seldom hope to do more than assist the client to achieve or recover average interpersonal competence. One must acknowledge that this goal is not one that is easily to be reached. But if the matter is to be left there, we must then say that the pastoral counselor in a liberal church confronts a more comprehensive assignment.

The pastoral counselor represents, and is involved in, a community of faith. This community of faith presupposes that salvation is social as well as individual, and social in the sense that it entails response to the Lord of *history* and responsibility with respect to institutional as well as with respect to interpersonal patterns. Liberal Protestantism stands in the prophetic tradition that assumes that men are responsible not only for their individual interpersonal behavior but also for the character (and evils) of the institutions within which (and interstitially between which) interpersonal behavior appears. This is the pragmatic meaning of faith. This pragmatic meaning of faith is a meaning that is integrally related to the nature and mission of the church. Any pastoral counseling that does not function in the direction of this generalized conception of vocation can turn out to be the opiate of the pious.

[23] Max Weber, *The Protestant Ethic*, p. 181.

One must acknowledge that pastoral care, insofar as it has been influenced by pietism or by the narrow type of psychotherapy described above, has yielded to the temptation to reduce the conception of the religious-ethical mission of the church, and likewise has reduced the conception of the vocation of the individual member of the church. Reformism, as Wennerstrom says, may militate against the pastoral counselor's entering into therapeutic communion with the distressed person. But the remedy is not to eliminate reformism. One should not confuse a prerequisite of the therapeutic process with a way of life.

Actually, the type of pastoral care which concerns itself only with interpersonal, subjective values to the neglect of social-ethical, institutional demands is very easy to come by in the American church today, even though the minister has had clinical training in pastoral care. I recall that the late H. Richard Niebuhr, following his systematic study of American theological education, told me that, in the past decade or two, courses on pastoral counseling of the truncated variety had become so much of a fad that the study of Christian social ethics had suffered from marked neglect; and he added that the courses in pastoral counseling rather conspicuously neglected the consideration of the relation between pastoral counseling and social-institutional ethics. The consequence is the alienation of the church from the redemptive powers of God in history.

It must be granted—indeed it must be emphasized—that these redemptive powers work against massive demonic obstacles in a technological society and in a society riven with racial tensions. This means that the identification of the enemy is not achieved by the conventional definition of mental health or of pastoral care. The truncated definition of mental health can be a recipe for alienation in the guise

of therapy. Confining attention to subjective values and to
demonic possession in the individual, it can by default give
aid to demonic possession in the society.

Augustine lived in an age like ours, and in face of pervasive disruption he extended the concept of demonic possession from the realm of the personal to the realm of the
cultural and institutional. Having been for years a professor
of rhetoric and drama, he projected the protagonist and the
antagonist of the play to the world stage, to the struggle
of the Two Cities. At the end of the nineteenth century
the elder Blumhardt in Germany revived an interest in
the concept of the demonic as it appears in the New Testament stories of healing. In face of the impending crisis of
capitalism his son, also a German Lutheran pastor, extended the concept of the demonic, as did Augustine, to
the cultural, economic-political realm. Jesus himself effected
a similar extension, a broadening and deepening of the
idea of the redemptive power of God, by relating his healing
activities to the wider struggle of the inbreaking Kingdom.

I recall from my experience as minister of a local church
an incident that brought home to me the broad span of
the struggle between the powers of the world and the
powers that conquer the world; also of the struggle between
"moral man and immoral society."

A member of my parish, a successful businessman, caught
in the vise of the depression, attempted without success to
commit suicide. In my conversations with him his persistent
question was, "Why shouldn't I have done it? My responsibility to my family was taken care of by the insurance. I
am nothing but a burden to them and to myself."

I could make no headway in responding to his question,
and in search of aid I called on Richard C. Cabot of Harvard. Cabot pointed out that this man had a faulty notion

of responsibility, for he had overlooked the fact that every time a person commits suicide he makes it more difficult for other people in distress to resist the temptation. This argument impressed the parishioner as well as me. But then the discussion came to the social issue, the meaning of the depression and the possible ways out. Pastoral psychology had to be supplemented by pastoral sociology, and also by the theology of culture.

Carl Wennerstrom says of William Ellery Channing that he was a man of "great soaring thoughts," but that he was embarrassed and frustrated in confronting the individual in distress, and that Theodore Parker was "a man of personal warmth, . . . always ready to help persons from any walk of life" and imbued with "concrete concern for them." This difference between Channing and Parker may have been largely a matter of temperament. In any event, Parker in the book cited by Wennerstrom made the first analysis of its kind I know of in American literature, an analysis of the great institutional powers in the nation (the power of business, government, school, and church); and Channing, besides promoting rationality and social reform, was bold and courageous enough to set forth the unorthodox doctrine of Patripassianism, that God the Father suffered in the person of the Son for the redemption of man. It would seem that both of them "linked the concrete enounter with the larger dimensions of ministry."

The concrete encounter with suffering is doubtless the alpha of authentic pastoral care, but under the Lord of history it demands to be linked with the larger dimensions of ministry. The omega is the inbreaking of the Kingdom through the power of the Spirit that both comforts the sufferer and forms the redemptive community. I know of no more succinct statement of the thrust of Christian faith in face of suffering and tragedy than that of Daniel Day Williams:

The Christian ideal of life envisions something higher than freedom from anguish, or invulnerability to its ravages. Its goal cannot be the perfectly adjusted self. In the world as it is, a caring love cannot but regard such a goal as intolerably self-centered. What does it mean to be completely adjusted and at peace in a world as riddled with injustice, with the cries of the hungry, with the great unsolved questions of human living as this? We see why in the end we cannot identify therapy for specific ills with salvation for the human spirit. To live in love means to accept the risks of life and its threats to "peace of mind." Certainly the Christian ministry to persons is concerned to relieve physical ills, anxieties, inner conflicts. But this relief of private burdens is to set the person free to assume more important and universal ones.[24]

Presupposed here is the conviction that the relief of "the more important and universal" burdens is indispensable for the reduction of the "personal burdens." Every personal problem is a social problem, and every social problem is a personal problem. Therefore, sociotherapy and psycho-therapy must advance together. Separated from each other, they yield something less than, indeed something other than, therapy.

Pastoral care, then, within the context of a community of faith, has the task of eliciting a sense of identity and vocation in a social world of tragedy and injustice, and in a world of new possibilities. These possibilities are mys-teriously available to those who, under the Great Task-master's eye, are of contrite and venturesome spirit; but ultimately they are hidden within his hands.

[24] Daniel Day Williams, *The Minister and the Care of Souls* (New York: Harper & Row, 1961), pp. 25-26.

The Vocation of the Lawyer

By James Luther Adams*

Is ours a secularized society? If so, what impact has secularization had upon the legal system? What is, or what should be, the place of religion, or (better) what sort of interaction, between law and religion, has obtained historically, and what sort is desirable, if any? These are questions that were confronted in the symposium. Our general assumption is that ours *is* a secularized society, a term that the panelists have ventured to define in somewhat varying ways. And I shall add to this variety, offering a more complex definition.

The principal concern of the present essay, however, is a narrower question, that regarding the relations between secularization and the profession of the lawyer. How has secularization affected the idea of the calling or vocation of the lawyer? And what is the relation of the profession of the law to the community in which it is exercised, and to community values?

Although I am a theologian and not a lawyer, I have had the temerity to attempt here to deal with these questions, looking at the profession "from the outside" and also from certain religious perspectives.

Toward this end I shall turn attention to the concept of vocation or calling, and to the concept of the professions. In order to bring to a particular focus the relation between the profession of the lawyer and the community values I shall center attention upon the idea of covenant, a concept that has figured largely for centuries not only in the sphere of religion but, also in modern times, in secular societies. First though we must attempt to clarify the meaning, or rather the several meanings, of the term *secularization.*

In much earlier times the lawyer, the doctor, and the priest were members of almost interchangeable vocations. One would have to go far back in history, however, to find this close combination of roles. Indeed, the division of labor with respect to these roles may be viewed as the mark of a stage in the history of civilization. In the past, however, the differentiation did not entail the narrow specialization and the fragmentation current today, for a commonly-held explicit faith, Christian or Jewish, still prevailed.

But these religious faiths (I say "religious" because some faiths deny that they are religious) came to be viewed as unacceptable by reason of

375

their otherworldliness, or because of their transcendental orientation (belief in God), or because of their authoritarian sanctions. In short, one encounters a variety of motives for secularization. It has not always been anti-authoritarian—for example, it is not so in communist Russia. Nor has it always held that the traditional faiths have been really other-worldly—the Marxist views them as "ideologies," as very worldly, as the "religious" protection of ruling-class interests offering "pie in the sky" to the exploited.

Yet, these complexities and variations do not exhaust the ambiguities attaching to the term *secularization*. A quite different usage (mainly so-ciological) of the term refers to a development that has taken place recur-rently within Christianity itself, and later within Judaism, a process favor-ing vigorous concern for this world. This process took place even though the transcendental orientation and the authoritarianism were retained. A harbinger of this change within Christianity is to be seen in the attack on the claim that the vocation of the monk or the nun is the highest among all callings. Initially, this attack was made for the sake of raising the status of the "secular" priest who works more immediately in the world. (Ac-tually, the noun *religious* still refers to the monastic vocation today.) This attack was carried through in the Protestant Reformation, with a some-what parallel attack coming from the Renaissance. A similar "secularization" is to be seen in the left-wing Reformers who urged that every Christian should be a monk *in the world*. Later on, religious leaders spoke of the "priesthood of all believers."

This process of secularization has been described in detail by Max Weber in his study, *The Protestant Ethic and the Spirit of Capitalism*,[1] an analysis of the dynamic brought into the common life by the Calvinist elaboration of a doctrine of vocation in the world. Here Weber centered attention on the vigorous economic activity promoted and given religious sanction by the Calvinists—he did not claim that Calvinism was the source of capitalism. He left for later study (never undertaken by him) the influ-ence of the Calvinist doctrine of vocation upon the political sphere, an influence issuing from the demand that every Christian should testify to the glory of God by striving to bring about a society of justice.[2]

Trained in the law, Calvin in Geneva aimed to relate religion and law, toward the end of institutionalizing religious and social values. Recogniz-ing the sinfulness of human nature, he even made room in a restricted way

---

1. M. WEBER, THE PROTESTANT ETHIC AND THE SPIRIT OF CAPITALISM (1976).

2. In the "secularizing" political thrust of Calvinism one can see a certain continuity with the religion of the Old Testament prophets. Indeed, according to Weber, they in their time played a role similar to that of the modern dissenting, free press. —Weber's study of Calvin-ism's doctrine of vocation has given rise to an extensive literature of comment and criticism. For the author's critique of Weber's presentation of "the Protestant ethic" *see* the chapter entitled *The Protestant Ethic with Fewer Tears*, in, IN THE NAME OF LIFE: ESSAYS IN HONOR OF ERICH FROMM (B. Landis & E. Tauber ed. 1971).

for the institutionalizing of dissent. Yet, his was on the whole a tight legal system. In time, however, and in other countries, the almost totalitarian character of the Geneva model was gradually transformed. In England in the seventeenth century, for example, the model was turned in a democratic direction by Neo-Calvinists and other Puritans. By many scholars, this turn is viewed as the origin of modern political democracy.

What we have been noting here is that the process of directing the Christian to work in the world is called a form of secularization. This kind of religion and this kind of secularization are not to be seen as opposites. Rather, they work hand in hand. Just here, then, a certain confusion ensues when the word *secularization* is defined as rejection of the transcendent reference (or belief in God). Because of possible confusion here, secularization defined as taking religion into the world of affairs has sometimes been called *secularity*.[3] The interaction between religion and law is at its maximum here.

There is, to be sure, a type of religion which rejects "secularity." We should pause here to take it into account, for it is a part of our secularized society, and it tends to minimize the interaction between religion and the legal system. In contrast to the "secularity" and the secularization we have been considering, is the narcissistic, privatized religion. This privatized religion tends to confine itself to personal and family concerns and to philanthropy. It leaves secularity to other agencies such as the state. In general, it does not in the name of Christian responsibility concern itself with public policy, except when that policy deals with personal vices and virtues. In actuality, however, it scarcely conceals its preferences in public policy, for example in the areas of crime, sexuality, and race relations. In contemporary parlance, it favors individual salvation as against social salvation. Individual salvation, it assumes, will through the conversion of individuals lead to social salvation. It does not recognize that every personal problem is a social problem, and every social problem a personal problem. This de-secularized religion appeared in early world-denying sects and in what is loosely called Pietism. It was also promoted by the revivalism beginning in the eighteenth century. Lyman Beecher in the next century affirmed in a famous sermon in New Haven (1811) that the Christian should not be directly concerned with the social issues of politics. Christian citizens should, instead, elect pious people to office and leave to them the decisions on social issues.[4] The discussion of public issues is viewed as inappropriate under religious auspices, that is, it is secular. Difficult it is to find a greater distance between piety and the legal system unless it be in the cult that leaves society to form an isolated enclave unspotted from the world.

---

3. *Cf.* Ogden, *Faith and Secularity*, in, GOD, SECULARIZATION AND HISTORY. ESSAYS IN HONOR OF RONALD GREGOR SMITH (E. Long ed. 1974).

4. L. Beecher, REFORMATION OF MORALS PRACTICABLE AND INDISPENSIBLE (New Haven Sermon 1814).

It is to be lamented that the widely-admired book, William James'
Varieties of Religious Experience, is almost entirely a study of privatized
religion. This book should not have been entitled *Varieties*, for it is strikingly lacking in variety with respect to types of religion. It may be taken
as a historical textbook on de-secularized, apolitical religion.[5]

I refer again to the term *secularization* in its more generally accepted
meaning, the rejection of belief in God or in transcendent reality. Here
again complicating, qualifying factors (both positive and negative) must
be taken into account. Secularization in the main has been associated with
a drive towards autonomy as against the heteronomy of authoritarian belief and against ecclesiastical control. This autonomy brought with it freedom of inquiry, a freedom exercised in liberal-religious groups as well as
in secular (especially scientific) groups and in the professions generally. I
leave aside here the discussion of the freedom of inquiry which among
religious groups has led to a rejection of traditional theism and to a new
kind of theology. Secularization, then, carries within it a variety of elements leading in opposite directions. Rejection of tradition in the name of
autonomy may be a path leading towards a new integrity and honesty,
growing out of freedom to criticize or to reject traditional language or
formulation. Or it may move in the direction of a highly serious humanism,
a very important element of our "secularized society." On the other hand,
secularization may become the occasion for the fragmentation of life and
even for the appearance of a relativism viewing ethical or religious values
as simply socially conditioned preferences. Law then may become merely
contingent. Here a sense of loss of center may lead to an attempt to "escape
from freedom" by adopting a new heteronomy of authoritarianism such as
one encounters in autarchic nationalism, or in National Socialism or demonic racism. The ethos of autonomy, when exhausted, passes over into
bloated heteronomy. There is nothing a jelly-fish wants so much as a rock.
Law then becomes blatantly arbitrary.

One of the most important aspects of secularization as rejection of ecclesiastical authority has been the emancipation of economic behavior from
church control and from religious sanctions. This process took place in
various ways in different countries. In the Neo-Calvinist thrust, as we have
seen, it claimed the religious motive of fulfilling vocation in the world. The
exercise of this vocation involved a rejection of chartered monopolies licensed by the church-state. This trend brought about a dispersion of economic power which we may call *localism*. This localism of economic behavior was accompanied by an analogous localism in the churches. This entailed the adoption of congregational polity in small, independent, voluntary, self-supporting, self-governing congregations demanding the separation of church and state— in short, a rejection of the established church
which was controlled mainly by church-state bishops and supported by

---

5. W. JAMES, VARITIES OF RELIGIOUS EXPERIENCE (1902).

general taxation. It is not surprising perhaps that many of the people who demanded the freedom of economic behavior were also leaders in the formation or maintenance of the new, "free churches," organizations which relied upon voluntary membership and voluntary financial support. This whole trend, as we have seen, was connected in certain ways with the secularization of exercising a religiously motivated vocation in the world. As Max Weber has reminded us, however, the new economic freedom eventually became largely secularized in another sense.[6] That is, it became largely secularized in the sense of abandoning the motive of testifying to God's glory, and in the sense of adopting the merely utilitarian, unreligious sanctions of economic activity for its own sake. The legal system was expected to protect the freedom of economic activity, and not to interfere.

One other aspect of secularization, as ordinarily understood, must be mentioned here because of its significance for the profession of the lawyer. The term *secularization* refers to the rejection by the professions of control at the hands of the church and for the sake of autonomy. But this emancipation would in many instances eventually issue in secularization through the abandonment of religious motivation. Here, as previously, we see a mixture of types of secularization, religious and unreligious.

Now, when we say that ours is a secularized society, we should mean that it contains various types of secularization (positive and negative), some emancipation from authoritarian religion, the emancipation of economic behavior from church controls and standards, a large component of "de-secularized" religion, churches that promote a religiously motivated "secularity," and widespread rejection of or indifference to any faith that claims transcendent reference of any kind. In addition to all this, the secularized society includes as a very important feature, a legal system in which explicit interaction between religion and law is largely absent.

Another way of characterizing our society is to say that it is pluralistic, offering freedom to disbelieve as well as to believe, and claiming the other freedoms that have emerged through the various types of secularization outlined here. Variations appear here in Protestant and Roman Catholic and Jewish circles. This pluralistic society is sanctioned by the Constitution, and the Supreme Court has ruled that a serious world-view disclaiming any transcendent reference is entitled to "religious" exemption from military draft.[7]

In the context of this total situation we turn now to a consideration of the nature and role of the vocation or profession of the lawyer. This is a task that must be viewed historically and necessarily in broad strokes. John Cardinal Newman, in his Dublin Lectures, reminded his Roman

---

6. WEBER, *supra*, note 1.
7. United States v. Seeger, 380 U.S. 163 (1965); *see also* Welsh v. United States, 398 U.S. 333 (1970).

Catholic audience that British culture always shall have been Protestant.[8] Thus we must say that however much our culture has become secularized through the abandonment of explicitly religious belief, it always shall have been Graeco-Roman and Judaic-Christian. By looking at the historical background of the professional vocation we may discern motifs that continue in some fashion as elements in modern history—one might call them persisting, protean vitamins.

Initially, the word *vocation* or *calling* possessed a strong religious connotation. In this context it is a mediating concept, a concept of relatedness, that is, between God and the religious community, or between God and the individual. It places the individual and the community in a cosmic relatedness. Abraham was called of God to leave the land of his fathers and to become the father of Israel. The Old Testament prophets were called of God to proclaim doom upon the unfaithful. They held that Israel had received a vocation among the nations. In later times the idea of vocation was individualized to provide religious orientation for the several callings within the community, as in the New Testament community. As we have seen, the term came to the fore in monasticism, in the West as well as in the East; and with the Reformers the concept was radicalized to make it apply to the cosmos of the multiform vocations in society.

The explicit concept of the professions does not, I believe, appear in the Old or the New Testament. An approximation to it appears more readily visible in Graeco-Roman thought and practice, particularly with respect to the functions of the lawyer and the doctor. In his book, *The Lawyer from Antiquity to Modern Times,* Dean Roscoe Pound observed that the lawyer advocate was so much viewed as a servant of the court that in earlier times in Greece he was not permitted to accept a fee from a client, for he was viewed as committed to the public good.[9] Later on, legal fictions had to be devised to enable the client to remunerate the advocate without jeopardizing the sense of justice that transcends special "interests." The profession of the law was closely associated with that of the trained orator, and in the Roman Empire the advocate often did not become learned in the law, but tended to resort to rhetorical tricks. In the fifth and sixth centuries advocates began the systematic study of law, and law schools with explicit disciplines grew up. The law recognized fees and fixed the scale. The main lines of discipline which have persisted since that time were established. The caution of caveat emptor was not appropriate for the client in facing the professional.

In Christian circles in the second century the fully-educated priest was expected to have studied rhetoric (which included the study of classical literature and its genres). This same breadth of training was evident al-

---

8. J. Newman, The Idea Of A University Defined And Illustrated (1873) (reprinted 1927).

9. Dean R. Pound, The Lawyer From Antiquity To Modern Times ch. 1 (1953).

ready in the education of the literary critic and the historian. Even in the second century the idea of systematic theology was already developed, and what one might call the profession of the theologian (the exegete and the apologist) took shape in impressive measure.

The concept of the professions was one of the great constructions of the Middle Ages, to be developed still further in the later period. In this view, the professional training requires the university. Indeed, before undertaking professional training the student is expected, indeed is required, to gain the right to wear the academic gown. The gown certifies that the student has been exposed to the various disciplines of learning; in short, he has become familiar with the characteristic value preferences of the culture (classical and Christian) and with the methods of rational criticism. As preparation for membership in the professions, the student is trained for a broad leadership role in the society, to transmit and criticize and give relevance to the values in a particular time and place. Writing of the pre-legal training of the lawyer, Albericus de Rosate in the fourteenth century enumerates "grammar, dialectic, logic, rhetoric, arithmetic, geometry, mathematics, music, astrology, moral philosophy, medicine, and literature."[10] Justifying this wide spectrum of studies for the lawyer, he writes that "legal science is commendable because it is more universal than other sciences; for other branches of knowledge deal with something particular; that one, however, deals with almost all sciences and especially with liberal ones."[11] This is a large order indeed. The professional is not only a servant of the court; he is also a critical student and servant of the community, of the culture at large.

When the student turns to the strictly professional training, he is to acquire specificity of function in terms of a rational theory of his professional skills so that he may understand and improve those skills. It has often been said that the modern professional initially learned the meaning of rationality from the philosophers of Scholasticism and from the medieval and the Renaissance jurists.

A third feature of the professions has become characteristic of the modern period. The members of the professions form themselves into autonomous associations that, supplementing the university training, define the standards of performance and provide sanctions in the face of their violation. Alfred North Whitehead has asserted that whereas ancient society was a "coordination of crafts for the instinctive purposes of communal life," modern society is a coordination of professions.[12] Through these autonomous associations each of the professions as a group becomes a major form of self-government. More than that, these associations have found

---

10.   E. Kantorowicz, *The Sovereignty of the Artist: A Note on Legal Maxims and Renaissance Theories of Art*, in SELECTED STUDIES 364 (1965).

11.   *Id.*

12.   A. WHITEHEAD, ADVENTURES OF IDEAS 72 (1933).

ways of transcending national and denominational boundaries. Thus, loyalties may extend beyond the state and the church. At the same time, we must note that some of the professional associations have shown features of trade associations and labor organizations. They provide information for the public and the government, but they also function as self-serving and even lobbying agencies.

We have observed that a second feature of the profession is the possession of a rational theory of the characteristic skills. In our day of high degree of specialization, this concern for specificity of function can readily militate against the broader leadership obligations: the concern for fundamental cultural values in a changing historical situation. Here we see an almost tragic aspect of the professional ethos. The more highly specialized a professional becomes—and this is an imperative demand in our world—the more the professional tends to neglect the broader obligations. I recall a formal professional meeting of chemists in which "the young Turks" reproached the elder chemists for ignoring their duties as citizens, particularly their duty to be concerned with public affairs and with the shaping of public opinion. In response, one of the elder chemists asserted that the young chemist should concentrate on his specialty, thereby gaining prestige as an eminent scientist. Having achieved this eminence, the chemist could more readily exercise influence in public affairs. The young Turks immediately redoubled their criticism, asking why the public should listen to a person who had schooled himself to become an idiot as a citizen. These young Turks were pointing to the fragmentation of the professions, a fragmentation in this instance accomplished in the name of science.[13]

The failure to stress the broader public responsibilities of the professional is fairly characteristic today in writings on the professions. A striking analysis of the role of the physician was presented by Supreme Court Justice Felix Frankfurter in an address entitled "A Lawyer's Dicta on Doctors," given at the Harvard Medical school.[14] Here Frankfurter emphasized the need for increasing cooperation between law and medicine. He

---

13. Another aspect of this fragmentation has to do with the performance of professional skills rather than with the broader responsibilities of leadership in the community at large. Specialization can move in the direction of dealing less and less with the client as a total person. Several decades ago in Greater Boston, I had the good fortune to be a member of the Boston Marriage Study Association. This organization brought together representatives of all the professions concerned with the family. The group not only studied the various professions involved; they even achieved tentative agreement on general goals. Beyond this, they formulated criteria in terms of which the clergy should undertake pastoral counseling, premarital, marital, and post-marital; and anonymous records were kept for common assessment. Moreover, each member of the group became available to other members when occasion seemed to make it expedient.

Mark Taylor's essay for the present symposium addresses itself to the problems and tasks of the lawyer as he/she attempts to confront the needs of the client as a whole person.

14. 1958 annual George W. Gay Lecture upon Medical Ethics, reprinted in HARV. MED. ALUMNI BULL., July, 1958.

then described the careers of four remarkable physicians, two of whom he knew through history, and two in person. Each of these model physicians made his contribution entirely within the confines of the professional skills of healing. To be sure, these contributions were of substantial, intrinsic significance. But not one word was said concerning the larger public responsibility of the doctor. This same element is lacking in a definition of the profession of the lawyer given by Roscoe Pound. He says that the term *profession* refers "to a group of men pursuing a learned art as a common calling in the spirit of a public service—no less a public service because it may incidentally be a means of livelihood."[15] It would not be at all difficult, of course, to cite the names of practicing lawyers who have been distinguished cultural leaders.

I have cited these reductionist definitions in order now to recall one type of conceptualization of the larger framework needed. For this purpose I select the concept of *covenant*. In its articulation in the Old Testament and in numerous subsequent versions, the idea of covenant was a theological concept, although in later times it has been secularized in varying ways. Alas, the word *covenant* is in many quarters mainly familiar only through the term "restrictive covenant."

Like the concept of vocation, *covenant* is a mediating concept, relating God and the community, as well as God and the individual in community. The basic idea, we now know, was in pre-Israelite times drawn from the realm of international affairs, the covenant between a conquering monarch and a subjugated people. In the Hebrew concept, God with a promise of faithfulness offers a covenant to which the people of Israel respond with a promise of faithfulness. Making a commitment is fundamental here, and one should note it is a societal commitment involving both the group and the individual. The God who offers the covenant has delivered the people of Israel from slavery in Egypt. The people are committed to work for a society of righteousness; they are responsible for the character of the society and its institutions. Having been slaves themselves, they are to be ever mindful of the needs of the deprived. At the same time the individual shares these responsibilities. The response of the people to God's offer is responsibility, both individual and collective.

The Old Testament covenant is always connected with law, and the law changes from time to time in important respects. Although law is an inextricable element, the violation of the covenant is not viewed as merely a violation of law; it is seen as a violation of trust and affection. A loving, righteous God has called (and holds) the society to a center. Loyalty is a centripetal power attracted by love to this center. Kings, priests, scribes, and people are bound together in one living tether, and they are measured by the embracing covenant between rich and poor, between high and low,

15. Quoted by Griswold, *The Legal Profession*, in TALKS ON AMERICAN LAW 263 (H. Berman ed., 2d 1971).

including the stranger.

The New Testament covenant through Jesus Christ breaks and transcends the kinship tie of earlier Hebrew culture, at the same time continuing and radicalizing universal motifs already in the Old Testament. The new covenant looks to the deliverance of all mankind from the dominion of evil, also a motif in the Old Testament. It gives every Christian the vocation and joy of witnessing to the Good News, and at the same time it accords religious status to each major function in the religious community. We cannot expound here upon the close relations between love and law in the gospels or in the theology of law and Spirit adumbrated by St. Paul. We should recall, however, that for several centuries the bishop at stated times in the week "held court" (*episkopalis audientia*) in order to exhibit, in contrast to pagan courts, a Christian conception of law informed by love.

For Christianity, as for Judaism, authentic law is not to be contrasted with love. The covenant is held together by both: the law provides structure and continuity, and love offers the dynamic that draws law beyond itself into the service of a broader and deeper community, as Judge Forer's presentation in the symposium amply shows. Each is distorted, or at least incomplete, without the other.

Professor Berman indicates how law and love belong in an embracing covenant when he says that law is "a process of creating conditions in which sacrificial love, the kind of love personified in Jesus Christ, can take root and grow."[16] Statements such as these may seem to approach the sphere of the impractical. This is particularly true in the face of the hard, workaday life of the lawyer concerned with doing his job in a complex and demanding legal system beset with a maze of rules and procedures.

At this point, one might profitably consider ways in which the profession of law under religious or under humanist motives can and does in important ways improve the rules and procedures. In order, however, to stress the broader functions and obligations of a profession, it may be helpful to cite some cases in which the profession has come short of the requisite concern, either with rules and procedures or with broad community responsibilities. These instances will appear at first blush to be extreme and atypical, but they do point to deviations by the shirking of responsibility—deviations to which all flesh is prone.

The violation or distortion of law occurs, no doubt most frequently, by reason of personal interest or greed. But the more massive deviations—and also the winking at deviations—issue from ideological, even demonic, commitments. I recall a conversation of several years ago with a former law professor who is presently in private practice. (I suppress his name, for I do not have permission to quote him.) In the conversation at a professional gathering I said that in the period of the McCarthy hysteria, many of the clergy came short of offering courageous dissent. But where were the

---

16. *Love and Law*, 56 Episcopal Theological Sch. Bull. No. 3 (1964).

lawyers? I asked. They had the special, professional responsibility to clear the air by boldly exposing the violation of elemental rights of due process. In response, this former law professor said that my reproaches were mild. A fairly typical comment among certain lawyers, he said, was of this sort: "The violation of the Bill of Rights is obvious and scandalous. But a good thing may be happening nevertheless. If McCarthy can paste the word *Communist* on the billboards of the party we oppose, perhaps we in the end can get rid of the New Deal. To be sure, some innocent people will have to suffer, but that will be a small price for the benefit."

One may say that this is the sort of thing that generally happens when feelings run high. But, obviously, the unusual situation of this sort is precisely the time when social responsibility is acutely needed.

Then consider another unusual situation in which ideological motives were endemic: the Sacco-Vanzetti Case. The accused were anarchists, and because they were immigrants, they had "un-American" political convictions. Here was another instance in which the legal system and the lawyers were being tested. Fifty years after the execution of the sentenced men, additional documents are still coming to light, the most recent being papers from the archives of A. Lawrence Lowell, President of Harvard University, who, with the President of M.I.T. and a retired probate judge, served on an advisory committee set up by Governor Alvan T. Fuller of Massachusetts. At the time, appellate review was not available according to Massachusetts statutes. The duty of the committee "was not clearly defined, but in fact they were asked to advise the chief executive whether they thought the defendants to be guilty and whether there was need for a new trial."[17] Although new evidence was said to be available, the committee advised against the holding of a new trial.

Between 1921 and 1927, additional important information had been discovered and offered by the defense for testing by trial. In light of this situation, Judge Thayer asserted, "[i]t is not imperative that a new trial be granted, even though the evidence is newly discovered, and if presented to a jury would justify a different verdict."[18]

Three days before the execution of the men, on August 20, 1927, the oft-dissenting Justice Oliver Wendell Holmes, Jr. denied a stay of execution determining that if the Massachusetts Constitution provided that a trial before a single judge was final, without appeal, this would be consistent with the United States Constitution. According to Justice Holmes, the only remedy for prejudice on the part of the judge would be executive clemency. This executive clemency was not granted by the Governor.

It became generally known later on that, some years before, this Gover-

---

17. Data referred to here were presented by the author of the well-known book on the case, Dr. Louis Joughin, in an address entitled, *Beyond Guilt or Innocence: the Responsibility of History,* read at a conference on *Sacco-Vanzetti: Developments and Reconsiderations—1979,* held at Boston Public Library, October 26-27, 1979 (unpublished).

18. *Id.*

nor, as a member of Congress, had approved the denial of a seat to his colleague, Victor Berger, who had been elected by the people of Wisconsin. These were his words:

> Berger characterizes the action of the House as a "crucifixion," and in a manner of speaking it is. It is the crucifixion of disloyalty, the nailing of sedition to the cross of free government, where the whole brood of anarchists, Bolshevists, I.W.W.'s may see and read a solemn warning.[19]

On the other side of the controversy, one can report that the only Irish and Catholic member of the Harvard Corporation strongly opposed President Lowell's conclusion that Sacco and Vanzetti were not entitled to a new trial. Moreover, William G. Thompson, chairman of the Boston Bar's ethics committee, gave almost the whole of his life for four years in service as chief counsel for the defense. Dr. Barbara Miller Solomon, Senior Lecturer at Harvard on the History of American Civilization, in her address on "Brahmins and the Conscience of the Community,"[20] reported in pungent detail the sharp divisions among the Brahmins of Greater Boston.

The Massachusetts Judicial Council, immediately after the executions, began a study of the law governing appeals in capital cases. Within three months, the Council formally recommended major statutory changes, proposing that a defendant's petition for a new trial should go directly to the full bench of the Supreme Judicial Court on the whole record of both facts and law. Legislative enactment came at last in 1939—twelve years later.

Michael A. Dukakis, attorney and Governor of the Commonwealth of Massachusetts, in his extensive Proclamation of July 19, 1977, summarized major factors in the miscarriage of the legal system under its custodians, including in pertinent part, the following:

> WHEREAS, The conduct of many of the officials involved in this case shed serious doubt on their willingness and ability to conduct the prosecution and trial of Sacco and Vanzetti fairly and impartially. . . .
> NOW THEREFORE, I . . . do hereby proclaim August 23, 1977, NICOLA SACCO AND BARTOLOMEO VANZETTI MEMORIAL DAY; . . . and I hereby call upon the people of Massachusetts to pause in their daily endeavors to reflect upon these tragic events, and draw from their historic lessons the resolve to prevent the forces of intolerance, fear and hatred from ever again uniting to overcome the rationality, wisdom and fairness to which our legal system aspires.[21]

Whatever one should say regarding the responsibilities of a lawyer not directly involved at the time in the Sacco-Vanzetti Case, the vital interaction between law and religion (and between law and humanism) requires

---

19. *Id.*
20. Read at the conference on *Sacco-Vanzetti: Developments and Reconsiderations - 1979, supra* note 16.
21. Joughin, *supra* note 17.

of all professions an active concern beyond the call of workaday duties and also beyond the call of career interests. The lawyer has a special responsibility in a time when confidence in the legal system is weak in many quarters.

A somewhat analogous situation has developed in the area of medical care. Not long ago, a dean of a major medical school asserted in conversation that the self-serving tactics of the doctors in their professional associations has so much tarnished the image of the physician that the medical schools find it increasingly difficult to enlist first-class students; indeed, an interschool committee was formed in order to correct the situation. Similarly, the weakening confidence of the populace in the political order is indicated in the decrease from 1892 to 1948 of the proportion of eligible voters participating in presidential elections from eighty-seven to fifty-seven percent.[22]

The professional stands always under the general expectation that he or she will serve the Commonwealth. Many are the areas in which professional and citizenship responsibilities call for alert concern: the third world craving for liberation, the bureaucratic organization of government, the extensive concentration of industry, "criminal justice," amnesty for war deserters, and the threat of nuclear self-destruction of humanity, to name a few.

Two problem areas that relate to the lawyer's work deserve emphasis here. First, there has been an increasing resort to litigation—everything must be handled by lawyers, a cause for a mounting proportion of national income going to the lawyer. Second, there is a temptation to manipulate the legal system for the sake of the client. Within the past week I have received a visit from a recent law graduate working in a large firm in North Carolina who expressed bitterly her increasing frustration by reason of the omission of truth in connection with advocacy. This is precisely the concern that Roscoe Pound noted in discussing the prohibition in ancient Greece of fees for the lawyer from the client.[23] Further efforts are required today among the lawyers themselves to find alternative devices for the sake of even-handed justice.

Cultural responsibility in the broader areas is not to be met without participation in the voluntary associations in which members do not work for their own gain. In these associations, different perspectives are brought into interaction toward the ends of achieving consensus and devising democratic strategies. In addition, systemic questions are raised and pressed. A clergyman who is a graduate of Harvard Business School has made a study of the associations in which members of his parish in Denver partici-

---

22. *See* B. Barber, "Mass Apathy" and Voluntary Participation in the United States (1948) (unpublished Ph.D. dissertation, Harvard University); and Barber, *Participation and Mass Apathy in Associations,* in STUDIES IN LEADERSHIP 477 (A. Gouldner ed. 1965).

23. POUND, *supra,* note 1.

pate. He found that they become involved ostensibly for the common good but that they join organizations in which their already-formed convictions and prejudices are supported. Thus, rather than engendering new and valuable insight, these organizations actually appear to promote fragmentation and mere self-interest. For reasons of this sort we may say of the citizen and especially of the professional person: "By their groups shall you know them."

Earlier sections of the present article have considered the composite responsibilities of the professions as well as the general covenantal framework for the understanding of authentic community. Edmund Burke two centuries ago gave us a modern classical statement defining the vital elements of covenant. It is within this structure that the interaction of law and religion can pose the crucial questions of ultimate concern. It was his conviction that "the spirit of religion" has been the integrating element of Western civilization.

> Society is indeed a contract. Subordinate contracts for objects of mere occasional interest may be dissolved at pleasure— but the state ought not to be considered as nothing better than a partnership agreement in a trade of pepper and coffee, calico or tobacco, or some other such low concern, to be taken up for a little temporary interest, and to be dissolved by the fancy of the parties. It is to be looked on with other reverence; because it is not a partnership in things subservient only to the gross animal existence of a temporary and perishable nature. It is a partnership in all science; a partnership in all art; a partnership in every virtue, and in all perfection. As the ends of such a partnership cannot be obtained in many generations, it becomes a partnership not only between those who are living, but between those who are living, those who are dead, and those who are to be born. Each contract of each particular state is but a clause in the great primeval contract of eternal society, linking the lower with the higher natures, connecting the visible and invisible world, according to a fixed compact sanctioned by the inviolable oath which holds all physical and all moral natures, each in their appointed place.[24]

---

24. E. Burke, Works vol. 2, 368 (1861).

GOD AND ECONOMICS

by
James Luther Adams

G. K. Chesterton once said that the most important question to ask about a new landlady is, What is her world view? In effect, he was saying that economics raises the question regarding world view. Economics cannot be confined to the study of the production and interchange of goods and services; it must also take into account the world view that informs these activities and which gives integrity and direction to human community. In short, the topic "God and Economics" brings us sooner than later to the question regarding the meaning of life and the resources for its fulfillment -- macroeconomics in an even broader sense than usually attaches to that term. It leads to a discussion not only of the meaning of meaning but also of the symbols that are pertinent for considering our topic. Indeed, it brings us to the question regarding the myths (and therefore also the root metaphors) which generally come into play in any treatment of religion and economics. We must briefly explain this conception of meaning and myth here at the outset in very broad strokes; and then we must indicate the limitations we aim to place upon the present discussion.

Being religious means asking the question of the meaning of our human existence. And what is the meaning of meaning in this context? It is the concern for significant relatedness. Wilhelm Dilthey long ago suggested that meaning or significance has to do with the relationship between the parts and the whole, a relatedness that holds past and present together in some continuity.[1] This conception of meaning may or may not include a conception of God, depending upon one's definition of the whole. Apart from that question we may close in on our topic by referring to two quite different conceptions of the relationship between the parts and the whole.

In ancient Israel, meaning, or significant relatedness, was immanently "located" within the arena of nature, society and history in contrast to the type of religion which envisages meaning primarily in interpersonal relatedness and which looks toward essential fulfillment outside or above history. For these ends symbols are created in society and history. They define and promote some sense of relatedness and continuity in human life.

An elaborated symbolization achieves what may be called a mythological articulation -- an imaginative, integrating, metaphorical conception of Whence and Whither within a temporal sequence. In a broad sense this sort of articulation may be spoken of as religious insofar as it provides, or aims to provide, a sense of identity and responsible vocation for the individual and the group. Some such mythological conception generally informs any economic philosophy.

We shall see presently that the outlook of Adam Smith and of
laissez-faire economic theory lives from such a myth. Previously
the world had been viewed as a machine, and before that, in ancient
Greece and the Middle Ages, as an organism. Such a myth appears
also in nineteenth-century conceptions of progressive evolution.
J. B. Bury, a non-theological historian of ideas, detected in the
idea of progress a residue, a secularization, of the idea of divine
Providence. Here we see myths that depend upon root metaphors
drawn from mechanics, biology and theology. These metaphors are
not only the consequence of experience; they are often its prerequisite. They create and order experience.[2]
    Strictly speaking, however, a myth is a story about the
gods. In Western tradition symbolic behavior is explicitly and
overtly religious when it presupposes activity of the divine in relation to the human -- a relationship between the whole and the
parts. In its Old Testament prophetic form, for example, it involves not only persons in their immediate interpersonal relations
or in the individual's relation to God but also in institutional
behavior. To be sure, this comprehensive, integrated view attaches
to a largely pre-pluralistic society.
    From this Old Testament prophetic perspective the con-
finement of religious meaning to interpersonal relations is a grossly
truncated sense of meaning or significant relatedness. In modern
terms we may say that this confinement represents an attempt, a
spurious attempt, to understand the human enterprise only psychologically and not also sociologically and politically. In contemporary individualistic existentialism the confinement assumes itself
to be concrete, but in actuality it is highly abstract; it is a mis-
placed concreteness that ignores the institutional framework and
support. It therefore ignores institutional behavior and responsibilities. It imprisons the flower within the crannied wall. In
the poem *Peter Bell* Wordsworth uttered protest against the failure
to recognize a broader relatedness.

> A primrose by a river's brim
> A yellow primrose was to him,
> And it was nothing more.

In the Old Testament tradition the sense of authentic ecology is an
ecology of grace. It is present in society and history -- in institutions as well as in personal experience -- though it may be interpreted in distorted, even magical, fashion.
    The present discussion of our theme will be limited to con-
sidering two major ingredients or models of tradition, the one from
the Old Testament and the other from the seventeenth century Radical
Reformation deriving its sanction from the New Testament. Both of
these models are versions of a great mythological invention, a
doctrine of covenant, one of the most influential metaphorical creations of the Jewish and Christian tradition. In important respects
these two models represent contrasting perspectives, even though
they are rooted in the same symbol. It is precisely because they
are contrasting perspectives regarding the divine-human relationship
that they are selected here for discussion. As we shall see, the

one perspective interprets meaning in terms of the integrity of relationships and responsibility in the total territorial community --
a broadly collective orientation; the other interprets meaning in
terms of the integrity and responsibility of the small group, the
gathered congregation -- a more narrowly collective orientation. In
both types of perspective institutions play a crucial, indispensable
role in the relatedness between the parts and the whole.

***

        In its initial religious form the shaping of the concept
of covenant was primarily the work of the Old Testament prophets,
though its origin and development are not confined to their influence. This covenant involves a deeper kind of personal relationship
than a contract and should not be confused with any form of bargained
pact. In general, covenant is a means whereby a transnatural,
transcendent deity is represented as binding his worshippers to himself by a sovereign act of grace eliciting a moral agreement and
calling them to obedient allegiance and faithfulness. It is an
agreement ostensibly entered into in voluntary consent (a historical
fiction). It forms a bond of loyalty for the sake of fellowship
with God and of harmonious living -- righteousness and peace. From
the human side this covenant is a commitment to what is deemed to
be an ultimate reality, a reliable though mysterious basis of confidence.
        There are various covenants, for example, with Abraham,
David and Moses as representatives. Thus the concept is a composite
one including the election of a people, a promise of land, a justification of possession of the land, a binding obligation upon the
king, a relating of the people as a whole to a divine purpose and
imperative, a divine sanction also for law and cultus. It may be
seen as an aspect of the development of the identity, unity and
vocation of a people, a harbinger of national survival but also a
humanitarian commitment looking toward eventual universality. A
dominant idea was the conviction that the covenant gives the promise
of God's power to liberate from enslavement, a promise already
initially manifest in the liberation from Egyptian bondage. This
identity and commitment includes the individual as well as the collective, the deprived as well as the privileged.
        In these developments there were various tributaries re-
flecting differing motifs and different social structures. In recent
scholarship much has been made of the invention of the metaphor of
covenant as a construct reminiscent of a suzerainty treaty between
a superior political power and a vassal. Insofar as this aspect of
the metaphor is emphasized, however, it can mislead one into assuming that the religious covenant is only a legal one between God
and Israel and that it is only for the collective. The basis of
the covenant is not so much law as it is affectionate response to
liberation from bondage arousing trust and faithfulness on the part
of the individual as well as of the collective.
        Violation of the covenant is not so much a breaking of
law as it is betrayal of trust -- a violation of a relatedness. The
violation brings judgment upon the people. George Foot Moore used

to sum up this aspect of covenant by defining a prophet as one who proclaims doom -- God's execution of judgment upon the faithlessness of the people. This "doom" threatens the entire people as a corporate personality. Yet, renewal of covenant is possible, for the divine purpose is to be fulfilled in the endtime.

Now, there are three features of this relatedness which are especially significant in our constructed model.

(1) The metaphor of covenant is a form of political rhetoric. Like the metaphors, the kingship of God, the kingdom of God, and the Messiah, it is drawn from the political realm -- an example of what Shailer Matthews called "transcendentalized politics."[3] As a political metaphor it embraces the whole of society in history. Nothing individual or collective, naturistic or human, inner or outer, personal or institutional, is excluded from meaning, from potential relatedness, before the Divine Majesty. No spatialization into a segment of relatedness is approved. This feature is characteristic of the exclusive monotheism of Israel, ("Thou shalt have no other gods before me").

This comprehensive conception lies behind the prophet's claim that God is the Lord of history, and also behind the warning of doom ("The Lord hath a controversy with his people"). The covenanted people are responsible for the character of the society as a whole, for institutional as well as individual behavior.

Martin Buber calls this idea of covenant "a special kind of politics, theopolitics." Meaning, significant relatedness, points to a holy ground, to an ultimate source and resource.

(2) The covenant belongs to all the people, and therefore it includes the deprived and the poor as well as the privileged, the weak as well as the strong. Righteousness and peace require concern and care for the poor and even the stranger at the gate. The nerve of a responsible society is the divine compassion engendering respect for persons regardless of status. There remains here a reminiscence of the pre-urban, more egalitarian, less corrupting, nomadic life when, it was thought, Israel was faithful to the covenant.

Ernst Troeltsch, considering this aspect of the ethos, asserted that the prophets were anti-urbanites representing the simple ethics of small agricultural business and common farmers, and that since the city and world politics (with the money economy) are here to stay the message of the prophets even in their own day was "impossible." Yet, their neighborly ethic "by leaping over all complicated cultural relationships to a humanely personal brotherliness achieved an immense world-historical significance."[4] It remains as a perennial antidote to the depersonalizing forces of "civilization."

(3) The meaning of life is grateful, affectional, inward response to the divine, gracious, creative, sustaining, liberating, transforming power, the ultimate source and resource of righteousness and peace. Accordingly, the covenant as a gift of this power is the basis for confidence, identity and vocation for the individual and the society before the unapproachable holiness of the divine.

Now, this conception of covenant is an "ideal type" -- in two senses of the term -- in the Weberian sense of being a descrip-

tive synthetic model accentuating selected features, and also in
the sense of providing a religious-ethical norm. The question remains, What were the ethical implications of the covenant for
economic behavior and institutions?

It is of course difficult to arrive at satisfactory,
comprehensive generalizations to cover the long history of Israel,
beyond asserting that the earlier rural, neighborly, tribal egalitarianism recurrently served as a challenge to the self-serving
economic and political power that came on the scene long after the
emancipation from Egypt. The criterion of impartiality finds expression again and again. Respect for the person was combined with
the view that there is no respect of persons with God. This combination of ideas is repeatedly evident in paradigmatic stories
reaching from the story about the prophet Nathan on through the
history.

The covenant provides sanction for the prophetic denun-
ciation of the indulgence of the elite in luxury, the pomp and
politics of the court, the callousness of the king and the palace
guard, international alliances, the conduct of war with horse and
chariot, and an enlisted army (in imitation of the great powers).
The egalitarianism is to be observed in practice in kinship obligations with respect to the possession and retention of property
by the owners and their kin, in laws regarding loans and security,
in the rejection of the *lex talionis*, in laws requiring humane
treatment and regulated manumission of slaves, in privileges for
the poor to glean in the fields, in the relief of the sabbatical
year with its care for the tender land, and also in the Utopian
ideal of the Jubilee every fifty years. To be sure, the contention
with powerful neighboring states and the necessity of maintaining
armaments, the need for a balance of trade, the crushing taxation,
gave advantages to the elites in their aggrandizement of power.
Economic and political powers, domestic and foreign, largely controlled the enterprise (partly for this reason the prophets proposed the need for a "Remnant").

We shall see something similar to this whole development
when we view an outcome of the second model of covenant. But no-
where in antiquity can one find outside Israel such a complex of
values or the theological sanction for these values, and also for
prophetic dissent, as one encounters in the doctrine of covenant
and covenant renewal.

***

The second and contrasting model of meaning or relatedness
is congregational polity. It comes to birth in the seventeenth
century in the gathered, covenanted churches of England and New
England, though it is rooted in earlier sectarian movements and
finds its sanction in the New Testament church. The term was also
familiar in secular usage. I once asked Dr. Geoffrey Nuttall, the
eminent British Congregationalist historian, to name the principal
sources of the term at this time. He replied by quoting a line from
the American musical, *Oklahoma*: "It was," he said, "bustin' out
all over."

393

A typical congregational covenant contained such phrases as a free community, a particular church, a communion of "visible saints" engaging to walk together by a voluntary consent in holy fellowship, to worship God according to His Word and under the headship of the living Christ. The believer was brought into the visible fellowship through confession of faith and adult baptism (the latter being a cause of dissension among the churches), "to make no difference of persons" and "bearing each other's burthens." The written covenant contained what might be called an abbreviated confession of faith, brief in order to avoid imposing upon the individual conscience an elaborate set of articles.

The Christians of congregational polity were Puritans who wished to purify the church and the society through recovering authentically Christian faith and fellowship and through finding the earthly center of religious life in the local congregation of believers. We may speak of this movement as being in the direction of localism. In place of a national covenant of Geneva or Edinburgh vintage -- or of Old Testament type -- these congregationalists (some of them being called "Independents") formed a covenant for each congregation.

Generally, however, each congregation recognized the living Christ in other congregations, and through "connectionalism" these congregations entered into cooperation with each other. These congregations protested against the centralized powers in the established church. They wished to be liberated from the hierarchical authority of bishops or clergy and from the association of the church hierarchy with the state and the monarch. They therefore promoted the separation of church and state, in order to place institutional authority in the self-governing congregation. Instead of a church for the masses they wanted a voluntary church only for believers. Here explicit faith, close interpersonal relations, and moral discipline were possible.

This self-governing congregation was to be self-supporting, thus rejecting financial support or control coming from non-believers or from coercive taxation at the hands of the political authority. Consequently, the passing of the collection plate (as well as the reading of the Bible) became a kind of sacrament. In this congregation every member in principle would have the right and responsibility of joining in the determination of policies (radical laicism).

What with the emphasis given to the reading of the Bible, a high premium was placed on literacy. These people wished to substitute participative coarchy for hierarchy. Not that the congregation considered itself to be autonomous. The principle of the consent of the governed was closely related to a doctrine and discipline of the Holy Spirit in accord with Scripture. In some degree, then, congregational polity was a pneumatocracy. The proponents of the polity appealed to the New Testament as sanction for the demand that the minister possess charismatic "gifts and graces." The congregation for its part was expected "to tast [sic] as it were the savour of his spirit."[5]

The principle of local autonomy entailed the struggle for freedom to form independent religious associations, a struggle that aroused persecution. This struggle was somewhat similar to that

394

right had been usurped by the clergy of the establishment. The Great Awakening was radically opposed to all ecclesiastical bureaucrats.

With regard to broader public policy Backus gradually moved in some measure away from the radical localism of the majority of Baptist pietists. This change is to be observed especially in his decision to support ratification of the new federal Constitution. He was the first Baptist of prominence to take this position, and he did so to the disappointment of most other Baptists, both clergy and lay. These Baptists were fearful of any substantial federal authority, retaining their adherence to radical localism and their distrust of democracy on any large scale. The reasons for his support of the ratification were the Constitution's exclusion of "all titles of nobility or hereditary succession of power" (ascribed status) as well as of religious tests, and also later the protection of freedom of religion and the prohibition of establishment afforded by the First Amendment. Equally important was his view that "the American revolution was built upon the principle, that all men are born with an equal right to liberty and property, and that officers have no right to any power but what is fairly given them by the consent of the people"; but he did not favor Jeffersonian Enlightenment formulations with regard to natural rights. His desire to protect freedom of religion was so strong that he approved of civil disobedience in face of even "legal" suppression of this freedom.

Backus believed that the health of the society depended upon freedom of individual conscience and upon the Christian character of the citizens. In this matter he was very optimistic. Jefferson thought the majority of citizens would become Unitarians; Backus believed the nation was destined to become Baptist. The bulk of his writings, however, were devoted to the definition of authentic Scriptural doctrine (as adumbrated in the Westminster Confession). Accordingly, he admonished obedience to the powers that be. But he apparently did not assert that the individual Christian in democratic society (in contrast to living in the society in which St. Paul found himself) is a part of these powers and is under obligation to attempt by institutional means to affect them. As a pietist he was perhaps too much of an anti-institutionalist, too much of an individualist, to sense that obligation.

This pietistic ethos did not, according to Dr. McLoughlin, prevent Backus from criticizing merchants, lawyers and the oppressors of the poor. But he did not view the economic establishment as requiring institutional remedies. He was too successful as an evangelist in converting prominent people, and perhaps he had been sufficiently successful as a farmer on his inherited land, to transcend his primary interest in the parts and to concern himself with the character of the whole economic structure. For this institutional criticism one would have to wait until the appearance of more prophetically oriented Baptists such as Francis Wayland (1796-1865), the fourth President of Brown University, and Walter Rauschenbusch (1861-1918), the proponent of the Social Gospel. (Congregationalists were also leaders in the Social Gospel Movement.)

Yet, with his congregational principle of separation of church and state, and the principle of the consent of the governed, also with his support for ratification of the federal Constitution and with his evangelistic appeal to the common man, Backus helped materially to shape the American ethos of the future. In these respects he maintained the heritage of the Radical Reformation stemming from the seventeenth century in England and New England. On the other hand, his pietistic lack of an institutional philosophy and his insensitivity to the prophetic conception of covenant did not help to prepare for combat with the new economic establishment that was the wave of the future.

***

Adam Smith observed that the isolated individual was persuaded by the evangelistic sect to believe that he has an eternal soul, thus gaining a new sense of his dignity and worth and of his freedom to accept the Gospel, but that after entering the sect he found himself in a tight vise of external discipline. Something analogous to this process of reversal was to be the fate of congregational localism -- and that in both the church and the business enterprise. At the outset this localism, as we have seen, promoted a dispersion of power and responsibility. Eventually, however, it found itself surrounded by powers, especially economic powers, which like a vise constricted freedom in the corporate community.

Adam Smith had identified the constrictor of freedom in the landed estates. (It is often overlooked that Smith was as much opposed to the unaccountable power of the owners of these estates as he was to commercial monopoly.) But his reliance upon free market and open competition was connected with his assumption that business enterprise would be small enterprise. He did not, could not, foresee the emergence of the mammoth corporation.

It is noteworthy that already in the 1830's President Andrew Jackson made vigorous attack on the special privileges of chartered corporations. Between the American revolution and 1801 state governments had created more than 300 corporations. Jackson's attacks on their special privileges under charters (attacks demanding competition) remind one of the attacks made upon chartered monopolies in the first half of the seventeenth century.

We cannot in the present discussion trace the development of corporate economic behavior in the first half of the nineteenth century. It will suffice if we indicate the emergence of the prophetic model with its concern for the character of the society as a whole in opposition to mere "localism." In our previous section we have centered attention upon the Baptists; now we may consider an opposing trend right within the churches of congregational polity, this time among the Unitarians.[9]

Radical criticism of the social system begins to appear in this group in the 1830's, the "age of Jackson." In 1832 the Rev. William Ellery Channing (Boston), a grandson of a signer of the Declaration of Independence, wrote "that the old principles of property are to undergo a fiery trial, that the monstrous inequalities of condition must be redressed, and that greater revolutions

God and Economics

than the majority have dreamed of -- whether for good or evil --
are to be anticipated." In the following year he renewed his
attack upon the accumulation of great wealth.

In 1841 Brook Farm (not exclusively Unitarian) was established with the purpose of substituting a system of brotherly
cooperation for one of selfish competition. It operated on a joint
stock proprietorship, and each member had free choice of occupation.
(Adam Smith half a century earlier had said that division of labor
was producing "dolts.") The Associationist Movement advocated a
plan for the democratic organization of industry.

In 1843 William Henry Channing, Ellery Channing's nephew
and biographer, attacked what he called "the degradations of our
present social state."

> The charity we need is justice -- justice in production, justice in
> distribution, the rallying cry today is social organization ....
> The error of the modern doctrine of liberty has been its tone of
> selfish independence; its idol has been individualism; its sin, law-
> lessness, its tendencies to anarchy.

Less than a decade later he wrote that liberalism "cannot stop
short of socialism. Mere modifications in government will in no
wise secure this integral development of human nature in all classes
which the conscience of the age demands."

In 1844 the Rev. James Freeman Clarke (in the latter part
of his career a Professor of natural religion and Christian doctrine
at Harvard) called for radical change in the system.

> The evils arising from want of organization appear most evidently
> when we consider this other great principle of modern society --
> freedom in the direction of industry. We have adopted the free
> trade principle in its fullest extent. We say, leave trade and in-
> dustry to regulate themselves. We say to Government -- 'laissez
> faire, let me alone' .... On the let-alone principle capital will
> always be able to take advantage of labor, and for the simple
> reason, the capital can *wait*, labor cannot.

John S. Dwight, the music critic who had been a member of
Brook Farm and an Associationist, emphasized the importance of the
social sciences for the battle against injustice. He spoke of
social science as "the second babe in the manger," the first being
Jesus.

Horace Mann, the principal education reformer of the
nineteenth century, called for "a laborious process of renovation
sustained by the power and resources of the government." "Wealth,"
he said, "wealth, by force of unjust laws and institutions, is
filched from the producer and gathered in vast masses, to give
power and luxury and aggrandizement to a few. Of production, there
is no end; of distribution, there is no beginning."

These Unitarians and Transcendentalists do not speak of
the congregational covenant, probably because the polity up to that
time had been supported by the state establishment and also because
of the regnant economic individualism in the denomination. They

399

speak rather of "Divine Love" and "Laws of Divine Justice." "Liberalism is of God, and ... its heaven-appointed end is social organization," said the younger Channing.

***

We have now come full circle, from the holistic pre-industrial society of the Middle Ages through the period when congregational, covenanted polity and capitalist free enterprise appear, to the beginning of the demand for socialism, a concern again for the whole in its relation to the parts. Viewing the longer historical development of the meaning of life as it has been surveyed in the present essay, we may say in simplified formulation that the Old Testament prophetic covenant was moral, religious and political, and that the historic congregational covenant was moral and religious but not (positively) political; religious socialism in opposition to capitalism is again moral, religious and political.[10]

The terms *capitalism* and *socialism* are weasel words. The same may be said,of course,regarding any key words that have persisted through a protracted period, for example, words like *God* and *liberalism*. During the past century and a half the terms *capitalism* and *socialism* have been undergoing considerable change. In the earlier part of this period capitalism was connected with the theory of the negative state which gives to the political order the economic function only of creating or maintaining conditions necessary for economic freedom and competition, necessary (that is) for the encouragement of the initiatives that release new energies and elicit capital investment.

Toward the end of the nineteenth century, however, new conceptions of economic responsibility began to emerge. The change is evident in the sphere of law. This change in legal thought has been described as a shift from emphasis on the rights of the individual will to the older "common-law idea of relation." (It is noteworthy that the term "relation" which is crucial for our definition of meaning appears here.) The individual with his "free contract" has been brought more and more (not without dust and heat) to recognize duties as well as rights, in terms of "social justice" instead of merely individualistic "legal justice." Thus the concept of meaning as mutually responsible relatedness within a societal framework was coming to the fore.

Roscoe Pound years ago characterized the change as a movement in the direction of a "feudal principle."[11] This restoration of a feudal principle was in part the gateway to the development of the welfare state where capitalism reluctantly became a mixed economy.

Meanwhile, great changes came in the technology of transportation and communication; also, the managerial revolution, with its hierarchy of salaried executives replacing the direction by the owners, evolved. In short, capitalism has passed through a number of phases, requiring differing definitions.

The definition of socialism likewise has assumed differing definitions extending all the way from anarchism to centralism.

400

Under its name have been such varied configurations as are suggested by the Social-Democratic Welfare states of Western Europe, the Leninist-Stalinist regimes of Russia and Eastern Europe to the various Third World regimes, not to speak of new African forms of socialism and the *Kibbutzim* of Israel. Moreover, within the past century in the United States socialist theory has borrowed from laissez-faire theory (particularly as skepticism developed regarding the adequacy of centralist socialism) and laissez-faire theory has borrowed from socialism (with the advent of the welfare state).

The old dictionary definition of socialism reads, "A political and economic theory of social organization based on government ownership." This definition is now in many quarters an anachronism, especially in face of current conceptions of democratic socialism.

In this connection we should look briefly at the development of religious socialism. Within the same decade as the Unitarian socialists were demanding social reorganization the movement calling itself "Christian Socialism" was initiated in the Church of England by F. D. Maurice and Charles Kingsley. Its purpose was to "Christianize socialism" and to "socialize Christianity." In practical terms it was mainly a cooperative movement and an experiment in adult education, but it became a stimulus for the criticism of the current capitalist economics. A similar movement was beginning in the German Lutheran churches. Roman Catholic neo-medieval socialist theory antedated these movements, for early in the century they were making radical attacks on capitalism as a form of modern chaos dissolving community and societal responsibility.

It is not surprising that these movements should appear in territorial churches accustomed to a national establishment rather than in churches that began by rejecting establishment. To be sure, the prophetic demands had been previously at a vanishing point. The quotations from the Unitarian socialists we have cited could be interpreted in part as the reappearance of the holistic perspectives of earlier Calvinist territorial covenant. (Troeltsch was wont to speak of primitive Calvinism as Christian Socialism.) Calvin, being a lawyer, was saturated with Old Testament law and covenantal lore. From the point of view of the congregational "Independents," however, the Genevan covenant was the inspiration for the non-Separatist Puritan attempt to replace the Anglican establishment with their own theocratic and coercive covenant.

For their part the religious socialists of the nineteenth century in England and the U.S.A. were coming to recognize that they faced a new, an economic, establishment, indeed that "automatic harmony" and "the invisible hand" had been frustrated by the crescent corporate, economic powers.

The emergence of the oligopoly of mammoth business corporations produces the paradox of the society of free enterprise: on the one hand it opened the way for a new freedom, a freedom that has produced an impressive array of goods and services and a rise in the standard of living for many, but on the other it has produced a system that provides new compulsion[12] at the hands of corporate and centralized powers largely unaccountable because in the

401

market they define the needs through advertising, and the markets
have not always remained free. In some respects these powers are
stronger than the government as well as stronger than the market.
Moreover, since economic congregational localism did not assume responsibility for consequences in the commonwealth, its conscience
could remain clear regarding the millions who have been left out,
millions now become billions in the Third World where the poor are
becoming ever poorer. A contemporary unconventional economist has
called this outcome "socialism for the rich" by reason of its advantages for the profits of the affluent.

Ellery Channing a century and a half ago had asserted
that the social system should be judged by its effects on the human
person. A major effect even upon those who contentedly live within
and from the corporate enterprise is to make them "kept" men and
women -- dissent is practically unknown among them, so much so that
Ralph Nader has suggested that we need a new Bill of Rights for
dissenters within the corporations.

Troeltsch long ago predicted that the enthusiasm for
political rights could not be maintained if the economic powers
could not meet the needs of body and mind in the general populace.
The present system has engendered or tolerated massive inequalities, inequalities in the forms of racism and sexism and also of
poverty at the gate of the affluent society. The richest 10 percent of our households receive 25.1 percent of our income while the
poorest 10 percent receive only 1.7 percent. Blacks earn 69 percent as much as whites; women who work full time earn only 56 percent as much as men. Some 80 percent of female workers labor in
"pink-collar" jobs. These jobs are segregated by race and sex.

Now, these inequalities are not to be remedied by government ownership of basic industries. Few people believe that government employees can be more efficient on the whole than employees
of private corporations. One can see, however, the possible advantage of government ownership of military production to remove
this segment from its inordinate political influence and from subsidies that syphon off profits to the private sector instead of
assigning them to the people as a whole.

If we add to the problems mentioned the issues raised by
the tax structure, by the multinational corporations with their
use of cheap labor abroad and their stripping of natural resources
to the profit of the developed nations, also by the ecological and
the energy crises, and by massive unemployment, we encounter areas
in which the wealthy and the middle class resist control. The
problem, as Dean Pound asserted, is that of injecting morals into
the law.

We have a national covenant called the Constitution. But
the working constitution includes all of the patterns or customs
that define our relatedness to each other. And these patterns in
appalling ways add up to "restrictive covenants" (actually, this is
the use of the term *covenant* most widely familiar).

Democratic socialism aims to break through these restrictive covenants. It urges that the democratic principles that have
obtained in politics should be applied to the economic sphere. In
the context of our present discussion the aim is that of combining

the prophetic sense of responsibility for the character of the society at large with the social ideals that came to birth in congregational polity -- the consent of the governed, participation in the process of making social-institutional decisions, the "bearing of each other's burthens," the dispersion of power and responsibility, the achievement of a just relation between the parts.

These values are now shared by people whose rootage is not in the explicit tradition of congregational polity, and they require application not only in the sphere of industry but also in education, in health services, and in the control of natural resources. The participation of the governed here would be calculated to re-personalize the individual participants in a pluralistic society which is now threatened by the giantism endemic in the culture.[13] The ways proposed (and in some places already attempted) include the introduction of worker participation in the determination of policies of the factory and the office, so that, for example, the workers may begin to own or participate in the control of the means of production and distribution. This strategy has already been adopted in Germany and Scandinavian countries. In Germany it is called *Mitbestimmung* (co-determination), and in order to make it effective labor representatives are being given training in special topics (investment, marketing, management) so they may serve with some competence on boards of trustees of corporations. Prime Minister Helmut Schmidt has asserted that this whole development is the major contribution of Germany since World War II to modern democracy.

Viewing the sluggishness of American concern for the inequalities in the society, Julian Bond has compared it to climbing a molasses mountain in snowshoes. We remain in what the prophet called the Valley of Decision, whether to worship the false gods of restrictive covenants and respectable hardness of heart or to "turn" in costing gratitude to the creative, sustaining, judging, forgiving, transforming Power that brings forth treasures old and new. This is the relatedness that gives meaning, identity and vocation to our pilgrimage. The alternative is affluent callousness and emptiness.

NOTES AND REFERENCES

1. W. Dilthey, *Selected Writings*. Edited, translated and introduced H.P. Rickman (New York: Cambridge University Press, 1976), pp. 215, 235.

2. Robert N. Nisbet, *Social Change and History* (New York: Oxford University Press, 1969), p. 5.

3. Speaking of "transcendentalized politics" Matthews says,

Our theology is not a system of philosophy, but an extension of the forms of social experience to religious belief. It is a sort of parable in whose plot can be read the history of the social experience of centuries. Its purpose is to make religious experience consistent with other experience and so reasonable.

The Atonement and the Social Process (New York: Macmillan, 1930), pp. 22, 25.

4. Ernst Troeltsch, *Gesammelte Schriften* (Tübingen: J.C.B. Mohr [Paul Siebeck], 1925) IV, pp. 57-58. The essay, "Galube und Ethos der Hebräischen Propheten," was first published in 1916.

5. Geoffrey F. Nuttall, *Visible Saints: The Congregational Way, 1640-1660* (Oxford: Basil Blackwell, 1957), p. 85.

6. Christopher Hill, *Society and Puritanism in Pre-Revolutionary England* (London: Secker and Warburg, 1964), ch. 14.

7. Nuttall, *op. cit.*, p. 142.

8. William G. McLoughlin, *Isaac Backus and the American Pietistic Tradition* (Boston: Little, Brown & Co., 1967); *Isaac Backus on Church, State, and Calvinism.* Ed. with an Introduction by William G. McLoughlin (Cambridge: Harvard University Press, 1968).

9. John MacNab, *Unitarian and Socialistic Ideas in the United States Prior to 1860* (Boston, 1953). A paper prepared originally for a Seminar in Intellectual and Social History of the Modern World, under Professor Crane Brinton at Harvard University, 1951. Privately printed.

10. Another way of describing the differences typologically is to say that although all of these perspectives have a cosmic or theological orientation, the prophetic covenant is microcosmic, mesocosmic and macrocosmic in scope -- it interprets meaning in terms of the individual, of the middle, infrastructural institutions, and also of the broader societal structures. The congregational covenant in the period we have surveyed gives no emphasis to the macrocosmic. This concern re-appears in religious and secular socialism.

The covenant conception in the Gospels has not been presented here, for the members of the primitive Christian churches had no opportunity to participate in the shaping of policies in imperialistic Rome.

11. Cf. Roscoe Pound, *The Spirit of the Common Law* (Boston: Marshall Jones Co.), chs. 1, 2, 7. A major thesis of this book is that modern legal history can be charted as a transition from "a feudal principle" (mutual relatedness of parties in obligations) to a "Puritan principle" (emphasis on individual rights) to a return to "feudal principles" (the restraint or limitation of individual and property rights).

12. This view was already set forth by Thomas Hobbes, summarized by C.B. Macpherson:

> The market makes men free; it requires for its effective operation
> that all men be free and rational; yet the independent rational de-
> cisions of each man produce at every moment a configuration of forces
> which confronts each man compulsively. All men's choices determine,
> and each man's choice is determined by, the market. Hobbes caught
> both the freedom and the compulsion of possessive market society.

The Political Theory of Possessive Individualism (Oxford: Clarendon Press, 1962), p. 106.

13. W. Alvin Pitcher discusses these problems of participation and also strategies available to the churches, in his essay on "The Politics of Mass Society," appearing in D.B. Robertson, ed., *Voluntary Associations. A Study of Groups in a Free Society* (Richmond: John Knox Press, 1966).